STUDIES IN ANCIENT ORIENTAL CIVILIZATION • No. 60
THE ORIENTAL INSTITUTE OF THE UNIVERSITY OF CHICAGO

Series Editors
Leslie Schramer
and
Thomas G. Urban

Gene B. Gragg. October 1997. Photo by Jason Smith

STUDIES IN SEMITIC AND AFROASIATIC LINGUISTICS PRESENTED TO GENE B. GRAGG

Edited by
CYNTHIA L. MILLER

THE ORIENTAL INSTITUTE OF THE UNIVERSITY OF CHICAGO
STUDIES IN ANCIENT ORIENTAL CIVILIZATION • No. 60
CHICAGO • ILLINOIS

Library of Congress Catalog Card Number: 2007929536

ISBN: 978-1-885923-41-7
1-885923-41-4

ISSN: 0081-7554

©2007 by The University of Chicago. All rights reserved.
Published 2007. Printed in the United States of America.

The Oriental Institute, Chicago

Series Editors Acknowledgments

The assistance of Katherine Strange Burke, Lindsay DeCarlo, and Katie L. Johnson is acknowledged in the production of this volume. Thanks are also due to Scott Branting, Director of the Center for Ancient Middle Eastern Landscapes (CAMEL) at the Oriental Institute, for his assistance with the maps.

The image on the cover comprises the beginning of "A Magic Prayer of Henoch" in Geʻez (folio 88 verso of University of Chicago Ms. 251, a Gospel of John with Magic Prayers, which is a codex forming part of the Goodspeed New Testament Manuscript Collection; courtesy of the Special Collections Research Center, University of Chicago Library). The text was first published by Gene B. Gragg in 1975.

Printed by Edwards Brothers, Ann Arbor, Michigan

The paper used in this publication meets the minimum requirements of American National Standard for Information Services — Permanence of Paper for Printed Library Materials, ANSI Z39.48-1984.

TABLE OF CONTENTS

List of Figures	vii
List of Maps	ix
List of Tables	xi
Foreword. *Gil J. Stein*	xiii
Preface. *Cynthia L. Miller*	xv
The Research of Gene B. Gragg. *Cynthia L. Miller*	xvii
Bibliography of the Publications and Communications of Gene B. Gragg. *Charles E. Jones*	xix
Gene B. Gragg as a Teacher. *Robert D. Hoberman*	xxv
Dissertation Committee Service. *Gene B. Gragg*	xxvii
1. The Afrasian Lexicon Reconsidered. *M. Lionel Bender*	1
2. *PQD* Revisited. *Stuart Creason*	27
3. 'May the Gods Preserve You!': The Variability of Injunctive **la* in Epigraphic South Arabian and Its Relation to Jussive Forms within South Semitic. *Joseph L. Daniels II*	43
4. *Littera ex occidente:* Toward a Functional History of Writing. *Peter T. Daniels*	53
5. The Story of *Mem u Zine* in the Neo-Aramaic Dialect of Bohtan. *Samuel Ethan Fox*	69
6. Prenasalization in Aramaic. *W. Randall Garr*	81
7. A New Masoretic "Spell Checker," or, a Practical Method for Checking the Accentual Structure and Integrity of Tiberian-Pointed Biblical Texts. *Richard L. Goerwitz III*	111
8. External Plural Markers in Semitic: A New Assessment. *Rebecca Hasselbach*	123
9. Semitic Triradicality or Prosodic Minimality? Evidence from Sound Change. *Robert D. Hoberman*	139
10. Akkadian-Egyptian Lexical Matches. *Alexander Militarev*	155
11. Constraints on Ellipsis in Biblical Hebrew. *Cynthia L. Miller*	165
12. The Ugaritic Alphabetic Cuneiform Writing System in the Context of Other Alphabetic Systems. *Dennis Pardee*	181
13. West Semitic Perspectives on the Akkadian Vetitive. *David Testen*	201
Contributors	215
Index	217

LIST OF FIGURES

7.1	Overview of Parser/Checker	115
7.2	Sample Parse Tree	116
7.3	*Accents*' Structural Interpretation of Genesis 1:1	117
7.4	Sample Error from *Biblia Hebraica Stuttgartensia*	121
12.1	Ras Shamra Tablet RS 12.063	190
12.2	Ugaritic Alphabet: Comparison with Hebrew Alphabet (Abecedary RS 12.063)	190
12.3	Ras Shamra Text RS 24.281	191
12.4	Ras Shamra Text RS 94.2440	191
12.5	Ras Shamra Text RS 16.265	192
12.6	Ras Shamra Text RS 16.265 Left Edge Showing Different Hand from That of Main Text	192
12.7	Ras Shamra Text RS 88.2215	193
12.8	Ras Shamra Text RS 92.2016, Line 40	193
12.9	Ras Shamra Text RS 16.270 Bearing Double Impression of Personal Seal of Ammistamru II	194
12.10	Ras Ibn Hani Bulla RIH 83/21 Bearing Triple Impression of Personal Seal of Ammistamru II	195
12.11	Ras Shamra Text RS 15.111, Line 4, Showing Two-wedged Archaic Form of {g} in {uġrt}	196
12.12	Ras Shamra Text RS 94.2440 Showing Imitative, Four-wedged Form of {ś}; (a) First Abecedary and (b) Second Abecedary	196

LIST OF MAPS

4.1	Information Given in Most Accounts of Writing Provided to the General Public	54
4.2	Map Illustrating Three Patterns of the Functional History of Writing: Adaptive Reuse, Misunderstanding Model, and Scholarly Input Model; as well as Adoption of Script	63

LIST OF TABLES

1.1	Afrasian Isoglosses	7
6.1	(Non-)Prenasalized Forms in Imperial Aramaic	83
9.1	Words Exhibiting the *šma: > šəmma* Change	140
9.2	Northeastern Neo-Aramaic Words Exhibiting Changes Similar to the *šma: > šəmma* Change	149
9.3	The Feminine Numerals	149
13.1	Literary Arabic Paradigms: The Imperative, the Negative Jusssive, and the Jussive	201
13.2	Old Babylonian Paradigms: The Preterite, the Precative, and the Vetitive	202
13.3	Akkadian High Vowels as Reflexes of Proto-Semitic *n	207
13.4	Past, Negated Past, and "Prohibitive" Formations in Chaha and Inor	209

FOREWORD

Gil J. Stein

The Oriental Institute, The University of Chicago

This volume of essays in honor of Gene B. Gragg appropriately celebrates and acknowledges the tremendous intellectual contributions of a remarkable scholar, a thoughtful mentor, and a giving colleague at the Oriental Institute of the University of Chicago. The essays are revised versions of papers presented at a symposium on comparative Semitics in honor of Gene's retirement held on May 21–22, 2004, at the Oriental Institute. The scope of these contributions seeks to emphasize the far-ranging scholarly impact of Gene's long and distinguished research career on the work of his colleagues and students.

Gene was born in Amsterdam, New York, and attended college at Loyola University of Chicago, from which he received his B.A. in Latin and Philosophy in 1960. He pursued his graduate studies in Linguistics at the University of Chicago, where he earned his Ph.D. in 1966. After a short stint as a Research Associate at the University of Amsterdam, Gene returned to Hyde Park and the University of Chicago in 1969. From 1970 onward, Gene has taught and conducted research in the departments of Linguistics and Near Eastern Languages and Civilizations, and served as a Voting Member of the Oriental Institute until his retirement in 2004.

Gene has played a major role as both an intellectual leader and as an able administrator through his roles as Chair of the Department of Near Eastern Languages and Civilizations from 1979 to 1985, and from 1997 to 2002 as Director of the Oriental Institute. In the latter position, Gene played a key role in overseeing the long and complex process of renovating and reinstalling the Oriental Institute's world class museum.

As a scholar, Gene has exemplified the vision of the Oriental Institute's founder, James Henry Breasted, in seeking to develop a truly interdisciplinary research center devoted to fostering a holistic understanding of ancient Near Eastern civilizations. Gene's personal contribution to this ideal has been through his rigorous and far-reaching integration of linguistics and ancient Near Eastern studies. He has also been a leader in the introduction of computer-based methodologies for the analysis and publication of ancient Near Eastern textual materials.

Gene's 1966 dissertation on Sumerian is still very widely cited as a breakthrough model for the application of formal linguistic theory and methods to the study of Sumerian grammar. This was published in 1973 as *Sumerian Dimensional Infixes* (Alter Orient und Altes Testament, Sonderreihe 5). Gene followed this up with a series of important publications on Sumerian grammar and syntax and on Sumerian literary texts such as temple hymns and the Fable of the Heron and the Turtle. He has also had a lasting impact in training several generations of students at the University of Chicago in this perspective through his teaching of graduate courses in Sumerian.

Moving beyond Mesopotamia, Gene broadened his intellectual scope to examine the broader macro-family of Afro-Asiatic languages. His major contributions to this field of study include publications and papers on both Semitic and Cushitic languages as diverse as South Arabian, Amharic, Tigrinya, Geʿez, and Oromo. As part of his deep commitment to this research, Gene spent a year in Ethiopia from 1974 to 1975 doing field research on the languages of this region. One of the most important publications to derive from this research is his *Oromo Dictionary*, published by Michigan State in 1982. He continues to make major empirical and synthetic contributions to the field of comparative Semitics and to the study of Afro-Asiatic languages.

Gene has also been a major innovator in the application of computers to the study of ancient Near Eastern languages. He played a key role in developing the pilot on-line presentation of Achaemenid Royal Inscriptions by writing the programs that allow for the parsing and grammatical analysis of these extraordinary texts from Persepolis. Gene continues to contribute to this research through his membership on the editorial board of the Persepolis Fortification Archive project chaired by Matthew W. Stolper.

Overall, Gene is one of the few people who have made significant contributions at all three key levels of scholarship — theory, method, and hard, empirical data. He has conveyed this knowledge to generations of students through his teaching and advising of graduate students. He has contributed major, far-reaching publications that have stood the test of time. And throughout this distinguished career, Gene has been a kind, humane, and good colleague.

It is an honor to present this volume to Gene as a small token of the tremendous respect and affection that we, his colleagues, students and friends, hold for him.

PREFACE

Cynthia L. Miller

All but one of the essays in this volume were originally presented at a Symposium on Comparative Semitics at the Oriental Institute in Honor of the Retirement of Gene B. Gragg on May 21–22, 2004. Thanks are due to Martha T. Roth for her leadership in organizing the symposium in Gene's honor and to the Department of Near Eastern Languages and Civilizations, the Department of Linguistics, the Division of the Humanities, and the College for sponsoring it. Thomas Urban and the staff of the Publications Office provided expert assistance in the production of the volume. Two of my graduate students assisted with the volume, thanks to the generous support of the Graduate School of the College of Letters and Sciences and the Etttinger Family Foundation. James C. Kirk compiled the index and proofread the first set of proofs. Wendy Widder proofread the final proofs. Christine Colburn, the Reader Services Manager of the Special Collections Research Center at University of Chicago Library, provided the image for the cover from Goodspeed 251, a Geʿez text that Gene published in 1975.

The symposium was centered around Semitic and comparative Semitic linguistics, the area of inquiry of most of Gene's students; two additional papers at the symposium (those by Bender and Militarev) directed our attention to his comparative Afroasiatic interests. An additional paper by Rebecca Hasselbach, who was recently hired to teach Comparative Semitics at the Oriental Institute, rounds out the volume.

The two Afroasiatic papers consider different aspects of connections between various branches of the Afroasiatic family. Lionel Bender, reconsiders the ratios of reconstructed forms derived from common Afroasiatic (or, Afrasian) terms in four language branches. His data suggest that Semitic has the strongest family inheritance from Afrasian, followed by Chadic, Omotic, and Cushitic. Alexander Militarev presents a number of Akkadian-Egyptian lexical matches, which he considers to be the result of contact rather than a common Afroasiatic origin.

Another pair of papers focuses on comparative Semitics. David Testen examines the origins the Akkadian vetitive on the basis of West Semitic analogues. Rebecca Hasselbach reconsiders the evidence for plural morphemes in the Semitic languages and proposes a new explanation for the fact that plural morphemes are diptotic rather than triptotic.

One paper, by Joseph Daniels, focuses on South Semitic by considering the range of syntactic constructions involving injunctive *la in Epigraphic South Arabic in comparison to jussive constructions in other South Semitic languages.

Three papers examine aspects of Biblical Hebrew; two use linguistic theory and one uses computational linguistics. Stuart Creason looks at the lexical semantics of the verb *pāqad* (the root *PQD* in the Qal stem) and proposes a single meaning for the verb with additional aspects of meaning contributed by the direct object and subject of the verb in various contexts. Cynthia L. Miller provides a linguistic account of the syntactic constraints on verbal ellipsis in Biblical Hebrew with attention to how poetry relaxes three of the constraints on verbal ellipsis that are found in prose. Richard L. Goerwitz describes a computer program that checks the pointing and accents of Tiberian biblical texts.

Three papers examine Aramaic. W. Randall Garr examines the phonological phenomenon of prenasalization in Imperial Aramaic, Middle Aramaic, and Mandaic within a dialectal and historical framework. The other two papers draw upon fieldwork in modern Aramaic dialects. Samuel Ethan Fox provides a traditional text in the Neo-Aramaic dialect of Bohtan and a grammatical sketch of its phonology and morphology. Robert D. Hoberman argues that prosodic structure rather than root structure played a crucial role in a sound change in Northeastern Neo-Aramaic dialects.

Two papers consider aspects of Semitic writing systems. Dennis Pardee considers the invention of the Ugaritic cuneiform alphabet in the context of other (linear) alphabetic writing systems. Peter T. Daniels considers the diffusion of West Semitic writing to Eurasia and beyond.

With this volume, we salute some (though hardly all!) of Gene's manifold achievements. Accepting his dictum that "philology without a theoretical perspective is blind" (1975b: 70), we are grateful to him for showing students and colleagues (not to mention several disciplines) that language study with a theoretical perspective knows no boundaries.

THE RESEARCH OF GENE B. GRAGG

Cynthia L. Miller

For over forty years, Gene B. Gragg has rigorously brought ideas and approaches from linguistics to bear on languages of the Near East and on several branches of the Afroasiatic language family. With joint appointments at the University of Chicago in the Department of Near Eastern Languages at the Oriental Institute and in the Department of Linguistics, Gene has conducted research that has been interdisciplinary in the truest sense of the term — in using linguistic theory and method to elucidate the structures of extinct or little-studied languages, on the one hand, and, on the other, in using data from those languages to explore problems in linguistic theory and method. However, describing Gene's research as interdisciplinary does not adequately capture the breadth and depth of his accomplishments either as a linguist or as a specialist of Near Eastern and East African languages.

Gene's doctoral dissertation and early research focused on Sumerian. Although primarily linguistic in orientation (1968a, 1972c, 1973a), he also published two early philological studies (1969, 1973b; see also 1997d). His dissertation (1966, published in a revised form as 1973e) applied the then still-new generative linguistic approach to the dimensional infixes in literary texts from the Old Babylonian period. By meticulously examining the distribution of the infixes within the prefix chain, the morphophonemic alternations of the infixes, their syntactic origins, and the semantic and/or syntactic function of the infixes with respect to the verb stem or the sentence as a whole, he was able to move beyond the standard view that the infixes are the result of concord between the verb and cognate adverbial phrases. At the same time, his linguistic analysis took into account the distinctive features of his ancient corpus, especially the problem of variants in different scribal copies of the same composition.

The problem of grammatical variation in ancient texts is a particularly vexing one for linguistic analysis, and so it is not surprising that Gene explored this topic in more detail (1972a), developing a method to measure the relative stability of grammatical elements in Sumerian texts, while examining possible factors that could influence variation (such as textual transmission, dialectal features of the text's place of origin, number of texts, phonological factors, individual scribal practice, diachronic linguistic features, and grammatical context). Another of his critical concerns in analyzing the syntax of ancient texts was whether the constructions analyzed represented the "total range of possibilities of Sumerian grammar, or a stylistic class, based on the actual, more or less statistically determined selective use literary Sumerian makes of these possibilities" (1973a: 134).

A year later in a seminal article entitled "Linguistics, Method, and Extinct Languages: The Case of Sumerian," he presented "a rationale for something between wholesale rejection and blind endorsement of the relevance of recent developments in linguistics for the study of ancient Near Eastern languages" (1973d: 78, n. 1). In this article he assessed the relationship of philological study of texts and linguistic analysis, noting that the decipherment, translation, and interpretation of texts — the purview of philology — must be the first step. A linguistic theory "with its accompanying heuristics" does not so much "provide miraculous answers to old unsolvable problems, as a new set of questions, or a better formulation of old questions, answers to which can be found in the old data" (1973d: 86). He described the "radical difference in point of view" (ibid., p. 86) between a theoretical linguist and a specialist in a particular language, especially with respect to the kinds of data available to the philologists of ancient languages as compared to the kinds of data needed for linguistic analysis. He urged linguists not to use linguistic terminology needlessly in their descriptions of ancient texts, but advocated "a philological-grammatical exposition oriented towards and informed by a linguistically responsible model" (ibid., p. 89). Throughout his career he has modeled this advice in his grammatical expositions of a wide range of languages and language families — the Semitic language family (1983b, 1997g) and Ethiopic (1997b), Geʿez (1997c, 1998c, 2004b), and Old South Arabian (1997f, 1997h); the Cushitic language family (2001b and Forthcoming b), Oromo of Wellegga (1976c), and Beja (2005 and 2006b); as well as three unaffiliated languages of the ancient Near East, Elamite (1994c), Hurrian (1992a, 1997e), and Urartian (1991c, 1992a).

From his early work on Sumerian, an extinct, isolate language with no surviving descendant languages (that is, a language that cannot be studied from either a comparative or a historical perspective), Gene turned next to research on South Semitic languages, ancient and modern, and to comparative and historical questions. As with Sumerian, his publications evince both philological and linguistic concerns; he published a Geʿez manuscript (1975b; the beginning of the text is reproduced on the cover of this volume) alongside studies that analyze the derivational morphology of Amharic (1970, 1987b), syntactic structures in Amharic (1972b) and Tigrinya (1974a), and lexical semantics (1978b, 1984b).

His interest in comparative and historical Semitic linguistics as well as his experience with Ethiopian Semitic languages led him to consider the possibility of contrasting Proto-Cushitic with Proto-Semitic — Proto-Cushitic, reconstructed from modern Cushitic languages, could serve as a control on the more tenuous reconstructions of Proto-Semitic, which must be recovered from mostly ancient and extinct languages (1982a: xv). Upon discovering, as Gene did, that "our knowledge of Cushitic was primitive in the extreme" with few of the materials necessary for historical reconstruction (1982a: xvi), most scholars would have looked elsewhere for data. Instead, he embarked upon a lexicographical project in the Cushitic language of Oromo, the third most widely spoken of all Afroasiatic languages (after Arabic and Hausa) and one of the five or six most important languages in Africa. The resulting *Oromo Dictionary* (1982a) remains the major lexical source for Oromo and includes more than 6,000 Oromo words with illustrative sentences for almost every main entry. More importantly, this research became part of the larger Cushitic etymological index (described in 1996b) and prompted further reflections on language contact (1980b) and lexicography (1988a, 1991b).

The potential of using computers for the electronic compilation of comparative linguistic data led Gene to computational linguistics. After completing CushLex, the electronic Cushitic etymological dictionary, he turned his attention to a database of comparative Afroasiatic. The Afroasiatic Index Project (described in 1996c and 1997a) is a computer database that will provide comparative lexical material for all branches of the Afroasiatic language family — Semitic, Egyptian, Cushitic (incorporating his earlier research in the Cushitic lexicon project), Omotic, Chadic, and Berber. He is also working on a collaborative project with Matthew Stolper to create an electronic study edition of the Achaemenid royal inscriptions (1996a, 1998a, b).

Gene's unbounded intellectual curiosity and rigorous linguistic method have served as a bridge between the often disparate fields of Semitic philology and linguistics, between the various sub-disciplines that study the ancient Near East, between the study of ancient languages by means of scribal corpora and modern languages by means of language helpers, and between users and developers of computer programs for linguistic and text analysis. In so doing he has inspired a generation of students and colleagues to expand their own research beyond disciplinary boundaries.

BIBLIOGRAPHY OF THE PUBLICATIONS AND COMMUNICATIONS OF GENE B. GRAGG (THROUGH 2006)

Charles E. Jones

1966

    Toward a Syntax of the Sumerian Verb: The Dimensional Infixes. Ph.D. dissertation, University of Chicago, Department of Linguistics. Chicago: University of Chicago.

1968

a   "Syntax of the Copula in Sumerian." In *The Verb 'Be' and its Synonyms: Philosophical and Grammatical Studies (3) Japanese/Kashmiri/Armenian/Hungarian/Sumerian/Shona*, edited by John W. M. Verhaar, pp. 86–109. Foundations of Language. Supplementary Series 1. Dordrecht: D. Reidel.

b   Review of *Sumerische Kultlyrik*, by Joachim Krecher. *Orientalia* 37: 371–81.

1969

    "Kes Temple Hymn." In *The Collection of the Sumerian Temple Hymns*, edited by Åke W. Sjöberg and E. Bergmann, pp. 155–88. Texts from Cuneiform Sources 3. Locust Valley: J. J. Augustin.

1970

    "Overt and Covert Categories in Derivational Morphology." In *Papers from the Sixth Regional Meeting, Chicago Linguistic Society, April 16–18, 1970*, pp. 262–69. Chicago: Chicago Linguistic Society.

1972

a   "Observations on Grammatical Variation in Sumerian Literary Texts." *Journal of the American Oriental Society* 92: 204–13.

b   "Semi-Indirect Discourse and Related Nightmares." In *Papers from the Eighth Regional Meeting, Chicago Linguistic Society, April 14–16, 1972*, edited by Paul M. Peranteau, Judith N. Levi, and Gloria C. Phares, pp. 75–82. Chicago: Chicago Linguistic Society.

c   "Sumerian and Selected Afro-Asiatic Languages." In *The Chicago Which Hunt: Papers from the Relative Clause Festival, April 13, 1972. A Paravolume to Papers from the Eighth Regional Meeting*, edited by Paul M. Peranteau, Judith N. Levi, and Gloria C. Phares, pp. 153–68. Chicago: Chicago Linguistic Society.

1973

a   "A Class of 'When' Clauses in Sumerian." *Journal of Near Eastern Studies* 32: 124–34.

b   "The Fable of the Heron and the Turtle." *Archiv für Orientforschung* 24: 51–72.

c   "Individual Research." In *Oriental Institute Annual Report 1972–1973*, pp. 35–36. Chicago: The Oriental Institute.

d   "Linguistics, Method, and Extinct Languages: The Case of Sumerian." *Orientalia* 42: 78–96.

e   *Sumerian Dimensional Infixes*. Alter Orient und Altes Testament, Sonderreihe 5. Kevelaer: Butzon und Bercker. [Originally presented as the author's thesis, University of Chicago, 1966]

1974

a   "Cleft Sentences in Tigrinya." *Journal of African Languages* 11: 74–88.

b   "The Cushitic Language Project." In *Oriental Institute Annual Report 1973–1974*, pp. 49–51. Chicago: The Oriental Institute.

1975

a   "Individual Research." In *Oriental Institute Annual Report 1974–1975*, p. 48. Chicago: The Oriental Institute.

b   "A Magic Prayer of Henoch from a Manuscript of the Goodspeed Collection of the University of Chicago." In *Proceedings of the First United States Conference on Ethiopian Studies, 1973*, edited by Harold G. Marcus, pp. 61–71.

Occasional Papers Series, Committee on Ethiopian Studies. Monograph 3. East Lansing: African Studies Center, Michigan State University.

1976

a "Individual Research." In *Oriental Institute Annual Report 1975–1976*, edited by John A. Brinkman, p. 51. Chicago: The Oriental Institute.

b "The NSF Ethiopia Project." In *Oriental Institute Annual Report 1975–1976*, edited by John A. Brinkman, pp. 42–43. Chicago: The Oriental Institute.

c "Oromo of Wellegga." In *The Non-Semitic Languages of Ethiopia*, edited by Lionel M. Bender, pp. 166–95. Occasional Papers Series, Committee on Ethiopian Studies. Monograph 5. East Lansing: African Studies Center, Michigan State University.

1977

"The Oromo Dictionary Project." In *Oriental Institute Annual Report 1976–1977*, edited by John A. Brinkman, p. 44. Chicago: The Oriental Institute.

1978

a "Individual Research." In *Oriental Institute Annual Report 1977–1978*, edited by John A. Brinkman, pp. 53–54. Chicago: The Oriental Institute.

b "Redundancy and Polysemy: Reflections on a Point of Departure for Lexicology Source." In *Papers from the Parasession on the Lexicon*, edited by Donka Farkas, Wesley M. Jacobsen, and Karol W. Todrys, pp. 174–83. Chicago: Chicago Linguistic Society.

1979

"Individual Research." In *Oriental Institute Annual Report 1978–1979*, edited by John A. Brinkman, pp. 91–92. Chicago: The Oriental Institute.

1980

a "Individual Research." In *Oriental Institute Annual Report 1979–1980*, edited by John A. Brinkman, p. 51. Chicago: The Oriental Institute.

b "Lexical Aspects of Oromo-Amharic Language Contact: Amharic Loanwords in Western Oromo." In *L'Ethiopie moderne: De l'avènement de Ménélik II à nos jours/Modern Ethiopia: From the Accession of Menilek II to the Present*, Proceedings of the Fifth International Conference of Ethiopian Studies, Nice, 19–22 December 1977, edited by Joseph Tubiana, pp. 107–24. Rotterdam: Balkema.

1981

"Individual Research." In *Oriental Institute Annual Report 1980–1981*, edited by John A. Brinkman, p. 51. Chicago: The Oriental Institute.

1982

a *Oromo Dictionary*. Monograph/Committee on Northeast African Studies 12. East Lansing: African Studies Center, Michigan State University, in cooperation with Oriental Institute, University of Chicago.

b Review of *The Gunnṣan-Gurage Languages*, by Robert Hetzron. *Journal of Near Eastern Studies* 41: 231–34.

1983

a "Individual Research." In *Oriental Institute Annual Report 1982–1983*, edited by Robert McC. Adams, p. 51. Chicago: The Oriental Institute.

b "Representation of Language Similarity in a Sample of Semitic." In *Ethiopian Studies: Dedicated to Wolf Leslau on the Occasion of His Seventy-fifth Birthday, November Fourteenth, 1981 by Friends and Colleagues*, edited by Stanislav Segert, András J. E. Bodrogligeti, Monica S. Devens, Maxine Rodinson, Sahle Sellasie, and Berhane Mariam, pp. 194–211. Wiesbaden: Harrassowitz.

1984

a "Individual Research." In *Oriental Institute Annual Report 1983–1984*, edited by Janet H. Johnson, p. 50. Chicago: The Oriental Institute.

b   "Polysemy and Derivation: Areal-Diachronic Perspectives." In *Papers from the Parasession on Lexical Semantics*, edited by David Testen, Veena Mishra, and Joseph Drogo, pp. 131–42. Chicago: Chicago Linguistic Society.

c   Review of *Etymological Dictionary of Gurage (Ethiopic)*, Vol. 1: *Individual Dictionaries*, Vol. 2: *English-Gurage Index*, and Vol. 3: *Etymological Section*, by Wolf Leslau. *Journal of Near Eastern Studies* 43: 343–46.

1985

"Individual Research." In *Oriental Institute Annual Report 1984–1985*, edited by Janet H. Johnson, p. 67. Chicago: The Oriental Insitute.

1986

"Individual Research." In *Oriental Institute Annual Report 1985–1986*, edited by Janet H. Johnson, p. 52. Chicago: The Oriental Institute.

1987

a   "Individual Research." In *Oriental Institute Annual Report 1986–1987*, edited by Janet H. Johnson, pp. 75–76. Chicago: The Oriental Institute.

b   "Paradigm Pressure, Lexical Pathology, and Lexical Replacement: The Development of the Weak Verb in Amharic." In *Language, Literature, and History: Philological and Historical Studies Presented to Erica Reiner*, edited by Francesca Rochberg, pp. 139–45. American Oriental Series 67. New Haven: American Oriental Society.

c   Review of *The Sumerian Language: An Introduction to Its History and Grammatical Structure*, by Marie-Louise Thomsen. *Journal of Near Eastern Studies* 47: 208–10.

1988

a   "Estimating Convergence and Conflict among Cognate Sets in a Cushitic Etymological Index." In *Papers from the International Symposium on Cushitic and Omotic Linguistics, Cologne, January 6–9, 1986*, edited by Marianne Bechhaus-Gerst and Fritz Serzisko, pp. 187–202. Hamburg: Helmut Buske Verlag.

b   "Individual Research." In *Oriental Institute Annual Report 1987–1988*, edied by Janet H. Johnson, p. 58. Chicago: The Oriental Institute.

1990

"Individual Research." In *Oriental Institute Annual Report 1989–1990*, edited by William M. Sumner, p. 75. Chicago: The Oriental Institute.

1991

a   "Individual Research." In *Oriental Institute Annual Report 1990–1991*, edited by William M. Sumner, p. 61. Chicago: The Oriental Institute.

b   "Lexicography of the Cushitic Languages." In *Wörterbücher: Ein internationales Handbuch zur Lexikographie*, edited by Franz Josef Hausmann, Oskar Reuichmann, Herbert Ernst Wiegand, and Ladislav Zgusta, pp. 2461–69. Handbücher zur Sprach- und Kommunikationswissenschaft 5.1. New York: Walter de Gruyter.

c   "Subject, Object, and Verb in Urartian: Prologue to Typology." *Aula Orientalis* 9: 105–12.

1992

a   "Hurrian and Urartian." In *International Encyclopedia of Linguistics* 2, edited by William Bright, pp. 188–90. New York: Oxford University Press.

b   "Individual Research." In *Oriental Institute Annual Report 1991–1992*, edited by William M. Sumner, p. 110. Chicago: The Oriental Institute.

1993

"Individual Research." In *Oriental Institute Annual Report 1992–1993*, edited by William M. Sumner, p. 91. Chicago: The Oriental Institute.

1994

a   "Babylonian Grammatical Texts." In *The Encyclopedia of Language and Linguistics*, edited by R. E. Asher and J. M. Y. Simpson, pp. 296–98. New York: Pergamon Press.

b   "Babylonian Grammatical Texts." In *Concise History of the Language Sciences: From the Sumerians to the Cognitivists,* edited by E. F. K. Koerner and R. E. Asher, pp. 19–20. New York: Pergamon Press.

c   "Individual Research." In *Oriental Institute Annual Report 1994*, edited by William M. Sumner, pp. 86–87. Chicago: The Oriental Institute.

d   Review of *The Hurrians*, by G. Wilhelm (translated from the German by Jennifer Barnes, with revisions by the author and a chapter by Diana Stein). *Aula Orientalis* 12: 247–49.

1995

"Less-understood Languages of Ancient Western Asia." In *Civilizations of the Ancient Near East*, Vol. 4, edited by Jack Sasson, pp. 2161–79. New York: Charles Scribner's Sons.

1996

a   "Achaemenid Royal Inscriptions." With Matthew W. Stolper. In *Oriental Institute Annual Report 1995–1996*, edited by William M. Sumner, pp. 85–86. Chicago: The Oriental Institute.

b   "CUSHLEX: a Cushitic Etymological Index." In *Cushitic and Omotic Languages: Proceedings of the Third International Symposium, Berlin, March 17–19, 1994,* edited by Catherine Griefenow-Mewis, and Rainer M. Voigt, pp. 43–58. Cologne: Rüdiger Köppe Verlag.

c   "Etymology and Electronics: Afroasiatic Index." *Oriental Institute News and Notes* 149: 1–4.

d   "Individual Research." In *Oriental Institute Annual Report 1995–1996*, edited by William M. Sumner, pp. 102–3. Chicago: The Oriental Institute.

e   "Mesopotamian Cuneiform: Other Languages." In *The World's Writing Systems*, edited by Peter T. Daniels and William Bright, pp. 58–72. New York: Oxford University Press.

f   "'South Arabian/Axumite' Depinto." In *Berenike 1995: Preliminary Report of the 1995 Excavations at Berenike (Egyptian Red Sea Coast) and the Survey of the Eastern Desert*, edited by Steven E. Sidebotham and Willemina Z. Wendrich, pp. 209–11. Leiden: Research School CNWS, School of Asian, African and Amerindian Studies.

1997

a   "The Afroasiatic Index Project." http: //oi.uchicago.edu/OI/PROJ/CUS/AAindex.html.

b   "Ethiopic." In *The Oxford Encyclopedia of Archaeology in the Near East*, Vol. 2, edited by Eric M. Meyers, pp. 278–80. New York: Oxford University Press.

c   "Geʿez Phonology." In *Phonologies of Asia and Africa (Including the Caucasus)*, edited by Alan S. Kaye, technical advisor Peter T. Daniels, pp. 169–86. Winona Lake: Eisenbrauns.

d   "The Heron and the Turtle: Sumerian Fable." In *The Context of Scripture*, edited by William W. Hallo and K. Lawson Younger, pp. 571–73. Leiden: E. J. Brill.

e   "Hurrian." In *The Oxford Encyclopedia of Archaeology in the Near East*, Vol. 3, edited by Eric M. Meyers, pp. 125–26. New York: Oxford University Press.

f   "Old South Arabian Phonology." In *Phonologies of Asia and Africa (Including the Caucasus)*, edited by Alan S. Kaye, technical advisor Peter T. Daniels, pp. 161–68. Winona Lake: Eisenbrauns.

g   "Semitic Languages." In *The Oxford Encyclopedia of Archaeology in the Near East*, Volume 4, edited by Eric M. Meyers, pp. 516–27. New York: Oxford University Press.

h   "South Arabian." In *The Oxford Encyclopedia of Archaeology in the Near East*, Vol. 5, edited by Eric M. Meyers, pp. 60–61. New York: Oxford University Press.

1998

a   "Achaemenid Royal Inscriptions Project." With Matthew W. Stolper. In *Oriental Institute Annual Report 1997–1998*, edited by Gene B. Gragg, p. 95. Chicago: The Oriental Institute.

b   "Achaemenid Royal Inscriptions from Persepolis in Electronic Form." With Matthew W. Stolper. *Oriental Institute News and Notes* 157: 1–5.

c   "Geʿez (Ethiopic)." In *The Semitic Languages*, edited by Robert Hetzron, pp. 242–60. Routledge Language Family Descriptions. New York: Routledge.

d   "Introduction." In *Oriental Institute Annual Report 1997–1998*, edited by Gene B. Gragg, pp. 3–6. Chicago: The Oriental Institute.

1999

"Introduction." In *Oriental Institute Annual Report 1998–1999*, edited by Gene B. Gragg, pp. 3–4. Chicago: The Oriental Institute.

2000

"Introduction." In *Oriental Institute Annual Report 1999–2000*, edited by Gene B. Gragg, pp. 3–4. Chicago: The Oriental Institute.

2001

a   "Introduction." In *Oriental Institute Annual Report 2000–2001*, edited by Gene B. Gragg, pp. 7–8. Chicago: The Oriental Institute.

b   "Kuschitisch." In *Historische Semitische Sprachwissenschaft*, edited by Burkhart Kienast, pp. 574–617. Wiesbaden: Harrassowitz.

c   "Preface." In *Letters from Egypt and Iraq 1954*, by Margaret Bell Cameron, pp. 5–6. Oriental Institute Special Publication 71. Chicago: The Development Office of the Oriental Institute, The University of Chicago.

2002

Review of *Syntactic Change in Akkadian: The Evolution of Sentential Complementation*, by Guy Deutscher. *Diachronica* 19: 403–8.

2004

a   "Bushes, Trees, and Networks in Afroasiatic." In *Papers from the 40th Regional Meeting of the Chicago Linguistic Society*. Chicago: Chicago Linguistic Society.

b   "Geʿez (Aksum)." In *The Cambridge Encyclopedia of the World's Ancient Languages*, edited by Roger D. Woodard, pp. 427–53. Cambridge: Cambridge University Press.

2005

"Morphology and Root Structure: A Beja Perspective." Proceedings of the Barcelona Symposium on Comparative Semitics, November 19–20, 2004. *Aula Orientalis* 23: 23–34.

2006

a   "Individual Research." In *Oriental Institute Annual Report 2005–2006*, edited by Gil J. Stein, p. 98. Chicago: The Oriental Institute.

b   "The 'Weak' Verb: Akkadian and Beja." In *The Akkadian Language in Its Semitic Context: Studies in the Akkadian of the Third and Second Millennium BC*, edited by G. Deutscher and N. J. C. Kouwenberg. Uitgaven van het Nederlands Instituut voor het Nabije Oosten te Leiden 106. Leiden: Netherlands Institute for the Near East.

Forthcoming

a   "Comparing Afroasiatic 'Templatic' Morphologies." In *Proceedings of the Simposio-International Group Comparative Semitic, Sitges, Spain, May 31–June 2, 2006*, edited by Gregorio del Olmo Lete.

b   "What Kind of Speech Community Is Represented by the 'Cushitic' Node?: Introduction to the Lexical Evidence." In *Proceedings of the 7th International Semitohamitic Congress, Berlin, September 13, 2004*, edited by Rainer Voigt.

GENE B. GRAGG AS A TEACHER

Robert D. Hoberman

While many of my memories of Gene's teaching, though more than thirty years old, are still vivid, others were brought back recently when I looked through my notebooks from his courses as I prepared these remarks. The fact that these notebooks are still on my shelves is in itself an indication of the importance Gene's courses had for my development as a linguist. I met Gene when I took his course on historical linguistics in the fall of 1972, my first term as a student in the Linguistics Department at the University of Chicago. In the following two years I took seminars called Questions in Semitic Linguistics that he co-taught, once with Carolyn Killean, an Arabist, and once with Stephen Kaufman, a specialist in Aramaic. The seminars and the general historical linguistics course, though naturally different in audience and material, were essentially the same in their intellectual approach, that is, a detailed discussion of challenging data of many sorts from many languages, using a wide variety of analytical modes. In the seminars, for example, two among the many topics Gene presented were Palmer's Firthian analysis of Tigré vowel harmony and Gene's own treatment of Amharic cleft sentences and relative clauses.

The course on historical linguistics was, in its overt organization, a chronological history of the field, but rather than a survey of antiques it was really an exploration of what each of the methodologies has to offer us today and how they complement one other. It was a combination of intellectual history and methodological tool kit for the working linguist. The course covered all the major developments of the nineteenth and twentieth centuries, starting with the Neogrammarians' Comparative Method, including a detailed treatment of Grimm's Law and Verner's Law, and then "contamination" (later known as analogy), internal reconstruction, and the structuralist treatment of phonemic change in terms of mergers and splits. Several specifically theoretical topics received serious examination: how internal reconstruction differs, and does not, from synchronic generative phonology; the generative view of language change as rule change (Kiparsky's formulation demonstrated with data from Akkadian dialectology); the effects of paradigmatic relations (then called transderivational constraints, now output-output constraints); and the Jakobsonian structuralist reinterpretation of sound change as change in systemic relations. Those are theoretical issues, but a big portion of the course examined empirical challenges to Neogrammarian and structuralist treatments of language change, particularly dialect geography (an image of the cycling sleuth of Calais, Edmond Edmont, sticks in mind) and variationist sociolinguistics. Gene attributed the notion that no dialect is completely consistent from the historical point of view — that everyone speaks a "transitional dialect" — to a direct chain of transmission from Rousselot to Martinet to Weinreich to Labov. The sociolinguistic approach to language change in progress, incidentally, which has since become one of the most productive branches of linguistics, was a fairly new and radical innovation at the time Gene taught this course. The illustrative problems Gene presented included many of the classics of historical linguistics but also many from his own work on languages ranging from Latin, French, and Dutch to Akkadian and Cushitic. My notebooks contain a wealth of descriptive details that are still thought-provoking. Gene clearly had put his full creative energies into designing the course. If he had turned his notes into a textbook, it would even now be one of the best.

Gene's work has dealt with a daunting range of languages: Sumerian, Hurrian, Cushitic languages, several ancient Indo-European languages, ancient and modern Semitic languages of Ethiopia, Akkadian, and Old South Arabian, with Latin and Hebrew always not far in the background. He has worked productively on phonology, morphology, syntax, and lexicography. He was interested enough in mathematical linguistics to show us Swadesh's equation for the retention of vocabulary over time,

$$t = \frac{\log rc}{2 \log r}$$

where t is the time-depth in millennia given an assumed constant rate of retention (r) in percentage per thousand years and a measured percentage of vocabulary shared by the two languages (c). This drew shocked gasps from many in the class, as I suspect it was expected to — a bit of sly humor. Gene was, early on, curious about the potential of computational linguistics. The first desktop computer I ever saw was Gene's little Radio Shack that he was using in his home office in 1978 to create and test algorithms for calculating relationships of languages within a family. This was an early stage of the research program that he has been actively pursuing in recent years, that is, the design of electronic database structures for the storage and comparison of lexical data and for electronic hypertext editions of complex ancient multi-lingual text corpora.

In 1974/1975 Gene was in Ethiopia collecting data for his dictionary of Oromo. I set off for my own dissertation fieldwork in Israel at the beginning of 1976, so we had only a brief opportunity to discuss my plans before I left, and he gave me free rein. I came back to the United States in 1978 and soon took a teaching position at another university, so again we had only infrequent contacts. (How did we live and work, pre-internet?). I had a mess of data and fairly little analysis, and I was beginning to panic. What did I have to say about my language that would be interesting to theoretical linguists? It was the hospitality shown me by Gene and his wife Michèle, and sometimes also their children Théo and Laura, that helped me over the hump. They welcomed me to stay in their home when I came to Chicago. In the evenings, after dinner and beer, I dumped my notebooks out on their dining-room table and Gene and I worked through the material. He astonished me by learning my language, which is a dialect of modern Aramaic, well enough so that when he came across in my draft words that I had not explained, he spotted them and asked about them. (I regret now that I never learned *any* of Gene's languages, but that seems to have made no difference to him.)

What inspired me about Gene's work when I was his student, and which still inspires me now, was a combination of four things that co-occur in very few environments:

(1) Alertness to up-to-date theoretical and methodological approaches of all sorts;
(2) Great depth of interest in the intellectual history of the field;
(3) A long-term commitment to the history and analysis of particular language families;
(4) Willingness to work with real live speakers of exotic, relatively little-studied languages in inconvenient places.

I was thrilled to be learning from someone who could teach a course on the development of generative linguistics and at the same time had cuneiform tablets on his desk. Gene remains for me the proof-by-example that one need not work in the most glamorous, competitive areas of theoretical linguistics, but one can be involved in a give-and-take with all streams and make lasting contributions on many levels, and that rigorous, creative teaching can be among those lasting contributions.

DISSERTATION COMMITTEE SERVICE

Gene B. Gragg

Although there are a few dissertations I unambiguously directed, and many more where I was clearly the second or third reader, I think "dissertations directed" in some cases would be an ambiguous category. As a "hyphenated" linguist-language person (and department member), I was often enough the "linguistics person" on some Near Eastern Languages and Civilizations dissertations and the "weird language person" on some linguistics dissertations. And in a number of dissertations with both data and linguistics orientation, it was sometimes difficult to tell who the real "director" was. However, participation in the dissertation process, as director or as reader, was always one of the most enriching (and demanding) of my career experiences. In that spirit, let me simply list a number of dissertation committees on which, according to what personal and department records I can consult, I had the privilege of serving.

1970	Callender, John B.	Coptic Nominal Sentences and Related Constructions
1975	Levi, Judith N.	The Syntax and Semantics of Nonpredicating Adjectives in English
1979	Mufwene, Salikoko S.	'Semantic Field' Versus 'Semantic Class'
1980	Collins, James T.	The Historical Relationships of the Languages of Central Maluku, Indonesia
1982	Fox, Samuel E.	The Structure of Morphology of Cairene Arabic
1983	Hoberman, Robert D.	Verb Inflection in Modern Aramaic: Morphosyntax and Semantics
1985	Zimansky, Paul E.	Ecology and Empire – The Structure of the Urartian State
1986	Cullen, John	Truth and Reference in English Complementation
1986	Yang, Zhi	A Study of the Sargonic Archive from Adab
1987	Layton, Scott C.	Archaic Features of Canaanite Personal Names in the Hebrew Bible
1987	Schick, Robert	The Fate of the Christians in Palestine During the Byzantine-Umayyad Transition, A.D. 600–750
1988	Eisele, John C.	Syntax and Semantics of Tense, Aspect and Time Reference in Cairene Arabic
1989	Tindel, Raymond D.	The History and Culture of Zafar
1989	Wheeler, Rebecca S.	The Lexical Entry of the English Verb Understand
1991	Crigger, Bette-Jean	"A Man Is Better Than His Birth": Identity and Action in Early Irish Law
1991	Jiang, Zi-Xin	Some Aspects of the Syntax of Topic and Subject in Chinese
1992	Miller, Cynthia L.	Reported Speech in Biblical and Epigraphic Hebrew: A Linguistic Analysis
1992	Nash, Peter T.	The Hebrew Qal Active Participle: A Non-Aspectual Narrative Backgrounding Element
1993	Burt, Clarissa C.	Parallelism in Jāhiliyya Poetry and the Northwest Semitic Connection
1993	Goerwitz, Richard L.	Tiberian Hebrew Pausal Forms
1993	Larson, Gary N.	Dynamic Computational Networks and the Representation of Phonological Information
1993	Long, Gary A.	Simile, Metaphor, and the Song of Songs
1993	Penney, Douglas L.	Towards a Prehistory of Biblical Hebrew Roots: Phoneme Constraint and Polymorphism
1995	Cohn, Rella Ann Israly	Yiddish Given Names-A Lexicon
1995	Creason, Stuart A.	Semantic Classes of Hebrew Verbs: A Study of Aktionsart in the Hebrew Verbal System

1995	Testen, David D.	Asseverative *La-* in Arabic and Related Semitic Particles
1999	Dobrin, Lise M.	Phonological Form, Morphological Class, and Syntactic Gender: The Noun Class Systems of Papua New Guinea Arapeshan
1999	Hemphill, Rachel	On the Perception/Production Interface in Speech Processing
2000	Karahashi, Fumi	Sumerian Compound Verbs with Body-Part Terms
2001	Ntihirageza, Jeanine	Quantity Sensitivity in Bantu Languages: Focus on Kirundi
2002	Suzuki, Hisami	Multi-modularity in Computational Grammar
2005	Conklin, Blane W.	Oath Formulae in Classical Hebrew and Other Semitic Languages

1. THE AFRASIAN LEXICON RECONSIDERED

M. Lionel Bender

1.1. Introduction

In Bender 2004, presented in San Diego, I compared 110 lexical items of Chadic, Omotic, and Afrasian, for which both *Chadic and *Omotic reconstructions are available and found that evidence for Omotic as descended from *Afrasian is considerably weaker than that for Chadic: about 9.5% of reconstructed Chadic roots were found to have *Afrasian sources, while only 3.9% of reconstructed Omotic roots do. Gene Gragg welcomed my suggestion of including Cushitic as likely to shed further light, leading to this paper. I extended the comparisons further to Semitic[1] when a new database for the latter came to my attention (Huehnergard 2000). In this paper, I limit the comparisons to those cases for which comparanda exist for all three Afrasian families and I also exclude five non-arbitrary items,[2] bringing the total to 105.[3]

1.1.1. Sources

Chadic items are taken from Newman 1977 and Jungraithmayr and Ibriszimow 1994. From the latter, I use only items found in two or all three branches of Jungraithmayr and Ibriszimow's Chadic. The Newman set of Chadic proto-forms differs from Jungraithmayr and Ibriszimow in that Newman reconstructs vowels, which Jungraithmayr and Ibriszimow do not, and Newman assumes a biliteral root, contrary to the traditional triliteral conception of *Afrasian, which is overly influenced by Semitic.

For Cushitic, I use Ehret 1987 sparingly.[4] My main sources for East Cushitic are Sasse 1979, 1982. To extend this to *Cushitic, I use: Beja (questionably North Cushitic) of Roper 1928; Agew (= Agaw) or Central Cushitic of Appleyard (personal communication); and for South Cushitic, Iraqw of Maghway 1989 (Iraaqw of Whiteley 1953, 1958 for some items) and Dahalo of Ehret, Elderkind, and Nurse 1989.[5] East and South Cushitic are considered as one family.

---

[1] In Bender 1997, I assume a structure of Afrasian in which Omotic and Chadic are independent branches, with all the others (Egyptian doubtfully, Semitic-Berber-Cushitic for sure, forming a third branch, which I call "Macro-Cushitic"). In view of the results of Bender 2004, I would go a bit further and say that the structure is 1: Omotic; 2: all the rest: 2.1: Chadic, and 2.2: Macro-Cushitic. Omotic is the first split-off.

I did not consider Berber here, for lack of an accessible database, nor Egyptian because of my uncertainty of how it should be classified.

The Omotic family tree used in this analysis is that of Bender 2003: 286:

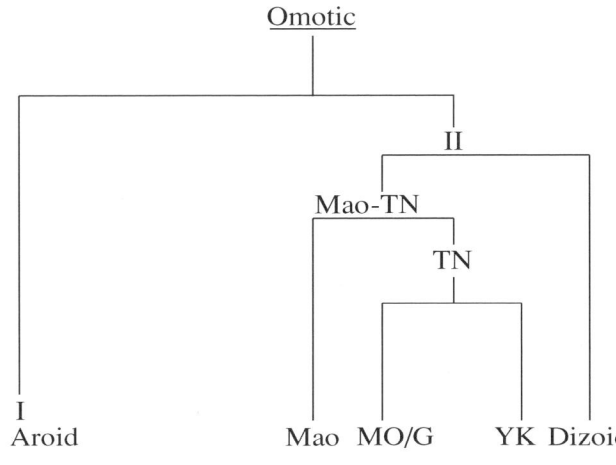

Notes: TN is the family having independent pronouns first-person singular / second-person singular ta/ne. MO-G is Macro-Ometo/Gimira. Macro-Ometo is Ometo plus C'ara. YK is Yem-Kefoid ("Janjero-Gonga").

[2] The five excluded items are four which are wholly or nearly wholly sound-symbolic: 'blow' of form **p-**, 'fly or jump' of form **pr-**, 'sneeze' **-tiš**, 'spit' **tuf**, and one Wanderwort: 'ten' **tom-**.

[3] I was fortunate to engage in stimulating personal correspondence with Gene Gragg, who urged extending the database to Cushitic; David Appleyard, who provided Agew proto-forms; Paul Newman, who encouraged me to use his Chadic proto-forms and updated one of them; John Huehnergard, who provided some additional Proto-Semitic forms; and Peter T. Daniels, who provided Bergsträsser 1983. None of these is responsible for any errors in data or interpretation in this work.

[4] Although I do not question herein Ehret's often dubious phonology, I had to reject a number of items for fantastic semantics, for example, 45: 'sit': 'sink, sink (down), live, exist, under, down, below'; 561: 'skin': 'people, folk, tribe, cowry shell, skin, flesh, body'. Ehret often includes specialized terms under a list gloss, for example, 'body hair, long hair, white hair', 'cut apart, cut off, cut repeatedly, cut up', and 'go along, go around, go before'. These are generally not used herein.

[5] There exists much disagreement about the status of South Cushitic. The consensus seems to be that it is part of East Cushitic rather than an independent family. Given the scant documentation of most languages, I have chosen to draw only on the two best-attested ones and treat them as coordinate to East Cushitic, so that there are three Cushitic families: North, Central, East-South.

Omotic items are from Bender 2003. Semitic is from Huehnergard (2000 and personal communication), supplemented by David Cohen 1970 and Bergsträsser 1983. The Huehnergard article is restricted to about 700 items having English derivatives listed in the main body of the dictionary.

There is still no definitive source on *Afrasian. The pioneering work of Marcel Cohen 1947 is useful because Cohen did not separate Omotic from Cushitic and because he used only Hausa from Chadic, so that Cohen is largely independent of Chadic and Omotic. Cohen does not give proto-forms, so I give approximations in cases that I accept as plausible. I also use the incomplete Diakonoff et al. 1993–97, which unfortunately covers only about one third of possible initials. This is supplemented by Diakonoff 1993. I did not use several recent sources because I consider them methodologically inadequate. In particular, Orel and Stolbova 1995 is skewed toward Chadic and neglects Omotic. In fact, Stolbova was a collaborator in Diakonoff et al. 1993 and contributed a rich Chadic database in that work also. I also added a few of my own reconstructions based on the current paper.

Following the pattern of Jungraithmayr and Ibriszimow and of Bender 1996–97, I establish grades of isoglosses, using bold, plain, or italic script.[6] There are some changes of orthography from the originals in the list of isoglosses.[7] Alternative glosses and other relevant information are given when space is adequate. An occasional comparative Nilo-Saharan form (graded III, II, I from strongest to weakest) is given from Bender 1996–97 and East Sudanic from Bender 2005.

1.1.2. Comparability

Jungraithmayr and Ibriszimow 1994 contains more proposed isoglosses for Chadic than those for other Afrasian families, though many are weak or possibly redundant. Partly to compensate for this in Omotic, I use representatives of all major branches in this order: Aroid, Mao, TN (the ta/ne family consisting of Macro-Ometo-Gimira, Yem, and Kefoid), and Dizoid. If an *Omotic reconstruction is posited, it is given following these, according to the grading set out in note 6. These do not always agree with Bender 2003 because my criteria here are slightly different. Note that occurrence in just Mao and TN is not considered as sufficient for an isogloss because Mao is closer to TN than to Aroid or Dizoid. Another point worth noting is that there are many cases for which Aroid and Dizoid share unique forms, although they are not in geographic proximity in most of their ranges. See Bender 2000 for discussion of the special relationship of Aroid and Dizoid: it seems that both have strong Nilotic substrata.

Since I added Cushitic and Semitic after establishing the gloss list on the basis of comparability of Chadic and Omotic, the Cushitic and Semitic lists are less complete than the others. Similarly to Omotic and following Tosco 2003, I list the main branches of Cushitic in the order North (= Beja), Central (= Agew), East, South, finally Cushitic with *. Beja is a single language, though some consider it coordinate to Cushitic rather than a member of Cushitic. Central is a small, fairly uniform family; some consider it a part of East Cushitic. East is very large, having two main divisions: Highland or Burji-Sidamo and Lowland. South is small and relatively poorly described; some consider it a part of East. I did not have access to Ehret 1980, which has been severely criticized by reviewers. I include in my data set here only Dahalo and Iraqw. The former West Cushitic is now generally accepted as being a distinct branch of Afrasian, namely Omotic.

---

[6] The grading is as follows:

*Chadic grading:
 found in all of West, Central, East Chadic **BOLD**
 found in any two of West, Central, East plain
*Cushitic and East Cushitic grading:
 found in three or more of Sasse's/Ehret's sub-families **BOLD**
 found in any two of Sasse's/Ehret's sub-families plain
*Semitic grading:
 Proto-Semitic or common Semitic **BOLD**
 found in West Semitic (not in Eblaite-Akkadian) plain
*Omotic grading:
 found in Aroid, M or TN, and Dizoid **BOLD**
 found in any two of Aroid, M or TN, Dizoid *italics*

In addition: *Agew in **BOLD**, *North Agew in plain.
Details on Omotic sub-divisions are similar (see Bender 2003).

[7] In the list of isoglosses, there are replacements for Jungraithmayr and Ibriszimow 1994 symbols: k' for ƙ, r' and s' for "r and s with dot under respectively." In the Diakonoff et al. 1993–97 items, symbol 8 stands for syllabic vowel or laryngeal. I have omitted some of the Diakonoff et al. 1993–97 diacritics as inessential for present purposes. I have replaced Newman's hl by ɬ. For uniformity, I have replaced a number of Huehnergard's Semitist symbols by IPA or Africa-alphabet symbols so that interdental fricatives are ð and θ respectively, lateral fricatives ɬ and ɬ', ejectives t', s', k', velar fricatives ɣ and χ, pharyngeal fricatives ʕ and ħ, glottal stop ʔ. The same and similar remarks apply to Dahalo and Iraqw, for example, -kk- for -k:-, -ɬ- for -hl-.

It must be noted that the lists of proto-forms are not strictly comparable. The Chadic list contains only proto-forms reconstructed in two or all three of Jungraithmayr and Ibriszimow's Chadic sub-families. The Omotic list contains proto-forms (or, in a few cases, forms that are frequent but not reconstructed) found in any one of the four sub-families: Aroid, Mao, TN, and Dizoid. The Cushitic list is similar in having Beja, Agew, and East and South Cushitic forms listed sequentially, with proto-forms used when available. It is not clear how much this skews the results, but Jungraithmayr and Ibriszimow 1994 are liberal in their criteria for what constitutes a proto-form and this helps balance it out.

There are about five times as many Chadic languages (150) as Omotic, so this tends to increase proposed proto-forms, especially on the liberal criteria used by Jungraithmayr and Ibriszimow 1994. There are over forty Cushitic languages and about thirty Omotic. Semitic has a vast literature and a long history of reconstructive work, though for lexicon it is scattered and not always easy of access. Extinct languages such as Akkadian, Ancient Hebrew, and Classical Arabic figure heavily into reconstructions. There are about seventy current Semitic languages. This does not take into account actual documentation in the literature, which is abundant for some languages (e.g., Arabic, Hausa, and Oromo), but weak to nearly lacking in many.

1.2. Analysis

Afrasian reconstructions are found for sixty-three of the 105 list items. Counting multiple cognates for some cases, the total of *Afrasian reconstructions is eighty-four. In judging cognates across families, I have not yet tried to apply supposedly regular correspondences such as those proposed in previous work, for example, the Egyptian Etymological project of Gábor Takács (1999). But note that proto-forms in the list were mostly reconstructed using standard methodology. Herein, I have tried to find a middle ground of plausibility in inspection. I am trying to find what the facts are, not to establish any particular grouping. I have no emotional attachment to any outcome. Subjectivity is regrettable: it can be reduced, but not avoided altogether in this kind of work, and more rigorous methodology can be applied in a later stage.

1.2.1. *Chadic < *Afrasian

These are sixty-one in number as follows (some items have two or three different cognates and several are questionable): 1, 6, 8, 9, 10, 11, 14, 16, 16, 16, 19, 21, 21, 22, 25, 27, 28, 29, 30, 32, 33, 34, 36, 36, 42, 43, 43, 46, 48, 49, 51, 52, 52, 52, 53, 54, 58, 58, 60, 60, 63, 63, 66, 70, 71, 71, 72, 73, 74, 75, 80, 82, 83, 84, 91, 98, 99, 101, 103, 104, 104. Here, as in all of sections 1.1–1.4, the reader will have to refer to the full isogloss list for the specific forms.

1.2.2. Cushitic < *Afrasian

There are twelve cases of *Cushitic < *Afrasian: 14, 25, 31, 36, 46, 60, 70, 73, 74, 79, 84, 85 and twenty-six cases of other Cushitic (Beja, Agew, East Cushitic) < *Afrasian: 1, 6, 21, 27, 28, 29, 38, 43, 47, 48, 49, 54, 57, 58, 62, 66, 71, 72, 72, 76, 80, 87, 90, 99, 101, 103 for a total of thirty-eight. Here I did not count South Cushitic (Dahalo and Iraqw) items because it is likely that South is a sub-family of East.

1.2.3. *Semitic < *Afrasian

The number of reconstructions for *Semitic is the lowest of the families (except *Afrasian itself). There are thirty-two cases of *Semitic < *Afrasian: 6, 8, 9, 10, 11, 16, 21, 25, 27, 30, 34, 36, 42, 47, 48, 58, 63, 63, 70, 73, 74, 76, 82, 83, 84, 91, 98, 99, 100, 101, 103, 104.

1.2.4. *Omotic < *Afrasian

I found twenty-one cases of *Omotic < *Afrasian: 1, 10, 21, 24, 28, 32, 36, 36, 38, 40, 51, 52, 57, 62, 70, 71, 71, 72, 78, 79, 87 and ten cases of other Omotic families < *Afrasian: 21, 28, 31, 53, 66, 76, 76, 87, 90, 101 for a total of thirty-one.

1.2.5. Adjustments

The number of choices varies by family, so that the role of chance correspondences must be taken into account: the more forms to compare, the more chance correspondences. The numbers of forms available for comparison to the eighty-four Afrasian forms are:

*Chadic: 422   Cushitic: 329, discounting Dahalo and Iraqw
*Semitic: 129   Omotic: 245

These numbers can be used as denominators to show the fractions of occurrences of *Afrasian-derived forms by family (to the third decimal point):

*Chadic < *Afrasian: 61/422 = .145
*Cushitic < *Afrasian: 12/329 = .036   Cushitic < *Afrasian: 38/329 = .117
*Semitic < *Afrasian: 32/129 = .248
*Omotic < *Afrasian: 21/245 = .086   Omotic < *Afrasian: 31/245 = .127

1.3. Discussion and Conclusions

I do not consider cross-family correspondences here (Chadic-Omotic, etc.).

It is clear that the number of Chadic reconstructed forms is exaggerated here because of semantic spread in many items and because the Jungraithmayr and Ibriszimow 1994 criteria are liberal. For example, the gloss 'burn' (Jungraithmayr and Ibriszimow 1994/2: 24) is detailed in Jungraithmayr and Ibriszimow 1994/1: 24–25 as having several subsidiary meanings: 'roast, fry', perhaps 'blow'. Some *forms are weakly attested, for example, *hl (= ɬ), found in three languages: Tangale, Kabalai, and Sumrai(?). Rather than try to disentangle all this, I simply used the totals of reconstructed forms as denominators (section 1.2.5 above). Of course, this strategy is subject to reservations, for example, can it be assumed that all reconstructed sets should be the same or nearly the same size? There are also the questions of accidental omissions of glosses from the data sets, relative ages (e.g., Chadic and Omotic are presumably older than Cushitic and Semitic), depth of scholarly investigation of the families, intrinsic properties of the language families, and historical particularities (such as language contacts).

From the ratios of section 1.2.5 above, one sees that Chadic and Semitic have about 14.5% and 24.8%, respectively, of their reconstructed forms presumably derived from *Afrasian. For Cushitic and Omotic, there is a complication in that not all comparisons are with proto-forms. For *Cushitic and *Omotic, the figures are 3.6% and 8.6% respectively. But if one takes into account comparisons with sub-families (Beja, etc., for Cushitic, Aroid, etc., for Omotic), the figures rise to 11.7% and 12.7% respectively.

Semitic has by far the strongest family inheritance from *Afrasian (about one-fourth of its proto-forms), followed by Chadic (about one-seventh of its proto-forms). Cushitic and Omotic are similar at about one-eighth of their forms (including sub-family forms). It is surprising that Cushitic trails even Omotic and that the figure for *Cushitic is so very low (3.6%). I think this indicates a need for reworking of Cushitic: most of Ehret's (1987) proposed proto-forms I considered here were rejected as unsatisfactory, and I found few new ones. If my idea of the Afrasian family tree is correct, the result for Cushitic should be much higher than for Omotic and similar to that of Semitic (Bender Forthcoming).

One must also keep in mind the mixed nature of reconstructed forms for all families except Omotic (where I used only my own, good or bad as they may be). In addition to several older sources, I made up some new proto-forms based on occurrences according to the structures I now accept. For *Afrasian, this means occurrences in any two of Chadic, Omotic, and Macro-Cushitic. For the last named, I accepted either Semitic or Cushitic or both. Of course Berber waits for inclusion and Egyptian also, if one can decide where it fits in. Non-contemporaneity is a mixed problem since Old Egyptian is not far in time from *Semitic and *Cushitic, though not as old as *Chadic and *Omotic, if my model is correct. There is some circularity here: assuming that a form found in Chadic and Omotic is of *Afrasian origin raises both *Chadic and *Omotic versus *Afrasian, but it is a necessary circularity, not a vicious circularity.

The Afrasian Isoglosses table (1.1) contains all 105 items. Of these, the twenty-one "best" items are those having cognates in all of *Chadic, Cushitic, *Semitic, Omotic or in three of these. Those in all four are four in number: 'come', 'eat', 'meat', 'urine' (by chance forming a simple sentence of the first three). The full list is: 1, 6, 10, 21, 25, 27, 28, 36, 48, 58, 66, 70, 71, 72, 73, 74, 76, 84, 99, 101, 103; see Selected Isoglosses. Note that in some cases, there is no single cognate set which runs through all families (e.g., #58 'hear' has one form in Chadic and Cushitic, another in Chadic and Semitic). Comments on the twenty-one "best" items follow:

1. 'ashes, etc.' All but Semitic. The third Agew form is 'earth' (#35 in the list). *Omotic bind ~ bend can be questioned. Diakonoff's -t' seems unjustified (-t is indicated).
6. 'bird'. In all but Omotic. The Diakonoff pər (and forms in Chadic-Cushitic-Semitic) may be from the symbolic form p_r 'fly, jump', which would invalidate this item. In Cushitic, I assume kim-bir.[8]
10. 'bone'. Absent in Cushitic and weak in Semitic. The vowel varies over a, o, u.
21. 'come'. This verb is discussed for its unusual conjugation in Bender 1990. t- is universal if one counts d- in Chadic, ʔtw/y- in Semitic, and aad/t- in Aroid of Omotic. As y- in all but Semitic if one counts ʔi in Cushitic.
25. 'cow, cattle'. One has to assume l- or ł- ~ š- to make this one work in all but Omotic.
27. 'cry, weep'. Not in Omotic. The form w_l is an isogloss for Chadic-Cushitic (Beja), but one has to assume ʔl also to bring in Semitic.
28. 'cut'. A weak isogloss depending on three *Afrasian forms. Universal: kat'- (Chadic kł ?, East Cushitic k'aɗ₁-, Semitic fis's', *Omotic k'aat'). fVt (pt in Chadic). t/dac ~ t/dyc (Omotic Aroid tic- ~ tec-).
36. 'eat, bite'. *Afrasian forms ʕm and k'am, which might be alternants, and tV8 (8 a laryngeal or syllabic vowel). Chadic has kám and also (Jungraithmayr and Ibriszimow) twy or (Newman) ti. Cushitic has Ehret's *-a/uɦim-. Semitic has h/ɦu/am. *Omotic has both t- and m-.
48. 'foot, leg'. Not in Omotic. I posit *Afrasian rgd/l on the basis of Chadic g₂rd (by root metathesis), Ehret's *ragad ~ rigid, and Semitic rigl.
58. 'hear, ear'. Not in Omotic. My *Afrasian ɗg and Cohen's šm: Chadic ɗ₂gw and km ~ łm, East Cushitic ɗe/og-, and Semitic šmʕ.
66. 'knee'. Marcel Cohen's Afrasian: gRb, Chadic: (Jungraithmayr and Ibriszimow) grp, Cushitic: Ehret's gʷilb ~ gulb, Omotic: TN: gurm+at. I do not include Semitic birk, though I wonder if this could be metathesis.
70. 'meat'. Universal. *Afrasian and *Cushitic ša, Chadic łw, Semitic ši?r (?), and *Omotic ac.
71. 'monkey, baboon'. Both Chadic and East Cushitic have roots containing g_l, Chadic also has a root containing k_r, while *Omotic has both gVr and k'ar. The lack of *Semitic is interesting: no monkeys in their environment?
72. 'moon, month'. Not in Semitic. There are two *Afrasian roots: arb found in Agew of Cushitic and in *Omotic, tVr in Chadic and Beja of Cushitic. The latter may be a Wanderwort, found also in some Nilo-Saharan and Niger-Kordofanian languages.
73. 'mouth'. *Afrasian has a monoconsonantal labial root; found also in Chadic as (Newman) ba, Cushitic as yaf ~ ʔaf, Semitic as p. Not in Omotic: I think ʔap in Mao is a loan from Amharic.
74. 'name'. The well-known Afrasian root sVm is found in Chadic and Semitic. Occurrences in Cushitic may be loans, and occurrences in Omotic certainly are.

[8] Alexander Militarev offered the comment that I am engaging in "long-range" comparisons à la Greenberg here with all the problems of that "method." For example, he says I missed an isogloss here in the Omotic #6 'bird' apt+i because I did not look at regular correpondences. But the comment is misguided because none of the sources I used suggested *Semitic or *Afrasian cognates to my Aroid form and the proto-forms I did use are based on standard methods, usually including regular correspondences. I do not accept Greenbergian "multilateral comparison" as a methodology, but rather as a heuristic which most of us make use of.

76. 'neck, nape'. Two weak *Afrasian forms kVš and kOm. N. Agew of Cushitic has k(ʷ)ərm and Dizoid of Omotic has kum; Semitic has kišād, Omotic Aroid has k'u/orc'+i and Mao has kitiš+. All this is doubtful.
84. 'sand'. Here, Marcel Cohen supports an *Afrasian form something like haS, for which I have Chadic gʷsk, for example, Hausa k'asa, *Cushitic haats', and Semitic fis's'. Not in Omotic.
99. 'tooth'. Diakonoff's *Afrasian sinn is reflected in Chadic (Newman) šan, Cushitic Iraqw sifino, zino, and Semitic šnn. Omotic is non-cognate.
101. 'urine'. Afrasian has several possible proto-forms: si/ant, wss ~ wsš, pVc'. Chadic has ps'r, wicē, Cushitic various, for example, Beja iša, East Cushitic sinɖ₁i-, Semitic θayn(at), Omotic TN šeš. These sibilantal forms could all be sound-symbolic.
103. 'water'. The *Afrasian m- root is reflected in Chadic (Jungraithmayr and Ibriszimow) ywm or (Newman) am, Cushitic may, and Semitic my. Omotic has no such form.

1.4. Afterword

My 2004 paper at the Thirty-second North American Conference on Afroasiatic Linguistics was aimed at the question of lexical evidence for Omotic being Afrasian, following on the negative outlook expressed in Bender 2003:xii. A negative outlook was expressed much earlier by Newman (1980).

In this paper, I think I have identified the cause of this negativity. There were two main past conceptions of *Afrasian: (1) a skewing toward Semitic or (2) the view that Afrasian has five or six equal branches — Berber, Chadic, Cushitic, Egyptian, Semitic, and possibly Omotic — with no sub-grouping. In my 1997 paper I proposed an "upside-down" view in which there is much internal structure and Semitic is, in fact, the most recent and most innovative branch. Using that approach herein, the number of plausible Afrasian proto-forms increases and Omotic figures into many of them. Thus the two likely Afrasian retentions of Bender 2003 is now increased to the thirty-one identified in section 1.2.4 above. Of course this comes at the expense of the former Cushitic, in which Omotic was the West branch.

Table 1.1. Afrasian Isoglosses
Cushitic in order: Beja, Agew, East, South, *Cushitic
Omotic in order: Aroid, Mao, TN, Dizoid, *Omotic

1. *ASHES* (cf. #35 'earth [Agew third form]', and #84 'sand')
    *Afrasian: Diakonoff et al. 1993–97:75: bət' (better: bət)
    *Chadic: **bt-**, **t(w)k**, pəlí, etc.; Newman 1977:2: bətu
    Cushitic: haš = 'dust' | **wəza**; tsVbVr+, **bət+a** | **darʕ+** | Dahalo: t̯'íliiɦa; Iraqw: daʔara | —
    *Semitic: —
    Omotic: bind+ | puus+ | bend+ | ts'iakn | *bi/end+

2. *BARK* (cf. #90 'skin')
    *Afrasian: —
    *Chadic: **ɓ-r**, **krp**, ɓkl/ɓlk, kɓr, lihè, etc.
    Cushitic: aɗif; šakar | **qaf**; sənkʷ+a | **k'olf+** | Dahalo: pák'o; Iraqw: k'afi | Ehret 1987:145: *k'aaf
    *Semitic: —
    Omotic: ɗaaki | tengo | k(')ol+ | orkn | —

3. *BEARD, CHIN*
    *Afrasian: —
    *Chadic: **grm**, **gs'm**, g-g, d₂m, ɓkm
    Cushitic: — | — | — | Dahalo: gátt'a; Iraqw: daamóo | —
    *Semitic: **ðak'ar**
    Omotic: buc+, s'/c'ir+ | — | buc+ | ts'(i)ar | *buc+, s'ir

4. *BEE* (cf. #47 'fly', and #61 'honey')
    *Afrasian: —
    *Chadic: **d-m**, **ym**, skn, mn, ɗʸm; Newman 1977:70: ami = 'honey'
    Cushitic: wiu | laɣl+a | **ka/in(n)+** | Dahalo: ɗíme; Iraqw: baʔaarmoo | —
    *Semitic: also 'honey': **nuhb**
    Omotic: ants' | — | matt+ | yans' | (y)ans'+

5. *BELLY, STOMACH* (occasionally 'chest' [Beja, second Dahalo form])
    *Afrasian: Marcel Cohen 1947:230bis: k'Vb
    *Chadic: **ɓtl**, gln, k'ɗ, gd, b₂kl, kt
    Cushitic: yam; gwadab | **gʷä/əzgʷ+** | Highland East Cushitic: *godoba | Dahalo: ɓágama; Iraqw: guraʔ; Dahalo: gíɗare | Ehret 1987:32: ***gʷadab**
    *Semitic: **kars'; b/p-t/š-n**
    Omotic: ʔak+ | — | — | — | —

6. *BIRD* (cf. #18 'chicken, fowl')
   *Afrasian: Diakonoff et al. 1993–97:34: pər (related to symbolic 'fly' pr?)
   *Chadic: yɗ ~ ɗt ~ ɗyk, s'-d, bk-, lay-, etc., púráámė, etc.; Newman 1977:6: ɗəy-
   Cushitic: kélai | dzäx+(äl)+ | **kimbir** | Dahalo: hétiiβe; Iraqw: s'irʔo | —
   *Semitic: **puur** ~ **ṣippur** (symbolic?)
   Omotic: apt+i | kap+ | kap+ | kap+i | ***kap+***

7. *BITE* (cf. #36 'eat')
   *Afrasian: —
   *Chadic: **k'-d**, k'-s
   Cushitic: finik; tam | ʔəŋ- | **k'aniin-, k'om-** | Dahalo: k'afi-; Iraqw: kifi- | —
   *Semitic: **nšk**
   Omotic: gaʔ- | šaat- | saat'- | wots'- | —

8. *BLACK*, *DARK* (cf. #20 'cold', and #78 'night')
   *Afrasian: Bender: -lm (?)
   *Chadic: **-lm, dk**, d-m, dp, rm, rs
   Cushitic: hádal; dil/ri | ŋətsir; (Kimant: <tsam-) | **dum-** | Dahalo: hímmaṯe; Iraqw: bóoʕ | —
   *Semitic: also 'dark': **θ'lm**
   Omotic: ts'an | tu/ot- | kar- | ts'an- | ***ts'an***

9. *BLOOD* (Mao < TN; Dizoid < Nilotic a)
   *Afrasian: Marcel Cohen 1947:335; Diakonoff et al. 1993–97:280: dm
   *Chadic: **br**, dm, b$_{(2)}$z; Newman 1970:10: bar
   Cushitic: boi | **bər+** | **ɗiig+** | Dahalo: ɗiiga; Iraqw: ts'eeree | ***bAr*** (?)
   *Semitic: **dam**
   Omotic: mak'as, zumʔ+i | [han+] | sut, hanna | [yarm] | —

10. *BONE* (first Dahalo item < Khoisan?)
    *Afrasian: Marcel Cohen 1947:225: k'Vs
    *Chadic: k's$_3$
    Cushitic: mitat | ŋats | **laf+**, mik'+ | Dahalo: [míttl'o]; Iraqw: fara | —
    *Semitic: **ʕaθ'm**; David Cohen 1970: Hebrew 'thorn': k'ōs'
    Omotic: k'o/us | — | mek'+ett+ | k'us | ***k'us***

11. *BOY, CHILD* (occasionally < 'bear (child)')
    *Afrasian: Bender: wl- (?)
    *Chadic: **w-l**, mr ~ rm, bzn; gr; wn; bl-
    Cushitic: ʔor | (ʔe)qwər-; ʔənfär+a | **ʔin(a)m+** | Dahalo: ɓóoreeṯe, g^{W}íttsa; Iraqw: garma | —
    *Semitic: **wald; b(i)n**
    Omotic: nas | me/al+ | naʔa | dad+u | ***na-*** (?)

12. *BREAST*, *CHEST* (occasionally 'suck(le)')

   *Afrasian: —

   *Chadic: **wɗ, p-ɓ,** n-n; kp; Newman 1977:18: wɔɗi = 'milk'

   Cushitic: daba; degát; nugw | **ʔa/əŋgʷ+** | **naʔs+, ʔəŋgʷ, nuug-** | Dahalo: gíɗare | *nuug-; Ehret 1987:463: ***ʔaŋgʷ+ ~ ʔuŋgʷ+** (?)

   *Semitic: **θady**

   Omotic: ami | — | ɗ/t'aam+ | t'iamu | ***ɗ/t'aam**

13. *BRING*, *CARRY* (cf. #51 'give' [Agew first form])

   *Afrasian: —

   *Chadic: **gr,** ɗgr, s-, ɓagi, etc.; Newman 1977:24: kərə

   Cushitic: hai | nax-s; məqʷ- | — | Dahalo: kaaʔ-; looʕ-; Iraqw: húuw | Ehret 1987:514: *heeʔ- (?)

   *Semitic: **nśʔ; wbl**

   Omotic: ba(ʔ)- | — | et- | baʔ- | *baʔ-

14. *BROTHER*

   *Afrasian: Marcel Cohen 1947:272: sn

   *Chadic: **ml,** sn, zr; Newman 1977:19: mahl- = 'friend'

   Cushitic: san | **za/än** | — | — | *san

   *Semitic: **ʔx**

   Omotic: iš+im, kan | — | ic+ | nan+u | *ic+

15. *BUFFALO*

   *Afrasian: —

   *Chadic: **kbn;** ɬ- (= 'cow'); dwk; Newman 1977:20: kəbən

   Cushitic: — | **kəw+a** | **gasar** | Dahalo: ɓeeʕa; Iraqw: sareeʕa | —

   *Semitic: —

   Omotic: [meek+ < Nilotic] | mi/en(d)+ | men+ | meen | *meen

16. *BURN* (cf. #43 'fire')

   *Afrasian: Marcel Cohen 1947:502: (w)k'd; ibid., 515: wbd; Bender: k'Vl/r (?)

   *Chadic: **kɗ, bɗ;** k-r, k(')-n, b₂s', hl, b(-)k, gl, yg; Newman 1977:106: b-kə = 'roast'

   Cushitic: li/aw; tiɓ-a | **bər-;** ɦaw- | ***bi/ark'-** (?), **gub-,** ah/ʔ- | Dahalo: guɓ-, ts'aak-; Iraqw: humíim | *bVr- (?)

   *Semitic: **ɬrp,** also 'roast': **k'ly,** also 'smelt, refine': **s'rp,** also 'become scorched': **rmɬ**

   Omotic: at- | k'i/en- | sok- | bonk-, kam+ak | —

17. *CAT*

   *Afrasian: —

   *Chadic: [**patu** < Kanuri], g₂zm, kalda

   Cushitic: bissa (symbolic?) | dVmmV+ | — | — | —

   *Semitic: —

   Omotic: — | — | agac+ | — | —

18. *CHICKEN, FOWL* (cf. #6 'bird')
   *Afrasian: —
   *Chadic: **kwd**; kwz
   Cushitic: kélai = 'bird'; andirhe | **dirw+a** | **lukk+** | Iraqw: kooŋki | *dir+
   *Semitic: 'fowl': **-wp**
   Omotic: — | wa+ | — | kobu | —

19. *CLAW, NAIL*
   *Afrasian: Diakonoff et al. 1993–97:32: pVr 'finger, nail'
   *Chadic: **pl-**, **glɓ**, krm
   Cushitic: nʔaf | **laŋ+** (?) | — | Dahalo: tsoolo; Iraqw: foqeni | —
   *Semitic: **θ'upr**
   Omotic: guš, šukum+a | s'uk'um | t'ung+ | šiš(k)in | **šukum**
   *Omotic form is areal (v. Nilo-Saharan 54, esp. Eastern Sudanic šokna ~ šukom)

20. *COLD* (cf. #8 'black, dark')
   *Afrasian: —
   *Chadic: **smɗ**, **ɗ-l**, kùsúk, ʔússú, etc., leilei, etc., kt, t-ɬ, dúk, etc.
   Cushitic: lʔa; ʔakil; amʔakwera | kämb- | **ɗamfi-, k'ab(b)-** | Dahalo: wíliʕine; Iraqw: ts'aaʔ | *k'amb-
   *Semitic: **k'rr**; **brd**
   Omotic: [k'až < Amharic], ta(t)s | — | c/šo+w | — | —

21. *COME* (cf. #52 'go')
   *Afrasian: Marcel Cohen 1947:25: y; Diakonoff et al. 1993–97:143: bH = 'go'; Bender: t-
   *Chadic: **b₂-**, w-, gr, d-, swk, sn, man, etc., l-; Newman 1977:26: (-)sə; , ibid., 27: imperative: ya
   Cushitic: ʔi | < *-Vnt- | -mtii, imperative: **áam-** | Dahalo: haʔ | Ehret 1987:454: **ʔim(t)-**
   *Semitic: **bwʔ**; **ʔty**; David Cohen 1970: ʔtw/y
   Omotic: aad/t- | kʷa- | y-, w- | yV- | *y-

22. *COOK* (cf. #16 'burn'; occasionally 'boil' [Agew second form])
   *Afrasian: Marcel Cohen 1947:312: s'ly
   *Chadic: **sry ~ swr**, **kwy**, **b(-)k**, **ɓɗ**, **s'p**; 'fry, roast', etc.: b₂s', gɮ, wùs, etc.; Newman 1977:28: da; ibid., 55: 'fry': surə, 56: kaw-.
   Cushitic: tikwi | **ca/əqʷ**; **bəl/r-**, **gi-s** | bol- | Dahalo: ɗak- | *bAl-; tVkʷ-(?)
   *Semitic: **bšl**
   Omotic: ʔuš- | — | katt-, et- | kats- | *katt-

23. *COUGH* (often symbolic [Chadic, East Cushitic])
   *Afrasian: —
   *Chadic: **wɬ**, tààríí, Newman 1977:29: ʼjaɬa; Jungraithmayr and Ibriszimow 1994 say this item is probably symbolic.
   Cushitic: šʼiš | ʔə(n)qʷ+ (?) | **[kʼuf(a)ʕ-]** | Dahalo: ʕeʕeð-, noun: ʕohoʔóna | —
   *Semitic: —
   *Omotic: pis/š- | ons- | — | — | —

24. *COUNT*
   *Afrasian: Diakonoff et al. 1993–97:6: 'pay, count, etc.' pad
   *Chadic: **ɗgn**, kn, b₂ɬ₂, nb
   Cushitic: ɗigwi | **ci/äb-** | **ɗik/g-** | Iraqw: fáar | *ɗig-
   *Semitic: **mnw**, also 'measure': spr
   Omotic: faid- | tiam- | paid- | fe/ad- | ***paid-**

25. *COW, CATTLE* (North Agew: also 'possessions')
   *Afrasian: Marcel Cohen 1947:432: l-
   *Chadic: ɬ-; naak, etc.; Newman 1977:30: ɬa (for form, cf. #28 'cut', and #92 'stand up')
   Cushitic: šʼa, yiwe | **ləw+; kəm+** | **šaʕ+**; plural: **loʔ+** | Dahalo: jáago, nát̪ʼetsa; Iraqw: ɬee, h/jikʷaa | Ehret 1987:241: *šaaʕ-; ibid., 337: (also 'cattle, herd'): ***ɬoo**, plural: **ɬoʔ-**
   *Semitic: **bakʼar; liʔ(at)**
   Omotic: waak+i | im+ | mi+ | ot+ ~ wet+ | —

26. *CROCODILE*
   *Afrasian: —
   *Chadic: **kdm**, ksr; Newman 1977:31: kədəm
   Cushitic: lɛma | — | — | Dahalo: gáɦatlʼe | —
   *Semitic: —
   Omotic: gur(gur)+ | — | — | — | —

27. *CRY, WEEP*
   *Afrasian: Bender: -l
   *Chadic: **wl**; k-k, kw, sʼw
   Cushitic: wau, walik, mile | — | ʔooy- < ʔoo y ('say' verb) | Dahalo: ʕaʕ-; Iraqw: ʕáaʕ | —
   *Semitic: **bky**; David Cohen 1970: ʔll
   Omotic: eep- | ya(a)p- | yep- | yeb | ***yep**

28. *CUT* (many varieties: 'chop', 'slice', etc.)

    *Afrasian: Diakonoff et al. 1993–97:55: fVt; ibid., 265: t/dac —> t/dyc; Bender: k'at'-

    *Chadic: **ɬ₂wl, pt, s'kr**; sìkkí, etc., dg, gl, kɬ, kn, ɓ-, ɗ-r, tíídà, etc., wɮ, grb; Newman 1977:33: ɬa

    Cushitic: wik, šitit, šikwib | **ka/äb-** | **k'er-, k'uur-, k'aɗ₁-, mur-**, goy- | Dahalo: ɦaβ₁-, k'eer; Iraqw: ts'áat | *kab- (?)

    *Semitic: Varieties: ʕɬ'd; fis's'; k's'b; **gbb ~ kpp**

    Omotic: ti/ec- | miints'-e | dob ~ dap, k'aat'- | k'aat' | *k'aat'-*

29. *DANCE*

    *Afrasian: Diakonoff et al. 1993–97:370: žeb

    *Chadic: **rw,** s₂wl, laka, etc., kama, etc., zb, d-r, w-r, kéènyè, etc.

    Cushitic: ar(i)d | **dzəm-** | **kirb-** | Dahalo: ɬeew; wirik-; Iraqw: niʕíim | —

    *Semitic: —

    Omotic: — | — | dub(b)- | — | —

30. *DIE* (cf. #65 'kill')

    *Afrasian: Marcel Cohen 1947:488: mwt

    *Chadic: **mwt**; Newman 1977:34: mətə

    Cushitic: ya(i) | **kət-** | **leʔ-, rays-** (?) | Dahalo: dzaa-; Iraqw: -gwáaʔ | —

    *Semitic: **mwt**

    Omotic: diʔ- | hee- | haib/k'-, k(')it- | šub- | —

31. *DIG* (or 'cultivate, plow' [Agew])

    *Afrasian: Bender: hud-

    *Chadic: **s'k-, ɓd,** -p, r-k, b₂zn, vùròk, etc.

    Cushitic: firik | g$^{(w)}$äz-, gəz- | **ɦaad-; k'ot-; dĭš-** | Dahalo: ɦ/ʕuɗ-; Iraqw: fóol | *ɦVd-

    *Semitic: **kry**; Bender: ɦpr

    Omotic: ko/uy- | hudz- | (y)iš- | — | —

32. *DOG*

    *Afrasian: Marcel Cohen 1947:189: kn_

    *Chadic: **kdn**; -d, kany, yn; Newman 1977:37: kər- (personal communication 2004: replace by: ada); Diakonoff 1993: kal/ra

    Cushitic: yáás | **gəzä/əŋ** | **ker+, kut+** | Dahalo: náʕeeṯe; Iraqw: seeʔaaj | Diakonoff 1993: *kal/ra

    *Semitic: Diakonoff 1993: **kal-b**

    Omotic: ke/an+, k'ask+i ~ ʔaksi | kan+ | kian+u | kan+a | ***kan+**

33. *DRINK* (cf. #36 'eat', and #103 'water')

    *Afrasian: Marcel Cohen 1947:296: šrb ~ sw

    *Chadic: **s₂w-**; Newman 1977:39: sa

    Cushitic: g^{w}a, gibit, šifi | **dza/əq-** | **ʕi/a/ug-** | Dahalo: maʔaw | —

    *Semitic: **šty**; 'drink one's fill': rwy, also 'absorb': ɬrb

    Omotic: wo/uc'- | iš- | ʔuy- ~ ʔuš- | wooʔ | **woc'*- (?)

34. EAR (cf. #58 'hear')

*Afrasian: Marcel Cohen 1947:82: 'hear': šm

*Chadic: **km ~ ɬm, aguɗ, lɛkwɔdi**, etc.; Newman 1977:40: šəmi

Cushitic: angwil | **ʔənqᵂ+** | **nabɦi+** | Dahalo: ʔágaddzo | *ʔankʼᵂ+

*Semitic: ʔθn, compare #58 'hear': šmʕ

Omotic: kʼaam+ | we/al+ | way+, hai+ | hai | *hai

35. EARTH (cf. #1 'ashes', #84 'sand')

*Afrasian: —

*Chadic: **kʼɬɗ**; sɛŋgá, etc.

Cushitic: bur, haš, di/e/abba | **bət+a** | **biy+** = 'sand' | Dahalo: guḍḍe | —

*Semitic: ʔarsʼ

Omotic: (h)am+ | kʼetsʼ+ | tul(l)+ | tu(u)r+ | *tul/r*

36. EAT (cf. #7 'bite', #33 'drink')

*Afrasian: Marcel Cohen 1947:60: ʕm; ibid., 246: kʼam; Diakonoff et al. 1993–97:208: tV8; East Sudanic: *C-am

*Chadic: hrɗ, kám, etc., **twy**; zm, gw̄se, etc.; Newman 1977:41: ti

Cushitic: tam, ʔam, kwiri | **qᵂ-** | **-kʼaam-** < *-kʔm- | Dahalo: ʕag-; Iraqw: gáaj | Ehret 1987:543: *-a/uɦim- (?)

*Semitic: ʔkl; lɦm; h/ɦu/am- (?)

Omotic: its- | m(a)- | m-, t(y)ʔa- | m- | *m-, t-*

37. EGG

*Afrasian: —

*Chadic: **drɬ₂**, kʼwái, etc.; Newman 1977:42: aši

Cushitic: kuhí | qäɣal+ ~ qᵂäräɣ+ | — | Dahalo: ʕógooe; Iraqw: qanɦi | —

*Semitic: —

Omotic: mol+, mukʼ+ | kial+ | mul | mu/ol+ ~ mialg+u | **mu/ol+**

38. ELEPHANT (first *Omotic, form perhaps areal; cf. Nilo-Saharan 299: Oŋor. TN perhaps < Cushitic)

*Afrasian: Bender: daŋ (?)

*Chadic: **gʸwn, lb**, tákyàl, etc., bkn; Newman 1977:43: gʸəwan

Cushitic: kwirib | dzan+a | **ʔarb+** | Dahalo: ḍokkóomi; Iraqw: daaŋᵂ | —

*Semitic: **pīl** (< Iranian?)

Omotic: dong+Vr, duur+o | tongVl+ | [zak+], dang+E(r)s+ | dor | ***da/ong+Vr**; *du/or*

39. EXIT, GO OUT (occasionally 'leave' [Agew second form]; cf. #52 'go')

*Afrasian: —

*Chadic: pt, gál ~ kál, etc., kàadé, etc., dōm, etc., b₂-; Newman 1977:60: pəta

Cushitic: — | **f-; ba-t-** | **baɦ-** | Dahalo: ḍik-; Iraqw: tiʔíit | *ba-

*Semitic: wśʼʔ

Omotic: wut- | — | kes- | kies-k | *kes-*

40. *EYE* (cf. #73 'mouth')

*Afrasian: Marcel Cohen 1947:63 unconvincing. Omotic < *Afrasian 'mouth': Marcel Cohen 1947:380bis: p~f~b ?

*Chadic: **ydn**; Newman 1977:46: idə

Cushitic: liilii | **ʔəl** | **ʔil+** | Dahalo: ʔíla; Iraqw: ʔila | Ehret 1987:326: ***ʔil+**

*Semitic: **ʕyn**

Omotic: aap+ | ap+ | aap+ | ap+ | **aap+**

41. *FALL*

*Afrasian: —

*Chadic: **d₂-, g₂ɓ**, prɗ, soor-, etc., tɗ, bəɗ-, və̀gə, etc., ŋgəɗi, etc.

Cushitic: di/eb, ɗi/eb | läb- | **kuf-** | Dahalo: luṭṭukum-; Iraqw: húuʔ | Ehret 1987:330: *ɬi/ap- (?); ibid., 352: *dlib- (?)

*Semitic: —

Omotic: — | — | — | wu(u)t- | —

42. *FAT, OIL*

*Afrasian: Marcel Cohen 1947:264: smn

*Chadic: **kɗʸr**, mɲàr, mavirə, etc., swn, mbūr, mààr, etc., ɗáwà, etc., ʔègéy, etc.; Newman 1977:95: mar

Cushitic: lʔa, gob | saɣʷ+a | ħayɗ-, verb: **ga/obʔ-** | Dahalo: ʔáɬ; Iraqw: diʕi; waħna | *gob; Ehret 1987:323: *laaʔ+

*Semitic: **šmn**

Omotic: durfi | — | — | kow | —

43. *FIRE* (cf. #16 'burn')

*Afrasian: Marcel Cohen 1947:244: k'lV

*Chadic: **-kw**, k-l; Newman 1977:48: aku, akʷa

Cushitic: nʔe | **läx+** | gi(i)r+ | Dahalo: ʔeega; Iraqw: ʔáɬa | —

*Semitic: **ʔiš(āt)**; David Cohen 1970: ʔšš

Omotic: noha ~ nu | tam+a | tam+a | tam+u | *tam+*

44. *FISH*

*Afrasian: —

*Chadic: **klp**, bgs, bn; Newman 1977:49: kərfi

Cushitic: [aši < Semitic] | [ʔas+a] | **kurɗ₁uum+ ~ murkuuɗ₁+** | Dahalo: mbaláβe; Iraqw: siimo | —

*Semitic: **nwn**

Omotic: toil+a | kook+ | — | — | —

45. *FIVE* (cf. #56 'hand')

   *Afrasian: —
   *Chadic: **bɗʸɬ**; Newman 1977:50: baɗə
   Cushitic: ɛi | **ʔankʷa** | **ke/on-** | Dahalo: ḏáwaṯṯe; Iraqw: kooʔán | —
   *Semitic: **xmš**
   Omotic: donk'- | k'us- | uc- | uccu | *uc*

46. *FLOWER* (Agew: 'fruit')

   *Afrasian: Diakonoff et al. 1993–97:35: pər
   *Chadic: **pl**, **bwiš**, **bòòcì**, etc.
   Cushitic: faar | fər+a | bis+ | — | Iraqw: ʕaji, ʕajúus | Ehret 1987:184: verb: fir-
   *Semitic: 'to blossom': **ʔbb**
   Omotic: uuš+ | — | — | uuš+ | *u(u)š+*

47. *FLY* (noun; cf. #4 'bee')

   *Afrasian: Bender: *Dbb
   *Chadic: **k'db**
   Cushitic: tifaa, var.: ɗiibáab | **tsənts+a** | — | Dahalo: ʕágooe, ɦíntote; Iraqw: baʔaarmoo | —
   *Semitic: **ðbb**
   Omotic: kusubo | ts'ing | wuts'+, uts+i | weng+i | —

48. *FOOT, LEG*

   *Afrasian: Bender: rgd/l
   *Chadic: **-s'm**, **g₂rɗ**, skr; Newman 1977:81: asə
   Cushitic: r/lagad | **ləkʷ+** | **ka/ob+**; **lVk+** (V = i, a, u), **magin+** | Dahalo: ḏakáʕa; Iraqw: jaaʔe | Ehret 1987:357: 'foot': ***ragad+ ~ rigid+** (?); ibid., 99: 'leg': *l/ɬukʷ+
   *Semitic: **rigl**; 'foot': **śapʕ**; David Cohen 1970: rgl
   Omotic: duut+i ~ root+i | tug+ | to(k)+ | aš+u | —

49. *FOUR* (cf. #97 'three')

   *Afrasian: Bender: pɗ
   *Chadic: **-pɗ**; Newman 1977:54: fʷaɗə
   Cushitic: faɗig | sädza | — | Dahalo: saʕála, ts'ijáɦi | —
   *Semitic: **rbʕ**
   Omotic: oydd+ | mets'- ~ bets'- | awd ~ o(i)d | kubm | *oyd-*

50. *FULL* (verb: 'fill, be full')

   *Afrasian: —
   *Chadic: **wn**, ng; Newman 1977:47: 'fill': n-(y-).
   Cushitic: verb: tib | verb: ʔəntaɣ- | verb: **-mg-** | Iraqw: háats' | —
   *Semitic: **mlʔ**
   Omotic: ts'ots'- | ts'oon | — | ts'ots' | ***ts'o-**

51. *GIVE* (second Beja item: auxiliary)

*Afrasian: Bender: tsa-; East Sudanic: *ti-n (cf. Mao)

*Chadic: **br**, tak, etc., tsá-, etc., oni, etc.; Newman 1977:57: barə

Cushitic: nuun, hi(w) | ʔəw-; naɣ- | **-ɦi/uw ~ hi/uw-** | Dahalo: heeʔ-, kaaʔ;ð- | *ɦ-w; Ehret 1987:525: ***-ɦ-**

*Semitic: **ntn**

Omotic: im- | ti- ~ ta- | im- | ats- ~ ta- | **im-**, **ta-*

52. *GO* (occasionally 'come', 'pass' [Agew])

*Afrasian: Bender: t- ~ d-ʔ; Marcel Cohen 1947:144: wd; Diakonoff et al. 1993–97:143: bH (= 'come')

*Chadic: **l-**; **dl**, **b₂-**, **ndòʔò**, **njaa**, etc., w-, dw, d-, dang, etc.; Newman 1977:58: d-, j-; Newman 1977:59: ɗə

Cushitic: ba(i), giig, sak | **fät-**; **däkʷ/xʷ-** | **dak'-** | Dahalo: ɗakʷ-, naaʕ-, roʔ- | *dakʷ

*Semitic: **hlk**

Omotic: t- | ya, hoy | ham- | tV- | *t-

53. *GOAT* (cf. #88 'sheep')

*Afrasian: Bender: dr

*Chadic: **wk- ~ kw-**, **s'kn**, **m-**, m-ɗ, d-r, Newman 1977:61: a(w)ku

Cushitic: yaa | fəntVr+a | **riʔ+** | Dahalo: héeri; Iraqw: ʔaari, leeʔi | —

*Semitic: —

Omotic: der+ti | šak+ | — | esk+u | —

54. *GOURD, CALABASH*

*Afrasian: Marcel Cohen 1947:226: kdd

*Chadic: **k'wd ~ kwɗ**, **ɗg**, **g-l**, ɬwk; Newman 1977:22: ɗ-ka

Cushitic: bawaala | bVɣʷ+a | — | Dahalo: kíβo, k'oodo; Iraqw: daɦaaŋw | —

*Semitic: —

Omotic: bot+ | — | bot+ | buda | **bot+**

55. *HAIR*

*Afrasian: —

*Chadic: yàɗ, g₂z-, skl, gr; Newman 1977:66: gasi; ibid., 176: = 'sinew, vein': t'iip'+

Cushitic: hami | tsəb/f+ | **rif+an** | Dahalo: t̪'íhi, t̪'át̪e; Iraqw: seʔeemi | —

*Semitic: **śaʕr**

Omotic: sits+i | — | — | sits+u | *sits+

56. *HAND* (cf. #45 'five')

*Afrasian: —

*Chadic: **k'mn**, dbr, r'iyáw, etc., sr, paka, etc.

Cushitic: ɛyi | nan | 'palm': **ganʕ+** | Dahalo: ɖaβa; Iraqw: dawa | —

*Semitic: **yd**, also 'palm': **rɦ**; Bender: ɦpn

Omotic: aan+ | kus+ | kuC+ | kuc+u | *kuc+

57. *HEAD*
　*Afrasian: Bender: mAt
　*Chadic: **kdn**; Newman 1977:67: ka
　Cushitic: girma | ʔaɣwär; **ŋat+a** | **matɦ+** | Dahalo: ʕani; Iraqw: saga | —
　*Semitic: also 'top': **rʔš**
　Omotic: mat+ | tok+ | tok+ | gel/r+i, moot+ | *mAt+

58. *HEAR* (cf. #34 'ear', and #67 'know')
　*Afrasian: Bender: dg; Marcel Cohen 1947:82: 'hear': šm; compare #34 'ear'
　*Chadic: **d₂gw**, km ~ ɬm, kl-
　Cushitic: maasuu | was- | **ɗe/og-** | Dahalo: ʔeeṯiṯ-; Iraqw: axáas | *m/was- (?)
　*Semitic: **šmʕ**
　Omotic: — | k'(i)eb- | si(s)- ~ ši(š) | siis- | *sis-*

59. *HIDE* (verb)
　*Afrasian: —
　*Chadic: **tgl**, gúɓé, etc., wesi, etc., ɓgw, ʔòmbìɗá, etc.
　Cushitic: kwibil/s, ʔar | təb-s | — | — | —
　*Semitic: —
　Omotic: ʔac- | -asa- | ac(')- > aš- | — | *ac-*

60. *HIT, BEAT* (occasionally 'pound, strike', etc.; cf. #65 'kill')
　*Afrasian: Diakonoff et al. 1993–97:272: dəkʷ; Bender: šbt' (?)
　*Chadic: **dwk** (= 'kill'), **ʦbɗ**, **kɗ**, **b₂g**, wr, dl, gb, pm; Newman 1977:68: ɬəɓə.
　Cushitic: t'a, 'touch': tah- | **tax-s/z-** | **ɗaw-, šok'-, tum-**; = 'touch, push': **-ta/uk'-** | Dahalo: paɦ-; Iraqw: táah, túuʔ | *tak'/h; Ehret 1987:350: *dlaʕ-
　*Semitic: **šbt'**, 'pound, strike': kšš ~ kwš, also 'strike, drub': ɬ'rb
　Omotic: gis'- | hedz- | (y)it- | — | —

61. *HONEY* (cf. #4 'bee')
　*Afrasian: —
　*Chadic: **d-m**, **skn**, **ym**, mn, ɗʸm; Newman 1977:70: ami (= 'bee')
　Cushitic: ʔau | **säɣar+** | **malab, zagm+** | Dahalo: t'aŋk'a, nala; Iraqw: danú | —
　*Semitic: **dišb ~ dibš**; also 'bee': **nuhb**
　Omotic: kur+ | — | es+ | is+ | *e/is*

62. *HORN* (cf. #10 'bone', and #99 'tooth')
　*Afrasian: Marcel Cohen 1947:266bis: kVs ~ kVš.
　*Chadic: **myk**, **gbn**, **ɓlm ~ plm ~ mlm**
　Cushitic: dʔa | gix | **gaas+** | Dahalo: ṯumpo; Iraqw: xarmoo | —
　*Semitic: **k'arn** (cf. Indo-European?)
　Omotic: k'uš+ | — | kal/r+, uš+ | uš+ | *k'uš+

63. *HOUSE, HUT*
- *Afrasian: Diakonoff et al. 1993–97:112: 'building': bVn; ibid., 139: bit
- *Chadic: **b-n, gd-, ɗáákìì,** etc., **zuguru**; lum, ku-li, etc., ʔàbùt, etc., dàrmà, etc.; Newman 1977:72: bən-
- Cushitic: gau, bekkar | **ŋən+** | **mi/an+** | Iraqw: xootɬ' | —
- *Semitic: **byt**; 'build, create': **bny**
- Omotic: eh+ | keT+ | kett+ | ʔii | *e/i+

64. *HYENA*
- *Afrasian: —
- *Chadic: **grn, b-r,** mwaɓulù, bóḷọkẹ, etc., dms, drl, gʸùlum, etc.
- Cushitic: galaaba, kárai, mirʔáfi | wək/x+a | **waraab+** | Dahalo: šúti; Iraqw: bahaa | —
- *Semitic: **ś'ab(u) ~ ś'ub(u)**, etc.
- Omotic: — | duul+ | — | — | —

65. *KILL* (cf. #60 'hit, beat')
- *Afrasian: —
- *Chadic: **dwk** (= 'hit'), bɗ, ɬ₂-; Newman 1977:75: d-
- Cushitic: dir | kəw- | -gši | Dahalo: ɓaɦ-, dzeʔeð-; Iraqw: gáas | —
- *Semitic: **k't(')l**
- Omotic: dees- | piy- | woɗ/t'- | wuuš- | —

66. *KNEE*
- *Afrasian: Marcel Cohen 1947:401: gRb
- *Chadic: **grp,** ɣwárùm, etc., gd; Newman 1977:76: gəfu
- Cushitic: gumba | **gərb** | **gi/ulb+** | Dahalo: gilli | Ehret 1987:61: ***gʷilb+ ~ gulb+**
- *Semitic: **birk**
- Omotic: buk'+ | kum+ | gurmat+, buk' | — | *buk'

67. *KNOW* (cf. #34 'ear', and #85 'see' [Agew third, *East Cushitic, *Cushitic second forms])
- *Afrasian: —
- *Chadic: **s-n,** bn ~ mn, yii, etc.; Newman 1977:78: sənə
- Cushitic: kan | ʔaq, -arq-; (ki/an-t-) | **-ɗeg- ~ -ɗog-; *arg-** | Dahalo: ɓar-, ʔeley-, hub-; Iraqw: xúuʔ | *kan-; Ehret 1987:375: ***ʔar-**
- *Semitic: **w/ydʕ**
- Omotic: ɗ/t'es- | al- | e/ar- | t'us- | *t'Vs-

68. *LAUGH*
- *Afrasian: —
- *Chadic: **gms₂, s₂wl,** gèllò, etc.; Newman 1977:79: gamsə
- Cushitic: faayid | ʔənqʷ-at- | — | Dahalo: k'ik'-; Iraqw: qaséem | —
- *Semitic: **ɬ'fik' ~ s'fik'**
- Omotic: yinc'- | — | miic'- | — | —

69. *LION* (= Agew: 'the maned one')

*Afrasian: —

*Chadic: **b-r**, kukum, etc., rbn, sèmkī, etc., jágádláu, etc.

Cushitic: haɗa | gämän+a | — | Dahalo: ɓaʔi, ṯeele; Iraqw: diraaŋ^W | —

*Semitic: **lbʔ**

Omotic: zob+ | — | — | baya, (h)aik(')+u | —

70. *MEAT* (cf. #25 'cow, cattle'; sometimes 'animal')

*Afrasian: Bender: ša-

*Chadic: **ɬw**, náámàà, etc., kùm, etc., vreŋ, etc.; Newman 1977:83: ɬəw-, = 'animal'

Cushitic: šaa | **si/əx+a** | **soʔ+**; 'cow': **šaʕ+** | Dahalo: daβi; Iraqw: fuʔni | *ša

*Semitic: **šiʔr**

Omotic: wah+a | os+ | ac+ | aš+ku | *ac+*

71. *MONKEY* (occasionally 'baboon' [Agew second, East Cushitic, Dahalo]; many variations)

*Afrasian: Bender: g_l, k'_r (?); East Sudanic: kOr+

*Chadic: **bd-**, **krm**, **gólógò**, **zúgúlì**, etc., mrn; Newman 1977:85: bədi

Cushitic: habek, lalúnkwi | dzaggVr+; cəcäw+a | **gelz+** | Dahalo: híβe; variety: góloβe | —

*Semitic: —

Omotic: k'aar+a, gay+, go/ur+, suud+ | — | ell+, k'ar+ | bei, bar/l+, gyɛru | ***gVr**, *k'ar*

72. *MOON, MONTH*

*Afrasian: Bender: arb+; Diakonoff et al. 1993–97:189: tVr = 'star'; t_r may be a Wanderwort

*Chadic: **t-r**, Newman 1977:86: təra

Cushitic: té/írig | **ʔarb/f+a** | leʕ+ | Dahalo: háge; Iraqw: ɬaħaaŋ | —

*Semitic: **wrx**

Omotic: arf+ | e/ams+ | as, (y)arf | ats+m/n | **ats*, *arf*

73. *MOUTH*

*Afrasian: Marcel Cohen 1947:380bis: -p-~-f-~-b-; Diakonoff et al. 1993–97:71: f8

*Chadic: **bk**, my, Newman 1977:88: ba

Cushitic: yaf | (Bilin: ʔäb) | **ʔaf+** | Dahalo: ʔáfo; Iraqw: ʔafa | Ehret 1987:191: **y/ʔaf+**

*Semitic: **p**

Omotic: [ʔap < Amharic?] | — | d/noon+ | eed+ | —

74. *NAME*

*Afrasian: Bender: sVm; also a Wanderwort, for example, Beja(?), TN, Dizoid

*Chadic: **sᴣm**; Newman 1977:90: səm

Cushitic: [sim] | səŋ^W+ | **magʕ+** | Dahalo: sáare, verb: sow-; Iraqw: ʔuma | Ehret 1987:447: ***si/um+**

*Semitic: **šm**

Omotic: nam/b+ | — | [sɪm] | [sɪm] | —

75. *NAVEL*
   *Afrasian: Diakonoff et al. 1993–97:76: bət'
   *Chadic: **b₂ɗ- ~ ɗb-**, tíncí, dùndí, etc., zbɗ
   *Cushitic: te/əfa | — | **ɦa/unɗur+** | Dahalo: júkku | —
   *Semitic: —
   Omotic: — | ušum+ | — | — | —

76. *NECK* (often 'nape', e.g., Ehret 1987:156; Ehret 1987:325)
   *Afrasian: Bender: kVš+ (?), kOm (?)
   *Chadic: **gdʸr**; Newman 1977:91: wəra
   Cushitic: ʔála, mok, mʔage | k⁽ʷ⁾ərm+gʷərgəm | **luk'm+** | Dahalo: ɗááʕeero; Iraqw: ʔisa | —
   *Semitic: **kišād; s'awwar**
   Omotic: k'u/orc'+i | kitiš+ | — | kum | —

77. *NEW*
   *Afrasian: —
   *Chadic: **mrb**, dáàlà, etc.
   Cushitic: noun: gɛyi | ʔazər- ~ ʔarəz- | **haar-** | Iraqw: ʕabɛn | —
   *Semitic: verb: ɦidθ
   Omotic: — | — | kal | k'al/r | k(')al/r

78. *NIGHT* (cf. #8 'black')
   *Afrasian: Diakonoff et al. 1993–97:174: 'dark': təhm
   *Chadic: **bɗ**; Newman 1977:92: bəɗi
   Cushitic: ha'wad, kuhii, mas | **qi/er** | **haw(ee)n+** | Dahalo: hiima; Iraqw: xʷeera, amasi | *qer- (?); Ehret 1987:549 = 'darkness, black': ***ham- ~ him**
   *Semitic: **layl(ay)**; verb: 'dark, shaded': θ'll, compare 'black'
   Omotic: ɗ/t'um, su/ot+i, gelt | — | t'um | goot+ | *t'um

79. *NOSE*
   *Afrasian: Bender: sin+
   *Chadic: **ntn**; Newman 1977:93: atən
   Cushitic: ginuf | **q⁽ʷ⁾əmb; əsəN** | **sVn+**, V = i, a, o, u | — | Ehret 1987:476: *ʔisŋʷ+ (?)
   *Semitic: **ʔanp**; David Cohen 1970: ʔnp (cf. #73 'mouth')
   Omotic: nuk+ | šint'+ | s/i(n)ɗ/t'+ | sint'+ | *sint'

80. *ONE*
   *Afrasian: Bender: mVt (?); Diakonoff et al. 1993–97:161: tak⁽ʷ⁾
   *Chadic: **kɗn,** m-ɗ, ɗk
   Cushitic: gal | **la-** | **mi/at-** | Dahalo: waṭṭúkʷe; Iraqw: wak | —
   *Semitic: **ʔaɦad; ʕašt**
   Omotic: [walak'a ~ kal(l)a < Nilotic] | iš+ | is | k'oi | —

81. PARTRIDGE, GUINEA FOWL, ETC.

*Afrasian: —

*Chadic: **zbl**, kwàɗáŋ, etc.

Cushitic: — | **dzəɣrVn+a** | — | Iraqw: 'guinea fowl': sakri | Ehret 1987:198: 'guinea fowl': *zagr+

*Semitic: —

Omotic: sa/el | — | — | — | —

82. PERSON, MAN (or 'people' [Agew?, East Cushitic second form])

*Afrasian: Bender: mt; Nilo-Saharan 176: (a)ta; Niger-Kordofanian: mt+

*Chadic: **mtm**, **b₂ln**, **mz**, **grm**, sùbúní, etc.; ɗafál, etc.; Newman 1977:96: mətu

Cushitic: ták | ʔəx+; **gərw+a** | **ni/a/um+; ge/or+** | Dahalo: gúɦo; Iraqw: hee | *gərʷ+

*Semitic: **unāš; mš**; 'man': **mt**

Omotic: eed | es+ | ats+ > ac/š+ | yaab | *e/ats

83. ROOT, VEIN (occasionally 'hair, etc.')

*Afrasian: Marcel Cohen 1947:260: sr(s) ~ šr(s)

*Chadic: **ɬ₂rw**, zm; Newman 1977:107: šar-

Cushitic: ɗai, gádam | [sər < Amharic] | **ɦizz+** | Dahalo: ḏára, hiḏḏe; Iraqw: deeʕaarmoo | —

*Semitic: 'root': **šurš**; 'vein, tendon': **širw/ʕ**

Omotic: c'aac'+ | — | t'e/amp+ | cwažu | —

84. SAND (cf. #1 'ashes', and #35 'earth')

*Afrasian: Marcel Cohen 1947:105: haS

*Chadic: **gʷsk**, for example, Hausa k'asa

Cushitic: i/assɛ | — | **biy-** = 'earth' | Dahalo: ndóoʕo; Iraqw: ɦasam | Ehret 1987:176: haats'+

*Semitic: Diakonoff 1993: ɦs's'

*Omotic: šam+i | šakiw+ | — | — | —

85. SEE (cf. #40 'eye', and #67 'know')

*Afrasian: Bender: ark'- (?)

*Chadic: **ngn**, **wl-**, gwl, k-t, myɗ, tl, lawan, etc., ɗi, etc., wee, etc.; Newman 1977:111: na

Cushitic: i/erh, ri/eh, šibib | q⁽ʷ⁾al- | **ʔarg-**; [ʔilaal < 'eye'] | Dahalo: waɦ-; Iraqw: ʔar | Ehret 1987:396: *ʔark'-

*Semitic: **rʔy**; also 'know': ʔmr, also 'watch, observe, guard': **nt'r**

Omotic: s/še- | — | beK- | se- | *se-

86. SEED (occasionally verb: 'sow' [North Agew])

*Afrasian: —

*Chadic: **wundel**, etc., krm; bdr ~ bzr, ídí, etc., āŋgās, etc.

Cushitic: habba; tɛra | fäz- | — | Iraqw: waraari | —

*Semitic: **ḏar**; Bender: za/erʕ

Omotic: maš+ | šok- | [zar/l < Amharic] | — | —

87. *SEW*
   *Afrasian: Bender: s/šak- (?); Diakonoff et al. 1993–97:195: tVl; ibid., 322: sVp
   *Chadic: **ɗmk, sool**, etc.; ráp, etc., tl, cəgə́n, etc., kápá, etc.
   Cushitic: fir; hayid | **saq/ɣ-** | — | Dahalo: hud̠-; Iraqw: híríit | —
   *Semitic: —
   Omotic: š/žak- | sip- | sip/k- | siip' | *sip-

88. *SHEEP* (cf. #53 'goat')
   *Afrasian: —
   *Chadic: tmk; Newman 1977:114: təmki
   Cushitic: *ʔn | [bäg+a < Amharic?] | — | Dahalo: héeri; Iraqw: beeʕi | —
   *Semitic: —
   Omotic: — | — | dor(s)+ | zun(k)+ | —

89. *SIT (DOWN)*
   *Afrasian: —
   *Chadic: **dmn, s'k** (?), ɗg-
   Cushitic: s'a, t'at'am | — | — | Dahalo: gwaɦ-; Iraqw: iutanaŋ | —
   *Semitic: also 'dwell': **wθb**
   Omotic: dok'- | kob- | — | — | —

90. *SKIN* (cf. #2 'bark')
   *Afrasian: Bender: gog+
   *Chadic: **zm, k-d**, zk, rə̀və̀k, etc., bkl, ɗk; Newman 1977:115: zəm
   Cushitic: ʔade, gale, sar | **ʔax+** | **gog+** < 'dry' | Dahalo: d̠iiʕ-, gino; Iraqw: dáaq | —
   *Semitic: gild ~ gald; 'hide': **mišk ~ mašk**
   Omotic: bic+, foot+i | k'e+, gonk'+ | goog/k+ | fat+u | *fAt+

91. *SLEEP*
   *Afrasian: Bender: (w)sn
   *Chadic: **(w)sn ~ swn**, ɲah, nùn, etc., kn, zb-, ywn; Newman 1977:116: s-n(-)
   Cushitic: diw, noun: nári | gändz- | **-hdi/ur- ~ -hudr-, raf+** | Dahalo: haddúra; Dahalo: ɓom-, giit̠-; Iraqw: gúuʔ | —
   *Semitic: **wšn; nwm**; noun: **šin-(a)t**
   Omotic: rat- | haal- > heey- | k(')e- | sok'- | —

92. *STAND (UP)*
   *Afrasian: —
   *Chadic: **wɬk**, dʸr, s'r-, dhlirre, etc.; Newman 1977:122: ɬa (for form, cf. #25 'cow, cattle', and #28 'cut')
   Cushitic: gad | **gʷ-** | **he/og-** | Dahalo: saad̠-; Iraqw: sifíit | —
   *Semitic: **k'wm**; also 'move': **ðwð**
   Omotic: wo(y)- | — | — | aš- | —

93. *STEAL*
  *Afrasian: —
  *Chadic: **mgr**, kr, s'r; Newman 1977:124: xərə
  Cushitic: gwihar, guhar | **k/qac-** < 'take' | — | Dahalo: aggʷiy-; Iraqw: fíis | *gwi-(?)
  *Semitic: **šrk'**
  Omotic: dib- | ho/ump- | — | — | —

94. *SUN*
  *Afrasian: —
  *Chadic: **p-t**; Newman 1977:126: fati = 'day'
  Cushitic: yiin | kʷar+a | — | Iraqw: ts'eeʕmá, looʔa | —
  *Semitic: **šmš**
  Omotic: hai ~ i/eyy | ab+ > aw+ | ab+ > aw+ | c'až ~ ts'iats+, kai | *kai*

95. *TAIL*
  *Afrasian: —
  *Chadic: **ks'r**, **spl**, ááyó, etc.; Newman 1977:127: kətər
  Cushitic: niiwa | **tsəmär+** | di/a/ub+ | Dahalo: rik'a; Iraqw: ɦaiso | —
  *Semitic: **ðnb**
  Omotic: go/ul+ | — | uN+ | — | —

96. *THIGH*
  *Afrasian: —
  *Chadic: **pwl**, **pnd**, gəmà, etc., gùrày, etc.
  Cushitic: dambe | — | **taf+** | Dahalo: luka; Iraqw: ʔorje | —
  *Semitic: —
  Omotic: — | — | — | bok(g) | —

97. *THREE* (Mao perhaps from Kwama or Surmic)
  *Afrasian: —
  *Chadic: **knɗ**; Newman 1977:132: k⁽ʷ⁾ən
  Cushitic: mehɛi | sä/əɣʷa | **saz(zi)ɦ-** | Dahalo: k'aβa; Iraqw: tám | Ehret 1987:218: 'three, four': *sazɦ-
  *Semitic: **θalāθ**
  Omotic: makkan | [tiazi] | keedz | kadu | *kAd+*

98. *TONGUE* (Dizoid perhaps from Nilotic)
  *Afrasian: Marcel Cohen 1947:436: lsn
  *Chadic: **ls₃-**, lyaaga, etc.; Newman 1977:134: ałəsi
  Cushitic: miid(al)aab | **lanq+** | ʕ/ʔarrab+ < ʔanrab+ | Dahalo: ʕéena; Iraqw: ts'ifraaŋ | —
  *Semitic: **lišān**; David Cohen 1970: laš-ān
  Omotic: adab ~ adim | -ts'il+ | int'Vrs+, ʔints'il | [yalb] | —

99. *TOOTH* (occasionally 'molar' [East Cushitic second form]; cf. #62 'horn')
   *Afrasian(?): Diakonoff 1993: sinn
   *Chadic: **sɜn**; Newman 1977:135: šan(-)
   Cushitic: kwire | **ʔərkʷ+** | **ʔilk+; gaws+** | Dahalo: kálati; Iraqw: sifino, zino | Ehret 1987:342: ***ʔiɬk+**
   *Semitic: **šnn**
   Omotic: ats(')+ | aats'+ | gaš+ | ac/š+u | ***at's+**

100. *TWO*
   *Afrasian: Diakonoff 1993: sn
   *Chadic: **sr**, belu, etc., rap, etc.; Newman 1977:137: sor(-)
   Cushitic: male | **läŋa** | **lam(m)-** | Dahalo: líima; Iraqw: ts'ar | Ehret 1987:444: ***ɬa(a)ma**
   *Semitic: **θn**; Diakonoff 1993: 'two equal parts': can-
   Omotic: k'asten | domb- | nam+ | t'aagn | —

101. *URINE* (sibilant forms perhaps symbolic)
   *Afrasian: Bender: si/ant+ (?); Marcel Cohen 1947:504: wss ~ wsš; Diakonoff et al. 1993–97:11: pVc'
   *Chadic: **ps'r**, kùrày, etc., wicē
   Cushitic: íša, verb: siw | verb: **tsa/əqʷ-** | **sindʲ-** | Dahalo: noun: sinṯ'a, verb: saaħaw; Iraqw: sooxaa | —
   *Semitic: **θayn(at)**
   Omotic: [šan < Amharic] | — | šeš | — | —

102. *WASH*
   *Afrasian: —
   *Chadic: **-pl, s'ɓ, bɗ**, bn, b₂s; Newman 1977:140: 'bathe': bəna, 'wash something': c-ɓə
   Cushitic: šigwiɗ, šuguɗ | **ʔənq-** | **ɗʲi/ak'-** | Dahalo: k'waṯ'ikuð-; Dahalo: paaħ-; Iraqw: hamáatɬ' | —
   *Semitic: **rħ; xś'**
   Omotic: šiɗ/ʔ- | kuš | mas- | — | —

103. *WATER* (cf. #33 'drink'; East Cushitic second form: 'flowing water')
   *Afrasian: Marcel Cohen 1947:485: mw/y, -n plural; Bender: may
   *Chadic: **ymn**; Newman 1977:142: am
   Cushitic: yam | **ʔaqʷ+** | **bik+ee,** wi/aʕ- | Dahalo: **maʔa** | *may
   *Semitic: **my**
   Omotic: nook'+ | haats'+ | aats'+ | (h)aai | —

104. *WHITE*

*Afrasian: Bender: b/pr- (?)

*Chadic: [**pr** < Niger-Kordofanian], ɓg; Newman 1977:145: p-( )

Cushitic: ɛl/ra | ca(ʔ)əd+ | **ʕazz-** | Dahalo: k'úuħuma; Iraqw: awak | —

*Semitic: verb: **brr**

Omotic: guit | kaaw- | — | gotn- | *gUt-

105. *WOMAN* (cf. #82 'person, man')

*Afrasian: —

*Chadic: **mn,** mkd, gə̀rə̀m̀, etc.

Cushitic: tak+at | ʔəxʷi/ən+a | — | Dahalo: gaana, nat̠'a; Iraqw: ʕameeni | —

*Semitic: David Cohen 1970: ʔd(d), ʔnθ, Bender: anš (?)

Omotic: ma+, amz+ | s/šaa | maats'/š+ | ba(a)y | *ma-

Abbreviations

Bender   author's reconstructions in this chapter
MO/G   Macro-Ometo/Gimira
TN   ta/ne family
YK   Yem-Kefoid ("Janjero-Gonga")

References

Bender, M. Lionel
  1990   "Coming and Going in Afrasian." *Afrikanistische Arbeitspapiere* 22: 19–34.
  1996–97   *The Nilo-Saharan Languages: A Comparative Essay.* Lincom Handbooks in Linguistics 6. Munich: Lincom Europa.
  1997   "Upside-Down Afrasian." *Afrikanistische Arbeitspapiere* 50: 19–34.
  2000   *Comparative Morphology of the Omotic Languages.* Lincom Studies in African Linguistics 19. Munich: Lincom Europa.
  2003   *Omotic Lexicon and Phonology.* Carbondale: Southern Illinois University Printing Service. (Available only from author at 401 S. Emerald Lane, Carbondale, IL, 62901, U.S.A.).
  2004   "Lexically Speaking: Is Omotic Afrasian?" (Unpublished paper given at the Thirty-second North American Conference on Afroasiatic Linguistics, San Diego).
  2005   *The East Sudanic Languages: Lexicon and Phonology.* Carbondale, IL: Lionel M. Bender.
  Forthcoming *Cushitic Lexicon and Phonology.*

Bergsträsser, Gotthelf
  1983   *Introduction to the Semitic Languages: Text Specimens and Grammatical Sketches.* Translated and annotated by Peter T. Daniels. Winona Lake: Eisenbrauns.

Cohen, David
  1970   *Dictionnaire des racines sémitiques: Au attestées dans les langues sémitiques,* Fascicule 1. Paris: Mouton.

Cohen, Marcel
  1947   *Essai comparatif sur le vocabulaire et la phonétique du Chamito-Sémitique.* Paris: Champion.

Diakonoff, Igor M.
  1993 "Hamito-Semitic Languages." In *Encyclopaedia Britannica*, Volume 22, pp. 722–30. Fifteenth edition. Chicago: Grolier.

Diakonoff, Igor M.; A. Militarev; V. Porkhomovsky; and O. Stolbova
  1993–97 "On the Principles of Afrasian Phonological Reconstruction." *St. Petersburg Journal of African Studies* 1–6.

Ehret, Christopher
  1980 *The Historical Reconstruction of Southern Cushitic Phonology and Vocabulary*. Berlin: D. Reimer Verlag.
  1987 "Proto-Cushitic Reconstructions." *Sprache und Geschichte in Afrika* 8: 180.

Ehret, Christopher; E. D. Elderkind; and Derek Nurse
  1989 "Dahalo Lexis and Its Sources." *Afrikanistische Arbeitspapiere* 18: 5–49.

Huehnergard, John
  2000 "Proto-Semitic Language and Culture." In *The American Heritage Dictionary of the English Language*, pp. 2056–68. Fourth edition. Boston: Houghton Mifflin.

Jungraithmayr, Herrmann, and Dymitr Ibriszimow
  1994 *Chadic Lexical Roots*. Two volumes. Berlin: D. Reimer Verlag.

Maghway, J. B.
  1989 "Iraqw Vocabulary." *Afrikanistische Arbeitspapiere* 18: 91–118.

Newman, Paul
  1977 "Chadic Classification and Reconstructions." *Afroasiatic Linguistics* 10: 1–42.
  1980 *The Classification of Chadic within Afroasiatic* (Rede uitgesproken bij de aanvaarding van het ambt van gewoon hoogleraar in de Afrikaanse Taalkunde aan de Rijksuniversiteit te Leiden op vrijdag 6 juni 1980). Leiden: Universitaire Pers.

Orel, Vladimir E., and Olga V. Stolbova
  1995 *Hamito-Semitic Etymological Dictionary: Materials for a Reconstruction*. Leiden: Brill.

Roper, E. M.
  1928 *Tu Beḍawiɛ: An Elementary Handbook for the Use of Sudan Government Officials*. Hertford: Stephen Austin and Sons.

Sasse, Hans-Jürgen
  1979 "The Consonant Phonemes of Proto-East Cushitic (PEC): A First Approximation." *Afroasiatic Linguistics* 7: 1–64.
  1982 *An Etymological Dictionary of Burji*. Kuschitische Sprachstudien 1. Hamburg: H. Buske.

Takács, Gábor
  1999 *Etymological Dictionary of Egyptian*, Vol. 1: *A Phonological Introduction*. Handbook of Oriental Studies 48. Leiden: Brill.

Tosco, Mauro
  2003 "Cushitic and Omotic Overview." In *Selected Comparative-Historical Linguistic Studies in Memory of Igor M. Diakonoff*, edited by M. Lionel Bender, Gábor Takács, and David L. Appleyard, pp. 87–92. Lincom Studies in Afroasiatic Linguistics 14. Munich: Lincom Europa.

Whiteley, Wilfred
  1953 *A Study of Iraqw: An Introduction*. Kampala: East African Institute of Social Research.
  1958 *A Short Description of Item Categories in Iraqw: With Material in Gorowa, Alagwa, and Burunge*. East African Linguistic Studies 3. Kampala: East African Institute of Social Research.

2. *PQD* REVISITED

Stuart Creason

2.1. Previous Work on *PQD*

Writing in 1958, E. A. Speiser remarked, "there is probably no other Hebrew verb that has caused translators as much trouble as *pqd*" (Speiser 1958: 21). The essential accuracy of his assessment is borne out by the fact that *pqd* has been the exclusive subject of at least two dissertations (Holler 1957, van Hooser 1962), one monograph (André 1980), and nine journal or encyclopedia articles (Scharbert 1960, Middelkoop 1963, Gehman 1972, Schottroff 1976, Grossfeld 1984, André 1989, Lübbe 1990, McComiskey 1993, Williams 1997), not to mention the uncounted monographs and articles in which it is considered in the context of some other issue, including, for example, the one from which Speiser's remark is taken. Yet, despite all this attention, the analysis of the meaning of *pqd* has not advanced much beyond Speiser's description of its semantic range and his one-sentence conclusion that immediately followed: "Its semantic range would seem to accommodate 'to remember, investigate, muster, miss, punish, number', and the like. Actually, however, this seemingly lawless profusion reduces itself readily to the single common denominator of 'to attend to with care'" (Speiser 1958: 21).

Within the extensive scholarly literature devoted to *pqd*, a single basic method can be discerned and, not surprisingly, when this method is applied to the same data by different scholars, it leads to essentially the same results. Briefly put, each scholar looks at all, or a sufficiently large number, of the examples of *pqd* and attempts to characterize what action is taking place in each example, using as many clues from the context as possible, including, for instance, the immediately preceding or following verbs that appear to be referring to the same action as *pqd*. Then, these examples are grouped into categories based on the similarity of the actions to which these examples are apparently referring. Finally, some scholars (notably Scharbert 1960, van Hooser 1962, André 1980, Grossfeld 1984, André 1989, and Williams 1997) attempt to provide a single "basic meaning" or *Grundbedeutung* that encompasses all these categories. Other scholars (such as Schottroff 1976 and Lübbe 1990) see this attempt as futile or unnecessary and suggest that *pqd* has multiple basic meanings.

Although no two scholars provide exactly the same number of categories (and, in some cases, subcategories) with exactly the same examples of *pqd* in each category, there is a general consensus. Nearly all scholars see at least seven distinct categories into which the examples of *pqd* can be placed: 1. 'to appoint', 2. 'to deposit, to entrust to', 3. 'to number, to record, to enroll', 4. 'to muster, to pass in review', 5. 'to punish', 6. 'to look after, to take an interest in', and 7. 'to miss, to check to see if present'. Some scholars, however, combine various of these categories into a single category. For example, Gehman (1972) and Williams (1997) combine the first two categories, Gehman (1972), Schottroff (1976), and Grossfeld (1984) combine the third and fourth, and Scharbert (1960) and Gehman (1972) combine the sixth and seventh. Furthermore, some scholars make additions to this list. For example, Gehman (1972) and Lübbe (1990) both add a category 'to pay a visit to, to make a social call' that is distinct from the category 'to take notice of'.[1]

When one of these scholars proposes a basic meaning for *pqd*, it is always some variation of Speiser's 'to attend to with care', although Scharbert explicitly adds the notion of authority to his proposed meaning. He defines the basic meaning as "jemanden oder etwas überprüfen," "kontrollieren," "nach dem Rechten sehen" (Scharbert 1960: 222). A similar idea is expressed by André, who says: "Als solche Grundbedeutung kann man etwa 'genau beobachten' annehmen, wobei oft das Urteil oder die Entscheidung, die aus der Beobachtung erfolgt, mit

---

[1] Grossfeld (1984) also adds a category 'to rule, be in charge of', and Scharbert (1960), Schottroff (1976), Grossfeld (1984), and Lübbe (1990) all add a category 'to order' that contains examples of *pqd* that clearly refer to a speech act.

einbegriffen wird" (André 1989: col. 709).[2] Though it is not always represented in the basic meaning proposed for *pqd*, the idea that *pqd* has something to do with what is done by someone in authority is common in the literature.

Despite the good efforts of all these scholars, all the previous work on *pqd* suffers, at some point or another, from three problems, two of which deal with broader theoretical issues in semantic analysis, and one of which is specific to the analysis of *pqd*. Each of these problems is considered in turn.

The first problem can be nicely illustrated by the first part of the quote from Speiser (1958): "there is probably no other Hebrew verb that has caused translators as much trouble as *pqd*." Speiser calls *pqd* a "Hebrew verb," when, in fact, it is no such thing.[3] *Pqd* is a root and there are, in Hebrew, eight different verbs that contain this root, (a Qal verb, a Niphal verb, a Piel verb, a Pual verb, a Hiphil verb, a Hophal verb, a Hithpael verb, and a Hothpaal verb).[4] These eight different verbs have different, though related, meanings, and it is important not to mix up the meaning of one of these verbs with the meaning of another. Most scholars are careful not to do this, although it is not uncommon to find in the literature examples of the Qal verb of this root listed alongside examples of verbs of other stems. For example, André (1989: col. 714) and Lübbe (1990: 12) both list examples of the Hiphil verb alongside examples of the Qal verb.[5]

Now, in fairness, one can argue that the meaning of a root is essentially equivalent to the meaning of the Qal verb that contains that root since the Qal is the basic stem and it instantiates the meaning of the root without any modification. That is a defensible position, but that step is not taken in this paper. In this paper, the only thing under consideration is the meaning of the eight Hebrew verbs that contain the root *pqd*, and in order to distinguish these eight lexical items from the root, they are cited according to their lexical form. So, the Qal verb that contains the root *pqd* is cited as *pāqad*, the Niphal verb as *niphqad*, etc.

The second problem can also be illustrated by the quote from Speiser: "There is probably no other Hebrew verb that has caused translators as much trouble as *pqd*. Its semantic range would seem to accommodate 'to remember, investigate, muster, miss, punish, number,' and the like." In his first sentence, Speiser makes reference to the work of translation, and in the second to the idea of "semantic range," an idea that has to do with the meaning of a word, not with its translation equivalents. Although various translation equivalents are often used to characterize the meaning of a word in another language, the meaning of a word in one language is something different than the various words that can be used to translate that word into another language. When someone is attempting to translate a word from one language to another, the meaning of that word is, of course, a very important consideration in how it is translated, but it is not the only consideration. The particular context in which the word is used as well as the words that are available in the language of the translation are also important. It is often best to translate the same word in different ways depending on the different contexts in which it is found, but these various translation equivalents cannot simply be listed in a lexical entry, or in a scholarly article, and then labeled the different "meanings" of the word that is being translated.

Again, nearly every scholar writing on *pqd* is aware of this problem and has avoided it in principle, but, in practice, it is often difficult not to reproduce in one's analysis of the Hebrew data the distinctions in meaning found

---

[2] André 1980, in contrast to André 1989, concludes that the root means "to determine the destiny," though this definition seems a bit too self-important, for example, in the rather mundane context of 1 Samuel 25:15, in which Nabal's servants are reporting to Nabal's wife how they had been treated by David's men, 'The men were very good to us. We were not mistreated and we did not determine the destiny of anything all the time that we traveled with them while we were in the field'. This verse is considered in more detail later in the paper, and it is only necessary to note at this point that it illustrates the fundamental problem with André 1980, namely, that it relies far too heavily on the uses of *pqd* when God is the subject and tends to ignore the more mundane examples such as this one. In this respect, André 1989 is a better treatment.

[3] A similar remark is made by Schottroff: "Im Hebr. kommen vom Verbum *pqd* alle Verbalstämme vor" (Schottroff 1976: col. 468).

[4] This same problem is illustrated by Hebrew lexicons in which all words that contain a particular root are listed following that root. This way of organizing a lexicon is certainly legitimate and can be quite helpful. What is not legitimate, and quite misleading, is listing all the verbs that contain that root in a *single* entry while listing all the nouns that contain that root in *separate* entries, as if all the different verbs were examples of a single lexical item, whereas all the different nouns were examples of separate lexical items. Simply put, the morphological means by which verbs are formed in Hebrew (that is, different vowel patterns and, in some cases, additional consonants affixed to the root) are precisely the same as those that are used to form nouns. The different vowel patterns and additional consonants make verbs of the same root as distinct from one another as the different vowel patterns and additional consonants make nouns of the same root distinct from one another.

[5] Lübbe (1990: 10) also lists examples of the Niphal verb alongside examples of the Qal verb.

in the language that is used to provide the various translation equivalents. A possible example of this problem is seen later in this paper in connection with the analysis of *pāqad* in 2 Kings 5:23–24 (section 2.4).

The third problem, the one specific to the work on *pqd* and also the one that has frustrated all the efforts to provide a single basic meaning for *pqd*, is that every scholar who has written on *pqd* has been attempting to characterize the wrong thing. Each of them has been attempting to characterize what action is performed by the subject of the verb *pāqad* in the contexts in which that verb is used. In this paper, it is argued that the meaning of the verb *pāqad* has very little to do with what the *subject* of the verb does. Rather, the meaning of *pāqad* has almost everything to do with what happens to the *object* of the verb in the various contexts in which the verb is used. What happens to the object of the verb remains consistent from context to context, though what the subject does to the object varies from context to context.

2.2. The Semantic Class of *pāqad*

Before an attempt is made to characterize what happens to the object of the verb *pāqad*, and thereby to define the meaning of *pāqad*, some support for this position is given from the syntax of this verb and what that syntax indicates about the semantic class into which this Qal verb falls. Almost every example of *pāqad* occurs with a direct object and, in many cases, the example also occurs with a prepositional phrase. Verbs that attest this syntax are verbs in which the subject acts upon the direct object and brings about a change in the direct object, and this change is more fully specified by the prepositional phrase. Two other verbs that fall into this category are the very common Qal verbs, *nātan* 'to give' and *śîm* 'to put, to place'. *Nātan* usually denotes a change in who possesses an object and the new possessor is indicated by the prepositional phrase, as in, for example, Genesis 24:53: 'The (Abraham's) servant brought out silver jewelry and gold jewelry and clothing, and he gave (them) **to Rebecca**'. *Śîm* usually denotes a change in the physical location of an object and the new location is indicated by the prepositional phrase, as in, for example, Deuteronomy 10:5: 'I (Moses) put the tablets **in the ark**'.

These two verbs also illustrate two of the three kinds of changes that a thing in the real world can undergo. A thing can undergo a change in its physical characteristics, or it can undergo a change in its physical location, or it can undergo a change in its status, that is to say, a change in how it is viewed by some individual or group, or, in other words, a change in its *metaphorical* location in a society or organization, that is, to what or to whom it is related in that society or organization.

It is important to note that these three kinds of changes are not mutually exclusive. In fact, they often occur together. In Genesis 24:53, for example, the understood objects of the verb *nātan* undergo a change of status. Once Abraham's servant gives the jewelry and the clothing to Rebecca, then, in the human society in which they live, the jewelry and the clothing are now recognized as being connected to Rebecca and under Rebecca's control in a way that they were previously recognized as being connected to Abraham's servant and under that servant's control. This change in status may also involve a change in location, but it does not usually involve a change in physical characteristics. Similarly, the object of the verb *śîm* undergoes a change of location. It may also undergo a change of status or a change in physical characteristics by virtue of its change in location, but not necessarily.

It is also important to note that the linguistic means by which changes in status are indicated are often identical to the linguistic means by which changes in location are indicated; that is to say, the same prepositions that are used to indicate a change in location are generally used to indicate a change in status, and that is why a change in status was defined as a kind of change in metaphorical, or non-physical, location.

Like the verb *nātan*, the Qal verb *pāqad* denotes a change of status. The subject of the verb acts upon the direct object of the verb and brings about a change in the status of the direct object and this change in status is more fully specified by the prepositional phrase. What remains consistent across contexts is the change in status that the direct object undergoes. What varies from context to context is exactly what the subject does to bring about this change in status, and that is why scholars have had such difficulty in determining a single meaning for this verb.

2.3. The Meaning of *pāqad*

What, then, is the meaning of the verb *pāqad*? It can be defined as 'to assign a person or a thing to what the subject believes is its proper or appropriate status or position in an organizational order'. More simply (and metaphorically), 'to put something where it is supposed to be in the overall scheme of things'. Now, in order to assign something to its appropriate status, it may be necessary to change its location or its physical characteristics, but those are aspects of the meaning of the verb as they arise in the various contexts in which the verb occurs, and most importantly, as they arise in connection with particular direct objects of the verb. They are not part of the meaning of the verb *in itself*. Furthermore, changing the status of something normally involves changing its relationship to something else in the overall scheme of things and, if the thing whose status is changed is a complex object with various parts, then changing its status may also involve changing its internal organization, that is, the relationships among that thing's various parts.

This definition immediately makes sense of a couple of features that scholars have long noted about this verb. First, it makes sense of the idea that the subject of the verb is someone in a position of authority. In order to change an object's status in some group or organization, one has to have a certain authority in that group; otherwise, the change in status will not be recognized by that group. Second, the common definition of this verb as 'to attend to with care, to look after' makes sense as well. In order to change the status of something, the subject must pay a certain amount of attention to that thing, and so, the translation of this verb as 'to take notice of' is often a perfectly acceptable translation, although it does not really convey the actual *meaning* of this verb very well.

2.4. Analysis of Selected Examples of *pāqad*

Having proposed a new definition for the Qal verb *pāqad*, it is now necessary to consider actual examples of this verb in order to determine whether this new definition accurately captures the meaning of the verb in the various contexts in which it is used. With that in mind, some examples of *pāqad* from each of the seven categories that scholars have proposed are examined in this section of the paper.

The first example to be considered is found in Deuteronomy 20:9, which is placed by all scholars in the 'to appoint' category. The text reads, 'After the officers have finished speaking to the people, they shall *pāqad* commanders of military-units at the head of the people'.[6] Translating *pāqad* as 'appoint' in this text is perfectly reasonable, and, of course, the English verb 'appoint' does denote a change in the status of the object that is brought about by someone who has authority over that object. The English verb 'appoint' does not, however, denote that the new status of the object is necessarily the proper or appropriate status for that object in that particular context, although that notion is clearly present in the context of this example. Deuteronomy 20 is about preparing the people of Israel to go into battle and when that is being done, it is more than appropriate that certain men be assigned to a position of authority at the head of the people who are going to be in battle. Something would be wrong or out of place if men were not assigned to this position.

The next example is found in 2 Kings 5:23–24, which is taken by André 1980 and André 1989 as an additional example of the 'to appoint' category, and by Schottroff 1976 and Lübbe 1990 as a separate category that they label 'to deposit, to entrust to'. It reads, 'Naaman said, "Please take two talents" and he (Naaman) urged him (Gehazi) and he (Naaman) wrapped two talents of silver in two bags and two changes of clothing and he (Naaman) gave to his (Naaman's) two servants and they carried in front of him (Gehazi), and he (Gehazi) came to the hill and took from their hand and *pāqad* in his house and sent away the men and they went'.

The interpretation of this example is difficult for at least two reasons and in order to understand it properly, it is necessary to consider the preceding context. In this chapter of 2 Kings, the prophet Elisha heals Naaman of leprosy and Naaman offers the prophet Elisha gifts in return. Elisha refuses these gifts, but Elisha's servant, Gehazi, slips

---

[6] In all the examples cited in this paper, the Hebrew verb is left untranslated and is represented in the translation by its lexical citation form without regard for the actual inflected form found in the original text.

away, chases after Naaman's chariot, and encounters Naaman a little way down the road. Gehazi tells Naaman that two young Ephraimite men have come to Elisha, and Elisha has sent him to request that Naaman provide these two men with gifts. Then the events of verses 23 and 24 take place.

The first difficulty in understanding these two verses is the identification of the referent of the various third-person masculine singular pronouns, in particular, the identification of the 'his' in 'his two servants'. In the translation above, these two servants were identified as Naaman's and this identification seems correct based on the preceding text. In verse 21, Gehazi is the only one who is said to chase after Naaman, and it is also stated that Naaman sees 'one running after him'. The word translated 'one running' is third masculine singular in form and is a reference, apparently, to Gehazi alone. The two servants, then, are Naaman's. These two servants take the items to Gehazi's house and then they, presumably, return to Naaman.

The second difficulty is the identification of the direct objects of the four verbs 'gave', 'carried', 'took', and *pāqad*, all of which are omitted in the Hebrew text. The omission of the direct object of a verb is not uncommon in Hebrew narrative when the direct object is recoverable from the context. In these cases, the direct object is generally understood to be identical in reference to the direct object of the immediately preceding verb. So, the most reasonable way to understand these clauses is to assume that the direct object of these four verbs is the same as the direct object of 'wrapped', namely, two talents of silver and two changes of clothing.

Understanding the direct object of *pāqad* to be the silver and the clothing poses a problem, however, for André, who wants to classify this example under the 'to appoint' category. While he notes that the clause can mean that Gehazi deposited the gifts in his house, he says: "In the light of Gen 39 (*Hi*) and Gen 40 above and of the fact that the direct or indirect object of *PQD* usually is personal, it is most likely that the objects left out are: 'he *PQD*-ed *two young men* (Gehazi's sons pretending to be the Ephraimites in the lie. *Cf* the punishment on his descendants, *v* 27) *in the house with the gifts*'" (1980: 119). He repeats this interpretation in André 1989, although without the reference to Gehazi's sons: "da aber *pqd* gewöhnlich ein menschliches Obj. hat, ist eher gemeint, daß er jemanden im Haus über die Geschenke bestellte" (André 1989: col. 714).

There are at least three serious problems with his line of reasoning. First, it relies on the identification of the two servants as Gehazi's and not as Naaman's, which seems unlikely. This identification is clearly required by the interpretation in André 1980. However, by 1989 André seems to have changed his mind. Now the person who is placed over these items is not Gehazi's two servants/sons, but a mysterious "jemanden," interjected into this text to save André's interpretation. There is no warrant whatsoever for bringing this "jemanden" into the story at this point.

Second, the interpretation makes no sense grammatically. The direct object of the three verbs other than *pāqad* (i.e., 'gave', 'carried', and 'took') must be the silver and the clothing. There is no other way to understand the text. If the direct object of *pāqad* is to be understood as different than the direct object of these three verbs, then it would be mentioned, as it is in the following clause: 'And he sent away the men'.

Finally, André's real problem seems to be that he has confused one of the translation equivalents of *pāqad* with the meaning of *pāqad*. The problem is not that *pāqad* must have a human object here. The problem is that the verb 'appoint' makes no sense as a translation of *pāqad* in this text, and since one of the meanings of *pāqad* is 'appoint' and since this example seems to fit into that category, then it is a problem that 'appoint' does not make sense as a translation of *pāqad* in this text.

The proper interpretation of the text is reasonably clear. Gehazi put the silver and the clothing in his house because that was the right place to put it if he wanted to keep it safe and yet did not want people to know that he had it. In this particular case, the notion of a change in the physical location of the silver and the clothing is predominant, and the notion of a change in the status of those objects is relatively weak. Nevertheless, it is still there. By putting the silver and the clothing in his house, Gehazi makes them his personal possessions, but ones that are kept hidden from others. They are secretly held possessions rather than publicly held possessions. His house is the place that the objects belong, if they are to have this status.

The next example to be considered is found in Numbers 1:1–3 and it is placed by all scholars in the 'to number, to record, to enroll' category. It reads, in part: 'The LORD spoke to Moses … "Raise the head of the entire congregation of the sons of Israel according to their families, according to the house of their fathers, by the enumeration of the names of every male according to their skulls from twenty years old and upward, everyone who goes out (with/as) a military unit in Israel. You and Aaron *pāqad* them according to their military units"'. The reason scholars place this example in this category is that, in this text, *pāqad* is used after the technical term for taking a census, namely, 'to raise the head'. In fact, Schottroff goes so far as to say, "In dieser Verwendung ist *pqd* Wechselbegriff zu *nś' rōš* 'die Zahl, Summe aufnehmen, zählen'" (Schottroff 1976: col. 472).

However, 'raise the head' and *pāqad* cannot simply be two different expressions referring to the single action of census taking. They must refer, rather, to two different actions, and the reason they must refer to two different actions is that the organizing principle mentioned in connection with the two expressions is different. The act of 'raising the head' is performed according to the men's families and their father's houses. The act of *pāqad*-ing is performed according to the men's military units. So, there is a two-step process here. First, the number of males over the age of twenty is determined for each family and house, and then those men are assigned to their proper position in a military unit. Now, the organization of the military units was undoubtedly based on the men's families and houses, but it did not simply reproduce the divisions of the men by their families and houses. It was a different organization that required a separate action, an action of *pāqad*-ing distinct from the action of 'raising the head'.

The use of *pāqad* to refer to the organization of military units is even clearer in Joshua 8:10 and for those scholars (Scharbert 1960, André 1980, André 1989, Lübbe 1990, Williams 1997) who have a category 'to muster' distinct from the category 'to number, to record', that is the category in which it is placed. The example reads: 'Early in the morning, Joshua *pāqad* the people, and he and the elders of Israel went in front of the people up (to) Ai'. There is no question as to what *pāqad* is referring to in this text. Joshua is gathering the people together in their military units in preparation for battle, or, more abstractly stated, Joshua is taking an object with internal complexity (the people) and re-arranging its parts so that it becomes something that fits into his overall plan (to capture Ai). Before Joshua *pāqad* the people, they were just a group of people. Afterward, they were an army, which is what he needed them to be in these circumstances.

It seems unquestionable that the meaning of *pāqad* in Joshua 8:10 is the same as its meaning in Numbers 1:3. Both examples refer to the organization of the people according to their military units. What is different, however, is the way that the two uses of *pāqad* should be *translated*. In Joshua 8:10, *pāqad* is best translated as 'muster' or possibly 'assemble' since the organization of the people into military units is for the purpose of engaging in battle on that very day. In Numbers 1:3, *pāqad* is probably best translated as 'organize' since there is not going to be a battle that day and the purpose is simply to prepare for possible future battles.

The essential identity of the meaning of *pāqad* in these two examples is not, however, seen by André and Lübbe. About Joshua 8:10, Lübbe writes, "The action is specifically military and therefore to be distinguished from meaning (f) [the category in which Numbers 1:3 is found]" (Lübbe 1990: 11). Lübbe is simply incorrect. Both actions are military, and so there is no distinction in meaning. André, writing about Numbers 1:3, says, "Gegenüber der Musterung eines Heeres sind zwei Unterschiede zu notieren: die Musterung wird von religiösen Führern ausgeführt und hat nicht einen Kampf zum Zeil, sondern die Wanderung durch die Wüste" (André 1989: col. 712). These objections are simply irrelevant. Moses was not exclusively a religious leader, and the preparations for the journey through the wilderness necessarily involved military preparations because the journey through the wilderness was going to involve military encounters.

Next to be considered are examples of *pāqad* that fall into the category 'to punish'. The discussion of these examples in the scholarly literature is complicated by the fact that they occur in four different syntactic constructions, one of which also occurs with the examples of *pāqad* that are placed in the category 'to look after, to take an interest in'. All scholars note these different constructions, as well as the overlap with the examples of *pāqad* that have a different "meaning," but they are generally at a loss to explain these facts. The concluding remark by Schottroff is representative, "Doch läßt sich eine strenge bedeutungsmäßige Abgrenzung allein aufgrund der Konstruktionen nicht vornehmen" (Schottroff 1976: col. 478).

From the standpoint of the position adopted in this paper, namely, that the verb *pāqad* has a single meaning, Schottroff's remark is unobjectionable, but there remains the question as to why four different syntactic constructions occur. In order to answer this question, the four constructions are considered in the most enlightening order, from the most complex to the simplest.

In the first construction, a word such as 'sin', 'iniquity', or 'guilt' occurs as the direct object of the verb and the one guilty of the sin is the object of a preposition, usually the preposition *'al* 'upon', but sometimes the preposition *'el* 'to, toward'. An example of this construction is found in Exodus 32:34. It reads: 'My messenger will go before you and on the day of my *pāqad*-ing, I will *pāqad* upon (*'al*) them their sins'. The meaning here is quite straightforward. In a world governed by a righteous and just God, if someone sins, and they do not receive the proper punishment for that sin, then something is wrong, or out of place. So, God, in his justice, takes that sin and puts it, metaphorically speaking, on the person who committed it. In God's righteous and just scheme of things, a sin belongs on the person who committed it, and if that sin is not on that person, then the sin is out of place in God's order and he needs to *pāqad* it onto that person.

In the second construction, the verb occurs without a direct object, but the one guilty of sin is still the object of the preposition *'al* or *'el*. This construction is most common in Jeremiah, but it also occurs in several of the other prophetic books. It is clearly a variation of the first construction in which the missing direct object is simply understood to be 'sin' or 'iniquity'. An example is found in Jeremiah 11:22. It reads: 'Therefore, thus says the LORD of hosts, "I am about to *pāqad* upon (*'al*) them. The young men will die by the sword; their sons and their daughters will die by famine"'. No specific sin is mentioned, but that is what is understood to be the object of the verb.

In the third construction, a word such as 'sin' or 'iniquity' occurs as the direct object of the verb, but there is no prepositional phrase. This construction is very rare. An example is found in Psalm 89:33. It reads: 'I will *pāqad* with the rod their transgression, and with plagues, their iniquity'. In this example, the one who has committed the sin is not explicitly mentioned but is clearly understood to be 'them', the ones who committed their transgression and their iniquity, whoever they might be in this context.

Finally, in the fourth construction, the person who is guilty of sin is the direct object of the verb. An example is found in Jeremiah 6:15. It reads: '"Therefore, they will fall among the fallen; at the time I *pāqad* them, they will stumble," says the LORD'. What is confusing about this construction is that the verb can be translated 'to punish', just as it can in the preceding two constructions, but this construction is *not* a reduced version of the first construction, the construction in which the sin is the direct object and the one being punished is the object of a preposition. In that construction, and in the two reduced forms of it, God was placing someone's sin in the proper place in the divine scheme of things. In this construction, God is placing *a person* in his or her proper place in the divine scheme of things. Now, if that person happens to be a sinner, then when God *pāqad* that person, things will not go so well for him or her. In contrast, if that person is one of God's favored individuals, then that person's situation will improve. In the latter case, the example of *pāqad* is placed by scholars in the category 'to look after, to take an interest in', and a different "meaning" is proposed for *pāqad*. The meaning, however, is the same in both cases, namely, God puts a person in his or her proper place in the divine scheme of things.

Williams is one of the few scholars who understands the connection between the examples of *pāqad* in the 'to punish' category that occur in the fourth syntactic construction and the examples of *pāqad* in the 'to look after, to take an interest in' category that also occur in this construction. He writes, "God 'attends' or 'takes note of' someone or something and acts accordingly, whether to bestow divine blessing or judgment. Thus, in positive contexts *pqd* is often glossed as 'be concerned about, care for, attend to, help' ... while in negative contexts it is typically glossed as 'punish'" (Williams 1997: 659). His analysis of the "meaning" of the fourth syntactic construction is correct, but it leads him to make a different sort of error; namely, he places all the examples that occur in the fourth construction in the 'to look after, to take an interest in' category and all the examples that occur in the other three constructions in the 'to punish' category. In other words, he does what Schottroff 1976 correctly said one could not do, that is, make a distinction in meaning based on syntax alone.

The final examples to be considered in this section of the paper are those that fall into the final two categories that scholars have proposed, the 'to look after, to take an interest in' category and the 'to miss, to check to see if present' category. As was noted above, some scholars combine these two categories into one and others add a third category, the 'to pay a visit to, to make a social call' category. Again, the fundamental problem is that scholars have concentrated their attention on what the subject does, rather than on what happens to the object, and the proposed meaning 'to take an interest in' represents the most general kind of description of the various actions that the subject does in the various contexts in which these examples occur. In none of these examples, however, does the translation 'to take an interest in' really capture the full meaning of the verb.

The first example to be considered in this category is Psalm 8:5–6, which reads: 'What is a man that you remember him, a human being that you *pāqad* him? You have made him a little less than divine beings; (with) glory and honor you have crowned him'. All scholars note that *pāqad* is used here in synonymous parallelism with the verb *zākar*, 'to remember', and, on this basis, they conclude that *pāqad* must therefore mean something similar to *zākar*, namely, 'to take notice of'. This line of reasoning is similar to the one taken in the analysis of Numbers 1:1–3, and it is as faulty here as it was there. Though it is true that God takes notice of humanity, the last half of verse 5 is saying far more than that. What it is saying is that God has placed humanity in its proper place in the divine order. That this understanding of *pāqad* is the correct one is made clear by the fact that verse 6, and the entire rest of Psalm 8, is concerned with describing exactly what that place is.

Another example that all scholars put in the 'to take an interest in' category is Genesis 21:1–2, although Lübbe 1990 and Williams 1997 also note that more than just mental activity is going on in this example. Lübbe makes this clear in his definition of the meaning of the category into which this example falls: "Think, with the implied intention of acting appropriately" (Lübbe 1990: 8). The example itself reads, 'The LORD *pāqad* Sarah just as he said and the LORD did for Sarah just as he had spoken. Sarah became pregnant and bore a son for Abraham'. What scholars fail to take into consideration in the analysis of this example is something of which all of them are fully aware, namely, that the LORD has previously promised Abraham that Sarah will bear him a son. Sarah, of course, is unable to bear a child, and, as a result, is not in the proper place in the divine scheme of things. So, the LORD must *pāqad* her, must put her in her proper place, and when he *pāqad* her, she becomes pregnant and bears a child, thereby fulfilling the promise that the LORD had previously made and setting things right in the divine scheme.

The next example, Judges 15:1–2, is placed by Gehman 1972 and Lübbe 1990 in the category 'to pay a visit to, to make a social call', which, for them, is a category distinct from the 'to take notice of' category. The example reads, 'After some time, in the days of the wheat harvest, Samson *pāqad* his wife with a kid-goat and he said, "Let me go in to my wife, to the inner chamber," but her father did not permit him to enter. Her father said to him, "I indeed thought that you had truly divorced her and (so) I gave her to your companion"'. The idea that Samson is merely paying his wife a visit "without the intention of remaining there permanently" (Lübbe 1990: 8) completely ignores the social context in which Samson's "social call" takes place. In the previous chapter of the book of Judges, Samson marries this woman, but then leaves at the end of the seven-day marriage feast after she betrays the secret of his riddle to her fellow Philistines. The woman is then given to Samson's companion as a wife. Later, Samson's anger subsides and he returns with the intention of, in André's words, "die Beziehung wieder anzuknüpfen" (André 1989: col. 713). It is to this action, an attempted reconciliation, that *pāqad* refers, not to a "social call."

That this understanding of *pāqad* is the correct one in this context is supported by the phrase, 'with a kid-goat', which Lübbe 1990 and Gehman 1972 ignore, and André 1989 appears not to fully understand. André writes, "Nach längerer Abwesenheit besucht Simson seine philistäische Frau und bringt ihr ein Zicklein als Gabe" (André 1989: col. 713). What André fails to see is the force of the preposition *bə*, here translated 'with'. One of the ways in which this preposition is used in Hebrew is to express the instrument by which an action is performed, and that is how it is being used here. Although it is true that the kid-goat is a gift, it is much more than that. The kid-goat is the *means* by which Samson hopes to *pāqad* this woman, which is to say, the means by which Samson hopes to re-establish what he believes is the proper status of this woman, namely, being his wife. If *pāqad* only refers here to 'paying a visit', then the use of an instrumental expression makes little sense, but it makes excellent sense if *pāqad* refers to Samson's attempt to re-establish his relationship with his wife.

Furthermore, understanding *pāqad* in this way makes better sense of the following clauses in this example. These clauses record a conversation that Samson has with the woman's *father*, rather than a conversation with the woman herself, but that is what is to be expected, given the social and economic context in which these events take place. When Samson leaves this woman at the end of the seven-day marriage feast, he naturally expects her to return to her father's house, where she would again be his responsibility and under his care and protection. So, in order for Samson to re-establish his relationship with the woman, he must first go to her father and give *him* the kid-goat (*contra* André 1989) as a form of compensation since it is the woman's father who has been wronged by Samson's action, and it is only her father who is able to re-establish the relationship. Unfortunately for Samson, it was not possible to re-establish this woman's status as his wife because her status had been changed in the intervening period of time. Having been given to another man, the woman cannot be given back to Samson.

A prepositional phrase also features in the next example to be considered. It is 1 Samuel 17:17–18, which reads, 'Jesse said to David, his son, "Take for your brothers this measure of grain and these ten loaves and make (them) go quickly to the camp, to your brothers. But these ten cuts of cheese you should bring to the commander of the thousand, and your brothers you should *pāqad* to/for peace/well-being, and their pledged thing you should take"'. Gehman places this example in the category 'to visit, to make a social call', and writes, "Closely related to this is the use of this verb with *ləšālōm*, 'to visit for peace', i.e., 'to bring greetings'" (Gehman 1972: 200).[7] Schottroff makes similar remarks, though he does not propose a separate 'to visit' category. He writes "das Verbum sich auf den Besuch von Verwandten bezieht, deren Befinden man in Erfahrung bringen möchte (*pqd lᵉšālôm* 'nach dem Befinden sehen')" (Schottroff 1976: col. 471). Finally, André places this example in the category 'to miss, to check to see if present' and writes, "Der junge David wird von seinem Vater zu seinen Brüdern geschickt mit dem Befehl: 'Sieh nach, ob es deinen Brüdern gutgeht' (m.a. W. 'prüfe, ob *šālōm* da ist oder nicht,' 1 Sam 17,18, vgl. v. 21, wo er nach ihrem Befinden *fragt*)" (André 1989: col. 710).

Although the interpretation of this example by these three scholars is not exactly the same in all details, the basic point that they make is that the expression "*pāqad* someone for peace" means 'to inquire about someone's well-being'. On this interpretation, the expression used here would approximate the Hebrew expression *šā'al lə* (someone) *ləšālōm*, which does have this meaning and in which both the word *šālōm* 'well-being' and the person about whose well-being one is asking are preceded by the preposition *lə*. This expression occurs in verse 21, as André notes, and its occurrence there is one of the reasons that André interprets this example as he does. Of course, one might ask, then, why the expression with *šā'al*, which is relatively common, was not used in this example, and the expression with *pāqad*, which is unique to this example, was. Or, put differently, what is different about the expression with *pāqad* so that it, rather than the expression with *šā'al*, was used here?

One answer to this question might simply be that the two expressions do not mean the same thing and so David's father Jesse is *not* instructing him to find out how his brothers are doing; rather, he is instructing him to alter the status of his brothers with respect to (their) well-being. Understanding this example in this way requires a rather subtle reading, with careful attention paid to the grammar of the two verses, and this interpretation is a bit more difficult to see than the interpretation of the example of Samson and his wife. Nevertheless, it seems preferable to the interpretations proposed by Gehman, Schottroff, and André.

According to the grammar of these two verses, the instructions that Jesse gives to David fall into two parts, indicated in the translation by the sentence break. In the first part, 'Take for your brothers this measure of grain and these ten loaves and make (them) go quickly to the camp, to your brothers', Jesse instructs David to do two things (take ... and make go quickly) and these instructions are expressed using imperative forms. In the second part, 'But these ten cuts of cheese, you should bring to the commander of the thousand, and your brothers you should *pāqad* to/for peace/well-being, and their pledged thing you should take', Jesse instructs David to do three things (bring ... *pāqad* ... take) and these instructions are expressed using imperfect forms.

Now, both imperative and imperfect forms can be used to express what the speaker wishes or desires, but the imperfect is the weaker of the two forms. It tends to be used when the force of the speaker's wish is mitigated in some way, for example, when the speaker is making a request of a social superior. That is clearly not the reason that the imperfect is used in this example because David is not Jesse's superior. So, the reason must lie in the nature of the instructions themselves. There must be some difference between the first and second parts of Jesse's instructions to David, and that difference would appear to be that the two instructions in the first part express what Jesse is *commanding* David to do and the three instructions in the second part express what Jesse is *requesting* that David do.

---

[7] Lübbe also puts it into this category, "In only one other instance is our meaning (a) ["to visit"] quite clearly applicable, viz 1 Sm 17:18" (Lübbe 1990: 8 n. 2).

That this interpretation is correct seems unquestionable, at least with respect to the two instructions in the first part of the example and the first instruction in the second part of the example. In the first part of the example, Jesse tells David to take the bread and make it go quickly to his brothers, and he has no reason to believe that there will be any obstacle to David's doing these two things. Jesse is commanding David to do these things and he expects them to be done. That is why the instructions are expressed as commands, with imperative forms.

In contrast, there *is* some uncertainty as to David's ability to carry out the first instruction of the second part of the example, the instruction that David bring the ten cuts of cheese to the commander of the thousand, that is, the commanding officer of David's brothers. It is possible that David might not be able to perform this action since the man might be unable, or unwilling, to see David when he arrives at the camp, or, less likely, that he might refuse to take the cheese from David. In this case, David will be unable to fulfill this instruction and so that is why it is expressed as a request, with an imperfect form, and not as a command, with an imperative form. This is something that Jesse wants David to do, but he realizes that he may not be able to do it.

Turning now to the second instruction of the second part, the instruction that David *pāqad* his brothers to/for peace/well-being. If this clause means that David is supposed to ask his brothers how they are doing, then it is quite strange that an imperfect verb is used. One would think that David would be commanded, not requested, to find out how his brothers are doing since Jesse surely wants to know this and there is clearly no obstacle that might prevent David from asking them. It is also strange that this request is made in the second part of Jesse's instructions to David. Since this request involves David's brothers, and not, apparently, the commander of the thousand, one would think that it would have preceded, rather than followed, Jesse's request that David bring the cheese to the commander.

However, if the request has nothing to do with finding out how his brothers are doing, but instead has everything to do with altering their status with respect to (their) well-being, then the use of an imperfect verb and the position of the clause in the second part of the example are not strange at all since the commander of the thousand is the one who has control over the well-being of David's brothers and David may or may not be able to influence the commander. Simply put, what Jesse is requesting of David is that he deliver the cheese to the commander and also do whatever he can to improve his brothers' standing with the commander. Jesse knows that David may or may not have the opportunity to do these two things and so the two requests are expressed with imperfect forms, rather than imperative forms.[8]

As was noted above, this example was placed by André in the category 'to miss, to check to see if present', rather than the category 'to look after, to take an interest in'. Not all scholars distinguish these two categories, and even those who do (Gehman 1972, Schottroff 1976, André 1989, Lübbe 1990, Williams 1997) describe the former category as a kind of extension of the latter. For example, Schottroff writes, "Die Bed[eutung] 'vermissen' ... ist ... wohl kaum die Grundbedeutung des Verbums, sondern ergibt sich resultativ aus der ergebnislosen Nachsuche nach Verschwundenem oder Abhandengekommenem" (Schottroff 1976: col. 471). Because of the relationship of these two categories, there is considerable disagreement among scholars as to which examples fall into the category 'to miss, to check to see if present', though all scholars agree that examples of *pāqad* that fall into this category are quite rare.[9]

Two examples from this category are considered in this paper. The first is 1 Samuel 25:15, which was briefly mentioned in note 2. It reads, 'The (David's) men were very good to us. We (Nabal's servants) were not mistreated and we did not *pāqad* anything all the time that we traveled with them while we were in the field'. In

---

[8] The interpretation of the final request, 'and their pledged thing you should take', is complicated by the uncertainty over the meaning of 'their pledged thing'. Two interpretations seem possible, either of which is compatible with the interpretation of *pāqad* as 'alter the status of your brothers'. The pledged thing is either an item that was given to the commander as a pledge that David's brothers would show up for the battle or it is an item pledged to David's brothers by the commander on the condition that they show up for battle. Whichever it is, Jesse is requesting that David take this item from the commander. In both interpretations, the action is one that relates to the commander, and not to David's brothers, and that is why the action is expressed with an imperfect and is found in the second part of Jesse's instructions.

[9] For example, Schottroff (1976: col. 471) insists that only 1 Samuel 25:15 and Isaiah 34:16 belong in this category; whereas André (1989: cols. 710–11), Lübbe (1990: 10, n. 6), Gehman (1972: 203) and Williams (1997: 661) all place 1 Samuel 20:6 in this category as well. Finally, Lübbe (1990: 10 n. 6) adds Isaiah 26:16 and Gehman (1972: 203) adds Jeremiah 3:16 to the list.

the context of this example, Nabal's servants have taken an extended excursion in the field with David's men and they are reporting back to Nabal's wife about how they were treated. That Nabal's men did not miss anything during this excursion is unquestionably the case, but to propose on that basis that *pāqad* here has the *meaning* 'to miss' misses something important to the understanding of *pāqad* in this context.

Given the context of this example, a more satisfactory accounting of the meaning of *pāqad*, and one that takes into account the activities of Nabal's servants with David's men, is that Nabal's servants did not have to attend to any of the practical matters that must be taken care of when traveling in the field for an extended time. These practical matters include, for example, such things as making sure that everything is packed in its proper place and that nothing gets left behind when camp is broken in the morning, so that it can be found again when camp is being made that night. When Nabal's servants were traveling with David's men, they did not have to take care of any of these practical matters. Others made sure that all the equipment, and the food, and so forth were available and ready to be used when they were needed. In this context, then, that is what *pāqad* means, namely, 'to put in the status of being ready and available for use any of the objects associated with travel in the field'.

The other example is 1 Samuel 20:6, which is the most commonly cited example of this category. It reads, 'If indeed your father (Saul) *pāqad* me (David), then you (Jonathan) shall say, "Truly David asked of me that he might go quickly to Bethlehem, his city"'. In this context, David is trying to determine if Saul wishes to kill him and so he intends to be absent from a meal that he is required to attend so that Jonathan can see Saul's reaction. If Saul responds angrily, then Jonathan will know that Saul has evil intentions toward David.

That scholars interpret this example of *pāqad* as having the meaning 'to miss' is reasonable since what is being anticipated is that Saul will take notice of David's absence at the meal and therefore will 'miss' him. It is, however, also reasonable to interpret this example as having the meaning proposed for *pāqad* in this paper, namely, to put David where he is supposed be in Saul's scheme of things, although, on this interpretation, *pāqad* would have to refer to an instance in which an unsuccessful *attempt* at *pāqad*-ing David was made. This interpretation is essentially the same as the one proposed for Judges 15:1–2 above, the example in which Samson intends to re-establish his relationship with his wife, but is unable to do so. Yet, that text still reads, 'Samson *pāqad* his wife with a kid-goat'. There is, however, another possible interpretation of this example, and it is considered in the next section in connection with the Niphal verb *niphqad*.

2.5. The Verb *niphqad*

The Niphal verb *niphqad* is the passive of the Qal verb *pāqad*, and scholars place the various examples of this verb into five categories that correspond to five of the seven categories into which they place examples of *pāqad*. The five categories are 'to be appointed', 'to be mustered', 'to be punished', 'to be looked after', and 'to be missing, to be missed'. Of the twenty-one attested examples of *niphqad*, fourteen fall into the final category, leaving only seven in the other four categories combined.[10] That so many examples of this verb occur in the final category is somewhat surprising since the corresponding category for the verb *pāqad* (i.e., 'to miss') was the rarest for that verb, and it was also the one that posed the most difficulty for the meaning proposed for *pāqad* in section 2.3 of this paper.

Excluding this final category for a moment, the meaning of the seven examples of *niphqad* that fall into the first four categories can easily be analyzed as the passive of the meaning proposed above for the Qal verb *pāqad*, namely, 'to be assigned to one's proper or appropriate status or position in an organizational order', or 'to be placed where one is supposed to be in the overall scheme of things'. An example that clearly shows this meaning is Nehemiah 7:1: 'When the wall was built and I had set up the doors, the gatekeepers and the singers and the Levites *niphqad*'. This example is taken from a section of the book of Nehemiah that records the successful completion of

---

[10] The seven are Numbers 16:29; Isaiah 24:22, 29:6; Ezekiel 38:8, Proverbs 19:23; and Nehemiah 7:1, 12:44. The fourteen are Numbers 31:49; Judges 21:3; 1 Samuel 20:18 (two times), 25, 27; 25:7, 21; 2 Samuel 2:30; 1 Kings 20:39 (two times); 2 Kings 10:19 (two times); and Jeremiah 23:4.

the wall of Jerusalem and the re-establishment of various positions of authority among the community of returned exiles, and the verb *niphqad* is generally translated 'were appointed'. That translation is a perfectly reasonable one and it is only necessary to make a remark similar to the one made above in connection with the example of *pāqad* found in Deuteronomy 20:9, namely, that the translation 'were appointed' does not necessarily indicate that the new status of the gatekeepers, the singers, and the Levites is the proper or appropriate status for these three groups in this particular context, although that notion is clearly present in this example.

As for the meaning of the final category, 'to be missing, to be missed', it too can be analyzed as the passive of the proposed meaning of *pāqad*, although, as was noted at the end of the previous section, it is somewhat problematic to analyze the meaning of *pāqad* as 'to *attempt* to assign an object to its proper status' which is how *pāqad* would have to be analyzed in those examples in which it apparently means 'to miss'. There is, however, an alternative analysis of the Niphal verb that avoids this difficulty and that may shed some light on the problematic Qal examples.

In this alternative analysis, the examples of *niphqad* that fall into the category 'to be missing, to be missed' are examples of the so-called "gerundive" use of the Niphal stem, in which the meaning of a Niphal verb can be analyzed as 'to be able to be X-ed, to be X-able', where X is the meaning of the corresponding Qal verb of the same root (for a brief treatment of this use, with examples, see Waltke and O'Connor 1990: 387). For example, the Qal verb *'ākal* means 'to eat', and the corresponding Niphal verb *ne'ĕkal* means 'to be eaten', or 'to be edible, to be able to be eaten'. In the case of the root *pqd*, the gerundive use of the Niphal verb *niphqad* would have the meaning 'to be able to be assigned to one's proper or appropriate status or position in an organizational order, to be able to be placed where one is supposed be in the overall scheme of things'. Now, an object that is edible is one that has not yet been eaten, and so an object that is *pāqad*-able is one that has not yet been *pāqad*-ed, in other words, one that is *not* in its appropriate position and so is "missing" from that position.

An example of *niphqad* that nicely illustrates this use of the Niphal stem is 1 Samuel 20:18: 'Jonathan said to him, "Tomorrow is the new moon and you will *niphqad* because your place will *niphqad*"'. This example occurs in the same context as 1 Samuel 20:6, considered in the previous section as an example of *pāqad* that means 'to miss'. In this example, part of Jonathan's response to David's plan is given. Jonathan notes that when David is deliberately absent from the meal with Saul, David will be *pāqad*-able, that is, missing from his proper position and, therefore, able to be placed in his proper position because David's place or position at the table will be *pāqad*-able; that is, it will not have its proper status because there will be no one in it.

If this analysis is the correct one, then it suggests another possible analysis of the examples of the Qal verb *pāqad* that have been placed in the category 'to miss'. These few examples may not, in fact, have the meaning proposed for *pāqad* in section 2.3, but may, rather, be examples of *pāqad* with a meaning separate and distinct from the proposed one. Under this analysis, this second meaning of *pāqad* would have arisen because of the semantic relationship of the verbs *pāqad* and *niphqad*. Since the passive verb, *niphqad*, is used with the meaning 'to be missing, to be missed', then the corresponding active verb, *pāqad*, came to be used with the corresponding active meaning 'to miss'. In this case, the meaning 'to miss' would not be an extension of the more fundamental meaning 'to look after', as scholars have proposed, but is, rather, a second meaning of *pāqad* only indirectly related to its first meaning.

2.6. The Verbs *hiphqîd* and *hophqad*

Next to be considered is the Hiphil verb *hiphqîd*, and although not all scholars who have written on *pqd* comment on *hiphqîd* (Gehman 1972, for example, does not mention this verb), those who have generally understand its meaning to be identical to the meaning of the examples of the Qal verb *pāqad* that fall into the two categories 'to appoint' and 'to entrust to, to deposit'. In fact, examples of these two verbs are often listed side by side by scholars (see, e.g., Schottroff 1976: cols. 473–74, André 1989: cols. 714–16, Lübbe 1990: 12 n. 9, Williams 1997: 661). However, the fact that examples of *hiphqîd* occur in only two of the seven categories proposed for *pāqad* indicates, at a minimum, that this verb has a more restricted or specialized meaning than *pāqad*. Its meaning is not simply identical to the meaning of *pāqad*.

How then can this more restricted meaning be characterized? The remarks made by Lübbe are especially apt. He writes, "The event described here may be viewed from two different vantage points, the one being the transfer of authority to an agent, the other being the subjecting of objects or persons to that agent's control. Thus the first describes the investing of authority to control in an agent, and the second describes the controlling activity to be experienced. No matter which aspect is more prominent in an occurrence, the event remains the same and the other aspect is always implicit" (Lübbe 1990: 12). More simply, the Hiphil verb *hiphqîd* denotes a situation in which a relationship of authority is established between two objects with the result that one of the objects will have authority over and responsibility for the other object. In most cases, the direct object of the verb is the one who is in a position of authority and the verb is translated 'appoint'. Less commonly, the direct object of the verb is the one who is placed under authority and the verb is translated 'entrust'. The Qal verb *pāqad* can, of course, also denote such a situation, but, unlike the Hiphil verb, its meaning is not *limited* to such a situation.

The more specialized meaning of *hiphqîd* as compared to *pāqad* is nicely illustrated by Numbers 1:48–50: 'And the LORD spoke to Moses, "Only the tribe of Levi do not *pāqad* and do not raise their head in the midst of the Israelites, but you *hiphqîd* the Levites over the tent of the congregation and over all its implements and over all that (belongs) to it"'. As was seen above in connection with verse three of this chapter of Numbers, the Qal verb *pāqad* refers, in this context, to the organization of the people into military units. In this verse, Moses is instructed not to *pāqad* the Levites nor to raise their head because they will not be part of the army nor will they receive a portion of the promised land. However, the Levites will have a position of authority over and will have responsibility for the tent of the congregation and the items connected to it. Therefore, Moses is commanded to *hiphqîd* them over these objects.

Now, if *hiphqîd* and *pāqad* were simply identical in meaning, then there would be a contradiction in this example, but there is no contradiction because the verb *pāqad* is less restricted in its meaning than the verb *hiphqîd* and so the exact meaning of *pāqad* in any given context depends on the context to a greater degree than the meaning of *hiphqîd*. In this particular example, the context restricts the meaning of *pāqad* to military organization and, as a result, it refers to a different activity than *hiphqîd*.

The Hophal verb *hophqad* is simply the passive of the Hiphil verb *hiphqîd*. It occurs only eight times, and its meaning is clear.[11] For example, 2 Chronicles 34:12 reads, 'The men were doing the work faithfully, and over them the Levites Yahat and Obadiah *hophqad*'. The relationship of authority that is established between the two Levites and the workers is clear in this context and so this example is usually, and appropriately, translated 'were appointed'.

2.7. The Verbs *piqqēd* and *puqqad*

The Piel verb *piqqēd* is the rarest of all the verbs that contain the root *pqd*, being attested only once (Isaiah 13:4). It is found in a military context and is a straightforward example of the so-called "intensive" use of the Piel, a use of this stem in which the Piel verb of a particular root is essentially synonymous with the Qal verb of that root but may have a slight nuance of more intensive action. The example reads, 'The sound of tumult in the hills, the likeness of a great people. The sound of a multitude of kingdoms, nations gathering together. The LORD of hosts *piqqēd* an army (for) battle'.

The Pual verb *puqqad* is nearly as rare as the Piel verb *piqqēd*, being attested just twice. It is simply the passive of the Piel verb (though neither example happens to occur in a military context), and therefore it is essentially synonymous with the passive of the Qal verb.[12] The example in Exodus 38:21 reads, 'These are the accountings of

---

[11] The only problematic example is found in Jeremiah 6:6: 'It (is) the city *hophqad*'. The form in the text is vocalized as a Hophal, but if this vocalization is correct, then the form is indefinite and masculine, but it must agree with a form ('the city') that is definite and feminine. This difficulty has led scholars to propose various emendations to the text. For example, André (1989: col. 719) suggests that the form be vocalized as a Niphal, which is possible, though it produces a syntax that is also difficult: the sentence would be a nominal sentence consisting of a pronoun, a definite noun, and an infinitive. Regardless of the exact resolution of this difficulty, the other examples of this verb are clear and straightforward.

[12] For this reason, it is possible that these two examples are not examples of a Pual verb, but rather examples of a Qal Passive verb, the Qal Passive being a verbal stem that is hypothesized to have existed in Hebrew, but which disappeared from the language. However, the presence of the Piel verb *piqqēd* in Hebrew makes this alternative analysis less likely, though still possible.

(the items of) the tent, the tent of testimony, that *puqqad* according to the mouth of Moses, (for) the service of the Levites', and the example in Isaiah 38:10 reads, 'In the gates of Sheol I *puqqad* (for) the remainder of my years'. In both cases, the meaning 'to be assigned to one's proper or appropriate status or position in an organizational order' is clear.

2.8. The Verbs *hithpāqēd* and *hothpāqad*

The last two verbs that contain the root *pqd* are the Hithpael verb *hithpāqēd* and the Hothpaal verb *hothpāqad*. They are both quite rare, each being attested only four times (the Hithpael in Judges 20:15 [two times], 20:17, and 21:9, and the Hothpaal in Numbers 1:47, 2:33, and 26:62, and in 1 Kings 20:27), and they are rarely considered by scholars. Only Scharbert 1960, Schottroff 1976, André 1980, and André 1989 make any comments about them, and these comments are all extremely brief. Schottroff correctly notes that "... die wegen der fehlenden Verdopplung des mittleren Radikals nicht als Reflexivstämme zum Pi., sondern als solche zum Qal mit infigiertem -t- aufzufassen sind ..." (Schottroff 1976: col. 468), and so these two verbs are most directly related to the Qal verb *pāqad* rather than to the Piel verb *piqqēd*.

As for their meaning, Scharbert and Schottroff both state that these two verbs are passive and always have the meaning 'gemustert werden' (Scharbert 1960: 214; Schottroff 1976: col. 468); whereas André defines each of them differently and includes in his definitions the notion of reflexivity, which is generally characteristic of verbs in Hebrew that have a prefixed *t*. He defines the Hithpael as "... soldiers presenting themselves fit for war," and the Hothpaal as "... soldiers brought to present themselves fit for war" (André 1980: 226).

The difference between a passive meaning 'to be mustered' and a reflexive meaning 'to muster themselves' is a rather subtle one. A reflexive would specifically indicate that the subject did something to itself; whereas a passive would indicate that something was done to the subject without specifying who or what did it. Even so, a reflexive meaning seems preferable for the four examples of the Hithpael verb *hithpāqēd*. All these examples are found in the context of the battle of the tribes of Israel against the tribe of Benjamin recorded in the last two chapters of Judges. The three examples in Judges 20 all occur in the same construction; that is, they all contain a subject, the verb, and a number. Judges 20:17 is representative, 'The men of Israel *hithpāqēd*, apart from Benjamin, 400,000 men carrying a sword, each one a man of battle'. In this example, and in the other two like them, the meaning is similar to that of Joshua 8:10 considered in section 2.4 of this paper, except that here the meaning is reflexive rather than active, 'The men of Israel, apart from Benjamin, gathered themselves together as an army'. In this case, a complex object (a large group of men) acts upon itself and re-arranges its parts so that it becomes something that fits into the overall plan (to fight Benjamin).

The fourth example, Judges 21:9, is a bit more interesting. It occurs after the battle when the Israelites are trying to determine who did not show up to fight, and it reads, 'The people *hithpāqēd* and there was not there any man from the inhabitants of Jabesh Gilead'. What apparently took place is that the men arranged themselves in their battle order; that is, they got themselves organized according to their appropriate status/position in the army, and it became easy to see which subgroup of the army was absent.

The examples of the Hothpaal verb *hothpāqad* are more clearly passive, though the example found in 1 Kings 20:26–27 could possibly be reflexive. It reads, '(Aram) went up to Apheq for battle with Israel and the Israelites *hothpāqad* and were provisioned and they went toward them'. In other words, the Israelites were gathered (or, possibly, gathered themselves) together in their military units in preparation for battle. The other three examples are also understood by Scharbert 1960 and Schottroff 1976 as referring to a military action, but it seems better to understand these examples as referring to the organization of the tribes with respect to the division of the land. That this is the case in Numbers 26:62 seems inescapable. It reads, '... they (the Levites) were not *hothpāqad* among the Israelites because a portion (of land) was not given to them among the Israelites'.

2.9. Conclusion

The Qal verb *pāqad* has a single meaning, which is, 'to assign a person or a thing to what the subject believes is its proper or appropriate status or position in an organizational order'. It has this meaning in every context in which it is used, although the direct object of the verb and what the subject must do in order to assign the direct object to its proper status will also contribute aspects of meaning to any given context. Since it is necessary to consider these other aspects of meaning when translating this verb, multiple translation possibilities exist for this verb depending on the context in which it is found. The only examples of *pāqad* that may not have this meaning are those in which the verb apparently means 'to miss'. These examples may attest a legitimate second meaning for this verb arising from the relationship of the Qal verb *pāqad* to the Niphal verb *niphqad*.

The meanings of the other verbs that contain the root *pqd* represent consistent variations of the meaning of *pāqad*. The Niphal verb *niphqad* is the passive of *pāqad* and means 'to be assigned to one's proper or appropriate status or position in an organizational order'. It also attests a gerundive meaning, 'to be *pāqad*-able, to be missing'. The Hiphil verb *hiphqîd* has a more specialized meaning than *pāqad* and denotes a situation in which a relationship of authority is established between two objects with the result that one of the objects will have authority over and responsibility for the other object. The Hophal verb *hophqad* is simply the passive of *hiphqîd*. The Piel verb *piqqēd* is essentially synonymous with the Qal verb but may have a slight nuance of more intensive action. The Pual verb *puqqad* is the passive of *piqqēd*. Finally, the Hithpael verb *hithpāqēd* is likely reflexive, 'to put oneself in one's appropriate status or position', and the Hothpaal verb *hothpāqad* is, apparently, always passive 'to be put in one's appropriate status or position'.

Bibliography

André, Gunnel
- 1980 *Determining the Destiny: PQD in the Old Testament.* Coniectanea Biblica. Old Testament Series 16. Lund: CWK Gleerup.
- 1989 "פָּקַד *pāqaḏ*." In *Theologisches Wörterbuch zum Alten Testament*, Vol. 6, edited by G. Johannes Botterweck and Heinz-Josef Fabry, columns 708–23. Stuttgart: W. Kohlhammer.

Gehman, Henry Snyder
- 1972 "Ἐπισκέπομαι, ἐπίσκεψις, ἐπίσκοπος, and ἐπισκοπή in the Septuagint in Relation to פקד and other Hebrew Roots: A Case of Semantic Development Similar to that of Hebrew." *Vetus Testamentum* 22: 197–207.

Grossfeld, Bernard
- 1984 "The Translation of Biblical Hebrew פקד in the Targum, Peshitta, Vulgate, and Septuagint." *Zeitschrift für die Alttestamentliche Wissenschaft* 96: 83–101.

Holler, R. K.
- 1957 The Meaning of PQD. Ph.D. dissertation, McCormick Theological Seminary.

van Hooser, Jack Boyd
- 1962 The Meaning of the Hebrew Root פקד in the Old Testament. Ph.D. dissertation, Harvard University Divinity School.

Lübbe, J. C.
- 1990 "Hebrew Lexicography: A New Approach." *Journal for Semitics* 2: 1–15.

McComiskey, T. E.
- 1993 "Prophetic Irony in Hosea 1.4: A Study of the פקד על Collocation and Its Implications for the Fall of Jehu's Dynasty." *Journal for the Study of the Old Testament* 58: 93–101.

Middelkoop, P.
  1963 "A Word Study: The Sense of PAQAD in the Second Commandment and Its General Background in the OT Regarding to the Translation into the Indonesian and Timorese Languages." *South East Asia Journal of Theology* 4: 33–47, 56–65.

Scharbert, Joseph
  1960 "Das Verbum PQD in der Theologie des Alten Testaments." *Biblische Zeitschrift* 4: 209–26.

Schottroff, Willi
  1976 "פקד *pqd* heimsuchen." In *Theologisches Handwörterbuch zum Alten Testament*, Vol. 2, edited by Ernst Jenni and Claus Westermann, columns 466–86. Munich: Chr. Kaiser.

Speiser, Ephraim A.
  1958 "Census and Ritual Expiation in Mari and Israel." *Bulletin of the American Schools of Oriental Research* 149: 17–25.

Waltke, Bruce K., and M. O'Connor
  1990 *An Introduction to Biblical Hebrew Syntax*. Winona Lake: Eisenbrauns.

Williams, T. F.
  1997 "7212 פקד." In *New International Dictionary of Old Testament Theology and Exegesis*, Vol. 3, edited by Willem A. VanGemeren, pp. 657–63. Grand Rapids: Zondervan Publishing House.

3. 'MAY THE GODS PRESERVE YOU!': THE VARIABILITY OF INJUNCTIVE *LA IN EPIGRAPHIC SOUTH ARABIAN AND ITS RELATION TO JUSSIVE FORMS WITHIN SOUTH SEMITIC[1]

Joseph L. Daniels II

3.1. Introduction

3.1.1. Particle *l-* as an Injunctive Element in Epigraphic South Arabian

Several studies have highlighted the formal ambiguity found in Epigraphic South Arabian between the prefixed imperfective verb and a possible jussive (*yqtl - yqtl*).[2] This ambiguity in *form* is often distinguished in *meaning* by the use of proclitic particles that convey an optative or injunctive force.[3] In particular, the Sabaic particle *l-* (<*la*) most often serves as an injunctive element within dedicatory texts, official decrees and proclamations, and devotional graffiti, thereby conveying a sense of intent, volition, or request. In this way, it is possible to differentiate between formally ambiguous verbs and determine narrative or injunction:

(1) *ʾbkrb w-ḥyw ʿttr ... hqny ... ḥmdm bdt **ḫmr-hmw** ʾlmqhw wldm dkrm ... **w-l-ḫmr-hw** wfy grbt-hmw*
(Ja 654/1–6, 9–10)

' ʾAbkarib and Ḥayûʿattar ... dedicated [to their lord ʾAlmaqah, master of Awwam, a bronze statue] in thankfulness that ʾAlmaqahū *granted them* a male child ... *may he* [ʾAlmaqahū] grant him the safety of their persons'

Although the use of this particle in topicalizing the injunctive force of the verb has been mentioned briefly in a few previous studies, a more complete examination of the syntactical conditions surrounding its use or non-use has been absent thus far.[4] In his section explaining verbal morphology, Beeston (1984: 20 [§ 7:8]; 1962: 26 [§ 22:2]) states only that *l-* (*la*) can precede either an infinitive [i.e., non-prefix conjugation verb] or an imperfect [prefix conjugation verb] and cites several examples. Most recently, Kogan and Korotayev (1998: 235) added two examples of the Sabaic imperative, but failed to comment on the variety of injunctive verbs preceded by *l-* (*la*) or standing alone. In sum, it is clear that the Epigraphic South Arabian texts exhibit several syntactical structures for expressing injunctions, including use of a non-prefixed verb (as in the Arabic "optative perfect" or the Akkadian stative with *lū*; see section 3.2.1 below) as well as a prefix-conjugation verb (as shared in the modern South Arabian and Ethiopic languages; see section 3.2.2 below).

In a broader study of the particle **la* and its use as an injunctive element, Huehnergard argued that it originally "served as an optional asserverative element which... could be prefixed to the predicate in verbal and non-verbal clauses to add emphasis to a statement, or to elements other than the predicate (especially the subject) to

---

[1] I would like to congratulate Professor Gragg on his well-earned retirement and I would like to personally extend my gratitude to him for his years of stellar guidance as my advisor and teacher.

[2] Although some evidence involving "weak" roots (*dymwtn* as opposed to *wl ymtn*) has been offered to argue for variant forms of indicative and jussive verbs, exceptions to these forms are also cited. Compare Kogan and Korotayev 1998: 235; Beeston 1984: 7 [§ 1:8]; Beeston 1962: 26 [§ 22:3]; von Höfner 1943: 10.

[3] This paper follows the common understanding of these two terms. As Huehnergard explains, the term "optative" means "that which expresses a wish or desire, often for a result that is unattainable or unexpected. The term 'injunctive' is intended to denote forms that signify intent, volition, or command, and to serve as a catch-all for the terms imperative, jussive, precative, and volitive" (Huehnergard 1983: 569, n. 1).

[4] It is important to note that the injunctive clause in Epigraphic South Arabian differs syntactically from the purpose clause which is also marked by the proclitic particle *l-* (*la*). Whereas the former often connects two meaningful clauses with co-ordinating *waw* (*w-*), the latter never uses this conjunction and generally follows verbs of commanding or ordering. For example, Ja 601/5–8 reads: *b-kn wqh-hmw mrʾ-hmw ... l ʿdrn b-ʿm ʾšʿbm ḫwln* 'when their lord ordered them... to help against the tribes of Ḫawlan' (purpose clause). Further, in line 15, the narrative changes to a wish: *w-l-s¹ʿd ʾlmqh ʾdm-hw bny šymm* 'may ʾAlmaqah bestow favor upon his subjects, the Banī Suḫaymum' (injunctive clause).

accentuate or topicalize them" (Huehnergard 1983: 592). This understanding of the origin and role of the particle has gained widespread acceptance (Lipiński 1997: 336 [§ 38.2]), however, little corroborating evidence from the Epigraphic South Arabian languages has hitherto been cited. In fact, the Epigraphic South Arabian texts (most notably Sabaic) offer several important examples in which the particle *la* exhibits a topicalizing function in both verbal and verbless clauses, all the while serving as an optional appendage.

The present study attempts to describe the various syntactical structures for expressing injunctions in Sabaic texts and relate the role of the particle *l-* (**la*) in effecting this force. Because of the inherently precative nature of dedicatory texts, the majority of examples derive from temple inscriptions and cultic rock graffiti in which the propitiant seeks safety, good health, or prosperity from the addressed deity. In this way, little confusion in interpretation arises regarding the intent of the writer. It is hoped that the semantic clarity of the text will shed some insight into its formal ambiguities.

3.2. Survey of Syntactical Environments for Injunctions in Epigraphic South Arabian

3.2.1. Injunctive *l-* with Prefix-conjugation Verb

As previously noted, Sabaic commonly uses the proclitic particle *l-* (**la*) affixed to a prefix-conjugation verb to express the injunctive (Kogan and Korotayev 1998: 235; Beeston 1984: 20 [§ 7:8]; Beeston 1962: 26 [22§ 2]). This jussive verb commonly has the energic *-n* (*<-an* or *-anna*) affixed to its last radical, whether followed by a non-affixed direct object or a pronominal suffix. In the cases in which the energic *-n* is graphically omitted, it is possible that a phonetic reduction to *-ā* could have replaced the full suffix. Such a reduction is seen in the pausal form in Arabic and the direct cohortative in Hebrew (Lipiński 1997: 355).

(2) Non-affixed direct object

    (a) **w-l-yzʾn** *ʾlmqh hwfyn-hmw b-kl sbʾt sbʾnn* (Ja 584/4–5)

       '*may* ʾAlmaqah *continue* to protect them in every expedition they undertake'

    (b) **w-l-yḫmrn** *ʾlmqh ṯhwn bʿl ʾwm ʾmh-hw hwn lhn lb-hw* (Ja 722/b–c)

       '*may* ʾAlmaqah Ṯahwan, lord of ʾAwwam, *grant* his female devotees a softening of his heart toward them'

(3) Pronominal suffix

    w-l-yḫmrn-hw *ʾlmqhw ḥẓy wrdʾw mrʾ-hmw* (Ja 667A/14–15)

    '*may* ʾAlmaqahū *grant him* the favor and goodwill of his overlord'

It is also important to note the disjunctive force of the proclitics *w-* (**wa*) and *f-* (**fa*) in effecting a semantic and syntactic separation from the preceding narrative. Although the proclitic *w-* (**wa*) appears more often than *f-* (**fa*) in Sabaic texts, both can be used to achieve the same force. In effect, the text's narrative enumerating the various reasons for the dedicant's offering ceases at this syntactic separation. The following injunctive verb then marks the dedicant's wish or intention for the future. Even further, it is possible to observe in a few texts a topicalized subject following the disjunctive particle *w-* (**wa*) yet preceding the marked injunctive verb. The standard *verb-subject-object* (VSO) word order in these instances is thus converted to *subject-verb-object* (SVO). Sabaic texts show a preference for resuming the verb with the particle *f-* (**fa*), but this particle is occasionally omitted.

(4) Disjunctive particle *w-* (**wa*) introducing an injunction

    b-ḏt hʿn ʿbd-hw b-hwt mrḍn **w-l-yzʿn** *ʾlmqhw s²rḥ grb ʿbd-hw bn kl mrḍm* (Ja 670/13–18)

    'because he [ʾAlmaqahū] delivered his servant from that sickness. *May* ʾAlmaqahū *continue* to preserve the body of his servant from every sickness'

(5) Disjunctive particle *f-* (**fa*) introducing an injunction

    w-ḫfr sṭrn **f-l yʿtbrn** *hwtr* (DSP 41/9)

    'and he carved out this inscription. *May* the Eternal *take* [it] *under his protection*'

(6) Disjunctive particle *w-* (**wa*) and fronted subject introducing an injunction

l‛s²m ... hqny ʾlmqh b‛l ʾwm ṣlmn ḏḏhbn **w-ʾlmqh l-yḫmrn** *s²rḥ grb-hw* (Ja 692/1–6)

'Li‛as²am ... offered ʾAlmaqah, lord of ʾAwwam, this bronze statue. *As for ʾAlmaqah, may he grant* protection of his body'

(7) Disjunctive particle *w-* (**wa*) and fronted subject introducing an injunction. (Note the optional use of *f-* [**fa*] in resuming the verb with the extraposed subject.)

w-ʾlmqhb *‛l ʾwm* **f-l-yḫmrn** *w-mt‛n w-rṯdn grb mrʾ-hw* (Ja 572/7–8)

'*As for ʾAlmaqah, lord of ʾAwwam, may he grant* (protection) and save and entrust (in safety) the body of his overlord [ʾIls²araḥ Yaḥḍ!ub]'

This syntactic structure (proclitic *l-* [**la*] + prefix-conjugation verb) parallels the common morphological structure of optative and injunctive verbs within several South Semitic languages. In Amharic and East Gurage (Selṭi), the first-person singular reflects injunctive *l-* affixed to the jussive stem: for example, *ləsbär*, *läsbär* 'let me break', respectively (Lipiński 1997: 375). Also, Ge‛ez positive injunctives may optionally be preceded by *la-*: for example, *yeqrab*, *la-yeqrab* 'let him approach' (Lambdin 1978: 150; Gragg 1998: 252 ff.). In each of the modern South Arabian languages, with the exception of Ḥarsūsi, the particle *l-* is affixed to the vocalic prefixes of the jussive verb in forming an injunctive: for example, Mehri *lərkēz* 'may he put (something) straight'; Jibbali *lqɔdər* 'may I be able'; Soqotri *lə ‛árəb* 'may he know' (Simeone-Senelle 1998: 403, 405 ff.). As discussed below (sections 3.2.3–4), the use of the preformative *l-* (**la*) on Sabaic injunctives is optional and the several examples of its non-use hint at its original asseverative force, which presumably added emphasis to injunctive verb.

3.2.2. Injunctive *l-* with Infinitive

Besides forming injunctions with proclitic *l-* (**la*) affixed to a prefix-conjugation verb, Sabaic dedicatory texts and cultic graffiti widely attest the use of this particle affixed to the infinitive.[5] The infinitive in Sabaic most often serves as a verbal noun, completing the sense of finite verbal predicates: for example, *wlyz‛n s²rḥ* 'may he continue to preserve'. It also appears commonly as a "converb," continuing the semantic and aspectual quality of the first verbal predicate in a series of related actions: for example, *flyḫmrn w-mt‛n w-rṯdn* 'may he grant (protection) and save and entrust (in safety)'. However, when prefixed with the injunctive proclitic *l-* (**la*), the infinitive digresses from the narrative and conveys optative or precative force.[6] Similar to the jussive, the infinitive occasionally has the energic *-n* (*<-an* or *-anna*) affixed to its last radical whether followed by a non-affixed direct object or a pronominal suffix. In each case, the injunctive infinitive is preceded by the particle *w-* (**wa*) or *f-* (**fa*) which, in turn, separates the injunction from the narrative. As the examples demonstrate, this syntactic construction strongly resembles the formal variety of the injunctive jussive.

(8) Non-affixed direct object. (Compare example [2].)

w-l-wz‛ *ʾlmqhw ḫmr-hmw ḫty w-rd!w mrʾ-hmw* (Ja 656/19–20)

'*may ʾAlmaqahū continue* to grant them the favor and goodwill of their overlord'

(9) Pronominal suffix. (Compare example [3].)

*ḥqn bn mʾbrm m‛hd s²msm ... **w-l-s²rḥn-hw** ‛ṯr* (DSP 60/1–5)

'Ḥaqqan, son of Maʾbaram, serves as a temple functionary of S²ams ... *May ‛A[th]tar preserve him*'

---

[5] Common convention refers to this unmarked verb as the "infinitive." However, owing to the ambiguous nature of the Epigraphic South Arabian script, it is impossible to ascertain the vocalic differences (if any) between the third person of the perfective, the active participle, and the infinitive. It has been argued that the **qattala*-stem (intensive, factitive) occasionally forms its infinitive as *tqtl(-t)*. See Kogan and Korotayev 1998: 236; Beeston 1962: 2 [§ 19:3]; von Höfner 1943: 59 [§ 51].

[6] It must be noted that the purpose clause formally resembles the injunctive clause in Sabaic. However, semantic distinctions often can be drawn easily from the two verbs involved. Whereas, the former employs verbs of commanding, bidding, and ordering, the latter rarely establishes a consequential or purposeful relationship between the two verbs. Instead, it expresses a wishful outcome or forthcoming desirable situation. In addition, the disjunctive particle *w-* (**wa*), which often precedes the injunctive verb, never precedes a purpose clause.

(10) Disjunctive particle *f-* (**fa*) introducing the injunctive infinitive. (Compare example [5].)

sṭr ... ws²bḫylt **fl wfy-hw** *'tr* (DSP 177/1–3)

'Was²abḫaylat wrote [this inscription] .... *May* 'A[th]tar *protect him*'

Conspicuously absent from this subset of injunctions is an example in which a topicalized subject precedes the injunctive infinitive. Indeed, we might speculate that the lack of an actor affix on the infinitive fosters an ambiguity between the subject and any following direct object. Thus, in all the text sources examined, the injunctive infinitive precedes the subject of the desired action. In those cases in which in a "fronted" subject is used to provide emphasis, a prefix-conjugation verb is required. Finally, it is important to note a grammatically ambiguous injunctive that can be categorized under either jussive or infinitive. Both the unvocalized Epigraphic South Arabian script and the rare use of the verb leave doubts about the formal structure of the injunction, even though the meaning remains quite clear.

(11) Ambiguous form: third-person feminine singular jussive or *qattala*-stem infinitive

l-tkrbn *s²msn b 'lt mṭll slmn...wqny-hw* (DSP 215/1–5)

'*May* S²ams, lordess of Muṭalil, *bless* Salmān... and his animal property'

The Sabaic root √*krb*, analyzed in detail by Beeston, occasionally denotes the 'blessing' conferred by a deity upon his propitiant.[7] This meaning bears close relation to the Akkadian verb *karābu*, defined by *The Assyrian Dictionary of the University of Chicago* (*CAD*) as "to pronounce formulas of blessing (said of gods)." If we interpret this form as the *t*-prefixed infinitive of the *qattala*-stem (see n. 9), then this injunctive demonstrates the proclitic *l-* (**la*) + infinitive construction. However, it also must be noted that the subject of the injunction is *s²ms b 'lt mṭll* 'S²ams, lordess of Muṭalil', both grammatically and semantically feminine. As noted in previous grammars (Kogan and Korotayev 1998: 234; Beeston 1984: 15 [§ 5:5]; Beeston 1962: 23 [§21:3]; von Höfner 1943: 69 [§58]), the feminine singular form of the prefix-conjugation shares this *t*-prefix (as an actor affix). The two forms, likely distinguished vocalically, thus parallel each other in shape and meaning.[8] Unfortunately, the energic *-n* sheds no light on the ambiguity since it is optionally affixed to both the infinitive and the jussive, as previously discussed (examples 4, 6, and 9).

Although it is well established that Arabic and Akkadian possess third-person injunctives formed from the non-prefix conjugation, examples derived from the South Semitic branch of languages (apart from Sabaic) are much harder to demonstrate. Indeed, previous studies have linked the morphological structure and syntactic features of the "optative perfect" in Arabic to the optative construction of "*lū* + stative" in Akkadian (Lipiński 1997: 360, 514–15).[9] However, in the case of the modern South Arabian and Ethiopian languages, such constructions seem to have been lost. Nevertheless, it is possible that an occasional vestigial form retains this nuance. In Selṭi (East Gurage), for example, the first-person plural of the jussive verb reveals an actor suffix, as opposed to the expected prefix:

(12) Selṭi: *lamsak***na** (<**la-* + *masak-na*) 'let us guide', **not derived from** (**la-namsak*) as opposed to the jussive *lamsak* (<**la-* + *'amsak*) 'let me guide', and *yamsak* 'let him guide'

---

[7] For a full discussion of the root and its variety of meanings, see Beeston 1981: 21–34. Beeston presents several lines of evidence supporting J. Pirenne's contention that the root in Epigraphic South Arabian at times denoted "binding" or "unifying," as related to the Arabic verb *karaba*. However, he also concedes that the Sabaic verbal noun *krbt* clearly denotes a deity's "blessing," as evidenced in Ja 692/10: *w-l-s²'d-hw krbtm w-'ṯmrm* 'may he bestow upon him blessings and crops'. Furthermore, several personal letters (inscribed on wooden sticks) attest the use of this verb in salutations and greetings: for example, YM 11738 *w-s²ymn* **l-ykrbn-k** 'may the [divine] Patron bless you'.

[8] Reconstructing the two forms produces only vocalic differences: **La-taKRuB* (third-person feminine singular, jussive), **La-taKRīB* (infinitive, *qattala*-stem).

[9] An important distinction between the two languages is the use of an injunctive particle. Akkadian requires use of the independent particle *lū* in forming non-verbal and stative injunctive clauses: for example, *lū šalmāta lū balṭāta* '(may you) be well and healthy!' (*CAD*, B, 55a). Arabic, however, derives its injunctive force from the original verbal construction and does not require an injunctive particle: for example, *ḥayyaka llāhu* '(may) Allāh preserve you!'; *raḥimahū llāhu* '(may) Allāh have mercy upon him!'

3.2.3. Injunctive *l-* with Non-verbal Elements

Besides serving as an injunctive affix upon verbal elements, Sabaic dedicatory texts and cultic graffiti also demonstrate the interesting influence that injunctive *l-* (*la*) has upon substantives and other non-verbal elements. When affixed to a non-verbal element, injunctive *l-* (*la*) renders the word as a wishful (often attainable) result or likely gain for the person to whom the text refers.[10] Namely, the Sabaic construction of injunctive *l-* (*la*) + non-verbal element renders the hope that "(a deity) may continue" or "bring forth" this idea to the text's author or tribe. The modified non-verbal element appears in a few different syntactic environments. It may serve as a relative clause in which the sense of a preceding injunctive verb is understood as also governing the clause. In a few cases, however, an appropriate injunctive verb is omitted altogether, and we must conclude that the relative clause retains the original sense of a commonly used verb.

(13) Injunctive relative clause governed by a preceding injunctive verb
w-l-sʿd-hmw ʾlmqh bʿl ʾwm ʾtmr w- ʾfql ṣdqm bn kl ʾrḍ!-hmw ... **w-l-ḏt nʿmt** w-tn ʿmn l-sḥmn w-bny btʿ (Ja 562/11–14)
'*may* ʾAlmaqah, lord of ʾAwwam, *grant them* good fruits and crops in all their lands ... *may* [ʾAlmaqah grant] *that which is prosperous* and success to Suḥman and the people of Bataʿ'

(14) Injunctive relative clause with an omitted verb
w-l-wḍʾ w-ṯbr ʾlmqh ... kl ḍ!r w-s²n ʾm ʾnmrm w-bny ḏ-ġymn w-s² ʿb-hmw ġymn **w-l-ḏt nʿmt** w-tn ʿmn l-ʾnmrm (Ja 564/24–26)
'*may* ʾAlmaqah humiliate and destroy... every enemy and foe of ʾAnmarum and the people of Ġayman and their tribe Ġayman; *may* [ʾAlmaqah bring forth] *that which is prosperous* and success to ʾAnmarum'

The use of the relative pronoun as a connector between the injunctive particle *l-* (*la*) and its modified non-verbal element eventually produced a periphrastic clause semantically equivalent to the *l-* (*la*) + jussive verb construction. It should be noted that the relative *ḏt* appears to be a "frozen" form and does not change according to the form of the governed verb.

(15) Injunctive periphrastic clause. (Compare with examples [2] and [4].)
w-l ḏt yzʾn tʾlb s²wf w-mtʿn ʾdm-hw (RES 3991/13–14)
'*may* Taʾlab [bring forth] *that which continues* to protect and save his devotee'

(16) Injunctive periphrastic clause. (Compare with examples [2] and [4].)
ʾlmqhw... w-l-ḥmr-hmw ʾwldm ʾḏkrm hn ʾm **w-l-ḏt ymtʿn** w-ḫryn ʿbd-hw (Ja 650/27–31)
' ʾAlmaqahū ... may he grant them healthy, male children; *may* [he bring forth] *that which saves* and delivers his servant'

Finally, the nominal element with injunctive *l-* (*la*) may appear in different contexts. On the one hand, it may stand alone in absolute form as an unbound hope or intention. On the other hand, it may stand in construct form bound with another word or pronominal suffix. As the examples below demonstrate, the actor effecting this wishful result — most often the cultic deity — is only seldom included in the injunction.

(17) Injunctive *l-* with substantive in absolute form
l-ḥym (DSP 29/1)
'May he have life!' (literally, '[May there be] life!')

(18) Injunctive *l-* with nominal clause in bound form
l-ḥy mḏmr (DSP 189/1)
'May the [tribe] Maḏmār have life!' (literally, '[May there be] life of the [tribe] Maḏmār!')

---

[10] It is important to draw a distinction between *injunctive l-* (*la*) and the other uses of the proclitic particle in Sabaic. When affixed to a non-verbal element, this particle can be used for purpose, dative of reference or association, ownership, and temporal or spatial motion. Unlike the other uses of this particle, *injunctive l-* (*la*) and its modified element tends to stand at the head of a nominal sentence or clause. See Beeston 1984: 54 [§ 34:3]; 1962: 55 for a full explanation and examples of the non-injunctive uses of *l-* (*la*).

(19) Injunctive *l-* with nominal clause in bound form
l-ḥywt y'rm (DSP 81/1)
'May Ya'rum have life!' (literally, '[May there be] life of Ya'rum!')

(20) Injunctive *l-* with pronominal suffix
l-ḥy-h (DSP 180/1)
'May he have life!' (literally, '[May there be] his life!')

Examples demonstrating the force of injunctive **la* upon non-verbal elements are rather uncommon in South Semitic outside of the Epigraphic South Arabian texts, but not altogether lost. In a few "frozen" phrases (generally optative in nature), it is possible to point to the use of the particle **la* as an injunctive element upon substantives and entire nominal clauses. In Ḥarsūsi, for example, common insults have preserved this use of the injunctive *l-* (*lə* < **la*):

(21) Injunctive *l-* with nominal clause
Ḥarsūsi: *lə-ḥébək wə-ḥāmēk bə-śəwēṭ!* 'May your mother and father burn in hell!' (literally, '[May they be] your mother and father in hell!')
lūk bə-ḥāmēk! 'Commit incest with your mother!' (literally, '[May you be] with your mother!')
(Johnstone 1975: 82)

3.2.4. Injunctions without *l-*

In a slightly different direction, it is necessary to note several examples in which the particle *l-* (**la*) is absent from the Sabaic injunctive verb. These unmarked injunctives attest the originally asseverative force of the particle and hint at the likely existence of a Sabaic jussive vocalically distinct from the imperfective form. In each instance, the dedicant's wishful hope or demand is clearly expressed in the mood of the verb, albeit without the injunctive particle *l-* (**la*). At times, the writer uses a disjunctive particle (*w-* [**wa*] or *f-* [**fa*]) to separate narrative from injunction.

(22) Injunctive infinitive without the particle *l-*
*w-nkrm **kwn** ḏn mṣdqn* (Gl 1533/11–12)
'*and may* this document *be annulled*' (literally, 'and annulled, may this document be!')

(23) Injunctive infinitive (energic form) without the particle *l-*
*sṭr bhl nzḥn **w-ṣrwyn** glln s²'-hw s²ms* (DSP 211/1–3)
'BHL NZḤN wrote [this inscription]; *may* S²ams *protect* the stone stela of his devotee'

At other times, the injunctive force of the verb alone seems to provide a meaningful separation from the narrative. One might argue that these verbs are variants of the Sabaic imperative,[11] however, it is not fully clear whether the subject (*s²ms*) is being addressed (imperative) or referred to (injunctive).

(24) Injunctive infinitive without the particle *l-* (note the absence of disjunctive *w-* or *f-*)
*sṭr slmn bn ṭmṭm **s²rḥ** s²ms br 'rk* (DSP 204/1–5)
'SLMN son of ṬMṬM wrote [this inscription]; *may* S²ams *preserve* [his] wheatfield'

(25) Injunctive infinitive (energic form) without the particle *l-* (note the absence of disjunctive *w-* or *f-*)
*sṭr slmn bn 'khl **s²wfn-hw** s²ms* (DSP 209/1–4)
'SLMN son of 'KHL wrote [this inscription]; *may* S²ams *guard over him*'

These non-prefix forms without injunctive *l-* (**la*), as well as the Sabaic imperative forms (see n. 11), most likely derive from an abbreviated jussive form preserving the modal vowel /u/ without actor affixes (**yaqtul* > **qtul*). Such is the case within the modern South Arabian languages in which the imperative is identical to the jussive

---

[11] Kogan and Korotayev (1998: 235) cite two definite examples of the Sabaic imperative found within the minuscule documents: YM 11749/2 *f-hmy hfn-k **f-t'lm** b-hmy* 'as for these [two] documents, sign them both as soon as they reach you'; YM 11742/2 *w- 'nt **f-s³ḥl-n** 'bd ḏ-DWRM* 'and you, take care about the client of ḏ-DWRM'. It is important to note that the imperative forms lack injunctive *l-* (**la*).

form without the actor prefix (Simeone-Senelle 1999: 404). Even further, the non-radical /w/ in the verb **ṣrwy-n** 'may he protect' (example [23]) likely reflects the vocalic quality of the reconstructed form.[12]

3.2.5. Injunctive *l-* in Clause-final Position

Finally, two peculiar cultic texts return our attention to the particle *l-* (**la*) as an optional injunctive element. As explained above, the variety of injunctive forms within Sabaic demonstrates a proclivity toward use of the particle but equally shows that the injunctive force of the verb renders the particle as a non-essential element. Whereas the particle may bear additional force in verbal injunctive clauses, it clearly provides the entire injunctive force to substantives and nominal clauses. In this way, it is possible for the speaker in Sabaic to express hope, volition, or intent by merely affixing the particle to various grammatical units such as jussive verbs, infinitives, substantives, relatives, etc. Oddly enough, in the following two texts we find injunctive *l-* (**la*), commonly understood as a proclitic particle in Sabaic, placed independently at the end of a verbal clause.[13]

(26) Injunctive infinitive (with pronominal suffix) isolated from non-proclitic *l-* (**la*)
 *sṭr bhl bn nzdh ... bywm hwkb glln s²rḥ-hw s²ms **l*** (DSP 203)
 'BHL son of NZDH wrote [this inscription] ... when he established this stone stela; *may S²ams preserve him*'

(27) Injunctive infinitive (energic form) isolated from non-proclitic *l-* (**la*)
 *sṭr slmn bn ʾkhl k-rʿy dʾnn w-hwfn ... kl dʾn-hw **l*** (DSP 214)
 'SLMN son of ʾKHL wrote [this inscription] as he tended his sheep; *may [S²ams] guard* over all of his sheep'

In each text, it is clear that the injunctive force of the verb itself allowed the author to initially omit the particle *l-* (**la*). The use of *l-* (**la*) in injunctive verbal clauses is generally optional, and thus, there would appear to be no meaningful semantic change. Non-prefix conjugation verbs (namely, infinitives and imperatives) particularly show this tendency to express injunction without use of *l-* (**la*). However, we are then faced with this question. Why do these two texts of different authorship place a *non-essential, proclitic* particle at the end of a verbal clause?

We might consider a few speculative answers to this question, although we are prevented from answering definitively due to the nature of the script and the paucity of relevant texts. First, I would argue that the focus of our attention should lie in the variability of *l-* (**la*) as an originally asseverative particle that came to be used almost exclusively with injunctives. The fact that the verb lost little injunctive force in itself is evident in the previous examples ([22], [23], [24], [25]) cited without the particle. Secondly, as Sabaic no longer used **la* in other asseverative functions, such as a vocative or direct object marker, it solely became associated with the injunctive verb even though its use was not semantically essential. In Geʿez, we find a similar case in which the only occurrence of **la*, outside of its injunctive use, is in the conditional particle *la-ʾəmma*. Sabaic texts, then, show a wide variety of syntactic environments in which the particle *l-* (**la*) merely reinforces the injunctive verb. Regarding examples (26) and (27), we might suppose that the post-placement of **la* performs the same function. This unexpected syntactic structure bears relation to the "enveloping" structure of the negative in some dialects of Mehri and Jibbali:

Mehri: *ʾəl səbēb-i laʾ* 'it's not my fault'; *ʾəl təhɛləz bɛy laʾ* 'don't nag me!'
Jibbali: *ʾɔl ɛɣbeðəš lɔʾ* 'don't anger him!'

Here, we might understand the first particle as providing initial negation to the statement, while the post-posed *laʾ* resumes the negative force at the end of the verbal clause. Similarly, it is likely that the injunctive verb in these Sabaic texts provided the initial sense of hope or precation, while the post-posed **la* resumed an equally injunctive

---

[12] Epigraphic South Arabian texts occasionally reveal the use of *matres lectionis*: for example, *ym - ywm* 'day', *byt – bt* 'house'. In the case of the form *ṣrwy-n* (<√ṣry), the long vowel /w/ (= ū, ō) may reflect compensatory lengthening on the modal vowel caused by loss of the prefix vowel (**yaqtul > *qtul > *qutūl*).

[13] It is common for Epigraphic South Arabian monumental texts to separate prepositions (*l-, b-, k-*) and conjunctions (*w-, f-*) from their modified elements by use of word dividers. However, in this case, the particle is not considered independent and it necessarily precedes the modified element directly.

force upon the entire verbal clause. However, further investigation on the nature of Sabaic syntax and grammar are necessary to provide more definitive answers.

3.3. Conclusion

This study aims to present a fuller understanding of the various syntactic structures employed in Epigraphic South Arabian (primarily, Sabaic) to express injunction. Through close analysis of cultic and ritual texts, it is possible to detail the various environments in which the particle *l-* (< *la*) provides an injunctive force upon the governed verb or clause. Although this injunctive particle is most often bound to a prefix-conjugation verb, several other syntactic structures obtain. Sabaic texts attest the particle governing infinitives, non-verbal elements, and, quite rarely, standing free-form in clause-final position.

It is likely that the particle is related to the North and West Semitic particle *la-/li-*, which also forms the precative (Lipiński 1997: 336 [§ 38.2]; 473–74 [§ 49.7, 49.12]). Lipiński (1997: 472ff.) argues even further that these particles are related to the Akkadian presentative *lū*, however, this free-form particle is absent in Epigraphic South Arabian and therefore cannot be substantiated using Sabaic evidence. We might speculate that the particle originally provided asseverative force upon the injunctive verb, as argued by Huehnergard (1983: 592), owing to the several examples in which the injunctive verb is not governed by the particle. Unfortunately, the unvocalized Epigraphic South Arabian script prohibits closer scrutiny of the subtle differences that may distinguish the injunctive from the indicative verb. Furthermore, the specialized vocabulary of cultic texts and the context in which they are borne may provide a degree of injunction by their very nature. Future archaeological studies in concert with the epigraphic analysis of in situ texts may give a better understanding. Finally, it is the hope of the author that this study may broaden our understanding of Epigraphic South Arabian syntax and its system of verbs.

Sigla of Inscriptions Cited

DSP	"Oriental Institute Dhamar Survey Project 1999–2003." n.p.
Gl	Maria von Höfner. *Inschriften aus Ṣirwāḥ, Ḥaulān*, Vol. 2. Sammlung Eduard Glaser 12. Vienna: Österreichische Akademie der Wissenschaften, 1976.
Ja	Albert Jamme. *Sabaean Inscriptions from Maḥram Bilqîs (Mârib)*. American Foundation for the Study of Man Publications 3. Baltimore: Johns Hopkins Press, 1962.
RES	J.-B. Chabot and G. Ryckmans. *Répertoire d'épigraphie sémitique publié par la commission du corpus inscripterium semiticarum*, Vol. 6. Paris: Imprimerie nationale, 1935.
YM	Yemen Museum Ṣanaʿa

Bibliography

Beeston, Alfred Felix Landon
    1962   *A Descriptive Grammar of Epigraphic South Arabian*. London: Luzac.
    1981   "Two Epigraphic South Arabian Roots: HYʿ and KRB." In *Al-Hudhud: Festschrift Maria Höfner zum 80. Geburtstag*, edited by Roswitha G. Stiegner, pp. 21–34. Graz: Universität Graz.
    1984   *Sabaic Grammar*. Journal of Semitic Studies Monograph 6. Manchester: Manchester University Press.

Chabet, J.-B., and G. Ryckmans
> 1929 *Répertoire d'épigraphie sémitique publié par la commission du corpus inscripterium semiticarum*, Vol. 5. Paris: Imprimerie nationale.
> 1950 *Répertoire d'épigraphie sémitique publié par la commission du corpus inscripterium semiticarum*, Vol. 7. Paris: Imprimerie nationale.

Gragg, Gene B.
> 1998 "Geʿez (Ethiopic)." In *The Semitic Languages*, edited by R. Hetzron, pp. 242–60. Routledge Language Family Descriptions. New York: Routledge.

Hetzron, Robert, editor
> 1998 *The Semitic Languages*. Routledge Language Family Descriptions. New York: Routledge.

von Höfner, Maria
> 1943 *Altsüdarabische Grammatik*. Leipzig: Harrassowitz.

Huehnergard, John
> 1983 "Asseverative *la and Hypothetical *lu/law in Semitic." *Journal of the American Oriental Society* 103: 569–93.

Johnstone, Thomas M.
> 1975 *The Modern South Arabian Languages*. Monographic Journals of the Near East 1. Malibu: Undena Publications.

Kogan, L., and A. Korotayev
> 1998 "Sayhadic (Epigraphic South Arabian)." In *The Semitic Languages*, edited by Robert Hetzron, pp. 220–41. Routledge Language Family Descriptions. New York: Routledge.

Lambdin, Thomas Oden
> 1978 *Introduction to Classical Ethiopic (Geʿez)*. Missoula: Scholars Press.

Lipiński, Edward
> 1997 *Semitic Languages: Outline of a Comparative Grammar*. Orientalia Lovaniensia Analecta 80. Leuven: Uitgeverij Peeters en Department Oosterse Studies.

Oppenheim, A. Leo, et al., eds.
> 1956– *The Assyrian Dictionary of the Oriental Institute of the University of Chicago*. Chicago: University of Chicago Press.

Pirenne, Jacqueline
> 1968 *Répertoire d'épigraphie sémitique publié par la commission du corpus inscripterium semiticarum*, Vol. 8. Paris: Imprimerie nationale.

Simeone-Senelle, Marie-Claude
> 1998 "The Modern South Arabian Languages." In *The Semitic Languages*, edited by Robert Hetzron, pp. 378–423. Routledge Language Family Descriptions. New York: Routledge.

4. *LITTERA EX OCCIDENTE:*
TOWARD A FUNCTIONAL HISTORY OF WRITING

Peter T. Daniels

A century and a half ago, Edward Hincks discovered Sumerian, beginning the spinning of the first thread of Gene Gragg's remarkable skein of achievements. Over a century ago, William Rainey Harper laid the cornerstone of the Haskell Oriental Museum, with its inscription "Lux ex oriente," setting the stage for Gene's scholarly home of the last forty years. A third of a century ago, I first encountered the ginger-haired generalist and was about to be astonished by an opening lecture on Afroasiatic that spanned the ages and the leagues to draw a complex and coherent picture of the history of the language phylum: another thread. He soon (and none too soon!) went off to Ethiopia to reinforce the threads of Cushitic, Ethiopic, and South Arabian studies. A quarter century ago, he wove all these threads and many more into a remarkable seminar on the ancient Near East as a linguistic area that drew participation from well beyond the Oriental Institute, in the sort of enterprise the University of Chicago was famous for encouraging.[1] Frequently through these years he has also borne the burden of administration, and the departments and Institute concerned are the better for it. And I must not omit the hospitality of him and Michele, which warmed the hearts of so many of us over the years. Thus I felt that to honor Gene, I must loom a seamless cloak, and not stitch together a patchwork quilt, to complement his own comprehensive works with a comprehensive account of the diversification and dispersal of West Semitic writing throughout Eurasia and indeed the world: *littera ex occidente*.

The approach followed here is called "functional" to contrast with the "formal" histories of writing that have prevailed so far.

4.1. The Formal History of Writing: I. Caricature

Map 4.1 represents what is included in most general accounts of writing provided to the general public. Writing began in Sumer, and somehow Egypt soon caught on. Some clever turquoise miners in the Sinai extracted the hieroglyphic alphabet to write Semitic, and eventually it turned into Phoenician.

Cadmus brought the letters to Greece, and the Greeks cleverly invented vowels, and brought them to Italy, where the Etruscans gave them to the Romans. The Romans would not give them away but insisted on their church using them for everybody. (But some crafty Scandinavians took them anyway and carved them on wood, turning them into runes, and some clever Irishmen made a code from them and carved them on stone, turning them into ogham.)

Meanwhile, the Greek church was happy to give them away, tailoring them to each of the recipients — Copts, Goths, Armenians, Georgians, and Slavs. (Twice, for the Slavs.)

And oh yes, there were Arabs in the east, who wrote very pretty, and Indians even farther east, who did not, and Chinese even farther east, who did, and made everyone around them write just like them, namely the Japanese and Koreans.

The foregoing summary is hardly short of ludicrous, but it reflects what can be found in popular treatments of writing. Recent years have brought a plethora of such books[2] — I will not even mention basic linguistics textbooks

---

[1] "Non-Semitic, Non-Indoeuropean Languages of Ancient Western Asia: A Typological and Areal Survey" (LING 431 = NELANG 402). The presenters were Gene B. Gragg, Colin P. Masica, Miguel Civil, Erica Reiner, Paul Zimansky, Hans Gustav Güterbock, Vijayarani Fedson, John A. Brinkman, Eric P. Hamp, and Howard I. Aronson. I was the unofficial Recording Secretary for that Winter 1979 seminar, and over the years several of the participants made copies of my notes. Unfortunately, no publisher could be persuaded of the value of the project.

[2] Once-popular books falling in this category include Clodd 1900 and Mason 1920; Moorehouse 1953 is a notch above (see Daniels 2002: 94–96). More recent volumes, including Jean 1992 and Robinson 1995, are discussed in Daniels 2000b. Albertine Gaur is a specialist in the

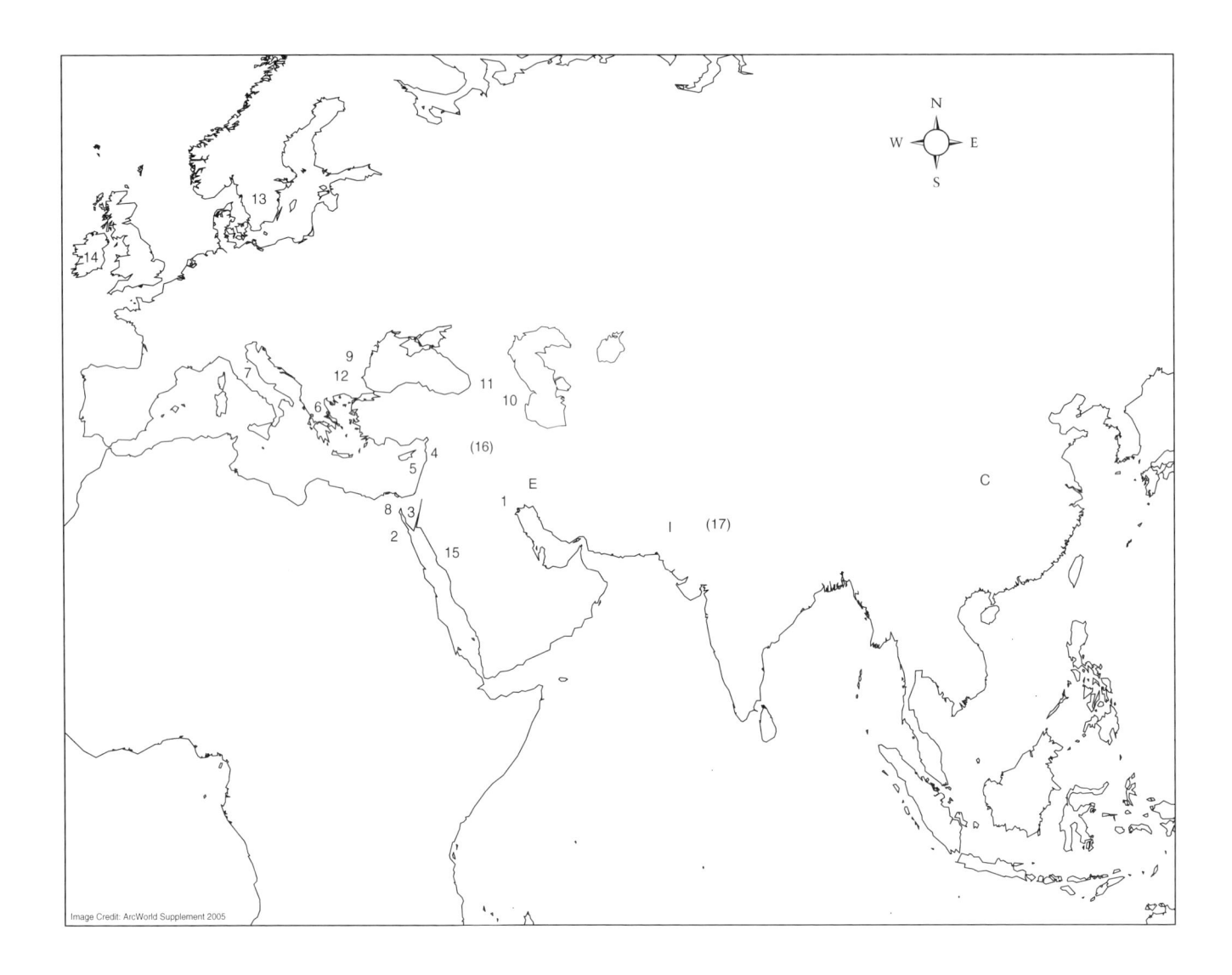

Map 4.1. Information Given in Most Accounts of Writing Provided to the General Public

1. Sumerian
2. Egyptian
3. Proto-Sinaitic
4. Ugaritic
5. Phoenician (Punic, Old Hebrew, Aramaic, Square Hebrew)
6. Greek
7. Roman
8. Coptic
9. Gothic
10. Armenian
11. Georgian
12. Slavonic (Glagolitic, Cyrillic)
13. Runes
14. Ogham
15. Arabic
(16.) Syriac
(17.) Indian

E   Elamite
I   Indus
C   Chinese

that find room for a few paragraphs or a few pages about writing systems. Not to be overlooked are encyclopedia articles. Juvenile encyclopedias[3] may be expected to resort to simplification, but in authoritative ones, it is disappointing to find spotty and outdated coverage.[4]

4.2. The Functional History of Writing: Laying the Groundwork

That, however, is far from the full story. Gene Gragg has devoted considerable attention to the less popular corners of both cuneiform studies and Semitic. I am precluded by the constraints on this symposium from going into the former, except as admonishment not to overlook the obscure. But West Semitic writing, with its background and all its ramifications, is a more than ample foundation for what can be considered the functional approach to the history of writing. What, exactly, is writing? Writing is *a system of more or less permanent marks used to represent an utterance in such a way that it can be recovered more or less exactly without the intervention of the utterer.*

The functional approach is grounded in my by now perhaps familiar sexpartite typology of writing systems (Daniels 1990). There are at least six ways for the units of a script to relate to the units of a language. (1) Sumerian cuneiform exemplifies *logography* — a logographic, or better morphographic, writing system, where each character represents an entire morpheme. (2) In a *syllabary*, each character represents a syllable. (3) In

---

writings of South Asia, and her history of writing (1984; illustrated almost entirely from the holdings of the British Museum) is reliable in that field, though less so in others. Ironically, for sociopolitical reasons she excludes South Asian writing from her history of calligraphy (1994; cf. Gaur 2000: 126); compare Salomon 1985 and other contributions to Asher and Gai 1985.

The latest crop includes Man 2000, Christin 2002, and even more disappointing, Sacks 2003. The jacket biography on Man's volume (2000) calls him "a historian and travel writer with a special interest in Mongolia." It is gratifying to find not only a brief discussion of Mongolian writing (ibid., pp. 279–80) and its history (ibid., p. 148) but also a mention of Phags pa script (ibid., p. 112) — though a mention of Phags pa without a mention of its immediate model, Tibetan script, is inexplicable. But he falls into the frequent trap of attributing the romanization of Vietnamese to French scholars (ibid., p. 280) rather than Portuguese missionaries. The main problem with the sumptuously illustrated volume edited by Christin is the translation. The French original is written by a large number of specialists (and, though there are gaps in coverage, a number of unusual topics are included), but the translators were unfamiliar with technical terminology in the field — and were not aware of their own unfamiliarity. (A passage from Durand 2002: "Thus the Akkadian for [gloss] would be: [transcription]. In syllabic Akkadian, the sentence would be notated as: [transliteration], which would be represented by twenty-three signs in paleo-Babylonian, using 'light' signs annotations. In a more recent system, the ideograms used would give: [transliteration], using only eight signs" [Durand 2002: 28]). Sacks's book (also issued in paperback with the title *Letter Perfect*) is a collection of ill-interpreted anecdotes filed into twenty-six batches (the French attribution of the Vietnamese alphabet recurs in Sacks 2003: 9).

[3] Typical encyclopedia articles are those by, surprisingly, I. J. Gelb in the junior high school–oriented *World Book Encyclopedia*. His article "Writing" describes in 1,200 words forerunners of writing and introduces the terms *logograph, syllabary*, and *pictography* only by implication suggesting that the Phoenician script is syllabic. Most of the 2,000 words of "Alphabet" recapitulate the history, but the term *syllabary* is avoided (Cypriote is "an alphabet of 56 signs, each standing for an intial consonant and a different vowel"). India is mentioned but not Southeast Asia or Inner Asia; there is a long paragraph on Cyrillic but no mention of Armenian (or the other alphabets of the Christian Orient; Gamkrelidze 1994). (Even under "Armenian," the student is wrongly told that "the Armenians cling to their own language, which is not closely related to any other language in the world" but not that their alphabet is distinctive.) We may hope that the successive paragraph openings "Chinese is the only major language that does not have an alphabetical system of writing" and "Japanese is based on Chinese, but the characters represent either syllables or words" do not represent Gelb's mis-statement but editorial interference.

[4] The *Encyclopædia Britannica* has not carried a unified, coherent treatment of writing in more than a century, since Peter Giles's 20,000-word masterpiece in the Tenth edition of 1902–3 (Daniels 2005: 510 with n. 19), which was subdivided and condensed in the supposedly definitive Eleventh edition. The Fourteenth edition, which was revised nearly every year between 1929 and 1973, between at least 1932 and 1960 carried a long article "Alphabet" by B. F. C. Atkinson written with an antiquarian slant and illustrated by a table purporting to show that the Greek alphabet derived from an ancient Indian alphabet. (The table is not mentioned in the text, and it is conceivable that it was prepared for a different article in the 1929 and 1931 printings.) At some point between 1961 and 1964, an abridgment by Joshua Whatmough, absent the offending table, replaced it. The Fifteenth edition of 1974 carries instead an extensive, competent treatment by David Diringer (d. 1969), "Alphabets." Inexplicable is a reference to "the recently discovered" Tocharian — for him, "Agnean and Kuchean" — which suggests the manuscript was prepared long, long before; even in Diringer 1948: 347–49, he refers to the discovery in 1890 (but not to the 1907 identification; Müller 1907). Probably coeval with the Whatmough abridgment are I. J. Gelb's "Writing" (a previous unsigned article "Writing" dealt with the development of handwriting in Europe), "Logogram and Syllabary," and "Pictography"; some passages in them are taken directly from *A Study of Writing*. They were expanded in the Fifteenth edition as "Writing, Forms of." The Fifteenth edition also includes an extensive article, "Calligraphy," covering most of the world; among its many contributors is Donald M. Anderson, whose 1969 book was the first to treat the scripts of South and Inner Asia from an aesthetic point of view. The *Britannica* article adapts his discussion of Syriac, omits his Inner Asia section entirely (so none of these scripts, though they are listed by Diringer, are illustrated), and severely condenses his treatment of South Asia.

In the 1985 reorganization of the Fifteenth edition, those three articles, as well as ones on cuneiform, Egyptian hieroglyphs, punctuation, and shorthand, were brought together under the omnibus heading "Writing." In 1988, Gelb's portion was replaced by David R. Olson's "The Nature and Origin of Writing," which includes nearly a page on "Chinese writing"; a separate section "Chinese Writing" of the same length, also

a *consonantary*, what I have called an *abjad*, each character represents a consonant. (4) In an *alphabet*, each character represents a consonant or a vowel (a segment, that is). (5) In an *abugida* (for which no satisfactory English term has been proposed),[5] each character represents a consonant plus a basic vowel, and other vowels are notated with additions to the base character. (6) In a *featural* script, shapes of characters correspond to phonetic features of the sounds represented.[6]

A functional history of writing, then, observes the changes in the relationship of the units of a script to the units of a language. The initial impetus for looking at such relationships was dissatisfaction with a consequence of I. J. Gelb's "Principle of Uniform Development," which states that "in reaching its ultimate development writing ... must pass through the stages of logography, syllabography, and alphabetography in this, and no other, order" (1952: 201).[7] In order to make the facts fit this formula, Gelb had to assert that the West Semitic signary is not an "alphabet" but a "syllabary," and that the Ethiopic signary is not a "syllabary" but an "alphabet."[8] These assignments of labels are counterintuitive, as the characters of the former denote segments and the characters of the latter denote syllables,[9] and the justifications for them cannot stand (Daniels 2000c).

Once the two "extra" script types, abjad and abugida, had been identified — in particular, once the distinction had been made between two completely different ways of notating syllables — certain facts about the origins of writing became apparent. First, every invention of a script in modern times (Schmitt 1980), where the inventor was not literate in any language but only knew by observation that writing existed (English and Arabic have most often been what is observed), is of a syllabary; I call the invention of writing *grammatogeny*, and when it is done by this sort of illiterate, *unsophisticated grammatogeny*.[10] What unsophisticated grammatogeny shows (and what has been confirmed by psycholinguistic investigation) is that it is syllables, and not segments, that are the smallest

---

signed by Olson, appears further on; and Søren Egerod's "The Writing System," also just short of a page, was not excised from his "Sino-Tibetan Languages" when it was moved to "Languages of the World." Diringer's "Alphabets," renamed "Alphabetic Writing" under "Systems of Writing," is now cosigned by Olson, but except for a few stylistic alterations and the removal of some passages that espouse a theory of origins different from Olson's — and the deletion of *symbol* and insertion of *phoneme* — the text is Diringer's. The opportunity was not taken to correct statements that are now known to be incorrect or at least uncertain, such as dating the origin of Brāhmī to the seventh century B.C.E. and Kharoṣṭhī to the fifth (it is most unlikely that any Indic writing predates Pāṇini, and it is all but certain that Brāhmī depends for its vowel notation on Kharoṣṭhī). As late as the 2002 DVD edition, Tocharian is still called "recently discovered." (The DVD edition cannot be used to study the *Britannica*'s materials on language and writing because all diacritics are merged into an underscore, e.g., "Brahmi and Kharosthi.")

[5] Salomon (1998: 15, n. 30) suggests "*akṣara* script" as more congenial for Indologists' use, but *akṣara* already means both "syllable" and "character of an Indic script," and adding a third sense in this semantic field could introduce confusion to a discussion. Alongside the terms I rejected (*neosyllabary* [Février 1948], *pseudo-alphabet* [Householder 1959], *semisyllabary* [Diringer 1948], and *alphasyllabary* [Bright 1992]) because they imply exactly the notion I am trying to refute — that the *abugida* is a kind of alphabet or a kind of syllabary — I have just come across *semialphabet* in the *Encyclopædia Britannica Micropædia* (though what is intended by the distinction "the syllabic Kharostī (sic) and semialphabetic Brāhmī" [s.v. "Indic Writing Systems"] is unfathomable). W. Bright denies having devised the term *alphasyllabary*, but it has not yet been found to occur earlier than his 1992 encyclopedia (in 1990: 136 he approved *semisyllabary*). Compare Daniels 1996b: 4 n. * and Bright 2000 for the different conceptualizations of *abugida* and alphasyllabary: functional vs. formal, as it happens. The words *abjad* and *abugida* are simply words in Arabic and Ethiopic, respectively, for the ancient Northwest Semitic order of letters, which is used in those languages in certain functions alongside the customary orders (in Arabic reflecting rearrangement according to shape, and in Ethiopic reflecting an entirely different letter-order tradition — both now attested in texts from Ugarit [Bordreuil and Pardee 1995, Pardee this volume]).

[6] Besides Korean, for which Kim (1988) and Sampson (1985) devised this term, the prevailing shorthand systems, Pitman, Gabelsberger, and Gregg, are featural, as is A. M. Bell's *Visible Speech* (1867).

[7] The unsatisfactoriness of the principle itself is discussed in Daniels 1990, 2001: 67 f.

[8] *A fortiori*, the Indic scripts are still more problematic for this view. In Kharoṣṭhī, devised for Gāndhārī Prakrit, each (Aramaic-derived) letter denotes a consonant followed by *a* and the other vowels are denoted by appendages for *e i o u*. (Closed syllables are all but nonexistent in Prakrits, so a vowelless consonant did not need to be notated [Salomon 1998: 15, n. 27].) In Brāhmī (ancestor of the scripts of South and Southeast Asia), vowel length and diphthong notations are found as well, introduced gradually (Masica 1991: 136), and it is difficult not to view these augmentations as reflecting the influence of Pāṇinian analysis. Gelb admits (1952: 188) to difficulties in classifying the Indic and Ethiopic scripts — asserting (incorrectly) that "there is not much difference in the vowel notation between the writings of the Semitic type on the one side and those of the Indic-Ethiopic type on the other." The optionality in the former is a huge difference.

[9] Swiggers (1984) attempts to save Gelb's classifications by invoking a semiotic distinction between *denoting* and *standing for*. However, while one can safely assert that West Semitic letters denote consonant(al segment)s but stand for syllables, one cannot say that Ethiopic letters denote syllables and stand for segments.

[10] The frequent juxtaposition of the Cherokee syllabary and Cree syllabics as examples of nineteenth-century Native American script inventions is misleading. Cherokee writing, with its array of eighty-five characters bearing no systematic relationship to each other or to the syllables they denote, was devised by the illiterate Sequoyah (Foreman 1938). Cree writing, with nine geometric shapes corresponding to consonants, presented in four rotations/reflections to denote the four vowels, was devised by the educated missionary James Evans (Nichols 1996). They typify unsophisticated and sophisticated grammatogeny respectively.

components of speech recognized by speakers who have not been trained in phonological analysis — by, for example, being taught to read an alphabet (Daniels 1992b). Second, the three independent inventions of a script in ancient times that we know of (Sumerian, Chinese, and Mayan) are also of syllabaries — *logosyllabaries*, in which each character denotes a morpheme *and* a syllable. Moreover, these three languages are distinctive in a similar way: their morphemes are, mostly, monosyllabic. Putting together these two observations, it becomes clear that when the minimal unit of speech (the syllable) and the minimal unit of language (the morpheme/word) coincide, the possibility of the foundation of writing arises.[11]

Writing cannot be a series of ideograms (marks representing "ideas") because ideograms are independent of language.[12] An octagonal red street sign can represent "stop" or "halt!" or "arretez" and so on in any language. Writing cannot even be purely a series of logograms, for every language includes stretches of speech that do not comprise identifiable content — names and grammatical morphemes. Thus any writing system must include a mechanism for representing sound independent of sense (DeFrancis 1989). The way logographic scripts achieve this is to reemploy logograms for their sound value alone, ignoring their semantic value — as in the familiar game called the *rebus*. A standard example is the use of a picture of a bee beside a picture of a leaf to conjure up the English word *belief*.[13]

In a language that is not monosyllabically organized, few homonyms or near-homonyms are available for the rebus principle to operate on. It is significant that neither any Indo-European nor any Semitic language hosted an ancient grammatogeny — and that the Incas of Peru created an impressive civilization using not a writing system, but a mathematical recording device using elaborate knotted cords, the *quipu* (Ascher and Ascher 1981). The language of the Incas is Quechua (Ostler 2005: 355–60). Quechua is not monosyllabic. But Sumerian, Chinese, and Maya are monosyllabic. The monosyllabic (proto-)Dravidian is thus a good candidate for the language underlying the Indus Valley script (Parpola 1994).[14] Monosyllabicity would be a useful criterion for identifying the language underlying the so-called Proto-Elamite script.

4.3. The Formal History of Writing: II. Soberly

The formal approach is well exemplified by a number of excellent works from, to fill in the round number omitted from the opening paragraph, half a century ago: by David Diringer (1948), James-Germain Février (1948), Marcel Cohen (1958), Johannes Friedrich (1966), and Hans Jensen (1969).[15] No one[16] has attempted such a survey since the latest editions of Diringer and Jensen in 1968 and 1969 — in particular, *The World's Writing Systems* (Daniels and Bright 1996) is not and was not intended to be a history of the forms of writing.[17] The contributors — some of them represented in this volume — were asked to describe how the world's writing systems represent their languages. The treatments of Inner Asian scripts — Iranian by Oktor Skjærvø (1996), Altaic by György Kara (1996) — much the most overlooked part of the world, grammatologically speaking — were especially eye-opening; over nearly two thousand years, through mutation after mutation of the *shapes* of the letters, *nothing happened* to the writing *system*. This sequence is thus a case where the formal approach adequately describes the history of the scripts.

---

[11] This principle was already recognized by Taylor (1899, 1: 34, 42 f.), but he was misled by the current faulty understanding of Sumerian and by Joseph Halévy's misconception of the nature of Sumerian; and it was recognized by Gelb (1952: 110 f.), but he was misled by his insistence on equating Egyptian "syllabography" with Sumerian, nor was the decipherment of Mayan, which provides a third independent example of ancient grammatogeny in a monosyllabic language, available to him (see Daniels 2002: 99).

[12] Ideograms must not be confused with pictograms — a *pictogram* is simply a small, often stylized, picture, which may have an ideographic, logographic, or phonographic function.

[13] This is used by I. J. Gelb (1961a). Gelb may also be the source of the familiar example "the Sumerian word *ti*, 'life', which is hard to draw in a sign, can be expressed through this device by the ARROW sign, which stands for *ti*, 'arrow', in Sumerian" (1952: 104); Chiera (1938: 55–57) describes the writing of the name "Kuraka" with the signs *kur* 'mountain', *a* 'water', and *ka* 'mouth'. Karlgren (1926: 34) offers Chinese *kʻiu* 'fur-coat' used for *kʻiu* 'to seek'.

[14] I find little or no merit in the claim of Farmer, Sproat, and Witzel (2004) that the Indus inscriptions do not represent writing at all. It may be noted that Parpola's linguistic map of the ancient Near East, presented in connection with his speculations about the homeland of Common Semitic (1994: 127), is based on Gene Gragg's 1979 map (see n. 1).

[15] Jensen's earlier editions are by no means so extensive or well documented as the final one.

[16] Haarmann 1990 and Coulmas 1996 are encyclopedic but not thoroughly reliable (Brekle 1991; Daniels 2002: 92).

[17] Data not otherwise referenced are from Daniels and Bright 1996.

Aramaic was the lingua franca of a vast region even before the accession of the Achaemenid (Persian) empire and became its chancery language. Texts using its twenty-two letter consonantal script are widespread, exhibiting the use of *matrēs lectionis* (non-etymological consonant letters) to suggest vowel quality: ⟨w⟩ for [u o], ⟨y⟩ for [i e], ⟨'⟩ for [ā].[18] Experiments in writing Iranian languages with Aramaic scripts presumably began in those times, but none are attested before the Parthian period (second century B.C.E.–second century C.E.). By the end of Parthian times, a standardized inscriptional form of the script had developed for the West Iranian language Parthian, and it remained in use into the Sassanian period. A Manichaean script, akin to Palmyrene and Old Syriac (Klugkist 1982: 215 f.), was used for several Iranian languages as well as Tocharian and Turkic. The East Iranian language Sogdian has its own script resembling the Syriac but not directly derivable from it; rather, Sogdian and Syriac appear to share an ancestor (Friedrich 1966: 138, Jensen 1969: 410).[19]

Whatever the specific ancestry of Sogdian script, it is clear that the script of the Turkic language Uyghur gradually emerged from it in the eighth century or so (Sims-Williams 1981: 359). *Matrēs lectionis* are still employed for most, but not all, vowels; ⟨w⟩ does double duty for [u] and [ü], ⟨y⟩ for [i] and [ï]. The Uyghur script was used for Mongolian from the beginning of the Mongol empire, and during the fourteenth century the Mongolian script proper emerged. Two further refinements, the West Mongol "clear script" and the script of the Tungusic language Manchu (Li 2000), can be considered alphabets, as all vowels are notated with unambiguous letters that do not also serve as consonants — the *matrēs lectionis* apotheosized.[20]

Thus over three thousand years, whether the Manchu script of the seventeenth century, or the abortive Buryat Mongolian briefly tried out in St. Petersburg in 1905, the inventory of letters and what they represent is barely changed from the Aramaic of the Achaemenid chancery or, for that matter, of the Fakhariyeh inscription of the ninth century B.C.E. (Kaufman 1982: 155–57).

This revelation by Skjærvø and Kara was astounding. What did it mean for the history of writing? It meant that, generation after generation, chancery after chancery, empire after empire, there was an unbroken chain of scribal training reaching back some three thousand years and across thousands of miles. From time to time, a new polity called for a new-looking script. From time to time, minor adjustments were made — sometimes as a result of sound change (such as the use of *lamed* for an interdental voiced fricative in Manichaean and Sogdian), sometimes as a result of deliberate improvement (such as the introduction of some diacritics in the "clear script"). But always the basic structure of consonant letters and descendants of *matrēs lectionis* for vowels persisted.

The Aramaic script itself diversified as various "national" chanceries developed their own styles, and from it eventually sprang the Syriac, Arabic, and Mandaic scripts still in use.

4.4. The Functional History of Writing: Three Patterns

Contrasting with historical sequences in which only the forms, but not the functions, of a writing system change are the sequences that involve functional changes. It appears that these can be sorted into three groups, according as the changes are all but incidental, are accidental, or are deliberate. The first can be likened — borrowing a term from the architectural preservation that has been such a feature of the city of Chicago — to "adaptive reuse." As when a factory is converted to residential lofts, or a courthouse to a public library, and the basic structure remains

---

[18] The details of how *matrēs lectionis* came into use remain under discussion (e.g., Cross and Freedman 1952; Cook 1990), but they are not important here: what I want to note is that they exist, and that from the beginning of attested Aramaic (language and script), they are a distinguishing characteristic of Aramaic as opposed to Phoenician; and then *matrēs lectionis* were borrowed for writing languages related more closely to Phoenician than to Aramaic — notably, of course, Hebrew.

[19] Christian Sogdian was also written with a development of Nestorian Syriac.

[20] This happened nowhere else. The incautious statement that Mandaic "vowel-indication ... goes beyond the function of the so-called *matrēs lectionis*" is sometimes found (Jensen 1969: 336, in this instance). Diringer claims "the consonants *alef, waw,* and *yod,* abbreviated, became vowels and are added as appendages to the consonants. The Mandæan alphabet has thus become in practice a syllabary similar to the Ethiopic script" (1948: 291) — even though Nöldeke had long since written "Wie unrichtig es ist, die mand. Lautbezeichnung mit der äthiop. zusammenzustellen, habe ich in Kürze in den Gött. Gel. Anz. 1869 St. 13 S. 504 zu zeigen gesucht" (1875: 11 n. 3). [Nöldeke's page reference is a misprint; Kuhn's bibliography (1906) registers (nos. 249 and 293) a review of Mandaic studies by Euting and by Petermann in *Göttingische Gelehrte Anzeigen* (1869: 481–501), and Nöldeke's typically incisive observations on Mandaic orthography are prompted by Petermann's invocation of similarity with Ethiopic.] Observing the details, however, reveals that not every vowel receives its own letter, and ⟨w⟩ and ⟨y⟩ represent /w y/ as well as /u o/ and /i/ and some /e/ (Daniels 1996a: 512).

intact but certain amenities are added unobtrusively, it sometimes happens that to an existing script, characters are added that augment the script in a way new to that script but constitute a minor subsystem (if that) within the overall script system.[21] Usually, additions simply increase the inventory of characters to correspond to differing phonological inventories.[22] In adaptive reuse, the additions represent the intrusion of characters that relate to their language in a way different from that of the inherited characters, but not in sufficient numbers to alter the inherited relation.

The second turns out to have been the most important sort of change in script typology. Only when a community attempts to imitate an existing writing system without having mastered it through a traditional course of scribal training does something new and different appear. Attempts to account for these innovations as the work of individual genius are unable to cite any evidence of accompanying sophisticated linguistic analysis that could have prompted, or been stimulated by, such intellectual activity.

Thirdly, when sophisticated linguistic analysis *is* present in a culture, deliberate changes and improvements in the nature of writing systems finally do come to the fore; sometimes, even the names of individual scholars who were responsible for the innovations are known.

The three sorts of change have been treated separately (respectively Daniels 2006, in press, and 2000a). They are brought together below.

4.4.1. Adaptive Reuse

The earliest adaptive reuse we know of appears in the creation of the Ugaritic script, which made a minimal step toward the recognition that different vowels can follow consonants: in addition to the twenty-seven letters common to both the Northwest and the South branches of West Semitic writing, corresponding to the twenty-seven consonants of early Northwest Semitic, there is an additional sibilant *s̀*, possibly devised for a Hurrian sound distinct from *s* and *š*; and there are two letters that proved to denote /ʾ/ when followed by /i/ or /u/ respectively. The inherited ⟨ʾ⟩ denotes /ʾ/ when followed by /a/. Syllable-final /ʾ/ is usually written with ⟨i⟩ (Tropper 2000: 33–39).

A very minor example of adaptive reuse with a functionally anomalous item is the Coptic alphabet. Coptic is written with the Greek alphabet augmented with six letters borrowed from Demotic Egyptian: ⟨š f h ḏ q⟩[23] — and ⟨ti⟩. Commonly, letters are invented for sounds that do not occur in the donor language while the complete original inventory is retained. The other new alphabets devised for the languages of the Orthodox churches on the basis of Greek — Gothic, Cyrillic, and so on — add some letters for consonants or vowels not provided for in the earlier alphabet. Almost all these alphabets retained letters not needed for spelling their languages because they represented numerals; Armenian and Georgian invented new shapes (Gamkrelidze 1994). Many examples are found in the widespread adoption and adaptation of Arabic writing throughout the Islamic world, usually systematically, sometimes not (Daniels 1997), where the letters for sounds peculiar to Arabic (⟨ṯ ḏ ṭ ḍ ṣ ẓ ġ⟩) are retained for spelling Arabic loanwords; Uyghur is almost unique in respelling Arabic loans in accordance with their borrowed form (Kaye 1996).

Typologically unusual is the *dropping* of the five letters ⟨ṯ ḏ ẓ ḫ ġ⟩ when the Northwest Semitic abjad came to be used for Canaanite languages, in both its Ugaritic form and its linear form (Sass 1988: 164; Naveh 1987: 42).[24]

Another example of seeming changes in the relation of script to language is found in another family of scripts that, like those of Inner Asia, is insufficiently studied: those of Southeast Asia. Here the ancestral forms were

---

[21] In Daniels 1990 such scripts were assigned to a separate "type," identified by the descriptor "augmented." This has not proven to be a useful analysis.

[22] In Daniels 2006, eight techniques for adapting scripts to the phonological systems of their language are exemplified: reduction of inventory, additions of letters, combinations of letters, alterations of letters, borrowing of letters, additions to letters, adding diacritics, and simplifications of letters.

[23] The Bohairic and Akhmimic dialects add ⟨ḫ⟩ as well (Ritner 1996).

[24] That this dropping was possible strongly suggests that at the time of this adaptation (Naveh [1987] makes it "by the twelfth century") the letters were not yet used as numerals for ordering lists or recording numbers. If they had been, they would have been retained like Greek qoppa and san.

abugidas — consonant-plus-basic-vowel scripts — learned from Hindu texts in Sanskrit, or Buddhist texts in Pali, depending on which area contacts were made in. The basic architecture of the scripts has not changed, but the phonetic material encoded has. Due both to phonological differences between the Indic source language (Sanskrit, Prakrits, Pali) and to changes over the centuries in the borrowing languages (Burman, Tai, Mon-Khmer, Malayo-Polynesian), distinctions that once represented voicing or aspiration, for example, now represent vowel quality, tone, or both.

4.4.2. The Misunderstanding Model

So far we have considered several of the chains of more or less strict adoption (section 4.3) or minor adaptation (section 4.4.1) of scripts, where the model script is well understood by the adapting scribes and is taken over largely intact. But there are two further ways that scripts are reused for new languages. The one that accounts for the Egyptian logoconsonantary, the West Semitic abjad, and the Greek alphabet is the Misunderstanding Model. It comes into play when the adopting scribes learn just a little of how a script works and apply that incomplete knowledge to writing their own language.

Given the monosyllabic understanding of the origin of writing (section 4.2), Egyptian with its Semitic-like bisyllabic bases was not a candidate for hosting an invention of writing *ex nihilo*. Left to their own resources, Egyptians might have come up with an elaborate accounting system functionally equivalent to the quipu. But Egypt was in close contact with Mesopotamia, and learned either directly or indirectly of Sumerian writing. Egyptians learned from Sumerian scribes that the same symbol was always to be used for the same morpheme. In agglutinative Sumerian, there was little change in phonological shape, so when rebus writing came to Sumerian, a character could be used for its V, CV, VC, or CVC sound value to render words unrelated to the original logogram's pictogram.[25] But because Egyptian morphemes change shape under inflection and derivation, all that remained constant was the consonants, so what Egyptian hieroglyphs denote is consonants only. Most signs denote two consonants, some denote three (distinguishing these from those that are used logographically is not always simple), and a few denote one consonant. Phonetic and semantic determinatives clarify the reading but complicate the orthography.

This in turn explains the West Semitic simple consonantary. All that Semitic-speakers understood of Egyptian writing was that symbols were supposed to represent consonants only, so they (merely) ran through their vocabulary, perhaps discovering minimal pairs, and realized that just twenty-seven or twenty-eight symbols would account for all their consonants.[26]

But the most familiar application of the Misunderstanding Model is the invention of the Greek alphabet. It is still often claimed that there is something special about the Greek language — or even the "Greek mind" — such that Greek or Indo-European "needs" to write the vowels, as opposed, of course, to Semitic languages, where the vowels "don't count," where they present "merely grammatical" information.[27] This is not true of vowels in Semitic, of course, nor is it true of the vowels in Indo-European. If it were, how would it have been possible for the Iranian languages to have been written with Aramaic scripts for over two thousand years? Not only do we have the Aramaic-based Iranian scripts described by Skjærvø (1996) — under names like Parthian, Middle Persian, Pahlavi, Sogdian, and Manichaean — we also have the modern use of (Aramaic-derived) Arabic script for Persian and many other non-Semitic languages.

---

[25] This appears to be a fairly late development, reimported for writing Sumerian grammatical morphemes *after* phonographic writing had been adopted by Akkadian (Cooper 1999: 71; Michalowski 2004: 26).

[26] The recently discovered inscriptions at Wadi el-Hol, Egypt, that predate but appear to be written with the same script as the Proto-Sinaitic inscriptions that have been interpreted as West Semitic (but see the reservations of Sass 1988: 45–50 — his conclusion that "it is possible at least to define the language of the texts as Northwest Semitic on the basis of their closeness in date and form of the letters to the Proto-Canaanite inscriptions" represents a most unscholarly conflation of script with language) have so far resisted interpretation, either as Egyptian or as West Semitic. Does this indicate that the West Semitic script family was actually devised for some other language entirely?

[27] These myths continue to be propagated to this day: "The adaption [sic] was possible partly through the Greek genius for tinkering and partly through the magical flexibility and aptness of the letters themselves" (Sacks 2003: 59). "The adapters used the twenty-two signs of the Canaanite alphabet, in which only consonants were noted down. To make them suitable for transcribing the Greek language, vowel signs had to be included" (Dobias-Lalou 2002: 233b).

So the old excuses of "had to write the vowels" and "Greek genius" will not do. The explanation for the "invention" of Greek vowels is simply that the first Greek writers, who got an explanation from a Phoenician scribe, did not understand what the Phoenician was telling them — or rather, what the Phoenician was saying. They got the concept that each letter represented the first sound of its name — *beyt*, *dalt*, *gaml*, and so on — they just did not get the first sounds of some of the names: *ʾalp*, *he*, *ḥet*, and so on — because those sounds were not phonemic in the Greek language. They thus thought that *ʾalp*, *yod*, *ʿayn*, and so on represented /a/, /i/, /o/, and so on. Note that this would not have happened if the source of the Greek alphabet had been an Aramaic forebear since the *matrēs lectionis* would have been available for indicating the vowels, eliminating the opportunity for misunderstanding. If an Aramaic script had been the model for the Greek alphabet, Greek orthography might have resembled Mandaic.

See map 4.2 for the geographical range of the Misunderstanding Model.

4.4.3. The Scholarly Input Model

The last of the kinds of reuse is in some ways the most interesting because it seems to be the only one that involves *deliberate* change, by people who have given deep attention to the nature of their writing system. It appears only in cultures that already had awareness of a grammatical tradition, so its name is the Scholarly Input model.

The most celebrated ancient grammarian, and the earliest identified by name, is Pāṇini and his school, whose task was the description and preservation of the ancient Sanskrit texts — which as far as we can tell were transmitted orally alone: there was no writing in India until generations after Pāṇini, in the time of Aśoka, emperor in the third century B.C.E. (There may have been some awareness of Greek writing, but it made no impact on Indian poetry or grammar.)

Yet, for some reason, and it is difficult not to attribute it to grammatical sophistication, in the far northwestern region of Gandhāra, a script came about that took consonant forms from an Aramaic script and added appendages to mark vowels other than /a/. Its name is Kharoṣṭhī. It is possible that the inspiration for these vowel marks was the *matrēs lectionis yod* and *waw*, though Kharoṣṭhī marks four vowels /i e o u/. A consonant with no vowel was attached to the following consonant — these are called conjuncts — one might even say that the sign for /a/ was the break between letters. The language written with Kharoṣṭhī has come to be called Gāndhārī, a Prakrit, and it had some further use to the north around the Tarim Basin and along the Silk Road (Salomon 1999).[28]

Much more influential in world history is the ancestral Indian script known as Brāhmī. This must have been developed on the model of some form of Kharoṣṭhī since it incorporates its features of marking vowels other than /a/, with appendages above, below, left, or right of the consonant letter, and combining consonants without vowels; but adds considerable sophistication based in Pāṇinian grammar, such as indication of vowel length and (eventually) characteristics of Sanskrit, including diphthongs and consonant-final words.

The second step in the chain of Scholarly Input script innovation takes us to Tibet. So far, all the languages in our chains have been Afroasiatic or Indo-European (with a tail of Altaic in the Inner Asia sequence): inflecting (and agglutinating) languages. But with Tibetan, we famously enter a land of isolating languages, where syllable-sized morphemes stand alone. It was thus eminently reasonable for the scholars who devised the Tibetan script, perhaps in the seventh century — according to tradition, Thon mi sam bho ṭa in 630 C.E. (Jensen 1969: 382) — by adapting some variety of Indic script, to largely abandon the conjunct device and introduce a dot after every syllable. Consonants entering into initial or final clusters are written adjacent to, above, or below their companions. The four vowels other than /a/ are strokes that accompany the resulting groups of consonants, above or below. Observe that there was a Tibetan grammatical tradition (Miller 1976).

---

[28] Richard Salomon at the 2005 meeting of the American Oriental Society (Philadelphia) announced the discovery of the ancient ordering of the Kharoṣṭhī vowels: (*a*) *e i o u*. He suspects influence of the Greek alphabetical order, but he also notes that in this order the vowel appendages move from high on the body of the character to low.

Yet another scholar now enters the stage: the Fifth Patriarch of the Sa skya pa school of Tibetan Buddhism, named 'Phags pa Blo gros rgyal mtshan. In 1264 the Mongol emperor Kubla Khan ordered him to devise a script that could be used for all the languages of the empire (including Tibetan, Uyghur, Mongolian, and Chinese), though in the event it was mostly used for Mongolian. It is an adaptation of Tibetan, mostly graphic, squaring up the letters and writing in columns rather than rows; with the innovation that the vowels other than /a/ are all written *below*, that is *after*, the consonant letters. The Phags pa script would barely warrant mention in this survey, were it not for the last step in the Scholarly Input chain.

The Korean tradition is very strong that the great fifteenth-century monarch King Sejong invented the Korean alphabet single-handedly (Lee 1997; Kim-Renaud 2000); that it was his brilliant idea to represent in the shapes of the consonant letters the portions of the vocal tract involved in producing the sounds they represent. (And the three basic vowel letters represent Heaven, Earth, and Man.) But it is much more credible that the king formed a commission to study the problem — and of course the scholars were familiar with Chinese phonological theory — and they studied other available scripts that were used for Buddhist scriptures. There is no denying the similarity of some Korean letters to some Phags pa letters (Ledyard 1997).[29] It seems quite plausible that coincidental similarity of one or another Phags pa letter to an organ of speech suggested to the Korean commission — or even to King Sejong himself — that all the letters be brought into some such relation. Further evidence of the Korean scholars' sophistication was that they were able to transcend the Chinese analysis of character-syllables into the "initial," that is, the opening consonant, and the "final," that is, everything else — and find letters for the medial vowel and the final consonant or consonants of each syllable, so that (originally) only twenty consonant letters and nine vowel letters were needed for thousands of syllables; for the letters were combined into syllable-blocks that from a distance resemble Chinese characters.

4.5. Conclusion

Thus West Semitic writing reached the very eastern edge of the Eurasian continent by 1446. A half century later, a Genoese adventurer headed west from the western extremity of the Eurasian continent, writing his logbook in the Roman alphabet, which thus became the first scion of West Semitic to reach the Western Hemisphere. But as signs on the streets of Chicago (and other cosmopolitan cities) make abundantly obvious, all its branches are represented in America: Arabic and Assyrian, Korean and Indian, Cyrillic and Roman — as well as one more variety that brings us back to Gene Gragg in a double way. Note in map 4.2 the dashed line crossing the Arabian Sea from, say, Goa or Bombay to Aksum. That represents the idea of the abugida principle — marking all vowels but /a/ — linking the Martomite Christians of the Indian coast with the users of an offshoot of South Arabian script in the Horn of Africa (Daniels 1992a). Maybe they were sailors; maybe they were missionaries: for the adoption of vowel marking (the very first instance of complete and consistent vowel marking in any Semitic script) coincides with the conversion of King Ezana in the middle of the fourth century. His inscriptions invoking pagan deities are unvoweled; his inscriptions invoking Jesus are vocalized.[30] A tantalizing remark by Johannes Friedrich, that similarities can be found between Ethiopian and Martomite liturgy (1966: 93), unfootnoted,[31] needs to be followed up.

The Ethiopic script makes us think of Gene Gragg not only because Ethiopic languages are one of his specialties, but also because it combines traits of seemingly distant cultures, which traits themselves resulted from minute grammatical scholarship.

He may not have made any of us into a Pāṇini, but he has certainly served as a model linguistic scholar who has inspired us for all these many years.

---

[29] Ledyard's dissertation (1966) remains the standard work on the history of the Korean alphabet. A typeset version published in Seoul in 1998 without the author's planned revisions does not supersede it; the author now repudiates certain changes he introduced into that publication (personal communication, 2006).

[30] Gragg (2004 [but written much earlier]) suggests that the vocalized Ezana texts be attributed to a second King Ezana over a century later. In more recent work (2006) he reverts to the traditional view.

[31] Gelb (1952: 279 n. 34) refers to Friedrich 1935: 17f.

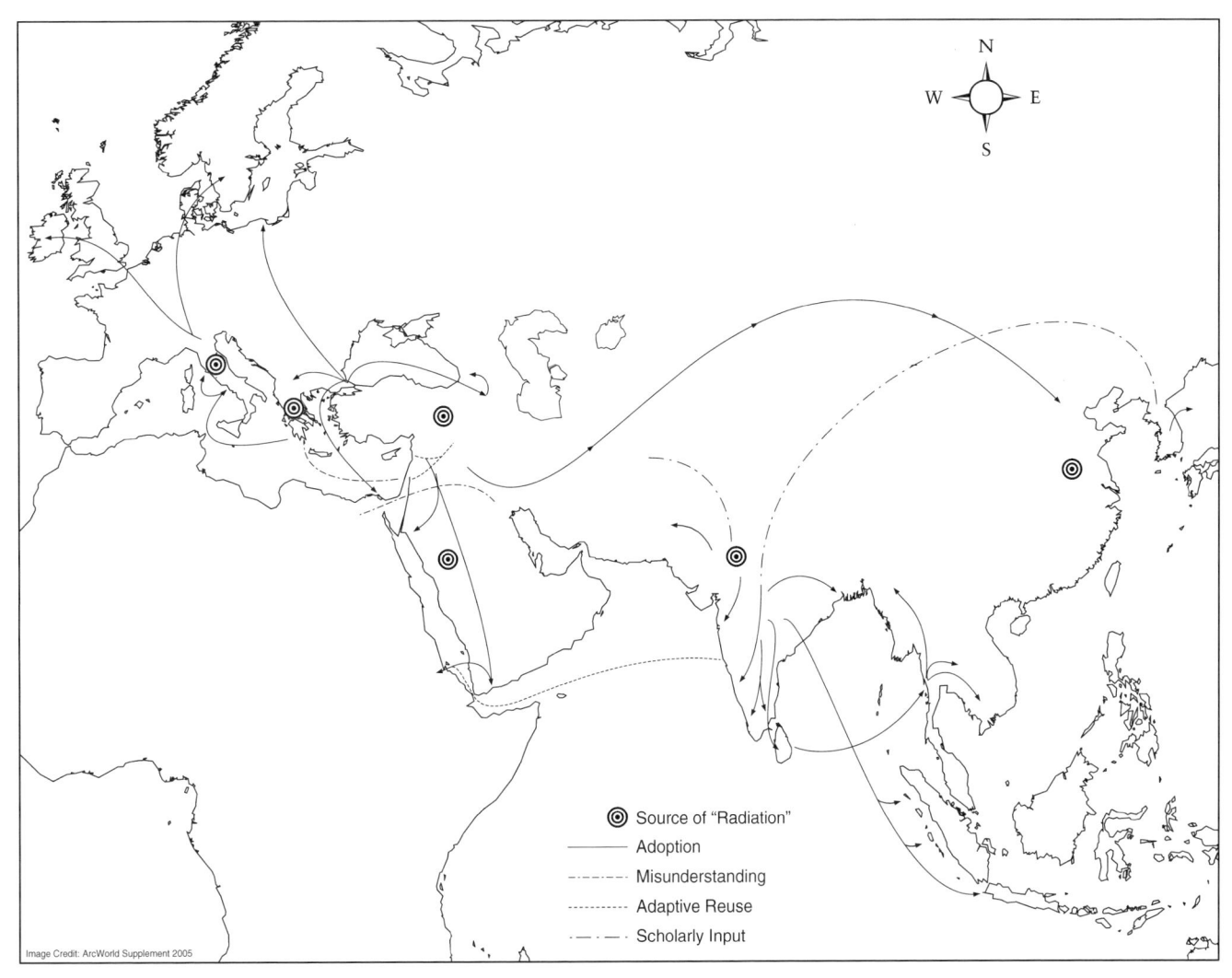

Map 4.2. Map Illustrating Three Patterns of the Functional History of Writing: Adaptive Reuse, Misunderstanding Model, and Scholarly Input Model; as well as Adoption of Script

Bibliography

Anderson, Donald M.
  1969 *The Art of Written Forms: The Theory and Practice of Calligraphy*. New York: Holt, Rinehart, and Winston. Reprinted New York: Dover, 1982.

Ascher, Marcia, and Robert Ascher
  1981 *Code of the Quipu: A Study in Media, Mathematics, and Culture*. Ann Arbor: University of Michigan Press.

Asher, Frederick M., and G. S. Gai, editors
  1985 *Indian Epigraphy: Its Bearing on the History of Art*. New Delhi: Oxford & IBH.

Bell, Alexander Melville
  1867 *Visible Speech: The Science of Universal Alphabetics; or Self-Interpreting Physiological Letters, for the Writing of All Languages in One Alphabet, Illustrated by Tables, Diagrams, and Examples*. London: Simpkin, Marshall.

Bordreuil, Pierre, and Dennis Pardee
  1995 "Un abécédaire du type sud sémitique découvert en 1988 dans les fouilles archéologiques françaises de Ras Shamra-Ougarit." *Comptes Rendus de l'Académie des Inscriptions et Belles-Lettres* (July–October): 855–60.

Brekle, Herbert E.
  1991 Review of *Universalgeschichte der Schrift*, by Harold Haarmann. *Zeitschrift für Sprachwissenschaft* 10: 297–303.

Bright, William
  1990 "Written and Spoken Language in South Asia." In *Language Variation in South Asia*, pp. 130–47. New York: Oxford University Press.
  2000 "A Matter of Typology: Alphasyllabaries and Abugidas." *Studies in the Linguistic Sciences* 30: 63–71.

Bright, William, editor
  1992 *Encyclopedia of Language and Linguistics*. Four vols. New York: Oxford University Press.

Chiera, Edward
  1938 *They Wrote on Clay: The Babylonian Tablets Speak Today*, edited by George G. Cameron. Chicago: University of Chicago Press.

Christin, Anne-Marie, editor
  2002 *A History of Writing: From Hieroglyph to Multimedia*. Paris: Flammarion.

Clodd, Edward
  1900 *The Story of the Alphabet*. New York: Appleton.

Cohen, Marcel
  1958 *La grande invention de l'écriture et son évolution*. Paris: Imprimerie nationale.

Cook, Edward M.
  1990 "The Orthography of Final Unstressed Long Vowels in Old and Imperial Aramaic." *Maarav* 5–6: 53–67.

Cooper, Jerrold S.
  1999 "Sumerian and Semitic Writing in Most Ancient Syro-Mesopotamia." In *Languages and Cultures in Contact*, edited by K. Van Lerberghe and G. Voet, pp. 61–77. Rencontre Assyriologique Internationale 42. Leuven: Peeters.

Coulmas, Florian
  1996 *The Blackwell Encyclopedia of Writing Systems*. Oxford: Blackwell.

Cross, Frank Moore, and David Noel Freedman
  1952   *Early Hebrew Orthography: A Study of the Epigraphic Evidence.* American Oriental Series 36. New Haven: American Oriental Society.

Daniels, Peter T.
  1990   "Fundamentals of Grammatology." *Journal of the American Oriental Society* 110: 727–31.
  1992a   "Contacts between Semitic and Indic Scripts." In *Contacts between Cultures: Selected Papers from the 33rd International Congress of Asian and North African Studies, Toronto, August 15–25, 1990*, Vol. 1: *West Asia and North Africa*, edited by Amir Harrack, pp. 146–52. Lewiston, New York: Edwin Mellen.
  1992b   "The Syllabic Origin of Writing and the Segmental Origin of the Alphabet." In *The Linguistics of Literacy*, edited by Pamela Downing, Susan D. Lima, and Michael Noonan, pp. 83–110. Typological Studies in Language 21. Amsterdam and Philadelphia: John Benjamins.
  1996a   "Aramaic Scripts for Aramaic Languages: Mandaic." In *The World's Writing Systems*, edited by Peter T. Daniels and William Bright, pp. 511–14. New York: Oxford University Press.
  1996b   "The Study of Writing Systems." In *The World's Writing Systems*, edited by Peter T. Daniels and William Bright, pp. 3–17. New York: Oxford University Press.
  1997   "The Protean Arabic Abjad." In *Humanism, Culture, and Language in the Near East: Studies in Honor of Georg Krotkoff*, edited by Asma Afsaruddin and A. H. Mathias Zahniser, pp. 369–84. Winona Lake: Eisenbrauns.
  2000a   "On Writing Syllables: Three Episodes of Script Transfer." *Studies in the Linguistic Sciences* (Urbana) 30: 73–86.
  2000b   Review of *Mysteries of the Alphabet*, by Marc-Alain Ouaknin; *The Alphabet versus the Goddess*, by Leonard Shlain; *The Alphabetic Labyrinth*, by Johanna Drucker; *The Story of Writing: Alphabets, Hieroglyphs and Pictograms*, by Andrew Robinson; and *Writing: The Story of Alphabets and Scripts*, by Georges Jean. *Sino-Platonic Papers* 98: 47–57.
  2000c   "Syllables, Consonants, and Vowels in West Semitic Writing." *Lingua Posnaniensis* 42: 43–55.
  2001   "Writing Systems." In *The Handbook of Linguistics*, edited by Mark Aronoff and Janie Rees-Miller, pp. 43–80. Blackwell Handbooks in Linguistics. Malden, Massachusetts: Blackwell.
  2002   "The Study of Writing in the Twentieth Century: Semitic Studies Interacting with Non-Semitic." *Israel Oriental Studies* 20: 85–117.
  2005   "Language and Languages in the Eleventh *Britannica*." In *Polymorphous Linguistics: Jim McCawley's Legacy*, edited by Salikoko S. Mufwene, Elaine J. Francis, and Rebecca S. Wheeler, pp. 505–29. Cambridge: MIT Press.
  2006   "On beyond Alphabets." In *Written Language and Literacy*, Vol. 9, Issue 1, pp. 7–24.
  In Press "Three Models of Script Transfer." (Paper presented at the annual meetings of the American Oriental Society, San Diego, and the International Linguistic Association, New York. To appear in *Word*).

Daniels, Peter T., and William Bright, editors
  1996   *The World's Writing Systems.* New York: Oxford University Press.

DeFrancis, John
  1989   *Visible Speech: The Diverse Oneness of Writing Systems.* Honolulu: University of Hawaii Press.

Diringer, David
  1948   *The Alphabet.* New York: Philosophical Library.

Dobias-Lalou, Catherine
  2002   "The Greek Alphabets." In *A History of Writing: From Hieroglyph to Multimedia*, edited by Anne-Marie Christin, pp. 233–40. Paris: Flammarion.

Durand, J.-M.
  2002   "Cuneiform Script." In *A History of Writing: From Hieroglyph to Multimedia*, edited by Anne-Marie Christin, pp. 20–32. Paris: Flammarion.

Farmer, Steve; Richard Sproat; and Michael Witzel
  2004   "The Collapse of the Indus-Script Thesis: The Myth of a Literate Harappan Civilization." *Electronic Journal of Vedic Studies* 11: 19–57. www1.shore.net/~india/ejvs/

Février, James-Germain
  1948   *Histoire de l'écriture*. Paris: Payot.

Foreman, Grant
  1938   *Sequoyah*. The Civilization of the American Indian 16. Norman: University of Oklahoma Press.

Friedrich, Johannes
  1935   "Einige Kapitel aus der inneren Geschichte der Schrift." *Archiv für Schreib- und Buchwesen*, neue Folge, 2: 8–18.
  1966   *Geschichte der Schrift*. Heidelberg: Winter.

Gamkrelidze, Thomas V.
  1994   *Alphabetic Writing and the Old Georgian Script*. Delmar: Caravan Books.

Gaur, Albertine
  1984   *A History of Writing*. New York: Scribner's.
  1994   *A History of Calligraphy*. London: British Library.
  2000   *Literacy and the Politics of Writing*. Portland: Intellect Books.

Gelb, I. J.
  1952   *A Study of Writing*. Chicago: University of Chicago Press.

Gragg, Gene B.
  2004   "Geʻez (Aksum)." In *The Cambridge Encyclopedia of the World's Ancient Languages*, edited by Roger D. Woodard, pp. 427–53. Cambridge: Cambridge University Press.
  2006   "Asia, Ancient Southwest: Scripts, South Semitic." In *Encyclopedia of Language and Linguistics*. Second edition, edited by Keith Brown, 1:512–18. Oxford: Elsevier.

Haarmann, Harald
  1990   *Universalgeschichte der Schrift*. Frankfurt: Campus Verlag.

Householder, Fred W., Jr.
  1959   "More on Mycenean." *Classical Journal* 54: 379–83.

Jean, Georges
  1992   *Writing: The Story of Alphabets and Scripts*. Translated by Jenny Oates. Abrams Discoveries. New York: Abrams.

Jensen, Hans
  1969   *Sign, Symbol and Script*. Translated by George Unwin. Third Edition. London: George Allen & Unwin.

Kara, György
  1996   "Aramaic Scripts for Altaic Languages." In *The World's Writing Systems*, edited by Peter T. Daniels and William Bright, pp. 536–58. New York: Oxford University Press.

Karlgren, Bernhard
  1926   *Philology and Ancient China*. Oslo: H. Aschehoug; Cambridge: Harvard University Press.

Kaufman, Stephen A.
  1982   "Reflections on the Assyrian-Aramaic Bilingual from Tell Fakhariyeh." *Maarav* 3: 137–75.

Kaye, Alan S.
  1996   "Adaptations of Arabic Script." In *The World's Writing Systems*, edited by Peter T. Daniels and William Bright, pp. 743–62. New York: Oxford University Press.

Kim, Chin-Wu
  1988   "On the Origin and Structure of the Korean Script." In *Collected Papers*, Vol. 2: *Sojourns in Language*, pp. 721–34. Seoul: Tower Press.

Kim-Renaud, Young-Key
- 2000 "Sejong's Theory of Literacy and Writing." *Studies in the Linguistic Sciences* (Urbana) 30: 13–45.

Kim-Renaud, Young-Key, editor
- 1997 *The Korean Alphabet*. Honolulu: University of Hawaii Press.

Klugkist, Alexander C.
- 1982 "Midden-aramese schriften in Syrië, Mesopotamië, Perzië en aangrenzende gebieden." Ll.D. proefschrift, Groningen.

Kuhn, Ernst
- 1906 "Versuch einer Übersicht der Schriften Theodor Nöldeke's." In *Orientalische Studien Theodor Nöldeke zum siebzigsten Geburtstag (2. März 1906) gewidmet von Freunden und Schülern*, edited by Carl Bezold, 1, pp. xiii–li. Gießen: Alfred Töpelmann.

Ledyard, Gari
- 1966 The Korean Language Reform of 1446. Ph.D. dissertation, University of California, Berkeley.
- 1997 "The International Linguistic Background of the Correct Sounds for the Instruction of the People." *The Korean Alphabet*, edited by Young-Key Kim-Renaud, pp. 31–87. Honolulu: University of Hawaii Press.

Lee, Ki-Moon
- 1997 "The Inventor of the Korean Alphabet." In *The Korean Alphabet*, edited by Young-Key Kim-Renaud, pp. 11–30. Honolulu: University of Hawaii Press.

Li, Gertraude Roth
- 2000 *Manchu: A Textbook for Reading Documents*. Honolulu: University of Hawaii Press.

Man, John
- 2000 *Alpha Beta: How Our Alphabet Shaped the Western World*. London: Headline.

Masica, Colin P.
- 1991 *The Indo-Aryan Languages*. Cambridge Language Surveys. Cambridge: Cambridge University Press.

Mason, William A.
- 1920 *A History of the Art of Writing*. New York: Macmillan.

Michalowski, Piotr
- 2004 "Sumerian." In *The Cambridge Encyclopedia of the World's Ancient Languages*, edited by Roger D. Woodard, pp. 19–59. Cambridge: Cambridge University Press.

Miller, Roy Andrew
- 1976 *Studies in the Grammatical Tradition in Tibet*. Studies in the History of Linguistics 6. Amsterdam and Philadelphia: John Benjamins.

Moorehouse, Alfred C.
- 1953 *The Triumph of the Alphabet: A History of Writing*. New York: Henry Schuman.

Müller, F. W. K.
- 1907 "Beitrag zur genaueren Bestimmung der unbekannten Sprachen Mittelasiens." *Sitzungsberichte der preussischen Akademie der Wissenschaften zu Berlin*: 958–60.

Naveh, Joseph
- 1987 *Early History of the Alphabet: An Introduction to West Semitic Epigraphy and Paleography*. Second revised edition. Jerusalem: Magnes.

Nichols, John D.
- 1996 "The Cree Syllabary." In *The World's Writing Systems*, edited by Peter T. Daniels and William Bright, pp. 599–611. New York: Oxford University Press.

Nöldeke, Theodor
- 1869 Review of works on Mandaic, by J. Euting and H. Petermann. *Göttingische Gelehrte Anzeigen* 481–501.
- 1875 *Mandäische Grammatik*. Halle: Waisenhaus.

Olson, David R.
- 1988 "The Nature and Origin of Writing." In *The New Encyclopaedia Britannica*. Fifteenth edition. Chicago: Helen Hemingway Benton.

Ostler, Nicholas
- 2005 *Empires of the Word: A Language History of the World*. London: HarperCollins.

Parpola, Asko
- 1994 *Deciphering the Indus Script*. Cambridge: Cambridge University Press.

Ritner, Robert K.
- 1996 "The Coptic Alphabet." In *The World's Writing Systems*, edited by Peter T. Daniels and William Bright, pp. 287–90. New York: Oxford University Press.

Robinson, Andrew
- 1995 *The Story of Writing: Alphabets, Hieroglyphs and Pictograms*. London: Thames & Hudson.

Sacks, David
- 2003 *Language Visible: Unraveling the Mystery of the Alphabet from A to Z*. New York: Broadway Books.

Salomon, Richard
- 1985 "Calligraphy in Pre-Islamic India." In *Indian Epigraphy: Its Bearing on the History of Art*, edited by Frederick M. Asher and G. S. Gai, pp. 3–6. New Delhi: Oxford & IBH.
- 1998 *Indian Epigraphy: A Guide to the Study of Inscriptions in Sanskrit, Prakrit, and the Other Indo-Aryan Languages*. New York: Oxford University Press.
- 1999 *Ancient Buddhist Scrolls from Gandhāra*. Seattle: University of Washington Press.

Sass, Benjamin
- 1988 *The Genesis of the Alphabet and Its Development in the Second Millennium B.C.* Ägypten und Altes Testament 13. Wiesbaden: Harrassowitz.

Sampson, Geoffrey
- 1985 *Writing Systems: A Linguistic Introduction*. Stanford: Stanford University Press.

Schmitt, Alfred
- 1980 *Entstehung und Entwicklung von Schriften*, edited by Claus Haebler. Cologne: Böhlau.

Sims-Williams, Nicholas
- 1981 "The Sogdian Sound-System and the Origins of the Uyghur Script." *Journal Asiatique* 269: 347–60.

Skjærvø, P. Oktor
- 1996 "Aramaic Scripts for Iranian Languages." In *The World's Writing Systems*, edited by Peter T. Daniels and William Bright, pp. 515–35. New York: Oxford University Press.

Swiggers, Pierre
- 1984 "On the Nature of West-Semitic Writing Systems." *Aula Orientalis* 2: 149–51.

Taylor, Isaac
- 1899 *The History of the Alphabet: An Account of the Origin and Development of Letters*. Two volumes. Second edition. London: Edward Arnold.

Tropper, Josef
- 2000 *Ugaritische Grammatik*. Alter Orient und Altes Testament 273. Münster: Ugarit-Verlag.

Woodard, Roger D., editor
- 2004 *The Cambridge Encyclopedia of the World's Ancient Languages*. Cambridge: Cambridge University Press.

5. THE STORY OF *MEM U ZINE* IN THE NEO-ARAMAIC DIALECT OF BOHTAN

Samuel Ethan Fox

5.1. Bohtan Neo-Aramaic and Its Speakers

The Bohtan dialect of Neo-Aramaic was spoken until 1915 in three villages called Ruma, Borb, and Šwata, which were located in the present-day Siirt province of Turkey, around fifteen kilometers east of the town of Pervari. In 1881 the three villages, many of whose inhabitants had recently converted to Catholicism from the traditional Church of the East, had altogether fifty households.[1] Their numbers at the time of emigration are unknown but were probably a few hundred.

In the spring or summer of 1915 the Bohtan Neo-Aramaic speakers escaped from a murderous attack on their villages, fled toward Armenian-controlled territory, and entered the Russian Empire via Yerevan. After the war and the subsequent upheavals in the Caucasus, they found homes in Azerbaijan at Khanlar and a German colony called Grünfeld near Ağstafa. Although long settled in the Soviet Union, they never became Soviet citizens.

On the night of June 13, 1949 Soviet soldiers knocked on their doors, gave them twenty minutes to assemble some belongings, and loaded them onto trucks, without any explanation. After a trip of seventeen days on the railroad in freight cars, and eighteen days down the Ob River on barges, they arrived at settlements in the Tomsk region of Siberia. There they remained in exile until 1956, when they were permitted to return to the Caucasus. The majority of those who had lived in Khanlar settled in there again successfully, but Ağstafa was less welcoming to the returnees, and many of them eventually relocated to Gardabani, just over the border in Georgia.[2]

In the 1990s the Bohtan Assyrians were once again uprooted. After the breakup of the Soviet Union, a combination of a severe deterioration in economic conditions and Georgian nationalism forced most of those who were living in Gardabani to leave. Around the same time, the war between Azerbaijan and Armenia over Nagorno-Karabakh led to the forced departure of many of the Christian Assyrians who were living in Azerbaijan. Most of them eventually settled in neighboring areas of the Russian Republic.

Currently most speakers of the dialect live in Russia in the towns of Krymsk (Krasnodarskiy Kray) and Novopavlovsk (Stavropolskiy Kray) on the northern fringes of the Caucasus. My estimate of the total size of the community is well under 1,000. Only a handful of Bohtan speakers live outside the former Soviet Union.

Bohtan is a northeast Neo-Aramaic dialect. The villages in which it was spoken until 1915 were located very close to the northwest edge of the area in which Northeastern Neo-Aramaic was spoken, and it is quite divergent from most other Northeastern Neo-Aramaic dialects. Its closest known relative is Hertevin (Jastrow 1988), which is very similar in most respects. The only previous discussion of the dialect is in Fox 2002, which outlines the major features of the phonology and morphology. A few major points are discussed below, with particular reference to the text.

5.2. Sound Changes

5.2.1. $\bar{a} \longrightarrow \bar{o}$

Bohtan has continued a sound shift whose beginning can be seen in the Hertevin dialect. Long *a* in the Hertevin dialect is low and back, in contrast to the higher, more forward short *a* (Jastrow 1988: 15), but in Bohtan long *a* has risen to *o*:

---

[1] I am indebted to Bruno Poizat for information on Bohtan collected by Jacques Rhetoré, who visited the Assyrians of Bohtan in the 1880s.

[2] The principal published source for the story of the Bohtan Assyrians and their exile to Siberia is Vartanov 1994.

Bohtan	Hertevin	Gloss
moye/mowe	*maye*	'water'
ona	*ana*	'I'
roba	*raba*	'big'
yotət	*'atet*	'you (masculine) come'

Generally *a* becomes *o* in stressed open syllables, but in some cases unstressed *a* has become *o* by analogy:

Bohtan	Gloss	Sound Change
potəx	'he opens'	regular change
potəxle	'he opens it (masculine)'	change by analogy

There is a strong penultimate stress,[3] and stress moves when a suffix is added:

arxe	'mill'
arxota	'mills'
kebən	'I (masculine) want'
kebənna	'I (masculine) want her'
abra	'son'
abreni	'our son'

In most dialects, adding a clitic to a word generally does not cause stress to shift, as in this Jilu example:

múdi	'what'
múdi-la	'what is it (feminine)?'

However, in Bohtan, even when clitics are added the stress usually shifts:

brota	'daughter, girl'
brotá-se	'also the girl'
bata	'house'
batá-la	'she is (in) the house'

In the verb paradigm, stress sometimes deviates from the usual strong penultimate pattern. The Bohtan preterite tense is formed by adding an L-set subject suffix[4] to the P stem.[5] A second L-set suffix can be added after the first to mark the object. But even when object suffixes are added so that the subject affix has become the penultimate syllable, it does not accept the stress.

qṭale	'he cut'
qṭále-le	'he cut it (masculine)'

Bohtan has a past marker *-wa*, which transforms the present tense into a past, and the perfect into a pluperfect.

yozi	'he goes'
yozí-wa	'he went'
štən	'I drank'
štə́n-wa	'I had drunk'

When object suffixes are added after the past *-wa* it becomes *-wo-*, but it does not receive the stress.

xowər	'he looks'
xowə́r-wa	'he would look'
xowə́r-wo-be	'he would look at it'

When *-wa* is added to a verb with the feminine singular ending *-a*, the *-a* becomes *-o* and receives the stress:

maxkiyó-wa	'she was talking'

But when an object suffix is added after *-wa*, the feminine ending keeps the stress, but the vowel reverts to *-a*.

patxá-wo-le	'she opened it (masculine)'

---

[3] Because the great majority of words have penultimate stress, stress is not marked unless it is *not* penultimate.

[4] Descended from Middle Aramaic *-li* 'to me', *-lāx* 'to you (masculine singular)', etc.

[5] Descended from the Middle Aramaic passive participle.

So long *a* sometimes becomes *o* in unstressed penultimate syllables, and fails to become *o* in non-penultimate stressed syllables. It is possible that this reflects an earlier more regular penultimate stress pattern in this dialect.

The change of long *a* to *o* in Bohtan is reminiscent of the change that occurred in Hebrew. The relation which some words bear to their cognates in other Northeastern Neo-Aramaic dialects is similar to that which Hebrew words bear to their Arabic cognates:

Arabic	Hebrew	Jilu	Bohtan	Gloss
banāt	bānōṯ	bna	bnota	'girls'
lisān	lāšōn	lišana	ləšona	'tongue'
ākil	oxēl	⁺axəl	oxəl	'eat'[6]

Turoyo, another form of Aramaic spoken only slightly south and west of the Bohtan dialect area, has undergone a change of long *a* to *o* as well, but in Turoyo this occurs in some cases where it does not in Bohtan:

Turoyo	Bohtan	Gloss
nóšəq	nočəq	'he kisses' (Jastrow 1988: 61)
nəšqo	načqa	'she kisses'
ʾabro	abra	'son' (Jastrow 1988: 3)

The ancestor of modern Turoyo, like Syriac and Babylonian Jewish Aramaic, seems to have had some instances of long *a* in final position which have later become *o* in Turoyo. However, this vowel evidently had been reduced to short *a* before the change of long *a* to *o* began in Bohtan.

5.2.2. *ay* —> *a*

In Bohtan, earlier *ay* has become long *a*, except before *ə* and *e*, where it remains:

ṣaydət	'you (masculine) hunt'
ṣadat	'you (feminine) hunt'
ana[7]	'well' (< *ayna*)
qmata	'before' (< *qmayta*)

Stressed long *a* derived from earlier *ay* is a long low front vowel [æ:]. Other cases of long *a* were created when a cluster simplified and a syllable containing a previously short *a* became open, and these are identical in sound to those derived from earlier *ay*:

| yara | 'she says' (< *yamra*) |
| yača | 'she comes' (< *yatya*) |

Unstressed tokens of long *a* are shorter and a little lower and so sound very close to short *a*. However, they contrast in the verb paradigm where *ptəxla* (< *ptəxlay*) 'they opened' is distinct from *ptəxla* 'she opened'. The phonetic difference between the two is very slight, and some younger speakers are not aware of it at all.[8]

5.2.3. Shwa Lowering

In Hertevin (Jastrow 1988: 15) *ə* varies between [ə] to [e], and there is no distinct short *e*. In contact with pharyngeal *ḥ* Hertevin *ə* goes as low as [a]. In Bohtan, *ə* varies more broadly, and this vowel is very often as low as [æ], regardless of environment. Lower tokens of *ə* are very close to *a*, but speakers do hear a difference between them: *kəmma* [cəmma] 'mouth' is distinct from *čamma* 'river' (< Kurdish *ç'em*).

In labial environments Bohtan *ə* becomes [ʌ]: *qow*[ʌ]*m-wa* 'he would get up'. This can also be heard on the tapes of Hertevin in words such as *qemli* (Jastrow 1988: 114).

---

[6] The cognate forms cited here are the masculine singular present participle of Hebrew and Arabic and the masculine singular J stem of Neo-Aramaic. The superscript + before the Jilu form indicates that the pronunciation is "emphatic."

[7] Some speakers have the form *ayna* for this word.

[8] When Fox 2002 was written I did not realize that there was a contrast between the two suffixes.

5.3. Morphology

5.3.1. Perfect Tense

In most Northeastern Neo-Aramaic dialects the P stem, which is a descendent of the Middle Aramaic passive participle, is used to form a preterite tense with L-set pronominal endings, continuing a pattern which was already common in Middle Aramaic forms like Syriac *qīm lēh* 'he stood' (Nöldeke 1880: 193). So in Bohtan we have these forms, similar to those found also in many other dialects:

ptəxli, ġzeli	'I opened', 'I saw'
ptəxlux, ġzelux	'you (masculine singular) opened', 'you (masculine singular) saw'
ptəxle, ġzele	'he opened', 'he saw'

Another sort of past tense based on the P stem is found only on the east and west extremes of the Northeastern Neo-Aramaic area. In these areas we find dialects that form past tenses by combining the P stem with the A-set pronominal endings which descend from the Middle Aramaic enclitic pronouns. At the east end of the Northeastern Neo-Aramaic dialect continuum we find two distinct patterns of this sort.

The first pattern is found in the group of Jewish dialects that include Halabja and Suleimaniya. In these dialects the P stem is combined with A-set endings to produce the preterite of intransitive verbs, while transitive verbs form their preterite with the L-set endings, as most Northeastern Neo-Aramaic dialects do. These forms from Khan (2004) illustrate this:

plíxli	'I opened'
kwīšna	'I went down'

On the other hand, in the dialect of the Jews of Urmi the P stem is combined with the A-set endings to produce a perfect tense which contrasts with the preterite (Garbell 1965: 69–71):

grišen	'I (masculine) have pulled'
mirex	'we have said'
grišli	'I pulled'
mirox	'you (masculine singular) said'

On the western end of the dialect continuum are Hertevin and Bohtan. Like Jewish Urmi, these dialects have a preterite on the usual pattern of P stem with L-set endings and a perfect which uses the A-set endings. In Hertevin the perfect is restricted in range and usage: it can be used only with stem I intransitive verbs and cannot be negated. In Bohtan, however, the perfect is employed quite freely:

ġzənna	'I have seen her'
mutwəxla	'We have put them'

It seems likely that a perfect tense based on the P stem and A-set pronominal suffixes must be a survival, occurring as it does at the opposite peripheries of the Northeastern Neo-Aramaic area. However, it is not clear whether Bohtan or Hertevin is more conservative, that is, whether the range of the perfect has become more restricted in Hertevin or more extended in Bohtan.

5.3.2. *-lal / -ləl*

Another interesting phenomenon in Bohtan involves a postposition. Hertevin (Jastrow 1988: 104), Bohtan, and Bespən (Sinha 2000: 159) all use a preposition *lal-* 'to, for'. In Bohtan alone, this also sometimes takes the form of a suffix on the preceding verb or a postposition:

yora	'he says'
yorá-lal duwaw	'he says to her mother'

This usage is comparable Kurdish suffix *-e* on verbs described by Blau (1975: 53):

çone mala wa	'ils allèrent chez eux'

A related form *-ləl* is also used as a postposition on nouns. Kurmanji makes extensive use of paired pre- and postpositions and sometimes uses the postpositions by themselves. In these examples the postposition *-ve* 'in' appears with the preposition *d* and by itself (Blau 1975: 54):

d xanîve   'dans la maison'
ço xanîk'ê xove   'elle rentra dans sa maison'

The use of *-ləl* as a postposition in Bohtan, both with and without an accompanying preposition, seems to derive from this pattern in Kurmanji.

əbbət xlulá-ləl   'in/by a wedding'
barmošé-ləl   'in the evening'

5.4. The Story of *Mem u Zine*

The following text in the dialect is a very brief version of the story of *Mem u Zine*. This story is very old and is regarded as the Kurdish national epic. It is told in several languages of the region, and examples in Kurdish, Neo-Aramaic, and Armenian are presented and discussed in Chyet 1991. The present version was recorded on 24 August 1985 in Gardabani, Georgian SSR.[9] The speaker is Lusya Gulyanova, who (as she says) was born in 1939 in Ağstafa, Azerbaijan.

In the morpheme-by-morpheme translation the verb stems and affix sets are indicated by superscript letters. Where a property of a word is internal, rather than expressed in a separate morpheme, it is represented in parentheses.

(1) ona lusya   wiyan   go   astafa, šetət   alpa-w   əčča   ma-w   tloti-w   əčča.[10]
    I   Lusya   be[P]+1FS[A] in   Ağstafa year-of   thousand-and nine hundred-and thirty-and   nine.
    Vsyo.[11]
    Everything.

(2) šəmmət d-aha[12]   hakowət   mamiolam   sətte   ziné-le.
    name-of of-this   story   mamiolam   lady   zine-is (M).

(3) ətwa   lətwa   to   m-olaha   lətwa.[13]   xa   mamiolam   iwa.
    there-was there-wasn't   more   from-God   there-wasn't.   a   mamiolam   there-was.

    p-xalmew   ġze-wa   xa   xalma.   xa   brota   yaćó-wa   laqrahan.
    in+dream+his   saw[P]+past   a   dream.   a   daughter present+come[J]+3FS[A]+past by-them.

(4) o[14]   brota   mpiló-wa   ləbbew.[15]   i   xa   axəsta   daryó-wa   sabatew.
    that   daughter fell[P]+3FS[A]+past   heart+his.   and   a   ring   put[J]+3FS[A]+past   finger+his.

(5) xa yoma qəmle   o   xalma   xləmle-le.   duwew   bobew[16]   yari,
    a day arose[P]+3MS[L]   that dream   dreamed[P]+3MS[L]+3MS[L]   mother+his   father+his present+say[J]+3P[A]

    "*ras* ġzet   p-xalmux   hatxa,   attu   əllət   susa,   xa   xaloma   didux
    "once saw[P]+2PS[A]   in+dream+your(MS) thus,   sit (imp. S) on   horse,   a   servant   your

    nubəl   ammux,   ptol-lux   ġzi-la   tləbtux."
    take(imp. S)   with+you (MS), search(imp. S)+2MS[L]   see(imp. S)+3FS[L]   fiancée+your(MS)."

---

[9] The recording was made by Vasili Shoumanov, to whom I am indebted for access to the tape, as well as much other help.

[10] In compound numbers, the conjunction *u* is suffixed to the previous word.

[11] Russian words are italicized in the text.

[12] *aha* 'this (feminine)' is an alternant of *aya*. Intervocalic *y* sometimes becomes *w* or *h* in Bohtan.

[13] Literally, 'There was, there wasn't, there was none better than God'. This is a standard introductory formula, found also in Fox 1997: 96 in a shorter form.

[14] The demonstrative *o* 'that', which is masculine in origin, is used for both masculine and feminine in Bohtan.

[15] Literally 'she fell (in) his heart'. This idiom is of Kurdish origin (Chyet 2003: 152), *dil k'etin*.

[16] 'His parents', literally, 'his father his mother'.

(6) tula   p-susa   tərwahan,   oyun   u   xalomew,   zila   patli-wa.
    sat^P+3P^L in+horse   two-of-them,   he   and   servant+his,   went^P+3P^L search^J+3P^A+past.

(7) tpəqla   b-xa   bata.   xoza   xa brota   hawla   toma   qam   bira,   malya
    met^P+3P^L in+a   house.   see^J(3P) a daughter behold there before well,   fill^J+3FS^A

    xa quqa   moye.   boqərra   maxkiyó-wa,   gaxki   ammaw.
    a jug   water. asked^P+3P^L   speaks^J+3FS^A+past, laugh^J+3P^A with+her.

(8) yora   "man-iwat?"   yara,   "ziné-na."[17]   boqərra   botar
    present+says^J(3MS) "who+you(FS) are?" present+says^J(3FS) "zine+am"   asked^P+3P^L about

    sətte   zine, tó-məndi   li   yara.
    lady   zine, nothing   not present+says^J(3FS)

(9) xroya   xa bena   xeta   xəš   xoze   palṭa   sətte zine.   maxke
    finally a   moment   other   already sees^J(3MS) goes-out^J+3FS lady zine.   speaks^J(3MS)

    ammaw,   dăle   aya o   brotá-la   ġze-la   p-xalmew.
    with+her, knew^P+3MS^L   this that   daughter+is(FS)   saw^P+3FS^L   in+dream+his.

(10) yorá-la   "a   brota,   kibən-nax."   yowəd
     present+says^J(3MS)+3FS^L   "this daughter present+want^J+1MS^A+2 FS^L" present+does^J(3MS)

     gaxka   ṭawla   ammaw.   kullen   maxkiyi   yawa   brota   rozi,
     laughs^J+3FS^A plays^J+3FS^A   with+her. all   laugh^J+3P^A gives^J+3FS^A daughter   agreement,

     kiba   gawró-le.
     present+wants^J+3FS^A marry^J+3FS^A+3MS^L

(11) zine   brotəd   baku   ġzela   wədle   gaxka   ammət sətte   zine.
     zine daughter-of   baku   saw^P+3FS^L   did^P+3MS^L   laugh^J+3FS^A   with   lady   zine.

     zine   mərró-lal   bobaw.   yara-t   sətte zine   kibe.
     zine said^P+3FS^L+to   father+her.   present+say^J+3FS^A+that lady zine   present+wants^J(3MS)

     "ona lébe-li."
     "I   not+loves^J(3MS)+1S^L"

(12) bobaw   yora   "ətlax   əlli   hodax: awdəx   la   qayti   marodahan."[18]
     father+her   present+says^J(3MS) "there-is+2FS^L on+me   thus: do^J+1P^A   not   reach^J+3P^A desire+their.

(13) yozu   xa   yoma   əl   diwan,   mamiolam   ammət   ṭləbtew   sətte zine.
     present+goes^J(3MS)   a   day   to   diwan,   mamiolam   with   fiancée+his   lady   zine.

(14) baku xoze   i   yora   "kulle   xe-le   manxapón-na   go d-o   diwan."
     baku sees^J(3MS) and present+says^J(3MS) "all+it one+is shame^J+1p. MS^A+3P^L in of+this diwan."

     maxke   yowəd   gošagóš,[19]   noše   šami.
     speaks^J(3MS)   present+do^J(3MS)   embracing   people   hear^J+3P^A.

(15) boba   duwəd   sətte zine-se   šami.   bobəd   sətte zine yorá-lal   duwaw,
     father mother+of   lady zine+also   hear^J+3P^A father+of   lady zine present+says^J(3MS)+to   mother+her

     "moy   awdəxna?   broteni   la   naxpəxna."
     "what do^J+1p. P^A daughter+our   not   be-shamed^J+1P^A

---

[17] This is a separate character, also named Zine.

[18] Literally, 'You have this on me: we will make (it so that) they will not reach their wish'.

[19] Compare Syriac *gašgaš* 'grope'.

(16) xrowe, yora boba, "Sa. dargušta mápluṭ-la m-bata.
finally, present+says[J](3MS) father, "go (imp. FS) cradle take-out(imp. S)+3FS[L] from+house.
o xena moy īt go bata, šot yoqəṭ. bata ṭrum-be nura.
that other what there-is in house let burns[J](3MS). house leave(imp. P)+in-it(M) fire.
maṭlat la naxpəxna."
in-order-that not be-shamed[J]+1P[A]"

(17) bata ṭorá-be nura, noše kiba bata mačmi, baku kole
house leave[J]+3P[A]+in-it(M) fire, people present+want[J]+3P[A] house extinguish[J]+3P[A], baku stands[J](3MS)
qam tara. yora, "p-kolən, kulle xe-le manxapən-na."
before door. present+says[J](3MS), "future+stand[J]+1MS all+it one+is shame[J]+1MS[A]+3P[L]"

(18) qam iwora əl ṭara, noše mašmé-la ki sətte zine hawlala
before entering[C] to door, people make-hear[J](3MS)+3P[L] that lady zine behold+is(3FS)
go čangəd mamiolam.
in arms+of mamiolam.

(19) bobət sətte zine šoma. qoyəm, mamiolam doré-lal zəndona.
father+of lady zine hears[J](3MS) gets-up[J](3MS) mamiolam puts[J](3MS)+to prison.

(20) brotéw-se b-lele yoma baxya parpaló-be əl boba, yara,
daughter+his+also in+night day cries[J]+3FS[A] begs[J]+3FS[A]+in-him to father, present+says[J](3FS),
"mápluṭ-le mamiolam m-zəndona."
"take-out(imp. S)+3MS[L] mamiolam from+prison."

(21) bobaw taxmən, qoyəm yorá-la, "broti,
father+her thinks[J](3MS), gets-up[J](3MS) present+says[J](3MS)+3FS[L] "daughter+my
p-torən-ne. sa, xuronax máxuš-la. ammət
future+let[J]+1MS[A]+3MS[L] go(imp. FS) friends+your(FS) assemble(imp. S)+3P[L] with
xuronax maššud, sun ṭrun-ne."
friends+your(FS) together, go (imp. P) let (imp. P)+3MS[L]"

(22) baku šoma, to-qmata yozi.
baku hears[J](3MS) more+before present+goes[J]+3P[A]

(23) yorá-lal mamiolam, "yadət-wo-le, mamiolam, hawda ṭləbtux
present+says[J](3MS)+to mamiolam, "know[J]+2MS[A]+past+3MS[L] mamiolam now fiancée+your(MS)
baxa gawra əbbət xlulá-ləl."
here marries[J]+3FS[A] by wedding+in

(24) ləbbəd mamiolam mamrí-le.
heart+of mamiolam pains[J](3MS)+3MS[L]

(25) xa bena lé poyəš,[20] sətte zine ammət xuronaw yača kiba
a moment not remains[J](3MS) lady zine with friends+her present+comes[J]+3FS[A] present+wants[J]+3FS[A]
yawó-le ṭroya.[21]
gives[J]+3FS[A]+3MS[A] let[C]

(26) oyun rešew ṭoyám-be i buləkəd dəmma b-hoya kəmmew-ləl, moyət.
he head+his carry[J](3MS)+in-it and spring+of blood future+be(3MS) mouth+his+in dies[J](3MS)

---

[20] Literally, 'a little time doesn't remain'. [21] Literally, 'to give him release'.

(27) sətte zine baxya, ṭalba m-olaha yara, "mamiolam mətle háyuna,
 lady zine cries^J+3FS^A asks^J+3FS^A from+God present+says^J+3FS^A "mamiolam died^P+3MS^L morning,
 ona matan bármoše-ləl, yomeni lá toyəm. maššud metəxna ṭamrí-lan."[22]
 I die^J+1FS^A evening+in day+our not end^J(3MS) together die^J+1P^A bury^J+3P^A+1P^L

(28) olaha ṣlawataw qbəlle-la, oyun-se mətla. tərwahan maššud ṭmərrán-na
 God prayers+her accepted^P+3MS^L+3P^L she+also died^P+3FS^L two-of-them together buried^P+3P^L+3P^L
 go xa todīt.
 in one coffin.

(29) aṭṭor noše yari ən aṣloye-wa anni ət bólahan wədlán-ne láġdode.
 then people present+say^J+3P^A if true+were they that face+their made^P+3P^L+3MS^L to+each-other

(30) yari ən aṣloyé-wa ibá-wa láġdode, bólahan b-howe
 present+say^J+3P^A if true+were present+want^J(3P)+past to+each-other face+their future+be(3MS)
 láġdode.
 to+each-other

(31) ən la *značit* xoṣáhan ṭari, xoṣahán moxa láġdode.[23]
 if not it+means backs+their leave^J+3P^A backs+their hit^J(3P) to+each-other

(32) baku go qawrá-se la ṭrele qətla marodáhan. yozí-wa b-lele
 baku in grave+also not leave^P+3MS^L reach^P+3P^L desire+their present+go^J+3P^A+past in+night
 xopə́r-wo-le bólahan xoṣáhan maqə́t-wo-le láġdode.
 dig^J(3MS)+past+3MS^L face+their back+their make-reach^J(3MS)+past+3MS to+each-other

(33) noše toxmənna, toxmənna, yari, "xa məndi īt baxa."[24]
 people think^P+3P^L think^P+3P^L present+say^J+3P^A "a thing there-is here"

(34) qəmle xa, zile ṣədle nawba. xoze moy? baku yote
 arose^P+3MS^L one went^P+3MS^L hunted^P+3MS^L ambush sees^J(3MS) what? baku present+comes^J(3MS)
 xopərre qáwrahan
 digs^J(3MS)+3MS^L grave+their

(35) xoṣahan madərre láġdode.
 back+their turns^J(3MS)+3MS^L to+each-other

(36) o noša-t ṣowə́d-wa nawba, xa sapa mxele, qṭále-le rešew.
 that man+that hunt^J(3MS)+past ambush, a sword hit^P+3MS^L cut^P+3MS^L+3MS^L head+his.
 xa tapakka dəmma pəlle bəl tərwahan, *i* xa kuba whele bəl
 a drop blood fell^P+3MS^L between two-of-them and a thorn became^P+3MS^L between
 tərwahan.
 two-of-them.

(37) xa magza mottula toma, yari man zole u ote baxa,
 an ax put^P+3P^L there, present+say^J+3P^A who goes^J+his and comes^J(3MS) in+here
 qoṭá-le o kuba.
 cuts^J(3MS)+3MS^L that thorn.

---

[22] Literally, 'together let us die, let them bury us'.
[23] Literally, 'their faces hit together'.
[24] Literally, 'there is something here'.

(38) man la qoṭá-le, ola lébe-le. *i* donəd bakuye b-dunye xena
who not cuts^J(3MS)+3MS^L God not+love^J(3MS)+3MS^L and time+of baku+plural in+world again

la howa sakri m-dunye.
not be(3P) be-lost^J+3P from+world.

(39) xləṣle.
ended^P+3MS^L

(1) I, Lusya, was born in Agstafa in the year 1939. That's it.
(2) The name of this story is "Mamiolam and Sitte Zine."
(3) Once upon a time there was a man named Mamiolam. He had a dream where a girl came to them.
(4) He fell in love with that girl, and she put a ring (on) his finger.
(5) One day he got up (after) he dreamed that dream. His mother and father said, "Once you have seen this in your dream, mount your horse, take a servant with you, and go look for your fiancée."
(6) The two of them mounted their horses, he and his servant, and they went looking.
(7) They happened upon a house. They saw a girl there in front of a well, filling a pitcher of water. They asked, she was talking, (and) they laughed with her.
(8) He said, "Who are you?" She said "I am Zine." They asked about Sitte Zine, but she didn't say anything.
(9) Finally, a little later, he saw Sitte Zine come out. He talked with her and he knew that this was the girl that he saw in his dream.
(10) He said to her, "Girl, I love you." He joked and played with her they were all talking (and) she agreed she would marry him.
(11) Zine the daughter of Baku saw him joking with Sitte Zine. Zine said to her father, she said that he loved Sitte Zine. "He doesn't love *me*."
(12) Her father said, "I promise that we will prevent them from achieving their wish."
(13) He went one day to the diwan (while) Mamiolam (was) with his lover Sitte Zine.
(14) Baku saw and said "I will shame them anyway in the diwan." He is talking (and) he was touching her (and) people were hearing.
(15) Sitte Zine's mother (and) father also heard. Sitte Zine's father said to her mother, "What should we do? Let us not be shamed (because of) our daughter."
(16) Finally her father said, "Go out. Take the cradle out of the house. Let everything else that is in the house burn. Set fire to the house so that we will not be shamed."
(17) They set fire to the house. People wanted to put out the fire, (and) Baku was standing outside the door. He said, "I will stand here (and) I will shame them anyhow."
(18) Before going in the door he told people that Sitte Zine was in the arms of Mamiolam.
(19) Sitte Zine's father heard and he got up and put Mamiolam in jail.
(20) His daughter cried day and night and begged her father, saying, "Take Mamiolam out of jail."
(21) Her father thought, he got up (and) said to her, "Daughter, I will release him. Go assemble your friends, go together with them (and) release him."
(22) Baku heard, he went first.
(23) He said to Mamiolam, "Did you know, Mamiolam, that your fiancée is getting married now here in a wedding?"
(24) Mamiolam's heart hurt him.
(25) In no time Sitte Zine came with her friends wanting to release him.
(26) He lifted his head and a spring of blood was in his mouth (and) he died.
(27) Sitte Zine cried (and) asked God, saying, "Mamiolam died this morning. I will die in the evening. Let our day not end. Let us die and be buried together."
(28) God accepted her prayer, (and) she died too. They buried the two of them together in one coffin.
(29) Then, people say if they were true, they will turn their faces to each other.

(30) They say that if they truly loved each other, their faces will be towards each other.
(31) If not, it means, they will leave their backs turned towards each other.
(32) Even in the grave Baku did not let them reach their wish. He would go at night, and would dig them up and would put their backs together.
(33) People thought (and) thought (and) said, "Something is going on."
(34) Someone went and stood guard. What did he see? Baku came and dug up their graves,
(35) He turned their backs together.
(36) The man that set the ambush hit (with) a sword (and) cut (off) his head. A drop of blood fell between the two of them, and a thorn appeared between them.
(37) They put an ax there. They said, "Anyone who passes by should cut that thorn."
(38) God would not favor whoever did not cut it, and the time of the "Baku's" in the world, they would not be lost from the world.
(39) It ended.

Abbreviations

1	first person
2	second person
3	third person
A	A-set (pronominal suffixes derived from Middle Aramaic enclitic pronouns)
F	feminine
imp.	imperative
J	J stem (stem derived from the Middle Aramaic active participle)
L	L-set (subject suffixes derived from Middle Aramaic -*l* 'to')
M	masculine
P	plural
P	P stem (stem derived from the Middle Aramaic passive participle)
S	singular
+	"emphatic" pronunciation

Bibliography

Blau, Joyce
    1975   *Le Kurde de ʿAmādiya et de Djabal Sindjār: Analyse linguistique, textes folkloriques, glossaires.* Paris: Klincksieck.

Chyet, Michael L.
    1991   And a Thornbush Sprang Up between Them: Studies on Mem u Zin, a Kurdish Romance. Ph.D. dissertation. University of California at Berkeley.
    2003   *Kurdish-English Dictionary.* New Haven: Yale University Press.

Fox, Samuel
- 1997 *The Neo-Aramaic Dialect of Jilu*. Wiesbaden: Harrassowitz.
- 2002 "A Neo-Aramaic Dialect of Bohtan." In *"Sprich doch mit deinen Knechten aramäisch, wir verstehen es!" 60 Beiträge zur Semitistik: Festschrift für Otto Jastrow zum 60. Geburtstag*, edited by Werner Arnold and Harmut Bobzin, pp. 165–80. Wiesbaden: Harrassowitz.

Garbell, Irene
- 1965 *The Jewish Neo-Aramaic Dialect of Persian Azerbaijan: Linguistic Analysis and Folkloristic Texts*. Janua Linguarum. Series Practica 3. London: Mouton.

Hetzron, Robert
- 1969 "The Morphology of the Verb in Modern Syriac (Christian Colloquial of Urmi)." *Journal of the American Oriental Society* 89: 112–27.

Hoberman, Robert D.
- 1989 *The Syntax and Semantics of Verb Morphology in Modern Aramaic: A Jewish Dialect of Iraqi Kurdistan*. American Oriental Series 69. New Haven: American Oriental Society.

Jastrow, Otto
- 1985 *Laut- und Formenlehre des neuaramäischen Dialekts von Mīdin im Ṭūr ʿAbdīn*. Third enlarged edition. Wiesbaden: Harrassowitz.
- 1988 *Der neuaramäische Dialekt von Hertevin (Provinz Siirt)*. Semitica Viva 3. Wiesbaden: Harrassowitz.

Khan, Geoffrey
- 2004 *The Jewish Neo-Aramaic Dialect of Sulemaniyya and Halabja*. Studies in Semitic Languages and Linguistics 44. Leiden: Brill.

Krotkoff, Georg
- 1982 *A Neo-Aramaic Dialect of Kurdistan: Texts, Grammar, and Vocabulary*. American Oriental Series 64. New Haven: American Oriental Society.

Nöldeke, Theodor
- 1880 *Kurzgefasste syrische Grammatik*. Leipzig: T. O. Weigel.

Sinha, Jasmin
- 2000 *Der neuostaramäische Dialekt von Bēṣpǝn (Provinz Mardin, Südosttürkei): Eine grammatische Darstellung*. Semitica Viva 24. Wiesbaden: Harrassowitz.

Vartanov, Il'ia
- 1994 *Assiriytsi v Sibiri: 1949–1956: Vospominaniia*. Chicago: Nineviia [in Russian].

6. PRENASALIZATION IN ARAMAIC[1]

W. Randall Garr

6.1. Introduction

To varying degrees, **n*C > C: in many Semitic languages (Brockelmann 1908: §61; Sanmartín 1995: 435–36; and Lipiński 2001: §27.3a).[2] This change is assimilatory in nature, and its governing condition is nearly universal. Nasals "tend to neutralize before following obstruents, where they tend to be homorganic with the obstruent" (Ferguson 1974: 6; see also Hajek 1997: 150). The process results in "total cluster assimilation" (Hajek 1997: 73).

In contrast, prenasalization adds a nasal segment to an underlying form (see Rosenthal 2006: §21; and, perhaps, Mustafa 1982: 16).[3] This phenomenon is also broadly attested in the classical Semitic languages but, unlike assimilation, tends to operate erratically and haphazardly.[4] In Middle Babylonian (sixteenth–eleventh centuries B.C.E.), though, its behavior is not erratic. There, prenasalization first attains a relatively systematic status.[5] It operates on nominals: for example, *zubbu* ~ *zumbu* 'fly', and such Standard Babylonian terms as *maddattu* ~ *mandattu* 'tribute', *puggulu* ~ *pungulu* 'very strong', and *mazzaltu* ~ *manzaltu* 'drain(age)'. It also operates on verbs, largely in the present-future form:[6] for example, *imaggur* ~ *imangur* 'he agrees' (*magāru*); see also *inabbu* ~ *inambu* 'he calls' (*nabû*), *inazziq* ~ *inamziq* 'he worries' (*nazāqu*), and especially *inaddin* ~ *inandin* ~ *inamdin* 'he gives' (*nadānu*). From a phonological perspective, Middle Babylonian prenasalization targets geminate, voiced stops and fricatives; a qualifying geminate cluster tends to be replaced by a homorganic sequence of nasal and singleton consonant: **bb* > [mb], **gg* > [ŋg], **dd* > [nd], and **zz* > [nz] (Aro 1955: 37; see also Gelb 1970: 76–77). The new prenasalized segment, whether orthographically represented by a dental (*n*) or bilabial (*m*), is not phonemic (von Soden 1995: §32a).

Prenasalization is also widespread later,[7] in a number of Aramaic dialects.[8] Within this group, prenasalization first becomes productive in Imperial Aramaic dialects (ca. 600–200 B.C.E.) (Kaufman 1992: 177a; cf. Folmer 1995: 705–6)[9] and continues intermittently into Middle Aramaic (ca. 200 B.C.E.–ca. 250 C.E.). But, with one stark exception (see Macuch 1965b: liii), it is rare in Late Aramaic (ca. 250–1200 C.E.). The reflexes of the second-

---

[1] I am grateful to John Huehnergard, Stephen Kaufman, and Oktor Skjærvø for critiquing an earlier draft of this article. I especially thank Richard Steiner for correcting the section on Papyrus Amherst 63 and freely sharing his unpublished material on the text. Finally, I appreciate the help I received from Paul-Alain Beaulieu, Moshe Bernstein, Klaus Beyer, Esther Eshel, Carol Genetti, Matthew Gordon, Douglas Gropp, Janet Johnson, Ulla Kasten, Marianne Mithun, Takamitsu Muraoka, John Ohala, Bezalel Porten, Jack Sasson, and James VanderKam.

[2] Throughout this study, two types of consonantal length are distinguished: a consonant which is lengthened by phonological operation, such as assimilation (C:); and a consonant which is morphologically or lexically long by assignment (CC).

[3] Note that prenasalization is not a dissimilatory process (see Blau 1970: 127, in conjunction with Ohala 1981: 188). Nor is it an assimilatory change somehow linked with vowel nasalization (see Hajek 1997: 190; cf. Southern and Vaughn 1997: 270–71, 281).

[4] For surveys, see Brockelmann 1908: §90A; and Mustafa 1982: 16–33.

[5] Initial signs of prenasalization, whose origin Poebel traces to Sumerian (1939: 148), already appear before the Old Babylonian period (Huehnergard 2005: 589). For Old Babylonian Amorite in particular, see Sanmartín 1995: 443–52, as revised by Streck 2000: 206, 220.

[6] For attested forms and citations, see Aro 1955: 35–36; and the Akkadian dictionaries.

[7] As in Middle Babylonian, prenasalization in Aramaic is "a phonetic phenomenon" (Kaufman 1992: 177a; cf. Spitaler 1952–54: 265 = 1998: 11). The nasal is recorded in old Aramaic loanwords: for example, *mandētu* 'information' < **ydʿ*, and *manḫalu* 'entering' < **ǵll* (e.g., Kutscher 1970: 374 = 1977: 117; and, with hesitation, Muraoka and Porten 2003: 16 n. 77). It also appears in cuneiform transliterations of proper nouns which, in Aramaic orthography, lack the nasal segment: e.g., חדוה = ᵁᴿᵁ*Ḫa-an-du-a-te* (AECT 3) and חבש = ᶠ*Ḫa-am-bu-su* (AECT 17) (e.g., Kaufman 1974: 121 n. 23; and Lipiński 1993–94: 145). See also the Palmyrean name *Mtbwl* = Μανθβωλείω[ν] (PAT 0271) (e.g., Cantineau 1935: 46–47; and Altheim and Stiehl *apud* Macuch 1965a: 89 n. 34e). Prenasalization, then, is an acoustic fact, even in cases where the orthography does not represent the nasal segment (e.g., Macuch 1965b: li; and 1976: 4–5; see also Southern and Vaughn 1997: 279; and, differently, Folmer 1995: 89–90).

[8] For the periodization and classification of the pre-modern Aramaic dialects adopted here, see Kaufman 1992: 173–75; and 1997: 114–18.

[9] For the possible roots of prenasalization in eastern Old Aramaic (ca. 1000–600 B.C.E.), see, for example, Muraoka 1983–84: 92; and NTA 3:8, 19:8, and 17*:1 (broken); contrast 15:5 and 23:1. For a western candidate, see KAI 317:4, and the discussion in Kottsieper 2000: 372–75 (reference courtesy of Wolfgang Röllig).

person masculine singular independent subjective pronoun are typical. The oldest, pre-Imperial form is a nasalless את (e.g., KAI 224:11.20). In Imperial Aramaic, the pronoun becomes אנת (e.g., TAD A6.16:3, B2.4:6, C1.1:34), and its nasal element persists into the language of Ezra (אַנְתְּ [Ezra 7:25]), Daniel (אנתה [אַנְתְּ "ק] [e.g., Daniel 2:29.31]), as well as other Middle Aramaic dialects (e.g., epigraphic Judean, Idumean, Palmyrean, and Nabatean). Thereafter, in Late Aramaic the prenasalized form is found only occasionally, as in Jewish Babylonian Aramaic (אנת [~ את]) and the orthography of Syriac (ܐܢܬ).[10] Another token of prenasalization is the noun 'nostrils, face'. This word, too, is nasalless in Old Aramaic (e.g., אפוה 'his nostrils' [KAI 224:2]). Then, in Imperial Aramaic, a nasal segment appears (e.g., אנפוהי 'his face' [e.g., TAD C1.1:133]), and it continues into biblical Aramaic (אַנְפּוֹהִי [Daniel 2:46, 3:19]), Qumran (e.g., א]נפוהי [11Q10 tgJob vi 8]), Jewish Babylonian Aramaic (אנפיה [~ אפיה] [e.g., b. Meg. 22b]), and Mandaic (*anpiḥ*). In both these cases, though, the new nasal corresponds to an etymological *n (see Ethiopic *'anta* and *'anf*, respectively). But not all prenasalized forms derive from *nC (e.g., Folmer 1995: 84–88; and Muraoka and Porten 2003: §3c), as biblical Aramaic of Daniel shows. There is no underlying *n in the *haphel* of סל״ק, yet the verb has a prenasalized variant: for example, הַסִּקוּ '(they) brought up' (Daniel 3:22) ~ לְהַנְסָקָה 'to bring up' (6:24). The *haphel* of על״ל has a nasalless origin with attested prenasalized outcomes: for example, הַעֵלְנִי 'bring me in!' (2:24) ~ הַנְעֵל 'he brought (him) in' (e.g., 2:25), and לְהֶעָלָה 'to bring (them) in' (5:7) ~ לְהַנְעָלָה 'to bring (them) in' (4:3). Likewise, a non-etymological nasal consonant makes a debut in *peal* prefix forms of יד״ע: for example, אִנְדַּע 'I will know' (2:9) and תִּנְדַּע 'you may know' (e.g., v. 30); see also מַנְדַּע 'knowledge'. Whatever triggers prenasalization in Aramaic, then, does not lie in the proto-form.

This study seeks to demonstrate the systematic nature of prenasalization in Aramaic (cf. Sanmartín 1995: 440; and, generally, Lipiński 2001: § 23.6). First, it isolates the conditions that govern this variety of prenasalization, especially in its formative period (section 6.2). Then, it traces the development and changes that occur as this phenomenon spreads in the post-Imperial period, starting with a sample of Middle Aramaic dialects (section 6.3) and ending with Mandaic (section 6.4). This study therefore seeks to characterize prenasalization in Aramaic within a dialectal and historical framework.

6.2. Imperial Aramaic

6.2.1. Consonantal Inventory

The following table (6.1) lists, in alphabetical order, the Imperial Aramaic forms that participate in prenasalization. Most forms occur in Egyptian documents. Some are taken from biblical Aramaic and Aramaic loanwords in Akkadian[11] — when they supply otherwise unattested information. Akkadian loanwords in Aramaic are included, too.

The list excludes four types of forms: (i) the preposition מן 'from', whose invariable form in the epigraphic Imperial Aramaic corpus suggests that *n is always preserved before a proclitic boundary (cf. biblical Aramaic); (ii) final *nun* perfects (e.g., זבנתן 'you bought' [TAD A3.10:5]), whose third radical is consistently preserved before an inflectional boundary and subsequent non-identical consonant (see Sanmartín 1995: 436; cf. Folmer 1995: 77 n. 196; Muraoka and Porten 2003: 11 n. 41, 13 n. 60; and, in this context, Voigt 2002–3: 144);[12] (iii) deverbal *qitl* and *qitlān* nouns (e.g., מנין 'number, amount') which, as in biblical Hebrew and Ugaritic, preserve the underlying proto-consonant in all phonological contexts (e.g., מנחה 'meal-offering'; see also biblical Hebrew מִנְחָה 'cereal offering, gift' and Ugaritic *mnḥ* 'delivery, tribute') (cf. Sanmartín 1995: 438 n. 25; and, differently, Levine 2002: 127);[13] and (iv) proper nouns, which can take idiosyncratic and linguistically non-representative forms.

---

[10] For Mandaic, see note 70 below.

[11] For a summary of applicable Aramaic loanwords in Akkadian, see Sanmartín 1995: 442 with n. 50.

[12] For the exceptional form נתתן (TAD A2.2:5), see Porten 1996: 94 n. 13; contrast Folmer 1995: 643 n. 218.

[13] Accordingly, מחתא in TAD A4.7:25 is misspelled; see מנחה in l. 21 (Folmer 1995: 81 with n. 242).

Table 6.1. (Non-)Prenasalized Forms in Imperial Aramaic

	Non-prenasalized		*Prenasalized*
[א]ביד	'your [fr]uit' (TAD C1.1:101) (Akkadian loanword)	אִנְבֵּהּ	'its fruit' (Daniel 4:9.11.18) (Akkadian loanword); see also
		אנבהון	'their fruit' (1Q20 apGen xi 12; see also xiii 17)
		אנפין	'face' (TAD A4.2:8.9)
אפיך	'your face' (TAD A2.1:2, A2.3:2, A2.4:2)	אנפיך	'your face' (TAD A3.3:3, A3.9:4)
אפיכי	'your face' (TAD A2.2:2, A2.6:2, D7.16:13)		
ב-אפנא	'in our presence' (TAD C3.28:1)	ב-אנפוהי	'in his face' (TAD C1.1:133)
את	'you (masculine singular)' (KAI 259:2)[14] (?)	אנת	'you (masculine singular)' (e.g., TAD A6.16:3, B2.4:6)
אתתה	'the woman' (TAD D23.1.II.9)	אנתה	'woman, wife' (e.g., TAD B2.6:32)
אתת	'wife of' (e.g., TAD C3.4:6)	אנתת	'wife of' (e.g., TAD C3.13:35)
		אנתתי	'my wife' (e.g., TAD B2.6:4)
		אנתו	'wifehood, matrimony' (e.g., TAD B3.8:45)
		אנתי	'you (feminine singular)' (e.g., TAD B2.3:26)
		אנת(ו)ם	'you (masculine plural)' (e.g., TAD A6.9:2, D2.10 fragment a:1)
		zambūru	'thyme' (?)
		ḫangaru	'dagger' (?)
חטה	'wheat' (TAD D4.4:3 [?])	חנטא	'the wheat' (TAD C3.28:104)
חטן	'wheat' (TAD B4.1:2)	חנטן	'wheat' (e.g., TAD D8.11:3)
		חנכה	'his palate'[15] (TAD C1.1:163)
מְחַן	'showing mercy' (Daniel 4:24) (*peal*)	חנתא	'gift' (TAD D7.9:1, D7.36:2)[16]
תדע	'it will (not) know' (TAD C1.1:122) (*peal*)	תִנְדַּע	'you may know' (e.g., Daniel 2:30) (*peal*)
		מנדע	'(to) know' (TAD D4.25:1) (*peal*)

---

[14] See Folmer 1995: 84.

[15] See, in this context, Greenfield and Sokoloff 1992: 88 with n. 75 = Greenfield 2001: 1:482 with n. 75.

[16] For the etymology, see Kaufman *apud* Porten 2002: 215 n. 2, below. But because its root is geminate, חנתא may not belong in this list; see also Ugaritic *ḥnt* 'mercy; plea'. Alternatively, חנתא may be deverbal, in which case see section 6.2.1.

Non-prenasalized		Prenasalized	
כדא	'the pitcher' (TAD A4.2.13)	*kandu*	'jar'
		כנדן	'jars' (e.g., TAD C3.7FV2:4, C3.7FV3:5)
		כנכר	'talent' (TAD A6.2:17)
כַּכְּרִין	'talents' (Ezra 7:22)[17]	כנכר(י)ן	'talents' (TAD A4.7:28, A4.8:27)
		kanšu	'donkey caravan' (?)
כעת	'now' (e.g., TAD A6.13:4, D1.32:14); see also	כענת	'now' (e.g., TAD A4.2:2, D7.16:6); see also
וּ־כְעֶת	'and now' (Ezra 4:17)	וּ־כְעֶנֶת	'and now' (Ezra 4:10.11, 7:12)
		מדינתא	'the province' (e.g., TAD A6.1:1, C3.19:14)[18]
מִדָּה	'tribute' (Ezra 4:20; see also 6:8; cf. 4:13) (Akkadian loanword); see also	מנדה	'payment, duty' (TAD D6.13 fragment d:1) (Akkadian loanword)
מדא	'tribute' (1Q20 apGen xxi 26; see also l. 27)		
		מנדע	'knowledge' (TAD C1.1:53; see also C1.1H:9)
		mandētu	'information'
מדעם	'something, anything' (e.g., TAD A2.1:10, A2.3:10, B4.1:3)	מנדעם	'something, anything' (e.g., TAD A2.5:4, C1.1:85, D20.5:2)
		מנדעמתא	'the things' (e.g., TAD C3.7GR2:23)
		manḫalu	'entering'; see also מנעל, below
		manṭaru	'bast'
		מנטרה	'watchfulness, guardpost' (TAD C1.1:82)
		מנפקה	'taking out, shipping' (e.g., TAD C3.7EV1:15)
ב־מציעתא	'in the middle/midst' (TAD C3.28:112)	ב־מנציעת	'in the midst of' (TAD A4.5:5.6, C1.2:7 [broken])
		ינדשו	'let them demolish' (TAD A4.7:8, A4.8:7) (*peal*)[19]
		תְּהַנְזִק	'it will harm' (Ezra 4:13) (*haphel*)
		מְהַנְזְקַת	'harmful (to)' (Ezra 4:15) (*haphel*)

---

[17] For ככרן 'talents', which was read in AP 83:29 and 50:9, see TAD C3.27:30 and D1.34 fragment b:2, respectively (see Folmer 1995: 86 n. 306, 93 n. 363).

[18] In this example, and morphologically similar suffixed feminine nouns (e.g., ספינתא 'the boat' [e.g., TAD A6.2:3.7] and תכונתה 'her money' [TAD B3.8:22.27]), it is unclear whether the *n*C sequence is separated by a vowel. In Palmyrean (section 6.3.1) and Qumran Aramaic (section 6.3.4), however, *n*C seems contiguous.

[19] For מדשה 'what is falling', which is "doubtlessly from נדש" (Kraeling 1953: 242 [ad 9:14]; see also Gropp 1990: 173 n. 14, with hesitation), Porten and Yardeni now read מרשה 'its beam' (B3.10:14), following Kutscher 1954: 237a = 1977: 41a.

	Non-prenasalized		*Prenasalized*
יחתון	'they will (not) go down' (TAD C1.2:6) (*peal*)	מנחת	'(to) descend' (e.g., TAD B3.7:10) (*peal*)
		הנחת	'bring down!' (e.g., TAD A3.8:13) (*haphel*)
מחתה	'(to) bring down' (TAD A2.5:6) (*aphel*)		
		ינטרנהי	'he will watch it' (TAD C1.1:208) (*peal*)[20]
		nungurtu	'(a kind of property)' (?)
		ינסח	'it will tear out' (TAD C1.1:156.210) (*peal*)
		ינסחוהי	'may they exterminate him' (KAI 228 A 14) (*peal*)
		מנסך	'(to) pour' (TAD C3.13:7) (*peal*)
		ינפי	'may he (not) sift' (TAD D7.5:4) (*peal*)
		תנפק	'you (may) go out' (e.g., TAD B3.12:22, D7.8:12) (*peal*)
		מנפק	'(to) go out' (e.g., TAD B3.11:3.4) (*peal*)
אפקני	'he brought me forth' (TAD A2.6:4) (*aphel*)		
		הנפקו	'they sent out' (e.g., TAD C3.7KV2:1.4.17) (*haphel*)
יהפק	'he will/should bring out' (TAD D7.14:3) (*haphel*)	יהנפק	'he will release, take out' (e.g., TAD A6.13:3.5, B2.7:11) (*haphel*)
תפק	'let her bring out' (TAD D7.7:8) (*aphel*)	תהנפק	'she will take out' (e.g., TAD B2.6:25.28) (*haphel*)
אפק	'bring out!' (TAD D7.7:6) (*aphel*)	הנפק	'take out!' (TAD C1.1:83) (*haphel*)
מפקן	'(they are [not]) bringing out' (TAD A2.5:3) (*aphel*)		
אצל	'I shall reclaim' (TAD B1.1:14) (*aphel*)	אנצל	'I shall reclaim' (TAD B3.3:13) (*aphel*)
		אהנצל	'I shall reclaim' (e.g., TAD B3.8:42, B3.11:10) (*haphel*)
תשא	'you shall carry' (TAD B1.1:13) (*peal*)		
		ינשא	'he will bear' (TAD C1.1:185) (*peal*)
		מנשא	'(to) carry' (e.g., TAD B8.1:14) (*peal*)
		יהנשג	'(he) will overtake/perceive' (TAD C1.1:199) (*haphel*)
		תהנשק	'(do not) kindle' (TAD C1.1:87) (*haphel*)
		אנתן	'I shall give' (e.g., TAD B2.1:7.13, C1.1:66) (*peal*)

---

[20] See also, perhaps, ינטר 'he will keep' (NSaq 37:5) and ינטרו 'let them guard' (26:7, 77 b 2).

Non-prenasalized		Prenasalized	
אתננה	'I would give it' (e.g., TAD A2.1:5; see also B1.1:11) (peal)	אנתננה	'I shall give it' (e.g., TAD B4.6:5, see also D7.29:5) (peal)
		תנתן	'you will give' (e.g., TAD B3.12:23.26.28) (peal)
יִתְּנִנַּהּ	'he gives it' (Daniel 4:14.22.23) (peal)	ינתנהי	'he will give it' (TAD D7.29:9) (peal)[21]
		תנתן	'she will give' (TAD B3.3:10, B3.8:26, D7.43:8) (peal)[22]
נתן	'we shall give' (TAD A4.10:13) (peal)	ננתן	'we shall give' (e.g., TAD B3.4:21, B4.4:11) (peal)
נתנהי	'we shall give it' (TAD A2.1:7) (peal)		
		תנתנון	'you give' (TAD D2.21:4) (peal)
יתנון	'they will give' (TAD D1.17 fragment b:8.9) (peal)	ינתנון	'they will give' (TAD B3.4:18, B4.2:6, D7.56:12) (peal)
		מנתן	'(to) give' (e.g., TAD A6.15:2, B3.4:12) (peal)
		אנתר	'I shall release/he released' (TAD B8.3:6) (peal/aphel)[23]
אַתַּרוּ	'shake!' (Daniel 4:11) (aphel)		
מסלק	'(to) ascend' (TAD B3.10:15) (peal)	מנסק	'(to) ascend' (TAD B3.7:10.13) (peal)
הַסִּקוּ	'(they) brought up' (Daniel 3:22) (haphel)		
		לְ-הַנְסָקָה	'to bring up' (Daniel 6:24) (haphel)
אעל	'I shall enter' (e.g., TAD D7.24:2) (peal)		
		תנעל	'you may come in' (TAD B3.12:22) (peal)
תֵעֲלֻן	'you will enter (?)' (TAD D23.1.VIII:10) (peal)		
		מנעל	'(to) enter' (TAD A6.7:7) (peal)
		הנעלת	'she brought in' (e.g., TAD B2.6:6, B3.3:4) (haphel)
הַעֵלְנִי	'bring me in!' (Daniel 2:24) (haphel)	הנעלו	'bring!' (TAD A6.10:7) (haphel)
לְ-הֶעָלָה	'to bring (them) in' (Daniel 5:7) (haphel)	לְ-הַנְעָלָה	'to bring (them) in' (Daniel 4:3) (haphel)
הֻעַל	'he was brought in' (Daniel 5:13) (huphal)		
		ענז	'goat' (e.g., TAD A4.10:10, D7.57:5)
		ענזא	'the goat' (e.g., TAD C1.1:166)
עִזִּין	'goats' (Ezra 6:17)		
		unqu	'Nackenstück' (?)
		צנפר	'a bird' (TAD C1.1:82)
צִפֲּרַיָּא	'the birds' (Daniel 4:11)	צנפריא	'the birds' (TAD C1.1:186.198)
		qenṣu	'handful' (?)

---

[21] The verb form יתן 'he will give' (AP 81:64) is now read יסן 'Jason' (TAD C3.28:5).

[22] For תתן 'she will give' (AP 81:24), see TAD C3.28:100 (תתו 'Tutu') (see also Folmer 1995: 93 n. 357).

[23] See also, perhaps, ינתר 'he will release' (NSaq 142:3). For הנת[ר]ת 'I (?) have (not) released' (4:4), Porten and Yardeni read הנ°ס°ת [ooo (TAD B8.7:4).

	Non-prenasalized		Prenasalized
		שנציו	'they did (not) succeed' (TAD A6.7:7.13) (Akkadian loanword)[24] (?)
שת	'year of' (KAI 228 A 1)	שנת	'year of' (e.g., TAD A4.5:2, D20.3:3)
שתא	'the year' (TAD D7.40:2)	שנתא	'(this) year' (e.g., TAD A4.1:2, C3.28:50)
		שנתא	'(jar) neck' (TAD D7.57:6) (?)

6.2.1.1. According to the table, prenasalization in Imperial Aramaic is distributed differentially across the phonetic spectrum. The dental stops (*t, d*) are most prone to prenasalization and account for approximately three-quarters (70%) of affected words. The voiceless bilabial stop (*p*) follows, adding another seventh (14%) to the tally. Over four-fifths (84%) of prenasalizing words are confined to these three phones.

The lesser targets of prenasalization subdivide into three categories: stops, which affect approximately one-fiftieth (2%) of the prenasalizing lexicon; fricatives, affecting approximately one-twentieth (5%) of the total; and emphatics, affecting slightly under one-tenth (9%). Among stops, the voiceless velar is prenasalized in two words (חנכה and כנכר), the voiced bilabial may be prenasalized in two cases (אנבה and *zambūru*), and the voiced velar might be prenasalized in two uncertain examples (*ḫangaru* and *nungurtu*). Among fricatives, prenasalization is favored by the sibilant group. The voiceless and voiced alveolars, as well as the correspondent of proto-Aramaic **ś*, undergo prenasalization a few times each (e.g., מנסך, ענז, and מנשא). The voiceless postalveolar fricative might prenasalize once (*kanšu*).[25] Even non-sibilant fricatives — the voiceless (*ḥ*) and voiced pharyngeal (ʿ < **ġ*) — prenasalize, albeit in a restricted manner (e.g., מנחת and מנעל). Finally, among emphatics the voiceless sibilant and voiceless dental can prenasalize (e.g., מנציעת and חנטא); the evidence for a prenasalized emphatic velar is weak (*unqu*).[26]

The last group of consonants does not prenasalize at all. Semivowels (*w, y*) and liquids (*l, r*) do not prenasalize in Imperial Aramaic. Nasals (*m, n*) do not prenasalize. Glottals do not, either (*ʾ, h*).

6.2.1.2. This synopsis suggests that specific features impact prenasalization in Imperial Aramaic. On the negative side, laterals, approximants, and glottal consonants block this change (Ladefoged and Maddieson 1996: 118–19). Nasal consonants prohibit it, too. On the positive side, non-glottal obstruents decidedly prefer the new prenasal element. That is to say, prenasalization targets the least sonorous segments in the language:[27] stops (voiceless before voiced), predominantly dental stops; fricatives; and related emphatics.

6.2.1.3. The synopsis also indicates that the rules governing prenasalization in Imperial Aramaic are different from those in Babylonian Akkadian (see Gropp 1990: 176 with n. 26; cf. Muraoka 1983–84: 91). Whereas prenasalization in Babylonian operates on voiced stops and fricatives, in Aramaic voiced and voiceless consonants jointly prenasalize. Moreover, prenasalization in Aramaic applies to a phone(me) that does not exist in contemporary Akkadian (*ʿayin* < **ġ*) (see Kaufman 1974: 120–21 n. 21). Accordingly, prenasalization in Imperial Aramaic is not directly related to its Babylonian forerunner (cf. Kutscher 1971: 106 = 1977: 56; Macuch 1976: 77; Coxon 1977: 255; Beyer 1984–2004: 1:92 n. 1; and Creason 2004: 401).[28]

---

[24] See Whitehead 1978: 132 n. 84
[25] See n. 37.
[26] For a possible parallel in later Idumean texts, see Lozachmeur and Lemaire 1996: 131–32.
[27] For the sonority hierarchy, see Laver 1994: 503–5.
[28] Folmer 1995: 89 considers the issue "moot."

6.2.2. Phonology

Although each case of prenasalization in Imperial Aramaic develops from a non-glottal obstruent, this phonetic/phonological condition alone does not account for the distribution of the sound change throughout the language. Minimal pairs remain. The prenasalized forms אנפין 'face' and צנפר 'bird', for instance, contrast with שפיר 'beautiful'. אנת(י) 'you' and אנתה 'woman, wife' prenasalize, but יתיר 'extra; more' and מיתתי 'you (feminine singular) die' (TAD B3.5:17) do not. In the same way, ינדשו 'let them demolish' differs from non-nasal שדר 'it sent' (TAD C1.1:101) and אשתדרו 'they intervened' (TAD A4.3:4).

6.2.2.1. The key lies in prenasalizing forms whose targeted cluster does not involve etymological *n.

*hVslVq   > hVssVq-
*Ciwdaʿ   > Ciddaʿ-
*haʿill   > haʿʿil(l)-
*karkar   > kakkar-

As the schema shows, each form passes through a common developmental stage before the onset of prenasalization. סל״ק, for example, usually participates in a sound change that neutralizes the second radical after a contiguous sibilant (e.g., *yislaq- > יסק 'there arises' [e.g., KAI 224:14.15.16 (Old Aramaic)]) (see Brockelmann 1908: §56gγ). יד״ע follows another pattern whereby its root-initial yodh (< *w) assimilates to the subsequent consonant in peal prefix forms (e.g., יִתֵּב 'it will sit' [Daniel 7:26]) (Kautzsch 1884: §43.1b; see also Brockelmann 1908: §268gα; cf. Huehnergard 2004: 143). על״ל usually inflects like other geminates; its first root letter doubles when the inflected form adds a *CV prefix (e.g., הַעֲלֵנִי 'bring me in!';[29] see also תַּדִּק 'it will crush' [Daniel 2:40.44] < דק״ק) (Bauer and Leander 1927: §§16f–h). When regular (morpho)phonological rules operate on these forms, each one develops a geminate cluster in due course.

כנכר/כַּכַּר requires additional comment. For when a reduplicated *CVC noun appears in the West Semitic languages, the second root letter is generally preserved:[30] for example, *qVdqVd > Ugaritic qdqd 'pate', biblical Hebrew קָדְקֹד 'pate', and, perhaps, Hatran qdqdn' 'the speckled one (?)' (H 1052); *sansin > biblical Hebrew סַנְסִנִּים '(date palm) branches'; or *dardar > biblical Hebrew דַּרְדַּר 'thistles', Arabic dardār 'elm (tree)', and Syriac dardrā 'thistle; ulmus campestris'. *karkar seems exempt (cf. Mustafa 1982: 22 [first possibility], on which cf. Tropper 2000: §33.115.44 [4]). Instead, the attested forms of *karkar abide by a different morphophonological patterning in which the second radical assimilates to its consonantal neighbor. This latter pattern is characteristic of Akkadian: qaqqadu 'head'; sissinnu 'date spadix' (see also Ugaritic ssn 'date branch/spadix'); and daddaru '(ill-smelling or thorny plant)', respectively (Brockelmann 1908: §91f, in conjunction with von Soden 1995: §57a).[31] By inference, כנכר/כַּכַּר may be an Akkadian loanword in Aramaic (see kakkartu 'round loaf of bread' and kakkaru '[one talent] metal disk; round loaf of bread'), whose presence in Northwest Semitic dates at least to the mid-second millennium B.C.E. (kkr 'talent' [ka₄-ka₄-ra (RS 16.205 + 192:20.22; see also 51.86:23 [broken])]) (cf. Růžička 1909: 7; and compatibly, Huehnergard 1987: 136). In the shift from *karkar > כַּכַּר, then, there arises a new, non-original geminate cluster (see Poebel 1939: 150, on Akkadian).[32] Thereafter, כנכר > כַּכַּר participates in the same sound change as do the inflected forms of native Aramaic סל״ק, יד״ע, and על״ל.[33]

6.2.2.2. A potential ambiguity arises in the case of prenasalized clusters which derive from an underlying *n (see section 6.1). For on the surface at least, it is uncertain whether the attested Aramaic forms preserve the etymological nasal (e.g., Whitehead 1978: 124 with n. 30; Mustafa 1982: 20–24; and Gropp 1990: 175; see also

---

[29] For the unusual shape and significance of the pretonic syllable, see Bauer and Leander 1927: §18t; and Rosenthal 2006: §20.

[30] For a common West Semitic exception involving a second radical bilabial stop, see Brockelmann 1908: §90a.

[31] For exceptions, see von Soden 1995: §57b; and George 1996.

[32] Because the condition governing prenasalization is regular, other non-productive interpretations of the attested prenasalized element are, in all likelihood, erroneous. Contrast, for example, Bergman 1968: 70; and, differently, Spitaler 1952–54: 265 = 1998: 11, arguing for an analogical nasal element; von Soden 1968: 178–80 = 1985: 113–17, positing nasal suppletion or root augmentation; or Macuch 1989: 22–24; and Militarev and Kogan 2005: lxxvi–lxxvii, on an infixed nun.

[33] Steiner (personal communication) and Lipiński 2001: §23.7 note the longevity of prenasalized כנכר. See Josephus, Antiquities 3.6.7 §144, equating Greek τάλαντον with what "the Hebrews call κίγχαρες" (translation Loeb).

Folmer 1995: 75 n. 185, 746), reinstate the historical nasal (e.g., Bauer and Leander 1927: §13e; and Muraoka 1983–84: 91), or represent a newly created nasal element (e.g., Müller 1991: 22). The phonological history of early Aramaic, however, eliminates all but one of these possibilities. After all, Imperial Aramaic is the linguistic heir of Old Aramaic (for a discussion, see Fales 1996: 56–57), and in Old Aramaic "[n]un is always assimilated to a following consonant" (Kaufman 1997: 119; see also Kutscher 1965: 38; cf. Beyer 1984–2004: 1:28, 89; Muraoka 1983–84: 92; and, somewhat differently, Kottsieper 1990: 60–61). At the time that Imperial Aramaic emerges, the underlying nasal of every *nC sequence is neutralized (e.g., *ʾanta > את 'you') (see, in this context, Spitaler 1952–54: 266 = 1998: 12; cf. Leander 1928: §6j; von Soden 1968: 175 = 1985: 109–10; and, emphatically, Sanmartín 1995:440). Subsequently, as in כַּבַּר and relevant forms of על״ל, יד״ע, and סל״ק, the recently minted geminate cluster participates in prenasalization (אנת > את) (e.g., Rosenthal 2006: §21, with hesitation; see also Blau 1970: 134). In Imperial Aramaic, the nasal segment of nC sequences is therefore new.

6.2.2.3. Because Imperial Aramaic inherits the phonological situation bequeathed by its Old Aramaic ancestor, it is not surprising that remnants from the earlier period persist (see Muraoka and Porten 2003: §§3a, d). For example, in the Bauer-Meissner contract of 515 B.C.E. the majority of *nC clusters replicate the pattern inaugurated in Old Aramaic: אצל 'I shall reclaim' (נצ״ל), תשא 'you shall carry' (נש״א), and אתננהי 'I shall give it' (TAD B1.1:11 [נת״ן]). One form, אנתן 'I shall give' (l. 10 [נת״ן]), signals that prenasalization is beginning to take hold. But there is also a less restrictive interpretation of this evidence (see, e.g., Macuch 1989: 22; and, generally, Gropp 1990: 171) inasmuch as Aramaic orthography, which is conservative in this respect, can mask the extent to which a subphonemic change is spreading throughout the language.[34] In which case, prenasalization may be more widespread than the one innovative form אנתן indicates (see Macuch 1971: 549; and, perhaps, Sanmartín 1995: 459).

Later, the outcome of C: varies considerably. In the early fifth century B.C.E., prenasalization recurs throughout the Cowley ostracon: ינתנו 'let them give' and ענז 'goat' (TAD D7.1:10). In the contemporary Clermont-Ganneau 152, old and new forms are juxtaposed in a single sentence: אפיכי 'your face' and אנפי 'my face', respectively (TAD D7.16:12–13) (see Porten and Greenfield 1968: 221 = Greenfield 2001: 1:45; and Greenfield 1968: 366 n. 41; cf. Muraoka and Porten 2003: §3a, end). But in AP 49, there is no visible trace of prenasalization: חטן 'wheat' (TAD B4.1:2) and מדעם 'something' (l. 3) (see Porten and Greenfield 1968: 221 n. 15 = Greenfield 2001: 1:45 n. 15). Subsequently, in the fourth-century Samaria papyri prenasalization returns to the Imperial standard and becomes, according to Gropp, "absolutely consistent": for example, אנת 'you' (WDSP 1:7.9), ינתן 'he will give' (e.g., 2:6, 3:6), and ננתן 'we will give' (e.g., 4:11, 7:14) (1990: 173 with n. 13). Yet toward the close of Imperial Aramaic something unexpected occurs. The third-century Uruk incantation (Geller 1997–2000, 2001), whose syllabic orthography can express prenasalization (see section 6.1), shows no trace of prenasalization: ⌈maḫ⌉-ḫe-te-e 'to lower him (?)' (l. 3 [*nḥt]), ḫa-[a]l-le-ta₅ 'I brought home' (l. 4 [*ʿll]), and ba-a-a-ta₅ 'in' (literally, 'between') (l. 28 [< *baynt]) (Beyer 1984–2004: 1:92–93). Clearly, prenasalization "did not yet completely become established in all varieties of [Imperial] Aramaic' (Folmer 1995: 706; see also Muraoka and Porten 2003: 15 n. 72). Old, non-nasal forms endure (see Kaufman 1974: 158).

Old forms are also characteristic of the Aramaic documents discovered at Hermopolis (TAD A2.1–7; late sixth–early fifth centuries B.C.E.) (see Kutscher 1970: 369 = 1977: 112). Their lexical distribution is wide indeed: for example, אפיך 'your face', מפקן 'bringing out' (נפ״ק), אתננה 'I will give it', נתנהי 'we shall give it' (נת״ן), and probably מפי 'Memphis' (TAD A2.2:3) < מנפי (e.g., TAD A3.8:7, B8.2:10, C3.27:2) (Porten and Greenfield 1968: 221 = Greenfield 2001: 1:45; and Greenfield 1968: 366).[35] 'Something, anything' usually appears in its old non-nasal form, too: מדעם (TAD A2.1:10, 2.3:10, 2.5:2).[36] In contrast, prenasalization is overtly marked only once: מנדעם (TAD A2.5:4).[37] Folmer raises the possibility that scribal conventions or "a local spelling tradition"

---

[34] See n. 7.

[35] A nasalless form of 'Memphis' also appears in the Saqqara texts (e.g., NSaq 136:2) (Beyer 1984–2004: 1:90).

[36] For derivations that align this prefixed form of יד״ע with others that exhibit the same non-nasal/prenasalized alternation in Imperial Aramaic, see, for example, Nöldeke 1875: §150; or Wright 1890: 145; contrast Kottsieper 1990: 51–54.

[37] Although אנשתה 'his household' (TAD A2.1:14, A2.4:3) may be a second instance, this word is otherwise phonologically problematic (Porten and Greenfield 1968: 220 = Greenfield 2001: 1:44); see also Middle Persian ANŠWTA (ʾNŠWTʾ) = mardōm 'mankind, people'. For etymological proposals, see Kutscher 1971: 116 = 1977: 66; and Porten 1996: 99 n. 4.

may differentiate the Hermopolis letters from those texts found at "Elephantine, where the spellings with *n prevail" (1995: 90). Kutscher, however, focuses on phonology. "It is very important to point out that unlike B[iblical] A[ramaic] and [the Aramaic dialect of] E[lephantine], there are more than twenty cases of assimilation of (and lack of dissimilation by) *n*" (1971: 104 = 1977: 54; see also Mustafa 1982: 20; and Muraoka and Porten 2003: §3a). And the phonological reading may well be correct, since the Hermopolis letters may betray another sound change that carries the "assimilation of ... *n*" one step further. At Hermopolis, nasal assimilation may cross a clitic boundary: הלה 'if not' (TAD A2.2:10) < *הן לה (see TAD C1.1:176) (note, especially, Greenfield 1968: 366–67; see also Porten and Greenfield 1968: 221 = Greenfield 2001: 1:45; Hug 1993: §B.I.3.1.1; and Hoftijzer and Jongeling 1995: 1:286);[38] cf., e.g., מן מפי 'from Memphis' (TAD A2.2:3). The important issue, then, is phonological rather than orthographic (cf. Gropp 1990: 175 n. 21). Hence, the near-absence of prenasalization at Hermopolis is linguistically significant. To all appearances, its dialect is a conservative island which is almost immune to prenasalization as attested in contemporary Aramaic-speaking communities.

6.2.2.4. In those dialects where prenasalization operates, it always affects the least sonorous geminate clusters in the Aramaic phonetic inventory. Yet two types of geminates tend to resist this change. Whitehead identifies the first, noting that "original CC is almost always preserved." For instance, "*all* the examples of pael and hitpael [*sic*] verbal forms" fail to prenasalize (1978: 124 with n. 31 [italics added]). *qattīl nominals do not prenasalize, either (Folmer 1995: 84). Unlike Akkadian (cf. Poebel 1939: 150), then, morphologically conditioned ("original") geminates are largely exempt from prenasalization (see Mustafa 1982: 14–15, 16). The other resistant cluster is delimited by structure; underlying its two segments lay two identical segments with an intervening morphemic boundary. The boundary may be inflectional, as in *mīt-tī > מיתתי 'you die'. Or it may be derivational, as in *mit-takil > מתכל 'relying' (TAD A2.7:2); see also * *'it-'aḥidū* > * *'it-taḥidū* > אתחדו '(they) were seized' (TAD A4.4:6). Prenasalization is blocked when C: originates as *CC or *C-C.

6.2.2.5. Though practically all words and forms abide by the rules of prenasalization, a few do not. In these cases, prenasalization does not operate on obviously secondary geminate clusters, whether derived by regular phonological or morphophonological rule. In one word, in fact, the underlying geminate seems original.

That word is צנפר 'bird' (pl. צנפריא). Its Aramaic cognates uniformly attest to a non-nasal geminate *pp*. Nor do the other Semitic cognates show that this underlying geminate derives from another source. In all probability, then, the cluster underlying צנפר is an original geminate (e.g., Barth 1894: 24; and Dolgopolsky 2004: 420; see also Nöldeke 1875: 119 n. 5), and its prenasalized surface form is phonologically exceptional (cf. Kottsieper 1990: 50, 54–57).

The other exceptions are more mysterious. The first, מנציעת 'the midst of' ~ מציעתא 'the middle/midst', is a morphological puzzle. It is claimed that these forms "must be ... of a rather rare pattern /mVqti:l/" in which a nominalizing *m*- is prefixed to the root מצ״ע (Muraoka and Porten 2003: 13–14 n. 62). But the alleged phonological development of **mVmṣī'at* > *mVṣṣī'at* (*mC > C:) is not attested in this language. Alternatively, מנציעת and מציעתא may reflect a feminine singular *qattīl nominal (Leander 1928: §43o‴).[39] This interpretation cannot be proven either, but it has the advantage of anticipating a Middle Aramaic change whereby *qattīl > *qantīl* (see section 6.3.5). In which case, מציעת > מנציעת forecasts the future. The last exception is *kandu* 'jar' / כנדן 'jars'. Inasmuch as the base form of 'jar' is best explained as *kadd,[40] non-nasal כדא — the attested singular determined form — meets linguistic expectations (cf. Folmer 1995: 86). As for the plural, כדין does not yet appear in Imperial Aramaic, though one example occurs in later Judean Aramaic (Mas 454:1).[41] Two other forms are attested instead. The later exemplar, from the late third century B.C.E., arguably indicates a broken plural: כֹּדָדֻן

---

[38] For a similar phenomenon in PAmh 63, see note 61.

[39] This word appears in other noun patterns, too: for example, Mandaic *miṣat* 'middle of' < **miṣ'-at* (see also Syriac and Babylonian Jewish Aramaic); and Targumic מציעא 'middle' < **maṣī'-*. Contrast Kogan 2005: 523.

[40] For the evidence, see Koehler and Baumgartner 1967–95: 2:439a = 1994–2000: 2:460b; and Huehnergard 1987: 136. Contrast Podolsky 1998: 199–200.

[41] Following the interpretation of Sokoloff 2003: 56a; contrast Cook 2004: 97–98.

(TAD D7.57:7) < *kadad-* (see עממא 'the people*s*' [TAD C1.1:98.189] < *ʿamam-* [singular **ʿamm-*]). The older example, from ca. 475 B.C.E., is nasalized: כנדן. It apparently shares its base with the singular. For just as *kandu* is the Babylonian reflex of כדא < *kadd*, כנדן develops from כדין < **kaddīn*. The two prenasalized forms of **kadd* violate phonological rule in the same way.

There is a feature shared by these exceptions. Prenasalized צנפר(יא) originates in **pp.* מנציעת evolves from **ṣṣ*. And *kandu*/כנדן is traceable to **dd*. The shared feature lies in the character of the prenasalizing geminates; they are among the least sonorous segments of Aramaic. From this perspective, then, the exceptional cases of prenasalization follow the phonetic/phonological model of the rule-driven prototypes (section 6.2.1.2). But they also represent a new development in the scope of prenasalization. The condition that blocks the prenasalization of original, morphologically defined geminates is already eroding in Imperial Aramaic.

6.3. Middle Aramaic

Despite its strong foundation in Imperial Aramaic, prenasalization does not spread quickly to later dialects. On the contrary, it spreads slowly and unevenly, as in Imperial Aramaic itself. Likewise, the linguistic tensions present in Imperial Aramaic are present in Middle Aramaic. Prenasalization is competing with older, non-nasal forms and, at the same time, is encroaching on new morphophonological territory. The patterns of Imperial Aramaic haltingly begin to unfold.

6.3.1. Palmyrean

In Palmyrean, prenasalization targets only secondarily formed geminate clusters. The second-person masculine singular independent subject pronoun, for example, has the form *ʾnt* (PAT 0555:4.7). The other prenasalized forms each have non-nasal variants (see Rosenthal 1936:40). *ʾntth* 'his wife' (e.g., 1787:3) has the variant *ʾtth* (e.g., 0770); see also *ʾtt* 'the woman' (0259 II 48; see also l. 127 [broken]). 'The city' appears as *mdyntʾ* (e.g., 0340 A 1) as well as *mdytʾ* (e.g., 1063:3); see also *mdynth* 'his city' (e.g., 1062 B 3) ~ *mdyth* (e.g., 1382:2) and *mdth* (0278:7) (see Cantineau 1935: 46). Or, among initial *nun peal* prefixed verb forms, 'give' can have a prenasal segment: *mntn* '(to) give' (0991:16) and *yntn* '(whoever) will give' (1981:7) ~ *ytn* 'he will give' (0259 II 6.70).

But the majority of Palmyrean forms do not overtly participate in prenasalization (see Nöldeke 1870: 96; and Mustafa 1982: 25). Except for the forms already listed, secondary geminate clusters derived from **nC* are not prenasalized in Palmyrean orthography:[42] for example, *ʾpy* 'according to' < **ʾanp-*, *ḥṭʾ* 'wheat' (PAT 0259 II 59) < **ḥinṭ-*, *ʿz* 'goat' < **ʿinz-*, and *štʾ* 'the year' (e.g., 2743:4) < **šant-*. Nor do initial *nun* roots, nouns as well as verbs: for example, *mqp* 'exit', *mqpn* 'export', *ʾpq* 'he spent' (1378:5), and *mpq* '(he who) exports' (0259 II 86.112) < **npq* (Cantineau 1935: 45–46; and Kutscher 1957: 19 = 1977: 21). Forms of **slq* and **ʿll* do not prenasalize: for example, *ʾsq* 'he brought' (e.g., 2743:4) and *msq* 'specified' (e.g., 0259 I 8); and *yʿl* '(whoever) brings in' (e.g., 2760:2) and *mʿl* '(he who) imports' (e.g., 0259 II 80), respectively. Other, miscellaneous forms are not prenasalized, either: for example, *kkryn* 'talents' (2634:5), *mdʿm/mdʿn* 'something, anything', and *mṣʿytʾ* '(the) middle' (0193:6). With a handful of exceptions, then, geminate clusters — whether secondary or original[43] — do not prenasalize in Palmyrean Aramaic. Prenasalization barely qualifies as a sound change in this dialect.

6.3.2. Nabatean

Prenasalization is more advanced in Nabatean (see Kutscher 1957: 19–20 = 1977: 21–22). According to the present evidence, the second-person singular independent subject pronouns are invariably nasalized: *ʾnt* (masculine) (e.g., NH 3:36)[44] and *ʾnty* (feminine) (e.g., 1:51). The nominal form *ʾnpy* 'the surface of' is

---

[42] Yet see n. 7.

[43] Contrast Cantineau 1935: 46, tentatively citing *rnbt* 'much' < **rabbat*, on which contrast PAT *dbnt!* 'what I built' (0570:1), following Nöldeke 1870: 103.

[44] For the second-person masculine singular pronoun *ʾntʾ* in NH 36:18.22 (cited, e.g., by Hoftijzer and Jongeling 1995: 1:85), Yardeni now reads *ʾnt* (ad loc.).

prenasalized (l. 33). And in at least one other noun, a prenasalized form alternates with its older, non-nasal variant: *'ntth* 'his wife' (e.g., CIS II 173:3–4) ~ *'tth* (e.g., Hackl, Jenni, and Schneider 2003: M.065.01:4); see also *šnt* 'year of' (e.g., K.006.01:8) ~ *št* (e.g., Z.025.01:3). Each time, the prenasalized form descends from a geminate cluster whose origin is **n*C (Cantineau 1930–32: 1:44–45; and Mustafa 1982: 25).

Whereas root-initial **n*C assimilates in *mṣb'* 'the stele, idol' (Hackl, Jenni, and Schneider 2003: N.060.25.01:1) and, perhaps, *mtn'* '(the) gift' (NH 3:43, 36:13; see also מתנא in TAD D8.3:7.11.16), elsewhere it undergoes prenasalization. Nominals such as *mnpqhm* 'their exiting' (e.g., NH 36:6.12) and, perhaps, *mnsb* 'carrying (?), loading (?)' (l. 30) participate in this sound change. Inflected verb forms do, too: for example, *'npqt* 'you brought out' (l. 24) and *tnpq* 'you will bring out' (ll. 2.22) < *npq;[45] or *'ntn* 'I will give' (4:14), *tntnwn* 'you will give' (4Q343 Letter nab Recto 5), and *mntn* '(to) give' (e.g., NH 2:9) < *ntn.[46] Prenasalization of Nabatean (**n*C >) C: > *n*C seems productive.

The remaining evidence for prenasalization in Nabatean is mixed. Apparently, the reduplicated noun *kkryn* 'talents' (NH 22:33) does not prenasalize. But *mnd'm* 'something, anything' does (e.g., 6:14, 9:6). Also, to judge from the nominal form *mn'lhm* 'their entering' (36:6.12), *'*ll* probably prenasalizes whenever a *CV prefix is added to the root. Prenasalization in Nabatean, then, often — but not always — occurs when the targeted geminate cluster is secondary (cf. Cantineau 1930–32: 1:44).

6.3.3. Aramaic Words in Iranian Texts[47]

The next stage in the development of Middle Aramaic prenasalization appears in Iranian texts. These texts are subdivided by period and their use of Aramaic words. First, in Parthian times (ca. 210 B.C.E.–224 C.E.),[48] the texts are written in a pastiche of Aramaic and Parthian words. Later, in Sassanian texts (224–651 C.E.), scribes "still wrote Aramaic words" (Skjærvø 1996: 520) but without their older literal and grammatical Aramaic values (Skjærvø 1995: 303). In this later period, Aramaic words are "a scribal devise [*sic*] to write the corresponding Iranian words" (e.g., MN = *az* 'from, than') (Skjærvø 1995: 287). Such ciphers, formerly known as ideograms or logograms, are labeled "heterograms." By convention, the Aramaic terms in Iranian texts of both periods are transliterated with capital letters.[49]

Prenasalization already begins in the Parthian period (Coxon 1977: 256). Among verbs, the imperfect form of 'give' is reasonably well-attested, and it is prenasalized in each occurrence: YNTN- and TNTNW(-). Among nominals, the evidence is weaker but corroborative. The second-person masculine singular independent subject pronoun is ANT ('NT), a *hapax legomenon* found in the very last Parthian inscription (Paikuli §48 [292 C.E.]). 'Woman' is ANTT ('NTT), another *hapax legomenon* appearing in a Greek-Aramaic bilingual from Georgia (KAI 276:3).[50] Still, the evidence is consistent: an underlying **n*C cluster has the Parthian reflex NC.[51]

The extent to which prenasalization operates elsewhere in Parthian texts is not certain. At Nisa, *haphel* forms of *'*ll* prenasalize: HNOLT (HN'LT) 'delivered (?)' and HNOLW (HN'LW) 'delivered (?)' (Sznycer 2003: 648 n. 20; see, however, Skjærvø 1995: 291). But the evidence ends there. No other native Aramaic word seems to participate in this change.

---

[45] For *ytpq* (CIS II 215:4) < *ytnpq (e.g., Kutscher 1957: 20 = 1977: 22), see Cantineau 1930–32: 1:81.

[46] For *y/ktn/bw* in NH 4:19, Yardeni now reads *ytnw* 'they may set' (2000: Errata). See Yadin et al. 2002: 1:253.

[47] For Iranian texts from the Parthian period, see Gignoux 1972: 42–68; and Skjærvø 1983. For Sassanian texts, see Gignoux 1972: 8–39; Nyberg 1964–74: 2:1–7; and 1988.

[48] The system itself may have originated earlier, though (see Ebeling 1941: 106; and Kutscher 1970: 393–99 = 1977: 137–42).

[49] For the current transliteration system, see Skjærvø 1996: 520; and 1995: 288. In cases where the Iranological system does not transparently convey the Aramaic term, a double transliteration will be used: the current system, followed by the more traditional Semitic equivalent as used by Gignoux 1972 and Nyberg 1964–74 (e.g., ANPE ['NPH] 'face').

[50] For a recent autograph, see Tsereteli 1998: 77 fig. 1.

[51] ŠNT 'year', however, probably does not represent prenasalization (see Ebeling 1941: 61). Less clear is the interpretation of ONBYN ('NBYN) 'grapes' (= Middle Persian ANBE ['NBH]). It may be structurally akin to biblical Aramaic אִנְּבָה. Alternatively, it may be related to Ugaritic *ġnb* (**qVtVl-*) or biblical Hebrew עֵנָב (**qital-*) (see Ebeling 1941: 14). In this latter case, a vowel separates the nasal and stop.

After the Parthian period, the evidence for prenasalization increases dramatically. One heterogram suggests the formation of secondary geminates: AZ ('Z) 'goat' < *ʿinz (cf. Skjærvø 1990: 97); see also the emended form GWBYTA (GWBYT') 'cheese' < *gubintāʾ (?). Other heterograms, however, take the next step. The new geminate prenasalizes in several common nouns such as ANPE ('NPH) 'face', MNGLA (MNGL') 'sickle',[52] and MNDOM (MNDʿM) '(some)thing'. Verb forms prenasalize, too. Indeed, initial *nun* verbs always prenasalize when their underlying form contains a *nC sequence: for example, YNSBWN-/YNSḆWN- 'take' < *yinsab- (*peal* imperfect); HNHTWN(-) (ḤNḤTWN[-]) 'put down' < *hanḥit- (*haphel* perfect); and YHNCLWN-/ YḤNCLWN- (YḤNṢLWN-) 'take away' < *yVhanṣil- (*haphel* imperfect). In Sassanian heterograms, secondary geminates are regularly prenasalized.

Ebeling suggests that prenasalization also affects original geminates (1941: 111). The evidence, however, is absent. Ebeling's own example of *tt (> *nt) > ND is a phantom. *dd does not prenasalize in GDE (GDH) 'Fortune, Fate' or ŠDRWN- 'send' (*pael*). *qattīl adjectives retain their old form: for example, +KBYR/KBYR 'great' and ŠPYL/ŠPYR 'good, lovely, pleasing'. Isolated nouns do, too: for example, ḴBA/KPA (KB'/KP') '(a measure)' and KKA (KK') 'tooth'. The only possible example of prenasalization is GNDA (GND') 'army' (e.g., Nöldeke 1875: §68; see also Nyberg 1988: 119–20). But even this example is unlikely, since GNDA (GND') is not Semitic in origin but Iranian, whence it was borrowed into Aramaic (e.g., Brockelmann 1928: 104; and, in detail, Rossi 2002). In Parthian and Sassanian Iranian documents, then, prenasalization in Aramaic words is restricted to secondarily formed geminates.

6.3.4. Qumran[53]

The Aramaic material discovered at Qumran shows further developments in the spread of prenasalization. In one, the sound change affects the geminate radical of the *pael* stem: חנבלו 'they damaged' (4Q532 EnGiants[d] ar 2 9) (Beyer 1984–2004: 2:49). This change, however, is not represented in other *pael* forms: for example, חבלת 'she (?) damaged' (4Q123a Levi[b] ar 3–4 5), חבלתון 'you damaged' (4Q203 EnGiants[a] ar 8 11), חֹבּלא 'they mutilated' (1Q20 apGen xiii 16), as well as מחבל 'ruined' (4Q531 EnGiants[c] ar 18 4 [passive]). Nor is it represented in *qattīl forms: e.g., ספיר 'sapphire' (4Q554 NJ[a] ar 3 ii 5; see also 2Q24 NJ ar 3 2 [broken]; 4Q196 papTob[a] ar 18 7; 11Q10 tgJob xii 3) and שפיר 'pleasant, beautiful' (4Q213a Levi[b] ar 1 16; see also 1Q20 apGen xx 2.4; 4Q202 En[b] ar 1 ii 3). In another development, scholars generally recognize a semantic distinction between non-nasal and prenasalized outcomes of (* ʾanp >) * ʾap:, at least in the Job targum: אפה 'his nose' (singular) (11Q10 tgJob xxxv 3.5) versus אנפוהי 'his face' (xxiii 4; see also vi 8 [broken]) (e.g., García Martínez, Tigchelaar, and van der Woude 1998: 89; see also Greenfield and Sokoloff 1992: 85 = Greenfield 2001: 1:479; cf. Fitzmyer 2004: 194). The innovations at Qumran therefore include an incipient *panel* stem and a limited phonemic status of prenasalization (see section 6.4).

Outside of these examples, prenasalization conforms to the pattern set in Imperial Aramic. A few terms strongly prefer a prenasalized realization: for example, אנתה 'woman, wife' (see also אנתּוֹ 'wifehood' [1Q20 apGen vi 10]), אנתה 'you (masculine singular)' (~ אתה [4Q246 apocrDan ar i 2.3]), and אנת(ו)ן 'you (masculine plural)' (~ את[ו]ן [4Q212 En[g] ar 1 ii 25]). And root-final *nun*, which is twice neutralized before an adjacent feminine suffix *t* — מדיתא 'the country' (4Q214a Levi[e] ar 2–3 ii 1) and מדיתון 'their city/province' (1Q20 apGen xxii 4)[54] — is elsewhere restored under this same condition: for example, מדינתא 'the province' (e.g., 4Q318 Zodiology and Brontology ar viii 7.7), [מ]דינתהון 'their [c]ity/[c]ountry' (11Q10 tgJob xxvii 8), as well as לבונתא 'the incense' (11Q18 NJ ar 20 5) and עדינתי 'my pleasure' (1Q20 apGen ii 14; see also l. 9). Under these limited circumstances, the preference for prenasalization is marked.

---

[52] For etymological discussions, see Cohen and Klein 2001: 251–60, and, briefly, Watson 2003: 89. For non-nasal Aramaic cognates, see מגל 'sickle' (KAI 315:15) and מגלא 'the sickle' (1Q20 apGen xv 10).

[53] For the present purposes, the evidence of Jewish Literary Aramaic will be limited to texts found at Qumran. For linguistic support, see Fassberg 2002: 24–26.

[54] For this latter form, contrast Kaufman 1983: 51–52 = 1984: 91–92.

Otherwise, prenasalization in Qumran Aramaic is phonologically consistent but is inconsistently represented in the orthography (Schattner-Rieser 2004: §6e; see also Cook 1998: 363). Several nominals, for instance, take two forms: for example, מנדע 'knowledge' (e.g., 4Q204 En[c] ar 1 vi 12; 4Q213a Levi[b] ar 1 14; see also 1Q20 apGen ii 22) ~ מדע (4Q212 En[g] ar 1 iv 13), [מנד]עם 'anything' (4Q196 papTob[a] ar 2 2) ~ מדעם̊ (4Q534 Birth of Noah[a] ar 1 i 4), חנטין 'wheat' (4Q351 Account of Cereal A ar i 2) ~ חטא (11Q10 tgJob xx 1), and שנׄתא 'the year' (4Q543 Visions of Amram[a] ar 1 3; see also 4Q545 Visions of Amram[c] ar 1a i 3 [broken]) ~ שתא (1Q20 apGen xii 15; 4Q550 PrEsther[a] ar 3).[55] *Peal* imperfect forms of יד״ע favor the prenasalized variant: for example, ינדע 'he will learn, understand, know' (1Q20 apGen ii 20; 4Q212 En[g] ar 1 v 15; see also 4Q534 Birth of Noah[a] ar 1 i 5 [broken]; 11Q10 tgJob xxix 9 [broken]) and תנדעונה 'you will know him' (4Q542 TQahat ar 1 i 2) ~ תדעון 'you will know' (4Q212 En[g] ar 1 ii 19; see also 1Q20 apGen i 4). The prenasalized variant is also favored among prefixed forms of נת״ן, but to a lesser extent: for example, אנתן 'I shall give' (1Q20 apGen xxi 12; see also l. 14), תׅנתן 'you will give' (4Q530 EnGiants[b] ar 2 ii + 6–12 [?] 14), ינתן 'he will give' (4Q246 apocrDan ar ii 8; see also 4Q197 Tob[b] ar 4 ii 5), תנתנון 'you will give' (4Q542 TQahat ar 1 i 10), and ינתנון 'they will give' (4Q196 papTob[a] ar 17 ii 14) ~ תתן 'you will give' (11Q10 tgJob xxvi 2), נתן 'we will pay back, give' (4Q530 EnGiants[b] ar 1 i 5; 4Q543 Visions of Amram[a] ar 2 1.2), and תתנון 'you will give' (4Q213 Levi[a] ar 2 7; see also 4Q203 EnGiants[a] ar 3 4; 4Q542 TQahat ar 1 i 5). In contrast, very few prenasalized forms of על״ל occur at Qumran: [י]נעול 'it does (not) come in' (11Q10 tgJob xxxvi 2; see also vi 3) ~ יעלון 'they will (not) enter' (4Q213 Levi[a] ar 1 ii 1), יעלן '(they [feminine plural]) enter' (1Q20 apGen xx 6), מעל 'entry' (11Q18 NJ ar 28 3; see also 1Q20 apGen xix 14; 4Q204 En[c] ar 5 ii 18 [broken]), אעל 'he brought (them) in' (4Q197 Tob[b] ar 4 iii 4), אעלת 'I was brought in' (4Q538 TJud ar 2 2), etc. Prenasalized forms of נפ״ק are a minority: for example, ינפק 'he will come forth' (4Q201 En[a] ar 1 i 5; 11Q10 tgJob xxxiii 3), אנפק 'he brought out' (1Q20 apGen xxii 14; see also v 27), and ינפק 'he sends forth' (11Q10 tgJob xxix 1) ~ יפוק '(whoever) will come forth' (1Q20 apGen xxii 34; 6Q14 Apocr ar 14 i 4; see also 1Q20 apGen xiv 13; 4Q540 apocrLevi[a]? ar 1 4 [broken]; 4Q541 apocrLevi[b]? ar 1 i 2; 4Q543 Visions of Amram[a] ar 28 1 [broken]; 11Q10 tgJob xxxi 2, xxxvi 5), יפק(ו)ן 'they come out' (xxxvi 5.7), מפק '(to) go out' (4Q209 Enastr[b] ar 7 iii 2; 11Q10 tgJob xxx 7; see also 1Q20 apGen xxii 30), and יפק{ו}ן 'they will send (them) out' (11Q10 tgJob xxxii 3; see also 1Q20 apGen xx 32 [broken]). So too, other, less frequent initial *nun* roots — for example, נט״ל, נת״ת, and נס״ב — are evenly distributed between prenasalized and non-nasal forms. In the Aramaic dialect of Qumran, then, prenasalization is both rule-driven and unsystematically expressed.

The degree to which prenasalization operates at Qumran is more restricted than in Imperial Aramaic (Cook 1998: 363). Not only is the change itself less diffused, but it seems to skip diagnostic words and forms which are prenasalized in the earlier period. For example, *aphel* forms of סל״ק are not overtly prenasalized: אסקת 'I offered' (1Q20 apGen xxi 20), אסקה 'he brought it up' (11Q18 NJ ar 13 4), מסקין 'offering' (4Q537 TJacob? ar 12 2), and אׄסקא '(to) offer' (4Q214b Levi[f] ar 5–6 i 3; see also 4Q214 Levi[d] ar 1 6 [broken]). 'Bird' is not prenasalized: צפר 'a bird' (11Q10 tgJob xxxv 8), צפרי 'birds of' (xiii 2), and צפריא 'the birds' (xxvi 6). Nor are מציעא 'the middle' (4Q554 NJ[a] ar 1 i 13), מציעיא 'the middle (gate?)' (ii 30), and [מצׄ]יעא '[the] mid[dle]' (5Q15 NJ ar 1 i 5). Despite its innovations, prenasalization in Qumran Aramaic is still in the process of developing.

6.3.5. Hatran

In Hatran Aramaic, prenasalization extends further. Like the western Aramaic dialect of Qumran, the *pael* can have an innovative form. *šdr* 'send' acquires a prenasal segment in H 342:13: *lšndrh* 'he will send him (?)' (Beyer 1984–2004: 2:50). The other innovation, which does not occur at Qumran, affects the *qattīl* adjective 'beautiful, good; (adverb) well, magnificently'. It can assume a conservative form, whether *špr* (H 309) or *špyr* (50:2). More often, though, it is prenasalized: *šnpr* (178:2, 389:1) and *šnpyr* (e.g., 23:2.5, 25:2.3, 52:3, 53:4, etc.) (e.g., Jensen 1919: 1045; and 1920: 27; see also Mustafa 1982: 26). At Hatra, prenasalization operates on original geminates of two different morphological classes.

---

[55] On the latter, contrast Collins and Green 1999: 40; and Crawford 2002: 122 (ad 4Q550a PrEsther[b] 3).

Like *šp(y)r ~ šnp(y)r*, a popular Hatran noun has non-nasal and prenasalized variants. By most accounts, that noun means 'Fortune, Fate'. Derived from **gadd-*, its inherited form is preserved in *gdˀ* (e.g., H 288 b 8, 297:2) and *gdh* 'his Fate' (74:4); see also the personal names *gdyhb* (e.g., 13:2, 23:2) and *ˁbdgdˀ* (27:7). Its innovative form has a pre-dental *n* (Caquot 1963: 87): *gndˀ* (e.g., 58:2, 235:1, 288 c 3), *gndh* (e.g., 79:1, 125:2), and *gndhwn* 'their Fortune, Fate' (79:10); see also *gndnˀ* 'the fortunate' (1039:1; see also 380 [broken]). Macuch, though, objects and counters that each form is lexically distinct: namely, *gdˀ* 'Fortune, Fate' (Mandaic *gada*; Middle Persian GDE [GDH]) and *gndˀ* 'army' (Mandaic *gunda*; Middle Persian GNDA [GNDˀ]) (1976: 7). But the objection is implausible (Altheim and Stiehl 1964–69: 4:243–45, 250–51). Hatran *gdˀ* and *gndˀ* appear in similar contexts: for example, *qdm mrn wgdh* 'before our lord and his Fate' (74:4) and *qdm brmryn wgndh* 'before Br-mryn and his Fate' (125:2). They also appear in identical phrases: for example, *gdˀ dy rmgw* 'the Fate of Rmgw' (406; see also 409 III 6–7) and *gndˀ drmgw* 'the Fate of Rmgw' (413 II 2–3); see also *lgdˀ rbˀ* (e.g., 408:3) and *lgndˀ r[bˀ]* (1053:2). Despite Macuch, then, Hatran Aramaic has two alternating forms of the nominal 'Fortune, Fate': an older, non-nasal *gd-*, and a more recent, prenasalized *gnd-*.

Prenasalization in Hatran is otherwise regular. 'Woman, wife' has a prenasalized form: *ˀntt* 'wife of' (H 35:3, 63:1). Initial *nun* verbs can restore an underlying **nC* cluster: *lnsb* '(whoever) will take' (281:3.9) (*peal*) and *lnpq* '(whoever) will bring out' (342:8) (*aphel*). *šntˀ* 'the year' may appear once (1039:4).[56] 'Because' is prenasalized, too: *mnṭlt* (344:7); cf. Palmyrene *mṭl*. Still, non-nasal forms may be recorded at Hatra as well (Beyer 1998: 127). Among the candidates, *lṭrh* (232 Va 4) and *lṭr* (016:6) may be *peal* forms of **nṭr* 'guard, watch, keep' (so, e.g., Degen 1973–74: 405; and Vattioni 1994: 90 [one possibility], respectively; cf. Aggoula 1991: 116). *ˁš* (034:1) may be an alternate form of **ˁz* 'goat' < **ˁinz-* (so Segal 1986: 72; and, tentatively, Vattioni 1994: 96). *lˁwl* (29:5) may be derived from *peal* **ˁll* (so, e.g., Hillers 1972: 55). For Vattioni, *mdˁn* in 74:8 may be a variant of *m(n)dˁm* (1981: 48, followed by Hoftijzer and Jongeling 1995: 2:598). To this extent, then, the phonological pattern in Hatran Aramaic resembles that of other Middle Aramaic dialects: the coexistence of prenasalized and non-nasal forms.

6.3.6. Papyrus Amherst 63[57]

Among the Middle Aramaic texts in this sample, PAmh 63 is the most difficult. Written in Demotic script by an Egyptian scribe to express an Aramaic dialect which the scribe may not have known, PAmh 63 is a gaggle of problems, of which two are particularly ominous. First, the entire text has not yet been published, except in translation (Steiner 1997). Second, the published sections do not necessarily establish the original text. The two teams that have studied the manuscript often disagree on a number of issues, including readings, grammar, interpretation, and translation. Textual judgments change over time, too. A canonical version of PAmh 63 is presently unavailable.

The research teams, however, agree on two important orthographic principles operating in this text. They agree that the Demotic script does not transparently express every Aramaic phone(me) (e.g., Nims and Steiner 1983: 262; and Vleeming and Wesselius 1985–90: 2:19). Sometimes, a Demotic form must be decoded and its Aramaic shape restored in order to make plain sense: for example, $r.k\bar{r}yk.^m$ = *lgryk* 'your feet' (XXI/4). Conversely, the teams agree that each segment in the Demotic script need not be phonetically salient. For example, whenever a non-alphabetic Demotic sign in PAmh 63 ends in *mn*, the final nasal is silent, even if that segment is in turn followed by a nasal phonetic complement (see Steiner 2000: 194 with n. 42; and, with less commitment, Vleeming and Wesselius 1985–90: 1:18): for example, $\bar{l}\bar{m}\bar{n}ryky^m$ (*mlyky*) 'your words' (XIX/7) ~ $m.ry^m$ (*mly*) 'my words' (XX/7), and $\bar{m}\bar{n}ny.my^m$ 'from the days of' (XVIII/8) ~ $\bar{m}\bar{n}y.mye$ (*mymy*) (XVIII/8). Stated broadly, the signs $\bar{m}\bar{n}, \bar{\bar{m}}\bar{\bar{n}}, \bar{M}\bar{n}$, and $\bar{l}\bar{m}\bar{n}$ do not establish prenasalization in PAmh 63.

---

[56] Contrast *šnt...* in the *editio princeps* (Bertolino 1996: 144).

[57] For a working translation, lineation, and references to prior literature on PAmh 63, see Steiner 1997. For the text's Middle Aramaic date, see, for example, Kaufman 1997: 117; for earlier assignments, see Steiner 1997: 310; and, differently, Vleeming and Wesselius 1985–90: 2:3–4.

Most of the evidence for prenasalization in this text is mixed. Prenasalization certainly occurs, but non-nasal and prenasalized forms also alternate in the orthography (see Folmer 1995: 92 with n. 350). For example, both genders of the second-person singular independent subject pronoun have two forms (see Kottsieper 1997: 428 n. 191): masculine ⌈e⌉.nt^m (⌈ʾ⌉nt) (XVII/7) and .nty^m [sic] (XV/3) ~ .t (ʾt) (XV/3; see also XVI/3), and feminine .nty^m (ʾnty) ~ ety^m (ʾty) (see, especially, XIII/17). 'Face' usually appears with a prenasal element, as in īnpyh.^m (ʾnpyh) 'her face' (XX/12), yet a non-nasal variant may be found in e.p.yn.^m (ʾpyn) 'our faces' (XI/9).[58] In other nominals, though, only prenasalized forms are attested: eynt⌈./y⌉^m (ʾntty) '⌈my⌉ wife' (XVI/7), šnt.^m (šnt ʾ) 'the year' (XVII/5.10), as well as the foreign word snm^mpr 'lapis lazuli' (XV/9–10).[59] In PAmh 63, then, prenasalization is a linguistic fact. It operates on secondary geminates, produces homorganic nasal-obstruent clusters (see Spitaler 1952–54: 259, 260 with n. 6 = 1998: 5, 6 with n. 6; cf. Vleeming and Wesselius 1985–90: 1:50, in conjunction with 2:21), and coexists with older, non-nasal forms.

The alternation between non-nasal and prenasalized forms of initial *nun* verbs is just as untidy. For example, the *aphel* of *npq usually shows prenasalization: īnp.kẇ (ʾnpqw) 'take out!' (XVIII/9) and īnp.kẇ 'I will take out' (l. 12). But a non-nasal variant may also be attested in ep.k⌈.⌉t^m (ʾpqt) 'I have taken out' (VIII/3). The *aphel* of *nḥt seems to have only non-nasal reflexes: for example, y.ḥ.t^m 'he would lay down' (V/9) and yḥ.tẇ 'let them be brought down' (XVIII/5 [passive]).[60] *Peal* forms are a hodgepodge, too. Imperfect forms of *nsy prenasalize: ynn̄sȳ (ynsy) 'he would carry' (V/10), yn̄sȳ (V/10), and yns̄ẇ 'let them lift' (VII/11). *nšq does not: y.š.k.^m 'let them kiss' (V/12; see also XVI/12). *nṭr has both forms: ytr̄.^m (yṭr) 'he will guard' (e.g., X/13) and t.nt⌈.⌉r.^m 'you protect' (XII/17). The reflexes of *nC in PAmh 63 therefore conform to the pattern that Segert describes: "Regressive total assimilation of the nasal /n/ to the immediately following consonant is very frequent,[61] but forms without assimilation are attested" (1997: 121).

Folmer adds that "there is also evidence for nC where n is not etymological" (1995: 92). For example, in inflected forms of *gll the prefixed verb can appear without a nasal element: t̄ḥ.r^m (tgl) 'you may (not) enter' (III/9) (*peal*). More often, though, the form is prenasalized: for example, hn⌈ḥ⌉r (hn⌈g⌉l) 'he brou⌈ght⌉ in' (XXI/9), hnḥr^m 'bring in!' (XX/9), hnḥ.rẇ 'they were brought in' (XVIII/2) (*haphel*), and mnḥ.r^m 'brought in' (IVA/10) (*aphel* passive). Similarly, the text may indicate two prefixed forms of *slq: non-nasal ⌈m⌉sk⌈m⌉ (⌈m⌉sq) '⌈is⌉ bring⌈ing⌉ up' (XVI/4) (*aphel*) and prenasalized m.^m⌈n̊⌉[.]⌈s⌉k^m h̄nn.⌈k⌉st^m (m⌈ns⌉q h⌈nq⌉st) 'in⌈deed⌉ you were/I was brou⌈ght⌉ up' (XVII/1–2) (*peal/aphel-haphel* passive).[62] Prenasalization does not, however, extend to the *peal* imperfect forms of *ydʿ: e.t.ʿ^m (ʾdʿ) 'let me know' (VI/2; see also l. 9) and yt.ʿ^m (ydʿ) 'let him know' (XIX/7). As in Imperial Aramaic, secondary geminates in PAmh 63 can, but need not, prenasalize.

The status of original geminates is not clear. Most do not have prenasalized forms: for example, k̇.t^m (gd) 'Fortune' (XIX/15) < *gadd, k.py^m 'my hands' (VI/3.9) < *kapp-, and m^m.bs̄m̄ (mbsm ʾ) 'perfumed' (XVI/13) (*pael* passive). Yet Steiner and Nims note a truly "unexpected case of nasalization < gemination" (1984: 102):[63] w̄y.m⌈n⌉rr.^m (wym[n]ll) 'and he was addressing' (XX/15) (*pael*); see also the orthographically moot forms wyl̄ m̄nr.r.^m (l. 13), w̄yM̄nrr.^m (XXI/2; see also XX/18, XXII/7), and m̄n̄nr.r.^m (mll) 'speak! (feminine singular)' (XIX/7) (*pael*). Indeed, this case is remarkable because prenasalization operates on an underlying geminate liquid.[64]

---

[58] Combining the reading of Vleeming and Wesselius 1985–90: 2:75 with the translation of Steiner 1997: 317b.

[59] s̄n̄w̄.ry.^m (snwry ʾ) 'blinding light' (XIII/6) may belong here, too.

[60] Contrast nn̄byh^m (nnbyg) 'let us cause to flow' (VI/6) and n̄byḥ (ʾnbyg) 'cause (it) to flow!' (XII/7) < *nbg (Steiner and Nims 1984: 101 with n. 49). Steiner has since corrected these readings (see Steiner and Moshavi 1995: 1266; and Steiner 1997: 313a, 318b), following Vleeming and Wesselius 1982: 501 and 1985–90: 1:62, 68, respectively.

[61] See also *min > m 'from' before a clitic boundary: for example, mhyk.r.^m (mhykl ʾ) 'from the palace' (XIX/8; see also XVIII/7). Contrast Nims and Steiner 1983: 266a.

[62] The interpretation of the participle follows Steiner and Nims 1985: 69; contrast Kottsieper 1997: 391–92.

[63] The other case cited is m̄nnr.r.^my.^m (m[n]rry ʾ) 'bitters' (VI/8) < *marrīr-. It was later retracted because the nasal, written with a non-alphabetic sign ending in mn, does not unambiguously represent a true nasal segment (see above).

[64] For another, disputed case, see Vleeming and Wesselius 1985–90: 1:91.

Vleeming and Wesselius adduce 'brothers' as an additional candidate of a prenasalized geminate.[65] This plural noun appears in two forms in PAmh 63, both of which are derived from *'aḫḫ-.[66] One form is eḥyky^m 'your brothers' (XI/4). The other is unusual: .nḥy 'my brothers' (l. 5). eḥyky^m has a conservative spelling. .nḥy is an innovation, for "'aḫḫay becomes 'anḫay." The innovation is "the dissimilation of doubled ḫa into nun-ḫa" (Vleeming and Wesselius 1985–90: 2:82). Here too, a morphologically conditioned geminate cluster prenasalizes.[67]

The evidence for prenasalization in PAmh 63 is relatively consistent. Secondary geminates, regardless of origin, can prenasalize. To this extent, PAmh 63 reflects an old pattern laid down in most Imperial Aramaic dialects (cf., in this context, Vleeming and Wesselius 1985–90: 2:23–24). But PAmh 63 shows that original geminates can occasionally prenasalize as well. For as in Qumran and Hatran Aramaic, the *pael* stem is affected once.[68] Still, PAmh 63 reflects a unique Middle Aramaic dialect. Prenasalization targets a geminate cluster that expresses morphological plurality and creates, in all likelihood, a highly marked form: *enḫ-* (plural) versus *eḥ-* (singular or plural); compare Qumran אף 'nose' versus אנפין 'face'. Prenasalization can also affect an original *and* highly sonorous geminate. Among the Middle Aramaic dialects, prenasalization is most evolved in PAmh 63.

6.4. Mandaic

Prenasalization in Aramaic is a definable yet circumscribed sound change. It is usually non-phonemic, and it largely targets low sonority, secondary geminate clusters. In Imperial and Middle Aramaic, it also operates on a small number of lexical items whose underlying geminate is original. Prenasalization is a distinctive feature which, because of its restricted scope, has limited-moderate effect on the vocabulary and grammar of a particular Aramaic dialect. But with the appearance of the Late Aramaic dialect of Mandaic (ca. third century C.E.), the scope of this sound change is no longer restricted. On the contrary, prenasalization becomes hyper-productive (see Macuch 1989: 25; 1990: 237; or, comparably, Sanmartín 1995: 443).

Mandaic prenasalization has some telltale signs of its Imperial Aramaic origin. Many nouns reflect this sound change: for example, *anpia* 'face', *hinka* 'palate', *mdinta* 'city', *minda(m)* '(some)thing', *'nza* '(nanny-)goat', *'nta/anta* 'woman, wife',[69] and *qunpud* 'hedgehog'.[70] Non-nasal and prenasalized forms alternate without phonemic consequence: for example, *apaiun ~ anpaiun* 'their face' in an early lead scroll (Macuch 1967: I a 47 and 35, respectively);[71] or *gabaruata ~ gambaruata* 'mighty deeds, miracles'.[72] It would seem that the inventory of affected consonants jibes with that of its Imperial and Middle Aramaic antecedents, too.

But the inventory of prenasalizing consonants is actually different and more extensive than in earlier Aramaic dialects. In Mandaic, for instance, only a minority of cases involve voiceless geminate obstruents (Macuch 1965b: §23d). Likewise, only a minority of prenasalized forms in Mandaic descend from secondary geminates. Like *gambaruata < *gabbār-* (cf. Macuch 1989: 24), most prenasalized forms are traceable to original geminates: for example, *gamba/ganba* 'side, border' < *gabb-*, *hambura* 'hole, opening' < *ḥabbūr-*, *zimbura* 'hornet, bee' < *dibbūr-*,[73] *sumbilta* 'ladder' < *sibbil-* (?), *'(u)mba* 'bosom' < *'ubb-*, *qumba* (~ *quba*) 'arch' < *qubb-*, and *šumbilta* (and variants) 'ear of corn; Virgo' < *šubbul-* (?). Further, the favorite prenasalized cluster in Mandaic is *ng* < *gg*: for example, *angaria/'ngaria* 'roof-demons' < *'iggār-* (Akkadian loanword), *gangarata* 'throat, tonsils' < *gaggar- < *gargar-*, *hinga* 'circle, dance'[74] < *hing-*, *hinga* '(a type of demon)' < *higg-*, *nangara*

---

[65] For an example in a foreign word, see the Babylonian toponym *s̄nnk.r^m* 'Esangila' (VII/5) < *-saggil-*; contrast Hatran *sgyl* (especially in H 107:6).

[66] For the plural base * 'aḫḫ-*, see Tropper 2000: §33.171.3; cf. Fox 2003: 64.

[67] Steiner (personal communication) notes a parallel example in some Greek versions of Genesis 46:21, where the Benjaminide name Ehi (אחי) is transliterated Αγχις, Αγχεις, or Αγχειν. See also Southern and Vaughn 1997: 278; contrast Knobloch 1995: 212, 311–12.

[68] Prenasalization might also affect *qattīl* nominals, if the nasal element in *mnnr.r.^m y.^m* 'bitters' (VI/8) is verified (see note 63).

[69] For Mandaic ' ~ *a*, see Macuch 1965b: §47, top; see also Nöldeke 1875: §26.

[70] The second-person independent subject pronouns probably belong here as well. But their morphology is not identical to the standard Aramaic model (see Nöldeke 1875: §75; and, differently, Macuch 1990: 235).

[71] For the date of the text, see Macuch 1967: 97.

[72] For the labialization of *n > m*, see Nöldeke 1875: §53, top; and Macuch 1965b: §22.

[73] For *z* < *d*, see Macuch 1965b: §36; see also Nöldeke 1875: §46; and, differently, Macuch 1990: 225–26.

[74] Note the analysis in Sokoloff 2003: 457b, s.v. חִנְגָּא III.

(~ *nagara*) 'carpenter' < **naggār-* (Akkadian loanword), *nangria* 'holes, pit(fall)s; plagues' < **naggar-*, and *tangara* 'merchant' < **taggār-* (Akkadian loanword); see also *sangara* 'prosecutor; advocate' and *šangaria* 'inflammation (?)'. Altogether, then, the conditions of prenasalization in Mandaic resemble its native Aramaic roots less than its areal predecessor, Babylonian Akkadian.[75] Mandaic prenasalization operates on voiced geminates, regardless of their origin.

The Mandaic variety of prenasalization has another innovative feature. It attains phonemic status.[76] The best example occurs in **maqtal* nominal derivatives of **ydʿ* 'know'.[77] The non-nasal derivative is *mada*, the generic term for 'knowledge' as well as the organ dedicated to thought and intelligence. Its prenasalized counterpart, *manda*, is more specific and charged. *Manda* expresses the central and fundamental doctrine of Mandean religion: γνῶσις (see also Macuch 1976: 6–7; 1986: 271; 1989: 23–24; and 1990: 236). Prenasalization may be phonemic in other, less certain forms as well: for example, *zadiqa* 'righteous man' versus *zandiqa* '(a religious heretic)',[78] or *masa* 'forearm' versus *mansa* 'copying'. Prenasalization is semantically distinctive in Mandaic.

It can be grammatically distinctive, too. For example, the original geminate cluster of the *pael* can participate in prenasalization and yield a new quadriliteral stem: the *panel* (see already Qumran, Hatran, and PAmh 63) (Nöldeke 1875: §163, in conjunction with Macuch 1965b: §195k). The attestations are few and diverse. In a rare case, non-nasal and prenasalized forms co-occur without noticeable semantic difference: namely, *habib ~ hambib* 'burn, grow hot'. In another rare case, both forms occur yet differ semantically: namely, *mqadar* 'be wounded' (passive participle) ~ *mqandran* 'be black' (feminine plural passive participle). More often, the prenasalized *panel* simply replaces the old *pael*: for example, *hambil* 'corrupt, destroy' < **ḥabbil-*,[79] *hangar* 'repress' < **ḥaggir-*, and *nandia* 'shake' < **naddī*; see also *tangar* 'trade, act as a merchant' < *tangara* 'merchant' (< **taggār-*). The same replacement also occurs in the corresponding passive-reflexive: *ʾtpanal*. The departure from its Imperial Aramaic roots could not be more striking. Not only does prenasalization in Mandaic target an original geminate, but it abides by Akkadian-like phonological parameters. In the end, this new variety of prenasalization barely resembles its genetic origins in Imperial Aramaic.

6.5. Conclusion

Prenasalization, **C: > nC*, is a productive sound change in Imperial Aramaic. The change is generally restricted to the least sonorous segments in the language, though the majority of prenasalizing clusters involve dental stops (*t, d*) and, to a lesser extent, the voiceless bilabial stop (*p*). There are also blocking conditions. Aside from a few lexical exceptions, the change is blocked if **C:* originates as **CC* or **C-C*.

Prenasalization spreads into Middle Aramaic. In Palmyrean, a handful of examples occur which involve underlying **nC*. In Nabatean, the number of prenasalized forms is growing, and the targeted cluster is expanding beyond the Palmyrean-like confines of **nC*. The same expansive trend appears in Iranian texts. The Aramaic dialect of Qumran shows two more innovations: the development of a *panel* form (חנבלו < **ḥabbil-*), and the development of a limited phonemic status attached to prenasalization. Hatran too reveals one *panel* form (*lšndrh* < **-šaddir-*), as well as one word whose original geminate prenasalizes (*gndʾ* < **gadd-*). Furthermore, a clear example of a prenasalized **qattīl* adjective appears in Hatran (*šnpr/šnpyr* < **šappīr*). The Aramaic represented in PAmh 63 is perhaps the most innovative of the Middle Aramaic dialects in this respect. Prenasalization occurs in secondary geminates that are derived from a variety of underlying clusters. More importantly, it occurs in geminates that are underlyingly original, in both verbs and nouns.

In a sense, prenasalization is at its apex in Mandaic. It is widespread indeed. But only a minority of prenasalized forms abide by the conditions governing its ancestral phenomenon in Imperial or Middle Aramaic. The majority

---

[75] See, for example, Kutscher, attributing the similarity to "spectacular Ak[kadian] influence" (1970: 404 = 1977: 147 [italics deleted]). See also Macuch 1965a: 85; perhaps 1976: 4; and, more generally, Herbert 1986: 6. Compare also, descriptively, Nöldeke 1875: §68.

[76] For isolated antecedents, see sections 6.3.3 and 6.3.4.

[77] For etymological discussions and their historical implications, see, for example, Lidzbarski 1915: xvii; and Macuch 1965a: 82–89. Contrast

Drower 1937: 12–13, and, more confidently, Lupieri 2002: 8, on which contrast Macuch 1965a: 83–84; and, differently, Gündüz 1994: 114.

[78] For the latter term, see Schaeder 1930: 274–88 (denying a relationship to *zadiqa*).

[79] Note also Hoffmann 1827: §17.4 on Syriac.

abide by an old, Babylonian-like rule which prenasalizes voiced geminates, whether secondary or original. Otherwise, prenasalization in Mandaic continues its Middle Aramaic trend: In verbs, the *panel* stem continues to take hold; and in nouns, the difference between *mada* and *manda* shows that prenasalization has attained a significant phonemic status. Among the Aramaic dialects analyzed here, prenasalization has developed to its greatest extent in Mandaic. The roots of this sound change, however, are only partly traceable to its Aramaic origins.

Abbreviations

AECT	Fales 1986
AP	Cowley 1923
b.	Babylonian Talmud
CIS II	Académie des Inscriptions et Belles-Lettres 1889–93
H	Hatran inscription (in Vattioni 1981 [nos. 1–341], 1994 [nos. 1–416; uncatalogued texts 01–037]; Beyer 1998: 113–14 [nos. 1039–1043], and 2002 [nos. 1044a–1055g])
KAI	Donner and Röllig 2002
Mas	Yadin and Naveh 1989
Meg.	Megillah
NH	Naḥal Ḥever documents in Yardeni 2000: 1:265–99
NSaq	Segal 1983
NTA	Lemaire 2001
Paikuli	Skjærvø 1983
PAmh 63	Papyrus Amherst 63
PAT	Hillers and Cussini 1996
RS	Ras Shamra excavation/tablet number
TAD	Porten and Yardeni 1986–99
WDSP	Gropp 2001

For documents of Qumran provenience, see Tov and Pfann 2002.

Bibliography

Académie des Inscriptions et Belles-Lettres
    1889–93   *Corpus Inscriptionum Semiticarum*, Part 2/1. Paris: Klincksieck.

Aggoula, Basile
    1991   *Inventaire des inscriptions hatréennes*. Bibliothèque archéologique et historique 139. Paris: Geuthner.

Altheim, Franz, and Ruth Stiehl
    1964–69   *Die Araber in der Alten Welt*. Five volumes. Berlin: de Gruyter.

Aro, Jussi
  1955   *Studien zur mittelbabylonischen Grammatik*. Studia Orientalia 20. Helsinki: Societas Orientalis Fennica.

Barth, Jacob
  1894   *Die Nominalbildung in den semitischen Sprachen, mit einem Wörter- und Sachverzeichnis*. Second edition. Reprint, Hildesheim: Olms, 1967.

Bauer, Hans, and Pontus Leander
  1927   *Grammatik des Biblisch-Aramäischen*. Reprint, Hildesheim: Olms, 1981.

Bergman, Ben Zion
  1968   "*Hanʿel* in Daniel 2:25 and 6:19." *Journal of Near Eastern Studies* 27: 69–70.

Bertolino, Roberto
  1996   "Une stèle inédite de Hatra." *Semitica* 46: 143–46.

Beyer, Klaus
  1984–2004 *Die aramäischen Texte vom Toten Meer, samt den Inschriften aus Palästina, dem Testament Levis aus der Kairoer Genisa, der Fastenrolle und den alten talmudischen Zitaten*. Two volumes. Göttingen: Vandenhoeck & Ruprecht.
  1998   *Die aramäischen Inschriften aus Assur, Hatra und dem übrigen Ostmesopotamien (datiert 44 v.Chr. bis 238 n.Chr.)*. Göttingen: Vandenhoeck & Ruprecht.
  2002   "Neue Inschriften aus Hatra." In „*Sprich doch mit deinen Knechten aramäisch, wir verstehen es!*": *60 Beiträge zur Semitistik; Festschrift für Otto Jastrow zum 60. Geburtstag*, edited by Werner Arnold and Hartmut Bobzin, pp. 85–89. Wiesbaden: Harrassowitz.

Blau, Joshua
  1970   *On Pseudo-corrections in Some Semitic Languages*. Jerusalem: Israel Academy of Sciences and Humanities.

Brockelmann, Carl
  1908   *Laut- und Formenlehre*. Volume 1 of *Grundriss der vergleichenden Grammatik der semitischen Sprachen*. Berlin: Reuther & Reichard.
  1928   *Lexicon syriacum*. Second edition. Reprint, Hildesheim: Olms, 1982.

Cantineau, J.
  1930–32 *Le nabatéen*. Two volumes. Reprint, Osnabrück: Zeller, 1978.
  1935   *Grammaire du palmyrénien épigraphique*. Reprint, Osnabrück: Zeller, 1987.

Caquot, André
  1963   "L'araméen de Hatra." *Comptes-rendus du Groupe Linguistique d'Etudes Chamito-Sémitiques* 9: 87–89.

Cohen, Chaim, and Jacob Klein
  2001   "'חרמש' and 'מגל' in the Bible and Their Parallels — Ugaritic *ḥrmtt* and Akkadian *niggallu*." In *Homage to Shmuel: Studies in the World of the Bible*, edited by Zipora Talshir, Shamir Yona, and Daniel Sivan, pp. 245–68. Jerusalem: Ben-Gurion University of the Negev Press/Bialik Institute [in Hebrew].

Collins, John J., and Deborah A. Green
  1999   "The Tales from the Persian Court (4Q550[a–e])." In *Antikes Judentum und Frühes Christentum: Festschrift für Hartmut Stegemann zum 65. Geburtstag*, edited by Bernd Kollmann, Wolfgang Reinbold, and Annette Steudel, pp. 39–50. Beihefte zur Zeitschrift für die neutestamentliche Wissenschaft und die Kunde der älteren Kirche 97. Berlin: de Gruyter.

Cook, Edward M.
　2004　　　Review of *A Dictionary of Judean Aramaic*, by Michael Sokoloff. *Maarav* 11: 95–101.
　1998　　　"The Aramaic of the Dead Sea Scrolls." In *The Dead Sea Scrolls after Fifty Years: A Comprehensive Assessment*, edited by Peter W. Flint, James C. VanderKam, with the assistance of Andrea E. Alvarez, 1:359–78. Leiden: Brill.

Cowley, A., editor
　1923　　　*Aramaic Papyri of the Fifth Century B.C.* Reprint, Osnabrück: Zeller, 1967.

Coxon, Peter William
　1977　　　"The Problem of Nasalization in Biblical Aramaic in the Light of 1 Q GA and 11 Q Tg Job." *Revue de Qumran* 9: 253–58.

Crawford, Sidnie White
　2002　　　"4Qtales of the Persian Court (4Q550[a–e]) and Its Relation to Biblical Royal Courtier Tales, Especially Esther, Daniel and Joseph." In *The Bible as Book: The Hebrew Bible and the Judaean Desert Discoveries*, edited by Edward D. Herbert and Emanuel Tov, pp. 121–37. London: British Library & Oak Knoll Press.

Creason, Stuart
　2004　　　"Aramaic." In *The Cambridge Encyclopedia of the World's Ancient Languages*, edited by Roger D. Woodard, pp. 391–426. Cambridge: Cambridge University Press.

Degen, R.
　1973–74　"New Inscriptions from Hatra (nos. 231–280)." *Jaarbericht Ex Oriente Lux* 23: 402–22.

Dolgopolsky, Aharon B.
　2004　　　"Etymology of Some Hamito-Semitic (Afroasiatic) Animal Names." In *Egyptian and Semito-Hamitic (Afro-Asiatic) Studies in memoriam W. Vycichl*, edited by Gábor Takács, pp. 417–36. Studies in Semitic Languages and Linguistics 39. Leiden: Brill.

Donner, Herbert, and Wolfgang Röllig
　2002　　　*Kanaanäische und aramäische Inschriften*, Volume 1. Fifth edition. Wiesbaden: Harrassowitz.

Drower, E. S.
　1937　　　*The Mandaeans of Iraq and Iran: Their Cults, Customs, Magic, Legends, and Folklore*. Oxford: Clarendon Press.

Ebeling, Erich
　1941　　　*Das aramäisch-mittelpersische Glossar Frahang-i-pahlavik im Lichte der assyriologischen Forschung*. Reprint, Osnabrück: Zeller, 1972.

Fales, Frederick Mario
　1986　　　*Aramaic Epigraphs on Clay Tablets of the Neo-Assyrian Period*. Studi Semitici (nuova serie) 2. Rome: Università degli studi "La Sapienza."
　1996　　　"Most Ancient Aramaic Texts and Linguistics: A Review of Recent Studies." *Incontri Linguistici* 19: 33–57.

Fassberg, Steven E.
　2002　　　"Qumran Aramaic." *Maarav* 9: 19–31.

Ferguson, Charles A.
　1974　　　"Universals of Nasality." *Working Papers on Language Universals* 14: 1–16.

Fitzmyer, Joseph A.
　2004　　　*The Genesis Apocryphon of Qumran Cave 1 (1Q20): A Commentary*. Third edition. Biblica et Orientalia 18/B. Rome: Pontificio Istituto Biblico.

Fitzmyer, Joseph A., and Stephen A. Kaufman
    1992   *Old, Official, and Biblical Aramaic*, with the collaboration of Stephan F. Bennett and Edward M. Cook. Part 1 of *An Aramaic Bibliography*. Baltimore: Johns Hopkins University Press.

Folmer, M. L.
    1995   *The Aramaic Language in the Achaemenid Period: A Study in Linguistic Variation*. Orientalia Lovaniensia Analecta 68. Louvain: Peeters.

Fox, Joshua
    2003   *Semitic Noun Patterns*. Harvard Semitic Studies 52. Winona Lake: Eisenbrauns.

García Martínez, Florentino; Eibert J. C. Tigchelaar; and Adam S. van der Woude
    1998   *Qumran Cave 11. II. 11Q2–18, 11Q20–31*. Discoveries in the Judaean Desert 23. Oxford: Clarendon Press.

Gelb, I. J.
    1970   "A Note on Morphographemics." In *Mélanges Marcel Cohen: Études de linguistique, ethnographie et sciences connexes offertes par ses amis et ses élèves à l'occasion de son 80ème anniversaire*, edited by David Cohen, pp. 73–77. Janua Linguarum, Series Maior 27. The Hague: Mouton.

Geller, M. J.
    1997–2000   "The Aramaic Incantation in Cuneiform Script (AO 6489 = TCL 6,58)." *Jaarbericht "Ex Oriente Lux"* 35–36: 127–45.
    2001   "Corrections." *Nouvelles Assyriologiques Brèves et Utilitaires*: 97.

George, A. R.
    1996   "The Akkadian Word for 'Moustache'." *Nouvelles Assyriologiques Brèves et Utilitaires*: 51–52.

Gignoux, Philippe
    1972   *Glossaire des inscriptions pehlevies et parthes*. Corpus Inscriptionum Iranicarum, Supplementary Series 1. London: Lund Humphries.

Greenfield, Jonas C.
    1968   "Dialect Traits in Early Aramaic." *Leshonenu* 32: 359–68 [in Hebrew].
    2001   *'Al Kanfei Yonah: Collected Studies of Jonas C. Greenfield on Semitic Philology*, edited by Shalom M. Paul, Michael E. Stone, and Avital Pinnick. Two volumes. Leiden: Brill; Jerusalem: Hebrew University Magnes Press.

Greenfield, Jonas C., and Michael Sokoloff
    1992   "The Contribution of Qumran Aramaic to the Aramaic Vocabulary." In *Studies in Qumran Aramaic*, edited by T. Muraoka, pp. 78–98. Abr-Nahrain, Supplement 3. Louvain: Peeters.

Gropp, Douglas M.
    1990   "The Language of the Samaria Papyri: A Preliminary Study." In *Sopher mahir: Northwest Semitic Studies Presented to Stanislav Segert*, edited by Edward M. Cook, pp. 169–87. Maarav 5–6. Santa Monica: Western Academic Press.
    2001   "The Samaria Papyri from Wadi Daliyeh." In *Wadi Daliyeh II: The Samaria Papyri from Wadi Daliyeh*, by Douglas Gropp, and *Qumran Cave 4. XXVIII: Miscellanea, Part 2*, by Moshe Bernstein, Monica Brady, James Charlesworth, Peter Flint, Haggai Misgev, Stephen Pfann, Eileen Schuller, Eibert J. C. Tigchelaar, and James VanderKam, pp. 1–116. Discoveries in the Judaean Desert 28. Oxford: Clarendon Press.

Gündüz, Şinasi
    1994   *The Knowledge of Life: The Origins and Early History of the Mandaeans and Their Relation to the Sabians of the Qur'ān and to the Harranians*. Journal of Semitic Studies, Supplement 3. Oxford: Oxford University Press.

Hackl, Ursula; Hanna Jenni; and Christoph Schneider
  2003   *Quellen zur Geschichte der Nabatäer: Textsammlung mit Übersetzung und Kommentar.* Novum Testamentum et Orbis Antiquus 51. Freiburg: Universitätsverlag; Göttingen: Vandenhoeck & Ruprecht.

Hajek, John
  1997   *Universals of Sound Change in Nasalization.* Publications of the Philological Society 31. Oxford: Blackwell.

Herbert, Robert K.
  1986   *Language Universals, Markedness Theory, and Natural Phonetic Processes.* Trends in Linguistics, Studies and Monographs 25. Berlin: Mouton de Gruyter.

Hillers, Delbert R.
  1972   "Mškn' 'Temple' in Inscriptions from Hatra." *Bulletin of the American Schools of Oriental Research* 207: 54–56.

Hillers, Delbert R., and Eleonora Cussini
  1996   *Palmyrene Aramaic Texts.* Baltimore: Johns Hopkins University Press.

Hoffmann, Andreas Gottlieb
  1827   *Grammaticae syriacae.* Libri 3. Halle: Impensis Orphanotrophei.

Hoftijzer, J., and K. Jongeling
  1995   *Dictionary of the North-West Semitic Inscriptions.* Two parts. Handbuch der Orientalistik 1/21. Leiden: Brill.

Huehnergard, John
  1987   *Ugaritic Vocabulary in Syllabic Transcription.* Harvard Semitic Studies 32. Atlanta: Scholars Press.
  2004   "Afro-Asiatic." In *The Cambridge Encyclopedia of the World's Ancient Languages*, edited by Roger D. Woodard, pp. 138–59. Cambridge: Cambridge University Press.
  2005   *A Grammar of Akkadian.* Second edition. Harvard Semitic Studies 45. Winona Lake: Eisenbrauns.

Hug, Volker
  1993   *Altaramäische Grammatik der Texte des 7. und 6. Jh.s v.Chr.* Heidelberger Studien zum Alten Orient 4. Heidelberg: Heidelberger Orientverlag.

Jensen, P.
  1919   "Erschließung der aramäischen Inschriften von Assur und Hatra." *Sitzungsberichte der Kgl. Preußischen Akademie der Wissenschaften zu Berlin, phil.-hist. Klasse:* 1042–51.
  1920   "Lesung und Ausbeutung der Inschriften." *Mitteilungen der Deutschen Orient-Gesellschaft* 60: 11–51.

Kaufman, Stephen A.
  1974   *The Akkadian Influences on Aramaic.* Assyriological Studies 19. Chicago: University of Chicago Press.
  1983   "The History of Aramaic Vowel Reduction." In *Arameans, Aramaic and the Aramaic Literary Tradition*, edited by Michael Sokoloff, pp. 47–55. Ramat-Gan: Bar-Ilan University Press.
  1984   "On Vowel Reduction in Aramaic." *Journal of the American Oriental Society* 104: 87–95.
  1992   "Languages (Aramaic)." In *The Anchor Bible Dictionary*, edited by David Noel Freedman, 4:173a–78a. New York: Doubleday.
  1997   "Aramaic." In *The Semitic Languages*, edited by Robert Hetzron, pp. 114–30. London: Routledge.

Kautzsch, E.
  1884   *Grammatik des Biblisch-Aramäischen, mit einer kritischen Erörterung der aramäischen Wörter im Neuen Testament.* Leipzig: Vogel.

Knobloch, Frederick W.
- 1995 "Hebrew Sounds in Greek Script: Transcriptions and Related Phenomena in the Septuagint, with Special Focus on Genesis." Ph.D. dissertation, University of Pennsylvania. Ann Arbor: UMI Dissertation Services.

Koehler, Ludwig, and Walter Baumgartner
- 1967–95 *Hebräisches und aramäisches Lexikon zum Alten Testament*. Five parts. Third edition, revised by Walter Baumgartner, Benedikt Hartmann, E. Y. Kutscher, Johann Jakob Stamm, Ze'ev Ben-Ḥayyim, and Philippe H. Reymond; edited by B. Hartmann, Ph. Reymond, and J. J. Stamm. Leiden: Brill.
- 1994–2000 *The Hebrew and Aramaic Lexicon of the Old Testament*. Five volumes, revised by Walter Baumgartner and Johann Jakob Stamm, with assistance from Benedikt Hartmann, Ze'ev Ben-Ḥayyim, Eduard Yechezkel Kutscher, and Philippe Reymond; translated and edited by M. E. J. Richardson, in collaboration with G. J. Jongeling-Vos, and L. J. de Regt. Leiden: Brill.

Kogan, Leonid
- 2005 "Lexicon of the Old Aramaic Inscriptions and the Historical Unity of Aramaic." In *Memoriae Igor M. Diakonoff*, edited by L. Kogan, N. Koslova, S. Loesov, and S. Tishchenko, pp. 513–66. Orientalia et Classica 8; Babel und Bibel 2. Winona Lake: Eisenbrauns.

Kottsieper, Ingo
- 1990 *Die Sprache der Aḥiqarsprüche*. Beihefte zur Zeitschrift für die alttestamentliche Wissenschaft 194. Berlin: de Gruyter.
- 1997 "Anmerkungen zu Pap. Amherst 63. Teil II–V." *Ugarit-Forschungen* 29: 385–434.
- 2000 "Der Mann aus Babylonien — Steuerhinterzieher, Flüchtling, Immigrant oder Agent? Zu einem aramäischen Dekret aus neuassyrischer Zeit." *Orientalia* 69: 368–92.

Kraeling, Emil G., editor
- 1953 *The Brooklyn Museum Aramaic Papyri: New Documents of the Fifth Century B.C. from the Jewish Colony at Elephantine*. Reprint, New York: Arno, 1969.

Kutscher, Eduard Yechezkel
- 1954 "New Aramaic Texts." *Journal of the American Oriental Society* 74: 233–48.
- 1957 "The Language of the 'Genesis Apocryphon': A Preliminary Study." In *Aspects of the Dead Sea Scrolls*, edited by Chaim Rabin and Yigael Yadin, pp. 1–34. Scripta Hierosolymitana 4. Jerusalem: Hebrew University/Magnes Press.
- 1965 "Contemporary Studies in North-Western Semitic." *Journal of Semitic Studies* 10: 21–51.
- 1970 "Aramaic." In *Linguistics in South West Asia and North Africa*, edited by Thomas A. Sebeok, pp. 347–412. Current Trends in Linguistics 6. The Hague: Mouton.
- 1971 "The Hermopolis Papyri." *Israel Oriental Studies* 1: 103–19.
- 1977 *Hebrew and Aramaic Studies*, edited by Zeev Ben-Ḥayyim, Aharon Dotan, and Gad Sarfatti. Jerusalem: Magnes Press/Hebrew University.

Ladefoged, Peter, and Ian Maddieson
- 1996 *The Sounds of the World's Languages*. Oxford: Blackwell.

Laver, John
- 1994 *Principles of Phonetics*. Cambridge Textbooks in Linguistics. Cambridge: Cambridge University Press.

Leander, Pontus
- 1928 *Laut- und Formenlehre des Ägyptisch-Aramäischen*. Reprint, Hildesheim: Olms, 1966.

Lemaire, André
- 2001 *Nouvelles tablettes araméennes*. École pratique des hautes études, Sciences historiques et philologiques 2; Hautes études orientales 34; Moyen et Proche-Orient 1. Geneva: Droz.

Levine, Baruch A.
    2002   "Ritual as Symbol: Modes of Sacrifice in Israelite Religion." In *Sacred Time, Sacred Place: Archaeology and the Religion of Israel*, edited by Barry M. Gittlen, pp. 125–35. Winona Lake: Eisenbrauns.

Lidzbarski, Mark
    1915   *Das Johannesbuch der Mandäer*. Giessen: Töpelmann.

Lipiński, Edward
    1993–94   "Aramaic Clay Tablets from the Gozan-Harran Area." *Jaarbericht "Ex Oriente Lux"* 33: 143–50.
    2001   *Semitic Languages: Outline of a Comparative Grammar*. Second edition. Orientalia Lovaniensia Analecta 80. Louvain: Peeters.

Lozachmeur, Hélène, and André Lemaire
    1996   "Nouveaux ostraca araméens d'Idumée." *Semitica* 46: 123–42.

Lupieri, Edmondo
    2002   *The Mandaeans: The Last Gnostics*, translated by Charles Hindley. Italian Texts and Studies on Religion and Society. Grand Rapids/Cambridge: Eerdmans.

Macuch, Rudolf
    1965a   "Anfänge der Mandäer: Versuch eines geschichtlichen Bildes bis zur früh-Islamischen Zeit." In *Die Araber in der Alten Welt*, by Franz Altheim and Ruth Stiehl, 2:76–190. Berlin: de Gruyter.
    1965b   *Handbook of Classical and Modern Mandaic*. Berlin: de Gruyter.
    1967   "Altmandäische Bleirolle." In *Die Araber in der Alten Welt*, by Franz Altheim and Ruth Stiehl, 4:91–203. Berlin: de Gruyter.
    1971   "Gesprochenes Aramäisch und aramäische Schriftsprache." In *Christentum am Roten Meer 1*, by Franz Altheim and Ruth Stiehl, pp. 537–57. Berlin: de Gruyter.
    1976   *Zur Sprache und Literatur der Mandäer*. Studia Mandaica 1. Berlin: de Gruyter.
    1986   "Hermeneutische Akrobatik aufgrund phonetischen Lautwandels im aramäischen Dialekten." In *On the Dignity of Man: Oriental and Classical Studies in Honour of Frithiof Rundgren*, edited by Tryggve Kronholm and Eva Riad, pp. 269–83. Orientalia Suecana 33–35. Stockholm: Almqvist & Wiksell.
    1989   *Neumandäische Chrestomathie mit grammatischer Skizze, kommentierter Übersetzung und Glossar*. Porta Linguarum Orientalium (neue Serie) 18. Wiesbaden: Harrassowitz.
    1990   "Some Orthographico-phonetic Problems of Ancient Aramaic and the Living Aramaic Pronunciations." In *Sopher mahir: Northwest Semitic Studies Presented to Stanislav Segert*, edited by Edward M. Cook, pp. 221–37. Maarav 5–6. Santa Monica: Western Academic Press.

Militarev, Alexander, and Leonid Kogan
    2005   *Animal Names*, with contributions by A. Arakelova, A. Belova, A. Kovalev, D. Nosnitsyn, E. Vizirova, and M. Yakubovich. Volume 2 of *Semitic Etymological Dictionary*. Alter Orient und Altes Testament 278/2. Münster: Ugarit-Verlag.

Müller, Hans-Peter
    1991   "Die Sprache der Texte von Tell Deir ʿAllā im Kontext der nordwestsemitischen Sprachen mit einigen Erwägungen zum Zusammenhang der schwachen Verbklassen." *Zeitschrift für Althebraistik* 4: 1–31.

Muraoka, Takamitsu
    1983–84   "The Tell-Fekherye Bilingual Inscription and Early Aramaic." *Abr-Nahrain* 22: 79–117.

Muraoka, Takamitsu, and Bezalel Porten
    2003   *A Grammar of Egyptian Aramaic*. Second edition. Handbuch der Orientalistik 1/32. Leiden: Brill.

Mustafa, Arafa H.
  1982 "Die sogenannte Geminatendissimilation im Semitischen." *Hallesche Beiträge zur Orientwissenschaft* 4: 13–39.

Nims, Charles F., and Richard C. Steiner
  1983 "A Paganized Version of Psalm 20:2–6 from the Aramaic Text in Demotic Script." *Journal of the American Oriental Society* 103: 261–74.

Nöldeke, Theodor
  1870 "Beiträge zur Kenntnis der aramäischen Dialecte. 3. Ueber Orthographie und Sprache der Palmyrener." *Zeitschrift für die Deutschen morgenländischen Gesellschaft* 24: 85–109.
  1875 *Mandäische Grammatik*. Reprint, Darmstadt: Wissenschaftliche Buchgesellschaft, 1964.

Nyberg, Henrik Samuel
  1964–74 *A Manual of Pahlavi*. Two parts. Wiesbaden: Harrassowitz.
  1988 *Frahang i pahlavīk*, edited by Bo Utas, with the collaboration of Christopher Toll. Wiesbaden: Harrassowitz.

Ohala, John J.
  1981 "The Listener as a Source of Sound Change." In *Papers from the Parasession on Language and Behavior: Chicago Linguistic Society, May 1–2, 1981*, edited by Carrie S. Masek, Roberta A. Hendrick, and Mary Frances Miller, pp. 178–203. Chicago: Chicago Linguistic Society.

Podolsky, Baruch
  1998 "Notes on Hebrew Etymology." In *Past Links: Studies in the Languages and Cultures of the Ancient Near East*, edited by Shlomo Isre'el, Itamar Singer, and Ran Zadok, pp. 199–205. Israel Oriental Studies 18. Winona Lake: Eisenbrauns.

Poebel, Arno
  1939 *Studies in Akkadian Grammar*. Assyriological Studies 9. Chicago: University of Chicago Press.

Porten, Bezalel
  1996 *The Elephantine Papyri in English: Three Millennia of Cross-cultural Continuity and Change*, with J. Joel Farber, Cary J. Martin, Günter Vittmann, Leslie S. B. MacCoull, Sarah Clackson, and contributions by Simon Hopkins, and Ramon Katzoff. Documenta et Monumenta Orientis Antiqui 22. Leiden: Brill.
  2002 "Letter Regarding Gift, Handmaiden, Allotment, and Pots (*TAD* D7.9)." In *The Context of Scripture*, edited by William W. Hallo and K. Lawson Younger, Jr., 3:215–16. Leiden: Brill.

Porten, Bezalel, and Jonas C. Greenfield
  1968 "The Aramaic Papyri from Hermopolis." *Zeitschrift für die alttestamentliche Wissenschaft* 80: 216–31.

Porten, Bezalel, and Ada Yardeni
  1986–99 *Textbook of Aramaic Documents from Ancient Egypt, Newly Copied, Edited, and Translated into Hebrew and English*. Four volumes. Jerusalem: Hebrew University Department of the History of the Jewish People.

Rosenthal, Franz
  1936 *Die Sprache der palmyrenischen Inschriften und ihre Stellung innerhalb des Aramäischen*. Mitteilungen der Vorderasiatisch-Aegyptischen Gesellschaft 41/1. Leipzig: Hinrichs.
  2006 *A Grammar of Biblical Aramaic*. Seventh edition. Porta Linguarum Orientalium (neue Serie) 5. Wiesbaden: Harrassowitz.

Rossi, Adriano V.
  2002 "Middle Iranian *gund* Between Aramaic and Indo-Iranian." *Jerusalem Studies in Arabic and Islam* 26: 140–71.

Růžička, Rudolf
    1909   *Konsonantische Dissimilation in den semitischen Sprachen.* Beiträge zur Assyriologie und semitischen Sprachwissenschaft 6/4. Leipzig: Hinrichs; Baltimore: Johns Hopkins Press.

Sanmartín, Joaquín
    1995   "Über Regeln und Ausnahmen: Verhalten des vorkonsonantischen /n/ im 'Altsemitischen.'" In *Vom Alten Orient Zum Alten Testament: Festschrift für Wolfram Freiherrn von Soden zum 85. Geburtstag am 19. Juni 1993*, edited by Manfried Dietrich and Oswald Loretz, pp. 433–66. Alter Orient und Altes Testament 240. Kevelaer: Butzon & Bercker.

Schaeder, Hans Heinrich
    1930   *Iranische Beiträge 1.* Reprint, Hildesheim: Olms, 1972.

Schattner-Rieser, Ursula
    2004   *Grammaire.* Volume 1 of *L'araméen des manuscrits de la mer Morte.* Instruments pour l'étude de l'Orient ancien 5. Lausanne: Zèbre.

Segal, J. B.
    1983   *Aramaic Texts from North Saqqâra with Some Fragments in Phoenician*, with contributions by H. S. Smith. Excavations at North Saqqâra, Documentary Series 4. London: Egypt Exploration Society.
    1986   "Arabs at Hatra and the Vicinity: Marginalia on New Aramaic Texts." *Journal of Semitic Studies* 31: 57–80.

Segert, Stanislav
    1997   "Old Aramaic Phonology." In *Phonologies of Asia and Africa (including the Caucasus)*, edited by Alan S. Kaye, 1:115–25. Winona Lake: Eisenbrauns.

Skjærvø, Prods O.
    1983   *Restored Text and Translation.* Part 3/1 of *The Sassanian Inscription of Paikuli.* Wiesbaden: Reichart.
    1990   Review of *Frahang i pahlavīk*, by Henrik Samuel Nyberg. *Kratylos* 35: 95–99.
    1995   "Aramaic in Iran." *Aram* 7: 283–318.
    1996   "Aramaic Scripts for Iranian Languages." In *The World's Writing Systems*, edited by Peter T. Daniels and William Bright, pp. 515–35. New York: Oxford University Press.

von Soden, Wolfram
    1968   "*n* als Wurzelaugment im Semitischen." In *Studia orientalia in memoriam Caroli Brockelmann*, edited by Manfred Fleischhammer, pp. 175–84. Wissenschaftliche Zeitschrift der Martin-Luther-Universität Halle-Wittenberg, Gesellschafts- und Sprachwissenschaftliche Reihe 17/2–3. Halle: Martin-Luther-Universität, Halle-Wittenberg.
    1985   *Bibel und Alter Orient: Altorientalische Beiträge zum Alten Testament von Wolfram von Soden*, edited by Hans-Peter Müller. Beiheft zur Zeitschrift für die alttestamentliche Wissenschaft 162. Berlin: de Gruyter.
    1995   *Grundriss der akkadischen Grammatik.* Third edition, in collaboration with Werner R. Mayer. Analecta Orientalia 33. Rome: Pontificio Istituto Biblico.

Sokoloff, Michael
    2002   *A Dictionary of Jewish Babylonian Aramaic of the Talmudic and Geonic Periods.* Dictionaries of Talmud, Midrash and Targum 3. Ramat-Gan: Bar Ilan University Press; Baltimore: Johns Hopkins University Press.
    2003   *A Dictionary of Judean Aramaic.* Ramat-Gan: Bar Ilan University Press.

Southern, Mark, and Andrew G. Vaughn
    1997   "Where Have All the Nasals Gone? *n*C > CC in North Semitic." *Journal of Semitic Studies* 42: 263–82.

Spitaler, Anton
- 1952–54 "Zur Frage der Geminatendissimilation im Semitischen: Zugleich ein Beitrag zur Kenntnis der Orthographie des Reicharamäischen." *Indogermanische Forschungen* 61: 257–66.
- 1998 *Philologica: Beiträge zur Arabistik und Semitistik*, edited by Hartmut Bobzin. Diskurse der Arabistik 1. Wiesbaden: Harrassowitz.

Steiner, Richard C.
- 1997 "The Aramaic Text in Demotic Script." In *The Context of Scripture*, edited by William W. Hallo and K. Lawson Younger, Jr., 1:309–27. Leiden: Brill.
- 2000 "Semitic Names for Utensils in the Demotic Word-list from Tebtunis." *Journal of Near Eastern Studies* 59: 191–94.

Steiner, Richard C., and Adina Mosak Moshavi
- 1995 "A Selective Glossary of Northwest Semitic Texts in Egyptian Script." In *Dictionary of the North-West Semitic Inscriptions*, by J. Hoftijzer and K. Jongeling, 2:1249–66. Handbuch der Orientalistik 1/21. Leiden: Brill.

Steiner, Richard C., and Charles F. Nims
- 1984 "You Can't Offer Your Sacrifice and Eat It Too: A Polemical Poem from the Aramaic Text in Demotic Script." *Journal of Near Eastern Studies* 43: 89–114.
- 1985 "Ashurbanipal and Shamash-Shum-Ukin: A Tale of Two Brothers from the Aramaic Text in Demotic Script." *Revue Biblique* 92: 60–81.

Streck, Michael P.
- 2000 *Die Amurriter. Die onomastische Forschung. Orthographie und Phonologie. Nominalmorphologie.* Volume 1 of *Das amurritische Onomastikon der altbabylonischen Zeit.* Alter Orient und Altes Testament 271/1. Münster: Ugarit-Verlag.

Sznycer, Maurice
- 2003 "À propos du passage de l'araméen au pehlevi." In *Mélanges David Cohen*, edited by Jérôme Lentin and Antoine Lonnet, with the assistance of Aziza Boucherit, Arlette Roth, Catherine Taine-Cheikh, and Omar Bencheikh, pp. 643–51. Paris: Maisonneuve & Larose.

Tov, E., and S. J. Pfann
- 2002 "List of Texts from the Judaean Desert." In *The Texts from the Judaean Desert: Indices and an Introduction to the* Discoveries in the Judaean Desert *Series*, edited by Emanuel Tov, pp. 27–114. Discoveries in the Judaean Desert 39. Oxford: Clarendon Press.

Tropper, Josef
- 2000 *Ugaritische Grammatik.* Alter Orient und Altes Testament 273. Münster: Ugarit-Verlag.

Tsereteli, Konstantin
- 1998 "Les inscriptions araméennes de Géorgie." *Semitica* 48: 75–88.

Vattioni, Francesco
- 1981 *Le iscrizioni di Ḥatra.* Annali dell'Istituto Universitario Orientale di Napoli, Supplement 28. Naples: Istituto Orientale di Napoli.
- 1994 *Hatra.* Annali dell'Istituto Universitario Orientale di Napoli, Supplement 81. Naples: Istituto Orientale di Napoli.

Vleeming, S. P., and J. W. Wesselius
- 1982 "An Aramaic Hymn from the Fourth Century B.C." *Bibliotheca Orientalis* 39: 501–9.
- 1985–90 *Studies in Papyrus Amherst 63: Essays on the Aramaic Texts in Aramaic/demotic Papyrus Amherst 63.* Two volumes. Amsterdam: Palache Instituut.

Voigt, Rainer
- 2002–3 "Die beiden Suffixkonjugationen des Semitischen (und Ägyptischen)." *Zeitschrift für Althebraistik* 15–16: 138–65.

Watson, Wilfred G. E.
   2003   "A Ugaritic Reference Grammar for the 21st Century." *Aula Orientalis* 21: 87–95.

Whitehead, J. David
   1978   "Some Distinctive Features of the Language of the Aramaic Arsames Correspondence." *Journal of Near Eastern Studies* 37: 119–40.

Wright, William
   1890   *Lectures on the Comparative Grammar of the Semitic Languages, with a General Survey of the Semitic Languages and Their Diffusion and of the Semitic Alphabet, Origin, and Writing*, edited by William Robertson Smith. Reprint, Amsterdam: APA-Philo, 1981.

Yadin, Yigael; Jonas C. Greenfield; Ada Yardeni; and Baruch A. Levine, editors
   2002   *The Documents from the Bar Kokhba Period in the Cave of Letters: Hebrew, Aramaic and Nabatean-Aramaic Papyri*, with additional contributions by Hannah Cotton and Joseph Naveh. Two volumes. Judean Desert Series 3. Jerusalem: Israel Exploration Society/Institute of Archaeology, Hebrew University/Shrine of the Book, Israel Museum.

Yadin, Yigael, and Joseph Naveh
   1989   "The Aramaic and Hebrew Ostraca and Jar Inscriptions from Masada." In *Masada: The Yigael Yadin Excavations 1963–1965, Final Reports,* 1:1–68. The Masada Reports 1. Jerusalem: Israel Exploration Society/Hebrew University of Jerusalem.

Yardeni, Ada
   2000   *Textbook of Aramaic, Hebrew and Nabataean Documentary Texts from the Judaean Desert and Related Material*. Two volumes. Jerusalem: Hebrew University.

7. A NEW MASORETIC "SPELL CHECKER," OR, A PRACTICAL METHOD FOR CHECKING THE ACCENTUAL STRUCTURE AND INTEGRITY OF TIBERIAN-POINTED BIBLICAL TEXTS

Richard L. Goerwitz III

7.1. Introduction

The orthography of biblical Hebrew manuscripts and scholarly printed editions encompasses not only traditional alphanumeric symbols, but also cantillation marks, or "accents," which indicate how the text should be chanted. These marks are difficult to typeset, and even the best scholarly editions contain various cantillation errors that have been introduced in the typesetting process. For example, the latest edition of *Biblia Hebraica Stuttgartensia* (Kittel et al. 1997 [BHS]), a generally accurate work, contains a significant number of accentual anomalies, on the order of one every fifteen pages. Some of these anomalies reflect features inherent in the base manuscript (Leningrad B 19a), but more often they reflect deviations in the printed edition from the original manuscript. Because most of these anomalies go unnoted in BHS, they are generally to be construed as errors, either in the editorial process, or, more typically, in the printing process.

In the past, eliminating such errors has proven impractical, both because of the quantity of the material, and because of the limited number of proofreaders who can efficiently locate and correct them. If human error could be eliminated from this aspect of the publication process, the potential benefits to publishers and their readers would be enormous. Not only would publishers be able to attain levels of accuracy and consistency not known since the time of the scribes who wrote the texts, but they would also be able to reduce substantially the resources consumed by the usual editing and proofreading cycles. This, in turn, would ultimately reduce the overall cost of providing such works to the public.

Fortunately, cantillation marks follow a grammar of their own that largely mirrors the syntactic structure of the sentence in which they occur. Although this grammar is not strictly context-free, it is possible to construct a grammar very close to it that is not only context-free, but also easily parsable. As a result, this grammar can serve as a basis for real-world computer-based automata that can efficiently locate accentual errors in scholarly editions of the Hebrew Bible.

The purpose of this study is to describe a system for automatically parsing, locating, and analyzing errors in the cantillation marks of modern scholarly Hebrew Bible texts. In the first half of the study (sections 7.2–4) I discuss this system in general terms, explaining how it is possible to construct it, and why I have taken the approach that I have. In the second half (sections 7.5–9), I describe a fast, practical, working implementation of it — a proof of concept.

Although this study focuses on the Tiberian cantillation system (as described in Yeivin 1980) and on BHS, the methods outlined here may be generalized and adapted to other cantillation systems and texts.[1]

7.2. Cantillation and Context-free Grammars

In his 1990 study, James Price claims that the Tiberian cantillation system (i.e., the cantillation system used in what most consider to be the best Medieval biblical manuscripts) can be formalized as a self-contained, computer-implementable, context-free accentual grammar. Context-free grammars are sets of rewrite rules, like the classic sentence structure rule, S —> NP VP ("a sentence consists of a noun phrase followed by a verb phrase"), which

---

[1] Yeivin's work is more concise and less theoretical than Wickes 1970 and hence far more useful here.

are often used to describe the syntax of a language. Although Price's study does much to systematize and elucidate the structure of the Tiberian cantillation system, he never actually offers a full set of such rules; that is, he does not offer a full context-free accentual grammar (Goerwitz 1994). Why? Because doing so, at least in the way he envisions the task, is simply not possible.

To illustrate why it is not possible to create such a grammar, let us examine the case of one particularly difficult accent, *revia*. *Revia* is a disjunctive accent that divides clauses marked by *ṭifḥa*, *zaqef*, and *segolta*, which denote even stronger breaks. *Revia* can be repeated within a verse, but it cannot follow itself too closely. If fewer than three words intervene between one *revia* and the next, the last *revia* turns into *pašṭa* (or, depending on syllable structure, into the variant form *yetiv*), unless this *pašṭa* would land within two words of the next *tevir* or *zarqa*, in which case a *tevir* or *zarqa* (depending upon the type of disjunctive clause) is used in its place (see Yeivin 1980: 226, 230, 234 for additional proximity and combinatory restrictions).

Note how important proximity is to the workings of these replacement rules. Although it is possible to conceive of a context-free grammar that handles all the various possible combinations, the problem is one of elegance. Context-free grammars do not represent concepts like "near" and "far" or "within x words" well. And an accentual grammar proper cannot represent word and syllable structures at all. Although it is sometimes possible to construct brute force grammars that simply list attested combinations, such grammars quickly become unwieldy and unnatural and are impossible to write.

This, then, is why, although Price's formalisms go a long way toward characterizing Tiberian accentual structures, Price wisely refrains from trying to offer a full accentual grammar. The Tiberian accents are simply too complex and multi-leveled to be captured elegantly or completely as a self-contained set of context-free rules.

7.3. Context-free Grammars and Tractability

The problem of capturing the Tiberian accents as a self-contained, context-free grammar is not only one of elegance and theoretical completeness, but also one of practical analysis and implementation. Even if we managed to construct a grammar that accounted for *revia* replacement and other such esoterica, and even if we could incorporate extra-accentual features such as word and syllable structures, the fact remains that there would still be no efficient, reliable, easily implementable method for programming a computer to process this grammar and to convert it into a parser.

The most powerful class of grammars that computers can deal with easily are those that can be converted into a type of *deterministic pushdown automaton* known as an "LR parser" (for more extensive discussions of these terms, see an introductory compiler textbook such as Aho et al. 1986). Grammars that fall into this category convert to small, very fast parsers that provide timely, efficient error recovery. Although it is often possible to handle grammars that fall outside this range by preprocessing the input with a so-called *lexical analyzer* (discussed in section 7.6), such an approach quickly becomes impractical for the sorts of phenomena we typically see in natural languages. Ambiguity is a particularly salient case in point (Tofte 1990).[2]

Because the Tiberian cantillation system contains many ambiguities (e.g., one cannot always tell a true *pašṭa* clause from a converted *revia* clause), the Tiberian Hebrew accentual system cannot be reduced, even with help from a lexical analyzer, to an LR-parsable grammar. It thus defies straightforward, computer-based analysis.

Despite apparent difficulties, though, the basic goal of machine-based analysis of the Tiberian accents is not altogether outside the realm of possibility. To realize it we must define our goal as simply being able to recognize errors in the accentuation of modern biblical editions. To achieve this goal we do not need to construct a full, theoretically elegant parsing system. Instead, we can settle for a simpler, slightly less accurate parser that brings us back into the realm of computational tractability, and allows us immediate access to a wide assortment of well-developed, reliable software tools and methods that will allow us to achieve our goal.

In a theoretical sense, such a move is "cheating." In practical terms, however, we are making precisely those

---

[2] GLR (generalized LR) parsers process ambiguous input but can only do so efficiently if that input has relatively few ambiguities (Tomita 1985).

concessions that enable us to develop a system that does what scholars and publishers really need it to do, namely to offer fast, practical help in analyzing and correcting the cantillation marks of modern Hebrew Bible texts that are based on Tiberian-pointed biblical manuscripts.

7.4. Cheating

Instances where "cheating" is most critical, that is, where we must misrepresent the grammar in order to obtain a working system, consist mainly in proximity/position restrictions, such as the *revia* —> *pašṭa*, *zarqa*, or *tevir* rule discussed above (section 7.2). Note also the case of *segolta*, which cannot be used if a *zaqef* or an *atnaḥ* has already appeared in a given verse. Often such phenomena can be re-cast as LR-parsable rules. But, as noted in connection with context-free grammars above, accomplishing this (if it is possible at all) comes only at the expense of verbosity and unnaturalness. And it makes the resulting grammar extremely difficult to write. The distribution of *segolta*, for example, can be handled by creating one special *atnaḥ* and two special *silluq* clauses, that is, an *atnaḥ* clause the first major divider of which is *segolta*, and a *silluq* clause the first major divider of which is either a *segolta* or an *atnaḥ* clause with a *segolta*. Such rules, however, are ugly; they will never capture generalizations about processes that involve syllable structure, or that boil down to questions of how musical patterns interact with the text's syntactic or semantic components (e.g., when should we use *segolta* in place of, say, *atnaḥ*, *zaqef*, or *zaqef gadol*?).

So instead of trying to capture generalizations in this way, we should simply give up and "cheat" — our goal being to reduce the complexity of our grammar to the point where it can be processed using simple, widely-available parser-generation software that can produce a real, working system. Such cheating does not prevent us from dealing with verses containing accents like *segolta*, or *pašṭa*, and *revia*. All it does is force us to accept a slightly lower standard of accuracy when validating them.

For example, to account for the distribution of *pašṭa* and *revia* in a simple, tractable way, all we need to do is ignore the *revia* —> *pašṭa* conversion rule, accepting as correct any sequence of *revia* followed by *pašṭa*.

Accepting as correct any sequence of *revia* followed by *pašṭa* means that our grammar now accepts as valid a few constructs that it really should mark as invalid. Acceptance of invalid constructs like this, however, does not cause difficulties within an actual, working parsing/error-detection system because the vast majority of errors introduced by the editing and typesetting processes consist of omissions and mindless mis-keyings. Only rarely are editors or typesetters creative enough in their mistakes to introduce ones that happen to correspond exactly to a concession (or "cheat") that we have allowed into our parser/error-detector's grammar (see section 7.9 for a discussion of where such mistakes are most likely to fool the working proof-of-concept system).

7.5. The Base Text

Having outlined the general theory on which an accentual parsing and error-detection system must operate, it is now possible to talk about the practical details of the particular implementation outlined here — what program modules make it up, how these modules interoperate, and what software-development tools were used to create them. Before discussing the system's implementation, however, let us consider briefly the data that this system will be analyzing. Let us consider, in other words, the nature and structure of the texts that the system is supposed to be parsing and checking.

In order for automated parsing and checking to work, we need texts set up in such a way that the computer can recognize the various accents. A good example of such a setup is the machine-readable *Biblia Hebraica Stuttgartensia* (BHS) edition distributed by the Center for Computer Analysis of Texts (CCAT) at the University of Pennsylvania. This edition — developed originally by the University of Michigan under grants from the Packard Humanities Institute and the University of Michigan Computing Center — utilizes a series of two-digit codes to represent the Tiberian accents.[3] For example, the two-digit code 73 stands for *ṭifḥa;* 80 stands for *zaqef;* 92 stands

---

[3] An online version of the CCAT BHS codebook is available, as of December 2006, at the following URL: http://www.wts.edu/hebrew/whmcodemanual.html.

for *atnah*. There are several ambiguous codes, such as 75 (which is either *silluq* or *meteg*), but these are all fairly easy to resolve (e.g., 75 is *silluq* if it comes just before *sof pasuq*). The beauty of a simple, clean system like that of the CCAT is that it is extremely easy for the computer to process and manipulate. Such a system therefore provides an ideal basis for a computer-based accentual parser/error-detector.

Consider, by way of contrast, the antithesis to the CCAT BHS (hereafter eBHS) texts: A proprietary coding system designed to work with a specific brand of typesetting or word-processing software. Such a system would provide no motivation for distinguishing between, say, *mahpak* and *yetiv*, or between *azla* and *pašṭa*. Why? Because the same graphic symbols are used in both cases. Remember that typesetting and word-processing codes exist mainly just to tell software where to print what symbols. And because *mahpak* and *yetiv* are the same symbol, as also are *azla* and *pašṭa*, there is no need in this context to use different codes to represent them. Unfortunately, in contexts such as automated error checking or format conversions, distinctions such as this are extremely important because without them vital structural information is obscured or entirely lost.

It might be added that proprietary typesetting or word-processing systems have a limited lifetime — usually the same as that of the software they are used with. This includes *Extensible Markup Language* (XML)-based coding systems, which (despite XML's current fashionableness) are not necessarily tractable or usable outside the context of the proprietary software used to create them.[4]

Unlike proprietary coding schemes, schemes like the one used in the eBHS text serve as efficient information repositories. They do not contain superfluous information. They convert readily into other formats. And they can be readily accessed, maintained, and corrected. Such schemes, therefore, are what we should be using as the basis for error checking. They may be stored in a platform-neutral state and then converted, as needed, into typesetters' native formats. In essence, the arguments for using a format like that of eBHS are the same as those for using structural or *content-based* (rather than presentation-based) markup schemes in general — a goal XML and its predecessor, SGML (Standard Generalized Markup Language), were, in theory, intended to attain.[5]

7.6. The Implementation

Having discussed both the theory on which a practical accentual parser/checker must operate and the data formats it prefers, it is now possible to discuss details of the proof-of-concept implementation offered here.

Stated briefly, the parser/checker offered here (which I call simply *Accents*) consists of two basic modules: (1) a lexical analyzer, and (2) a parser. The first module, the lexical analyzer, translates accentual codes into a form that the next module, the parser, can utilize. The parser then restructures these accents into a simple human-readable parse tree (see fig. 7.1), and flags any errors it detects. The parser itself is fairly abstract and deals only with generic representations of the accents it is processing. Although the parser is, in theory, agnostic about what lexical analyzer is used and what coding system the lexical analyzer operates on, in actual fact I have written only one lexical analyzer for it, which is tailored specifically for the eBHS texts mentioned in the preceding section.

One key point about the *Accents* program is that it is small and conceptually very simple — simple enough to be implemented using off-the-shelf tools like C (ANSI), YACC, and Lex.[6] C has been around since the 1970s, and is ubiquitous. YACC, a simple language for generating LR parsers, is a standard component of most stock Unix and Unix-like systems. Lex, a tool for creating modules that break data streams down into so-called "tokens," is also a standard Unix utility. Versions of YACC and Lex exist for many different operating systems besides Unix.

---

[4] XML is a metalanguage for defining the syntax of markup (e.g., "tags" like <body></body>) in documents. Markup/tags give structure to what would otherwise be plain character data. XML markup syntax is formally defined using *document type definitions* (DTDs) or *schemas*. The XML specification itself is controlled by the World Wide Web Consortium (http://www.w3.org/XML/). When people talk about XML they are typically talking about document instances that conform to one or another XML DTD or schema. XML itself is not a markup language or document format, and it defines the actual semantics of markup in only limited ways. Contrary to popular belief, there is nothing intrinsic to XML that prevents one from using it in obtuse or proprietary fashions.

[5] See Coombs et al. 1987 for further, if early, discussion of the distinction between markup intended for presentation, like "color" or "boldface" codes, and markup intended to delineate real underlying textual structures like paragraphs and sections.

[6] ANSI C is the version of C defined by the American National Standards Institute Committee X3J11. Draft standards began in the late 1980s. The latest official standard is ANSI/ISO 9899–1990.

```
                    ┌──────────────────┐      Raw Machine-Readable Input
                    │ Lexical Analyzer │◄─────        (e.g. eBHS)
                    └──────────────────┘
                             │
                             ▼
                    ┌──────────────────┐
                    │      Parser      │─────► Human-Readable Parse Tree
                    └──────────────────┘
```

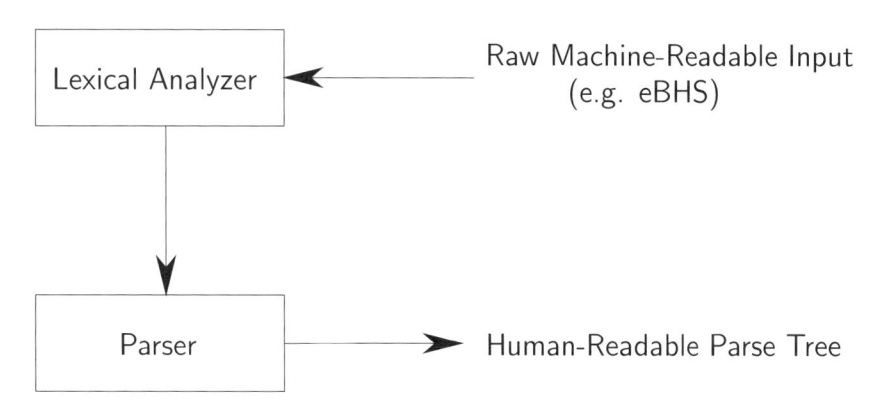

Figure 7.1. Overview of Parser/Checker

They are well-understood, reliable, readily available tools.[7] Because of their reliability and ready availability, ANSI C, YACC, and Lex were natural choices as the implementation languages for *Accents*.

Without turning this paper into a tutorial on YACC and Lex (which, like all software, will seem outdated and quaint within a few decades of their creation), let me nevertheless pause for just a moment to review what modules written for these tools look like and how they work. YACC grammars are written in a notation linguists will easily grasp and Lex files make extensive use of a commonly used pattern-matching language called *regular expressions* (see, e.g., Friedl 2002). YACC and Lex therefore serve as useful tools for explaining how *Accents* is put together and how it functions.

The YACC portion of *Accents* consists of a series of rules of the form:

```
LHS : RHS
```

where LHS ("left-hand side") represents a node in a given accentual parse tree having RHS ("right-hand side") as its child, or children. When several rules have a common LHS component, they may be grouped together, in which case a simple slash is written instead of the repeated LHS. By convention, "terminal" symbols, that is, symbols that form the leaves of the parse tree, are written in capital letters:

```
silluq-clause : silluq-phrase
              | tifcha-clause silluq-clause
              | tevir-clause silluq-clause
              | zaqef-clause silluq-clause
              | atnach-clause silluq-clause
silluq-phrase : SILLUQ
              | MEREKA SILLUQ
            etc.
```

The above YACC input rules may be read, in English, as follows:

1. A silluq-clause consists of either
    (a) a silluq-phrase
    (b) a tifcha-clause then a silluq-clause
    (c) a tevir-clause then a silluq-clause
    (d) a zaqef-clause then a silluq-clause, or
    (e) an atnach-clause followed by a silluq-clause
2. A silluq-phrase consists either of
    (a) SILLUQ, or
    (b) MEREKA then SILLUQ

---

[7] Lex and YACC were developed at Bell Laboratories in the 1970s — YACC by Stephen C. Johnson, and Lex by M. E. Lesk and E. Schmidt. Both were shipped as standard Unix utilities as early as version 7 (1978). See Institute of Electrical and Electronics Engineers (IEEE) Std1003.2 (POSIX Shell and Utilities) for the most recent applicable standard.

The actual rules found in the *Accents* source code are, in reality, considerably more complex than the ones given above.[8] The *Accents* source code, for example, characterizes the cantillation mark *ṭifḥa* in such a way that it cannot occur after *zaqef* within a *silluq* clause. What it does, in other words, is to prevent rule 1c above from applying to the output of rule 1d. Doing this is not terribly difficult, but to explain fully how it is done would require a rather lengthy digression. It is enough here merely to note that the same basic principles illustrated above apply to the full grammar.

What YACC does is to take the entire set of syntax rules that make up the *Accents* grammar and turn these into a working parser. This parser may then be used to process the Bible verse-by-verse, building linear sequences of accents up into two-dimensional trees (e.g., fig. 7.2) — or else reporting any failures to do so, presumably due to errors in the text.

```
              silluq-clause
            /              \
    ṭifḥa-clause        silluq-clause
         |                   |
        ...             silluq-phrase
                          /        \
                      MEREKA      SILLUQ
```

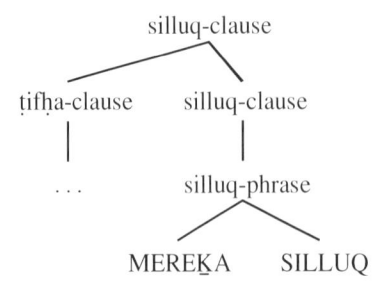

Figure 7.2. Sample Parse Tree

In order for the parser to do its work, something has to convert the accent "codes" present in the actual Hebrew text into symbols the parser can recognize, like MEREKA and SILLUQ. As noted above, this conversion is handled by the lexical analyzer.

The lexical analyzer is generated via Lex from a set of directives or "rules" that map specific patterns in a machine-readable input stream to tokens (terminal symbols) that a parser can understand. The following Lex rule, for example, tells Lex to send an ATNACH token to the parser whenever it encounters the characters "9" then "2" on its input stream:

```
92              { return ATNACH; }
```

All Lex rules have this same general form. Basically, the material at the left-hand margin lists the character sequence to look for. The remainder of the line contains computer code written in the C programming language, which tells the lexical analyzer what to do when it finds that character sequence. Here are several more examples:

```
01              { return SEGOLTA;     }
65{TEXT}05      { return SHALSHELET;  }
80              { return ZAQEF;       }
85              { return ZAQEFGADOL;  }
81              { return REVIA;       }
```

The TEXT string above is a macro that expands to an expression that matches non-numeric characters. That macro is defined elsewhere in the Lex input file.

In a few cases the Lex rules become considerably more elaborate than what we see above, as, for example, when the rules must distinguish *munaḥ+paseq* combinations that are simply that from ones that are actually the elusive (and graphically identical) accent *legarmeh*. The Lex rules also handle verse and/or so-called Betacode delimiters (used by older eBHS texts to mark books, chapters, and verses; they are now obsolete).

---

[8] The term *source code* refers to human-readable computer instructions, which must be converted or *compiled* into something a computer can execute, that is, into a computer program. See note 9 below for information on obtaining the *Accents* source code.

7.7. Running the *Accents* Program

Accents is provided as a source-code distribution. This means that people who want to use it must compile it into executable form; that is, they must themselves convert the C, YACC, and Lex files into a program their computer can actually run. Doing this is not difficult for those who have worked in C, or its daughter language, C++. On Unix and Unix-like systems, compiling is likely to require nothing more than a run of the included *configure* script and an invocation of the standard program-building utility, *make*. (Those who are not accustomed to compiling executables from source should contact their information technology support staff and avail themselves of a local Unix programmer or systems administrator.)

Once set up, *Accents* can be set to work, from a command-line interface (in Unix terms, a "shell"; in Microsoft Windows terms a "command window"), directly on eBHS-format texts, which must, incidentally, be in Unix LF (as opposed to DOS CR-LF, i.e., carriage return-linefeed) format. *Accents* simply reads the text from the "standard input" and sends a list of verses it has processed to the screen or "standard output," flagging errors as it finds them. Alternatively, it can take its input from one or more files specified on the command line. Systems with no concept of standard input or a command line will not support *Accents*, at least as it is currently configured. Those not familiar with command-line interfaces should again consult their local information technology support staff.

Under Unix (or any Unix-like operating system), for example, *Accents* would normally be invoked as follows:

```
accents -p < name-of-your-eBHS-file
```

where *name-of-your-eBHS-file* is the full pathname of the file where your eBHS text resides, and where *-p* is a command-line switch that tells *Accents* to print trees for the verses it parses.

The trees that *Accents* outputs to the computer screen are not nearly so elaborate as the one depicted above in figure 7.2. Rather, *Accents* outputs its parse trees using a simple, indented, text-only notation. The digits at the left-hand side of each line of output indicate the degree of nesting. Literal accent names such as *ṭifḥa*, *munaḥ*, and *atnaḥ* appear at the innermost clausal levels, with no preceding digit. For an example of this notation, see figure 7.3, which shows a piece of *Accents*' actual output (on the left), and depicts graphically (on the right) how this output relates to an actual Hebrew verse (in this case, Genesis 1:1). Read the right side of this figure in reverse order, following the natural order of the Hebrew words at the bottom.

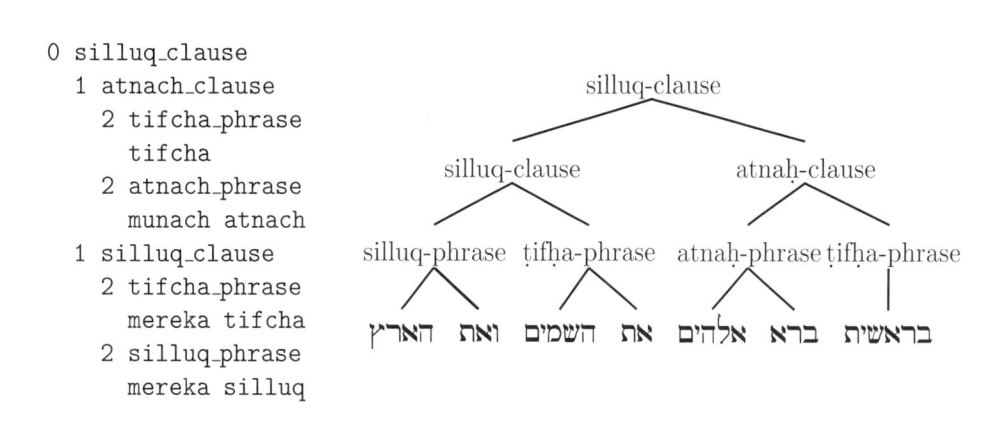

```
0 silluq_clause
    1 atnach_clause
        2 tifcha_phrase
            tifcha
        2 atnach_phrase
            munach atnach
    1 silluq_clause
        2 tifcha_phrase
            mereka tifcha
        2 silluq_phrase
            mereka silluq
```

Figure 7.3. *Accents*' Structural Interpretation of Genesis 1:1

When invoked with the *-p* command-line option, *Accents* reports errors as part of the accentual parse trees it produces (see section 7.8 for a full discussion of this feature and its potential usefulness to editors, proofreaders, and typesetters). If no *-p* command-line switch is provided, *Accents* merely lists parsing errors as it finds them and emits *book chapter:verse* references for each verse it has successfully processed, for example:

```
Gen 1:1
Gen 1:2
Gen 1:3
```

```
Gen 1:4
Gen 1:5
...
Exod 4:8
Exod 4:9
accents warning 7 (yyparse): error encountered in Exodus 4:10
Exod 4:10
Exod 4:11
...
```

Although on some computer systems error output does not end up quite where one might expect it to, notice of an error will normally precede reference to the verse that caused the error, at least when running in this mode. If *-e* is supplied on the command line, error messages are suppressed, and only those verses that contain errors are listed on the screen. In other words, if you type

```
accents -e < name-of-your-eBHS-file
```

you will see, instead of the above output, only references to verses containing errors, namely

```
...
Exod 4:10
...
```

Note that the *-e* option will also work with the *-p* option. Using these two options together tells *Accents* to display trees for only those verses that contain accentual errors.

7.8. Full Example

To illustrate the utility of *Accents* for editors, proofreaders, and typesetters, let me offer a full, real-life example of how it manages to ferret out, with relative ease, a subtle error that made its way into both BHS and eBHS.

Above the second letter of the ninth word of Exodus 28:1 in the Leningrad Hebrew Bible manuscript (B19a) there appears to be a stray mark — a dot that sits over, and very slightly to the right of, the somewhat more darkly drawn accent *revia* (see fig. 7.4). The trouble with this stray dot is that it does not look like a stray dot unless one's attention is called directly to it as a possible error. As a result, the dot makes the *revia* (which looks something like a period) look very much as though it were, instead, the lower member of the colon-like accent, *zaqef*.

The seeming reasonableness of this reading, visually speaking, is evident in BHS, where the editor of Exodus, G. Qwell, without any comment at all, transcribes the accent as *zaqef*. As one might expect, Qwell's oversight also appears in eBHS, where it has gone probably undetected until now. This type of error, which would be virtually impossible to eliminate from traditional, hand-proofread biblical editions, is caught easily by *Accents*, which, when applied to Exodus 28:1 (invoked with the *-p* option), produces the error report shown at the bottom of figure 7.4.

Notice that in the error report, *Accents* manifests some confusion about where exactly the error occurs (it omits a preceding *munaḥ* and marks the segment containing the error as a *tevir*-clause). As noted above, this sort of confusion is not uncommon. *Accents* must often throw out a few tokens or terminal symbols before it can reset itself well enough to continue parsing. Usually a quick look at the manuscript, printed edition, or electronic text in question (any of which may prove to be the error's source) is all that is required to pin down where the error that *Accents* reports actually lies.

7. 9. Known Shortcomings

As noted above (section 7.4), there are a few accentual errors that *Accents* will not always catch. These are listed in the comments to the YACC parser code, as found in the *Accents* source code distribution. Salient examples include (1) *pašṭa* for what should be *gereš* and (2) some cases of *yetiv* for *mahpa$\underline{k}$*, and the reverse. These are very easy errors to make, from an underlying data-encoding standpoint, particularly when using naive optical character recognition to input character codes. Fortunately they are not common in eBHS, and they are not visually difficult to spot in print-outs (the slant of the mark and/or its position will be completely wrong).

Occasionally the accentuation of a verse is also just too bizarre for *Accents* to handle. In Exodus 20:1–17, for example, the doubly accented ten commandments cause *Accents* to spew an amusing series of error messages. Those who attempt to run *Accents* themselves should simply ignore these messages. The same situation occurs in the second version of the ten commandments in Deuteronomy 5:6–21. Although *Accents* handles some doubly accented verses quite elegantly (e.g., Genesis 35:22), such verses are more the exception than the rule.

Sophisticated users wanting a deeper understanding of these problems, or of any others that surface, are invited to try out the *-d* option, which causes *Accents* to emit profuse diagnostic messages that can often be of help in determining what it is "thinking." Under Unix or Linux, for example, one might type

```
accents -d < text 2>&1 | less
```

It is possible to separate out only those diagnostic messages that seem particularly relevant for a particular problem by piping *Accents*' output through a standard Unix filter program, such as *egrep*. For example, to obtain a list of superfluous or unrecognized accents encountered during parsing, one might type

```
accents -d < text 2>&1 | egrep 'Unrecog' | more
```

Note, however, that with the *-d* option, *Accents* runs considerably more slowly than it does without. (It runs fastest when invoked with just the *-e* option.) Running *Accents* with the *-e* option (with or without the *-d* option) may cast light onto subtle parsing issues, that is, onto why *Accents* is flagging an error.

Another issue is the whole concept of "errors," a term that mirrors closely the simplistic way in which *Accents* views Hebrew accents. In *Accents*' view a given accentual sequence either passes or is flagged as bad. There are no gray areas. In real life, however, there are gray areas. Accentual sequences may violate purported accentual "rules" without rendering the text erroneous in a strict sense. Another way to view the system described here might therefore be as an anomaly detector — that is, a system for locating sequences of accents that merit attention, either because they reflect errors, or else because they constitute interesting deviations from the norm. I have generally used the term "error" here simply because it is a more natural one for information scientists, and because, in the great majority of cases, the *Accents* program seems in fact to be finding errors (rather than debatable "anomalies") in the text.

One final issue worth mentioning here is that *Accents* can currently process only the twenty-one prose books of the Hebrew Bible. The three poetic books, Psalms, Proverbs, and Job, have yet to be integrated into the distribution. There were three reasons for this omission. First of all, I had limited resources at my disposal to devote to the project. Secondly, my knowledge of the poetic cantillation system was limited, and I simply was not as comfortable designing for these accents as I was for the prose ones. Thirdly, it made sense to start with the prose accents because the prose books constitute about ninety percent of the Hebrew Bible.

If time and resources permit, or if some new source of funding appears on the horizon, I will extend the system to cover the poetic books. In the meantime, if some other scholar would like to make the required modifications, he or she would have my blessing (see note 9 for directions on how to obtain the source code).

7.10. Concluding Remarks

The central intellectual question that this paper addresses is whether the fairly complex Tiberian Hebrew accentual system can be re-cast as a simple, computationally tractable "grammar." Theoretically, the answer to this question is "no." Practically, however, the answer is "yes." *If* we are willing to extend our grammar so that it accepts not only valid accentual constructs but also a few (unlikely) erroneous constructs as well, we can, in fact, reduce that grammar to a simple, computationally very tractable form.

The fact that our grammar can be reduced to a simple, computationally tractable form has enormous practical consequences. As noted at the outset of this paper, it means, for one thing, that it is possible now for scholars and publishers to produce accentually correct biblical editions. It also means that they can easily construct tools for asking questions of the data such as:

1. In what range of accentual clause types does accent X occur in manuscript or edition Y?
2. How does manuscript/edition Y's use of accent X differ from that of manuscript Z?
3. Where in manuscript Z did the scribe make the most accentual errors, and what sorts of errors did he tend to make?

As proof of this concept, that is, as proof that we can construct a practical computer-based tool that can analyze biblical Hebrew cantillation marks, this paper has introduced *Accents*. *Accents* is a simple tool for analyzing and validating the accentuation of machine-readable Tiberian texts. It is obviously not the last word in accentual validation, but it is practical, stable, and very fast. Most importantly, however, it offers *prima facie* evidence that it is possible to construct practical, working automata based on an almost-correct accentual grammar that can efficiently and reliably locate errors in machine-readable Hebrew Bible texts.[9]

---

[9] To acquire the source code for *Accents* contact the author at richard@goerwitz.com. At least through the end of 2007, the source code will also be available at http://www.goerwitz.com/software/accents/accents-1.1.4.tar.gz.

7. A NEW MASORETIC "SPELL CHECKER" FOR CHECKING ACCENTUAL STRUCTURE 121

Original Manuscript

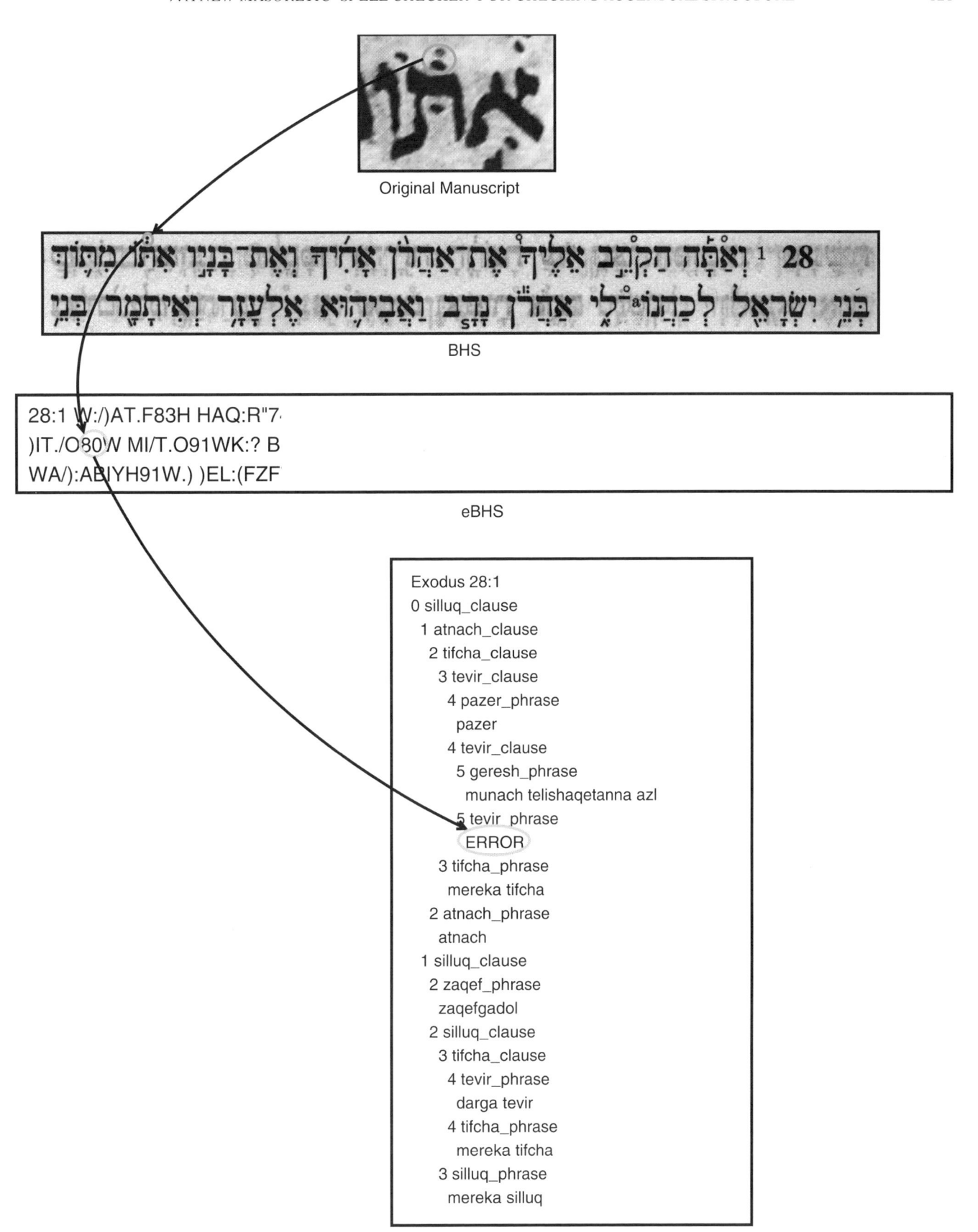

BHS

```
28:1 W:/)AT.F83H HAQ:R"7
)IT./O80W MI/T.O91WK:? B
WA/):ABIYH91W.) )EL:(FZF
```

eBHS

```
Exodus 28:1
0 silluq_clause
 1 atnach_clause
  2 tifcha_clause
   3 tevir_clause
    4 pazer_phrase
     pazer
    4 tevir_clause
     5 geresh_phrase
      munach telishaqetanna azl
     5 tevir_phrase
      ERROR
   3 tifcha_phrase
    mereka tifcha
  2 atnach_phrase
   atnach
 1 silluq_clause
  2 zaqef_phrase
   zaqefgadol
  2 silluq_clause
   3 tifcha_clause
    4 tevir_phrase
     darga tevir
    4 tifcha_phrase
     mereka tifcha
   3 silluq_phrase
    mereka silluq
```

Accents Output

Figure 7.4. Sample Error from *Biblia Hebraica Stuttgartensia*

Bibliography

Aho, Alfred V.; Ravi Sethi; and Jeffrey D. Ullman
   1986   *Compilers, Principles, Techniques, and Tools*. Reading: Addison-Wesley.

Coombs, James H.; Allen H. Renear; and Steven J. DeRose
   1987   "Markup Systems and the Future of Scholary Text Processing." *Communications of the ACM* 30: 933–47.

Friedl, Jeffrey E. F.
   2002   *Mastering Regular Expressions*. Second edition. Sebastopol: O'Reilly.

Goerwitz, R. L.
   1994   Review of *The Syntax of Masoretic Accents in the Hebrew Bible*, by James D. Price. *Journal of the American Oriental Society* 114: 276–77.

Kittel, Rudolf; Karl Elliger; and Wilhelm Rudolph
   1997   *Biblia Hebraica Stuttgartensia*. Fifth edition. Stuttgart: Deutsche Bibelgesellschaft.

Price, James D.
   1990   *The Syntax of Masoretic Accents in the Hebrew Bible*. Studies in the Bible and Early Christianity 27. Lewiston: Edwin Mellen Press.

Tofte, Mads
   1990   *Compiler Generators: What They Can Do, What They Might Do, and What They Will Probably Never Do*. Berlin and New York: Springer-Verlag.

Tomita, Masaru
   1985   *Efficient Parsing for Natural Language: A Fast Algorithm for Practical Systems*. Kluwer International Series in Engineering and Computer Science 8. Boston: Kluwer Academic Publishers.

Wickes, William
   1970   *Two Treatises on the Accentuation of the Old Testament: Taʿame emet on Psalms, Proverbs, and Job; Taʿame kaf-alef sefarim on the Twenty-one Prose Books*. Library of Biblical Studies. New York: Ktav.

Yeivin, Israel
   1980   *Introduction to the Tiberian Masorah*, edited and translated by E. J. Revell. Society of Biblical Literature Masoretic Studies 5. Missoula: Scholars Press.

8. EXTERNAL PLURAL MARKERS IN SEMITIC: A NEW ASSESSMENT

Rebecca Hasselbach

8.1. Introduction

The derivation of the external plural markers attested in Semitic languages is still one of the most puzzling problems regarding the reconstruction of Early/Proto-Semitic.

It is usually assumed that the feminine plural morpheme *-āt- and the masculine nominative and oblique plurals *-ū and *-ī are Common Semitic since they are, at least in vestiges, preserved in most Semitic sub-branches. Other external plural markers, such as *-ān(V), *-aw, and *-ay, are restricted to specific languages or morphological environments and most commonly do not represent the primary plural marker in the languages in which they occur. Most of the latter plural morphemes are also attested in other Afroasiatic sub-branches. Thus, they probably belong to the common stock of Afroasiatic morphemes and cannot be considered secondary innovations within Semitic. In fact, the analysis and reconstruction of plural markers in Semitic is only possible when we take the various forms attested in other Afroasiatic languages into account.[1]

Another question that has not yet been answered satisfactorily is why external plural markers exhibit a diptotic case system in Semitic as opposed to the triptotic case system of the singular and most broken plural patterns in those languages that preserve the full case inflection.[2] Although this problem has been recognized before, no convincing explanation for this rather idiosyncratic phenomenon has been given so far.

The present study attempts to summarize the current state of research concerning external plural markers and to suggest a reconstruction for the most common plural morphemes in Semitic based on evidence from Semitic and other Afroasiatic languages.

8.2. Evidence

Afroasiatic languages share a common set of morphemes that are used to mark plurality. The following section briefly summarizes the main Afroasiatic evidence, starting with non-Semitic data, followed by the most common attestations in Semitic.

The most widely attested constituent of external plural markers in Afroasiatic languages other than Semitic is /w/. Egyptian most commonly uses the masculine plural markers -w and -ww — although the /w/ is not always expressed in the writing — and the feminine plural markers -t and -wt.[3] Other Afroasiatic languages similarly have external plural markers containing /w/. In Chadic, we find plurals such as -aw, -ūwa and -āwā (Zaborski 1976: 6; Newman 1990: 12; Voigt 1999: 19).[4] The Berber language Tuareg uses the plural markers -awan, -iwan, and -aw for the masculine and -awin, -iwin, and -awat for the feminine (Ratcliffe 1998: 103; Zaborski 1976: 3–4;

---

[1] I am particularly honored to dedicate this study to Gene Gragg, who is not only one of the leading scholars in Semitics, but has also devoted a great part of his work to the investigation of Afroasiatic languages in general. My thanks also go to Janling Fu for his helpful corrections. All opinions and errors are, of course, my responsibility alone.

[2] Languages to be counted among these are Akkadian, Ugaritic, and Classical Arabic. Old South Arabian might have preserved the full case system as well, but because of the absence of any indication of short vowels in the orthography this cannot be proven with certainty. Geʿez has a diptotic case system in both the singular and plural — accusative versus non-accusative — that is the result of the loss of final short /i/ and /u/. This final vowel loss caused the merger of the nominative and genitive singular.

[3] The feminine form -wt seems to be less frequent than -t (Schenkel 1983: 203, 209; Zeidler 1992: 197). It is unclear whether the /w/ of the Middle Egyptian plural morphemes is consonantal or vocalic. Schenkel seems to treat them as consonantal at this period (1983: 173–209), while standard grammars like Allen's simply state that /w/ was most likely a consonant in Middle Egyptian and perhaps, in some cases, vocalic, without specifying its exact status in the plural (Allen 2000: 16).

[4] Hausa has a set of three different plural morphemes which are used for biconsonantal nouns, -unā, -uwā, and -ukā, as in tāfī > plural tāfunā 'palm of hand', ʾabu > plural ʾabūbuwā 'thing', and garī > plural garūruwā 'town' (Ratcliffe 1998: 108).

Petráček 1965: 229).[5] A wide range of plurals in /w/ is also attested in Cushitic languages, where forms like -wa, -uwwa, -awwa, -iw, and -ōwo are used in various languages (Zaborski 1986: 295).[6] All these forms show that the formation of external plural markers with /w/ is a common feature within Afroasiatic languages.[7] However, components of /w/ are only a sub-set of external plural markers in these languages.

In Tuareg, the most common plural markers are -în for the feminine and -än for the masculine.[8] Furthermore, Tuareg has several less common suffixes to mark plurality, including -ân, an ending -a that is only used for the feminine, and a plural marker -t, which is rare and only used for four nouns denoting family relations (Ratcliffe 1998: 103).

In Hausa, singular nouns — all of which end in a vowel — usually form their plural by vowel ablaut. Singulars ending in /ī/ and /ē/ change their final vowel to /ā/ or /ai/, while singulars in /ā/ or /ō/ change their vowel to /ī/ or /ū/. The final /ā/ in the singular is a characteristic of the feminine (Ratcliffe 1998: 105). Furthermore, Hausa has a rare plural suffix -anī, as in garmā (singular), garēmanī (plural) 'trenching hoe' (Ratcliffe 1998: 109).[9]

Cushitic languages have multiple variants of plural markers. The most common morphemes are compounds of -t, such as -et, -at, -ut, -ūte, and -ti; compounds of -Vy, such as -ay, -eyyi, -iyye, -eyye, etc.; others with -n, as in -an, -ān, -ane, -anu, -en; and with -m, as in -ma, and -mu (Zaborski 1986: 294–96).[10] The basic components of these plural markers, the consonants /w/, /y/, /t/, and /n/ are also known from Semitic languages.

The most common external plural marker in Semitic is the plural marker *-āt, which is primarily associated with the feminine. It is attested in all major languages, as in Akkadian šarrāt- 'queens', Classical Arabic banāt- 'daughters', Hebrew məlākôt < *-āt 'queens', Syriac malkātā (emphatic state), Geʿez, where it is not gender dependent, as in nəgəstāt 'queens' and nabiyāt 'prophets' (masculine plural), and in Old South Arabian and Ancient North Arabian.[11]

The second most frequent external plural markers in Semitic are the masculine nominative and oblique plurals *-ū and *-ī. Both forms together are only attested in a limited number of languages, including Babylonian Akkadian, šarrū 'kings' (nominative) and šarrī (oblique), Classical Arabic muʿallimū- 'teachers' (nominative) and muʿallimī- (oblique), Ugaritic malakū- (nominative) and malakī- (oblique), and perhaps Old South Arabian, where two forms for the masculine plural in the construct are attested, bnw and bny, which probably indicate the same diptotic case system as found in Babylonian Akkadian, Classical Arabic, and Ugaritic.[12] Remnants of this diptotic system also seem to be preserved in Yaʾudic texts from the eighth century B.C.E. that have mlkw for the nominative masculine plural and mlky for the oblique plural (Moscati 1964: 88; Retsö 1997: 272).

Other Semitic languages only preserve one of the two markers, usually the original oblique case, while the nominative form was lost. This loss was caused by a general collapse of the case system in these languages. Examples of the masculine plural *-ī can be found in Hebrew məlākîm (nominative + oblique) 'kings', Syriac malkīn (nominative + oblique), Mehri -īn (Johnstone 1975: 20), and probably as a vestige in Geʿez on plural nouns with pronominal suffixes, as in ʾahgur 'cities', but ʾahgurika 'your cities' (nominative + oblique).[13] In both

---

[5] Voigt states that there might be traces of /w/ in Berber (Voigt 1999: 17). The feminine plural -awat is extremely rare and only used for one noun, while the other plural markers with /w/ are primarily used with nouns that are biradical (Ratcliffe 1998: 104). The marker -aw is equally rare and only used for two nouns (ibid.).

[6] Afar, for example, uses the plural marker -wa on masculine nouns that end in a consonant, as in lubak > plural lubakwa 'lion', ʾalib > plural ʾalibwa 'tendon'. It also makes use of a plural marker -ōwa for biradical nouns that have a base CaC, such as ʾaf > plural ʾafōwa 'language' and han > plural hanōwa 'milk' (Ratcliffe 1998: 113).

[7] Consequently, Voigt reconstructs a "Proto-Hamito-Semitic" plural marker *-wV (Voigt 1999: 19).

[8] Ratcliffe considers the feminine plural marker -în an innovation of Berber (Ratcliffe 1998: 104).

[9] Hausa further has apophony between the singular, dual, and plural of certain nouns, as in singular digdigē, dual digādigī, and plural dugādugai 'heel' (Ratcliffe 1998: 109), where the dual and plural endings -ī and -ai resemble the Semitic oblique endings of the plural and dual, only that their distribution is the opposite from Semitic.

[10] These are the plural markers that have parallels in Semitic languages. Cushitic languages also have external plural markers with /l/ and /k/, although these seem to be inner Cushitic innovations (Zaborski 1986: 298). In the Cushitic language Afar, the most common plural marker is -itte, which has a kind of default status and is used when a masculine noun ends in a vowel, although the plural marker itself is feminine, as in bagu > plural bagitte 'stomach', sāku > plural sākitte 'morning' (Ratcliffe 1998: 111).

[11] For Ancient North Arabian, see Macdonald 2004: 504; for Old South Arabian, see Nebes and Stein 2004: 461.

[12] For the attestations, see Beeston 1984: 29 and Nebes and Stein 2004: 461. In Ancient North Arabian (Dadanitic) the masculine plural construct is attested as bnw 'sons of', which might indicate the preservation of the diptotic case system, but no oblique forms have yet been found (Macdonald 2004: 504).

[13] This /i/ is etymologically long.

Hebrew and Aramaic -īm/n is only used for the absolute masculine plural, not for the masculine plural construct or before pronominal suffixes.

Old Akkadian, Assyrian, Hebrew, and Aramaic have a variant oblique plural marker -ē and -ay < *ay. In Old Akkadian and Assyrian, this -ē plural is used for all masculine oblique forms, such as šarrē 'kings' (bound and unbound),[14] while in Hebrew and Aramaic this form is only used for masculine plural constructs, including masculine plural nouns with pronominal suffixes, as in Hebrew malkê 'kings' (masculine plural construct) and malkênû 'our kings'.[15] The forms in Hebrew and Aramaic have been explained as the result of an analogy with the oblique dual *-ay (Bauer and Leander 1991: §64f; Gray 1934: §209), but this explanation is rather unsatisfying since the Akkadian plurals in -ē have to be derived from the same basic form. An alternative explanation is to assume an independent plural marker *-ay that is not originally connected to the dual.[16]

A plural marking morpheme /w/ and compounds thereof are attested in numerous Semitic languages. This /w/ can appear either as part of external plural markers or be part of broken plural patterns. Examples of the former include the external plural -aw in Geʿez, which is used for a limited set of six biconsonantal nouns: ʾabaw 'fathers' from the singular ʾab, ʾafaw 'mouths' from ʾaf, ʾaxaw 'brothers' from ʾəxʷ, ʾədaw 'hands' from ʾəd, ʿədaw 'males' from ʿəd, and ʿədaw 'trees' from ʿəḍ (Lambdin 1978: 21). A number of nouns in Syriac and other Aramaic dialects similarly form their plural by the insertion of /w/, although this construction is primarily attested in connection with the feminine plural, as in ʾaṯrəwāṯā 'places' from the singular ʾaṯrā (emphatic state), lebbawāṯā 'hearts' from lebbā, and nahrəwāṯā 'rivers' from nahrā.[17] None of these words contains /w/ as root consonant.[18] It has also been suggested, that a plural ending -aw underlies certain forms of plural nouns with pronominal suffixes in Aramaic, such as Imperial and biblical Aramaic -why, presumably < *-awhî (Cross 2003: 354).[19] Certain biconsonantal nouns in Classical Arabic similarly insert /w/ before the feminine plural marker, such as sanat-un 'year', plural sanawāt-un, ʾaḥawāt-un 'sisters' from the singular ʾuḫt-un, and ʾiḥwat-un 'brothers' from the singular base ʾaḫ-un. In Classical Arabic, /w/ is also found in certain broken plural patterns that are used for singular stems containing a long vowel, mostly /ā/, less often /ū/, as in fāris-un 'horseman', plural fawāris-u and ṭūmār-un 'scroll' plural ṭawāmīr-u (for further examples see Fischer 1987: §97). In Mehri, we find the feminine plural forms -ōtən and -ʾawtən, but it is not certain whether or not the diphthong /aw/ is original in these forms (for the attestations, see Johnstone 1975: 20).

The last external plural marker to be mentioned in this context is -ān. This form is attested in Geʿez, where it is used for the plurals of animate masculine nouns and masculine plural adjectives, although masculine nouns can also be pluralized by the "feminine plural" -āt.[20] Examples in Geʿez include mašaggerān 'fishermen' from the singular base mašagger, liqān 'elders', and ṣādəqān 'righteous' (masculine plural adjective). A morpheme -ān in connection with the plural is attested in various other Semitic languages. In Classical Arabic, -ān is part of the broken plural formations fiʿlān-un and fuʿlān-un, as in ǧīrān-un 'neighbors' from the singular ǧār-, ġizlān-un 'gazelles' from the singular ġazāl-, and fursān-un 'horsemen' from fāris-. These two plural patterns are primarily used for individual plurals — as opposed to collectives — and for living beings, although their usage was expanded to other categories (Fischer 1987: 54). An individualizing morpheme -ān is attested in Akkadian, where it is used for both singulars and plurals, as in šarrāqān- 'a particular thief' and šarrāqānū 'a certain group of thieves', ilū 'gods' versus ilānū 'a certain group of gods' (von Soden 1995: §56r; Huehnergard 1998: 198).[21]

---

[14] Lipiński (2001: 245) takes the -ē as simple allophone of -ī.

[15] In Samaritan Aramaic, the plural generally seems to have the same form as the original dual, -em and -en < *-aym/n (Macuch 1982: 277).

[16] See, for example, Retsö 1997: 272–74, who takes -ay as an original masculine plural marker that acquired dualic function by a secondary restrictive process, and Cross 2003: 356.

[17] For this type of plural and more examples in various dialects of Aramaic, see Nöldeke 1875: 167 and 1982: 56; Bauer and Leander 1962: §53j; Fassberg 1990: 136; Muraoka and Porten 2003: 73–74.

[18] Fassberg states: "The plural markers /-awan/, /-awat/, /-awata/ on nouns ending in /-u/ as well as nouns ending in /-a/, /-e/, and even consonants is a general Aramaic feature" (1990: 136).

[19] A more common derivation of this suffix is *-ayhu > *-ayu > *-aw > ō and then a reattachment of the third-person masculine singular pronominal suffix *-hī resulting in -ōhî (Bauer and Leander 1962: §171).

[20] As, for example, in nabiyāt 'prophets' (masculine plural).

[21] Lipiński assumes that the plural endings -ānū/ī in Akkadian only spread from the Old Babylonian period on. This spread was caused by the decline of the dual suffix -ān (Lipiński 2001: 246). Although it is true that this type of plural is used more frequently in later dialects of Akkadian, the morpheme itself is most likely nevertheless ancient and related to similar morphemes in other Afroasiatic and Semitic languages.

Similar plural formations are found in Syriac, such as *rabbānē* 'masters' from the singular base *rabbā'*, *šalīṭānē* 'rulers', and *qašīšānē* 'priests' (Nöldeke 2001: 51).[22] Furthermore, the morpheme *-ān* is attested in Hebrew, where it is primarily used to form abstracts, as in *gā'ôn* 'pride', *hāmôn* 'noise', *rə'ābôn* 'hunger', but also rarely for collectives, as in *pərāzôn* 'rural population' (Gesenius et al. 1910: §85u).[23] The various forms in Geʿez, Akkadian, Aramaic, and Hebrew most likely go back to the same original morpheme *-ān*. Since this morpheme frequently has the function of either individualizing or particularizing, Kienast suggested that it originally marked a plural of a certain number that is closely related to the dual ending *-ān(i)* (Kienast et al. 2001: 137). Although I would agree that *-ān* is connected to a particularizing function in most languages in which it is attested and probably had a similar function originally, I would not go as far as Kienast and connect it to the dual.[24]

A particular case is the absolute feminine plural *-ān* in Aramaic, as in *malkā* 'queen', plural *malkān*. It is disputed whether this feminine plural marker is original and related to the forms found in Geʿez and Akkadian, or whether it represents a secondary form within Aramaic that was produced by analogy with the masculine plural *-īn*.[25] Aramaic is the only Semitic language in which the feminine plural is marked by a morpheme *-ān*. Furthermore, the feminine plural marker *-āt* is regularly used in the construct and emphatic state. Thus, it is more likely that this marker is indeed not directly related to the *-ān* morphemes attested in other Semitic languages but reflects a secondary development within Aramaic.

In summary, we can reconstruct six morphemes that are used as external plural markers or compounds thereof in Semitic:

(a) *-ū /*-ī, primarily used for the masculine plural dependent on case;
(b) *-āt, mostly, but not exclusively, used for the feminine plural;
(c) *-w- and its various compounds used for both broken plural formations and as part of the external plurals *-aw/-awāt*;
(d) *-ay, mostly used in the same environments as the oblique plural marker *-ī*; and
(e) *-ān, used for the animate masculine plural and "particularizing" plural formations.

Most of these basic elements, or at least their consonantal constituents, are also attested in other Afroasiatic branches, as has been shown above. Thus, the consonantal elements *t* and *n* and the glides *y* and *w* that underlie the most common plural formations in Semitic, Egyptian, Chadic, Berber, and Cushitic can be considered components of a set of morphemes that were used to mark plurality in Afroasiatic. It is more difficult to determine the vocalic elements of these morphemes in other Afroasiatic branches than Semitic. What we seem to be able to reconstruct are the elements *-ān, probably *-aw, and other compounds including /w/ such as *-awa/āt, which are mostly used for biradical nouns, *-at, and perhaps *-ay. It is not clear whether it is possible to reconstruct a common Afroasiatic external plural marker *-āt. Diakonoff suggested that the Somali feminine plural *-ō(d)* and Hausa *-oči* might be derived from *-ātu, but this derivation is not certain (Diakonoff 1965: 64). The common Semitic masculine plural markers *-ū* and *-ī* are also rare in other Afroasiatic branches, in case we can connect them to certain forms in Hausa at all, or unless we take them as products of /w/ and /y/.[26]

---

[22] There are numerous examples in Syriac in which the suffix *-ān-* is not used for human or living beings, such as *'ebbānē* 'fruits', *besmānē* 'fragrances', *gawnānē* 'colors', etc. (Nöldeke 2001: 51). Common to most words quoted by Nöldeke that take the plural *-ānē* in Syriac is that they represent individualized collectives that were subsequently pluralized.

[23] The suffix *-ān* is also used for abstracts in other Semitic languages, as in biblical Aramaic *dakrānayyā'* 'remembrance' and *minyān* 'number' (Bauer and Leander 1962: 195), Syriac *mawtānā'* 'plague' and *benyānā'* 'building' (Nöldeke 2001: §128), and Geʿez *raš'ān* 'old age' (Dillmann et al. 2003: §122).

[24] A particularizing or individualizing function in the plural is not restricted to the morpheme *-ān*. Bloch argues that there is a tendency in Modern Hebrew to form previously non-existing individualizing plurals from collectives, such as *'ofot* 'pieces of chicken' from the collective *'of* 'chicken', etc. (Bloch 1989: 124).

[25] For the interpretation of the feminine plural *-ān* as secondary, see Moscati 1954a: 41; 1964: 92; Lipiński 2001: 247. For the opposite interpretation, see Retsö 1997: 276.

[26] The Berber masculine plural *-ən* might be derived from *-una, but this derivation is uncertain as well (Diakonoff 1965: 65). For the derivation of these long vowels from glides, see section 8.3 below.

8.3. Previous Reconstructions

Three different types of reconstruction have been proposed for the masculine plural morphemes *-ū (nominative) and *-ī (oblique) and the feminine plural *-āt. Two of these assume an underlying phonological development that applies to both the masculine and feminine forms; the third derives these morphemes from various nominal suffixes. The three basic types can be summarized as follows:

(a) The direct derivation of the long plural vowels from the corresponding short (case) vowels of the singular by a process of lengthening.[27]

(b) The derivation from the singular base of a noun by the insertion of a specific plural morpheme, usually /w/ or its vocalic equivalent /u/, less often /y/.[28]

(c) A derivation mostly without phonological changes to the singular base or case vowels by assuming different abstract/collective endings that are attached to the singular base (Brockelmann 1908: 452; O'Leary 1969: 193; Kuryłowicz 1973: 39; Retsö 1997: 275).

Approaches *a + c* and *b + c* are not mutually exclusive.

The first derivation, that is, the lengthening of the singular (case) vowels, is thought to result in the following paradigm:[29]

	masculine singular	masculine plural	feminine singular	feminine plural
nominative	*kalbu	> *kalbū	*malkatu	> *malkātu
genitive	*kalbi	> *kalbī	*malkati	> *malkāti
accusative	*kalba	> **kalbā	*malkata	> **malkāta

According to this reconstruction, we would expect a triptotic case system in the plural since there is no apparent reason why the accusative singular vowel /a/ should not have been lengthened by the same process as the short case vowels of the nominative and genitive.[30] Several suggestions have been made as to why we find a diptotic system in these external plurals instead. Diakonoff assumed that the diptotic case marking in the plural is a vestige of a time when Semitic/Afroasiatic generally only recognized two cases (Diakonoff 1988: 64).[31] Gray proposed that vestiges of the original accusative plural *-ā still exist in the plural morpheme -ān attested in Geʿez and maybe in the Akkadian plural markers -ānū and -ānī (Gray 1934: §205). Yet another suggestion was made by Kienast, who argues that there was no original plural -ā because -ā originally had the function of a "status determinatus" (Kienast et al. 2001: 143).

Although there seems to be evidence that the earliest Semitic personal names partly exhibit a different case system than the system found in Classical Arabic, Akkadian, and Ugaritic, they nevertheless use the same basic three vowel markers as attested in later languages (Streck 2000: 282–90). In addition, this early inflectional system seems to contain a fourth case in the singular, marked by -Ø, that could be used for the same basic functions as the other vowel-marked categories (Streck 2000: 282). The assumption that the external plurals preserve an original diptotic case system is therefore rather unlikely. Furthermore, there is no reason why the plural should not have undergone the same case expansion as the singular. The interpretation of the attested variants of the -ān morpheme as a vestige of an original accusative plural is equally problematic. This -ān element is, as mentioned

---

[27] See, for example, Wright 2002: 145; Brockelmann 1908: 441 for the feminine plural; Moscati 1954a: 50 and 1964: 87; Kuryłowicz 1973: 145 for the feminine plural *-āt; Diakonoff 1988: 64; Lipiński 2001: 245; Kienast et al. 2001: 143.

[28] See Vycichl 1958: 176 for both the verbal and nominal system; Petráček 1965: 228; Zaborski 1976 and 1986 for Afroasiatic parallels of plurals with /w/-insertion; Voigt 1999: 19; Tropper 2004: 208–9.

[29] For the sake of simplicity, the reconstructed forms are given without mimation/nunation since these are not of immediate importance for the reconstruction of the external plural markers. Mimation/nunation should, of course, be assumed for the unbound forms of the noun.

[30] This problem has been pointed out before; see, for example, Retsö 1997: 271.

[31] Diakonoff further assumes that the external plural markers had their origin in the feminine, reconstructed as *-ât, where it seemed that the plural was produced by the lengthening of the vowel /a/ of the feminine singular marker. This "lengthening" of the vowel for the indication of the plural was then transferred to the masculine plural by analogy (Diakonoff 1988: 64). In the earlier version of his treatment of Afroasiatic languages, Diakonoff considered the lengthening of case vowels as one of various different ways to mark plurality, including the insertion of /w/, primarily used in Egyptian, and a hypothetical plural formation -āw and -āy for masculine nouns without mimation which reflect the suffixation of an assumed plural marker /ā/ to the nominal base (Diakonoff 1965: 63–64). The -ān- plural would be the corresponding form with nunation, that is, -ā-n-u (nominative) and -ā-n-i (oblique; ibid.).

in section 8.2 above, primarily found in Geʿez as animate masculine plural and in Akkadian, where it is analyzed as individualizing/particularizing suffix (von Soden 1995: §61i; Kienast et al. 2001: 129), in vestiges in Hebrew terms like *pərāzôn* 'rural population', where it reflects a collective, and in some plural formations in Syriac, such as *rawrəḇānē* 'magnates'. The Hebrew form in particular indicates that we are not dealing with a remnant of an accusative plural that originated in the same process as the external masculine plural markers *-ū* and *-ī*. Hebrew plurals and duals exhibit mimation, not nunation. Consequently, the final *-n* on *pərāzôn* does not reflect the same morpheme as the mimation of the plural and dual but is part of an undividable morpheme *-ān*. This ending *-ān* is an original abstract/collective marker that is not derivationally connected to the Semitic masculine plural *-ū* and *-ī*.[32]

This reconstruction has further been criticized because the masculine plural and feminine plural do not seem to lengthen the same morpheme. In the masculine plural it is the case vowel that is lengthened, while it is the vowel of the feminine singular marker *-at* in the feminine plural (Zaborski 1976: 2).

The second phonological approach attempts to explain the masculine and feminine plural markers by insertion of a glide that causes the lengthening of the respective vowels by contraction. There are two possible positions for the addition of a glide, either directly after the nominal base or after the singular case vowels. The two different possibilities will be discussed separately.

The most common reconstruction of the two is the suffixation of /w/ or its vocalic equivalent /u/ ~ /ū/. This analysis is primarily based on comparative evidence from Egyptian. Egyptian has the aforementioned external markers *-w* (masculine plural) and *-wt* (feminine plural), which are interpreted as being directly related to the Semitic plural markers *-ū/-ī* and *-āt*.[33]

Petráček reconstructs a plural morpheme *-ū* that is attached to the nominal base, as exemplified by Classical Arabic *muslim-Ø-ū-na*, where {Ø} reflects the masculine marker and {ū} the nominative masculine plural (Petráček 1965: 227).[34] This {ū} is supposedly also the base for the feminine plural *-wt* in Egyptian, which Petráček analyzes as *sn-ū/w-t* 'sisters' and the feminine plural in Classical Arabic, for which he assumes the development *muslim-w/ū-at-un* with the underlying contraction of **wa > ā* (Petráček 1965: 228). Zaborski similarly connects the Semitic external plurals to a plural morpheme /w/ that is attested in Egyptian, Berber, and Cushitic.[35] Voigt reconstructs two Proto-Afroasiatic plural markers, **-wV* and **-aan*. In Semitic, the sequence **-wu* presumably contracted to **-ū*, while the sequence **-wi* resulted in the long vowel **-ī* attested in the oblique masculine plural (Voigt 1997: 222; 1999: 19). The feminine plural marker reflects the same basic development **-wat > *-aat* (Voigt 1999: 15). The same approach is found in a recent article by Tropper, who suggests a case neutral plural morpheme {ū} = {uu} for the nominal and verbal system (Tropper 2004: 208). Both Tropper and Voigt reconstruct the feminine plural on nouns and the predicative adjective (= stative) with final /t/, that is, as **-āt*. The stative feminine plural in *-ā* in Semitic is considered a secondary development resulting from the loss of the original /t/ (Tropper 2004: 204; Voigt 1999: 12).[36]

The basic development as suggested by Petráček, Voigt, and Tropper can be represented as follows:[37]

---

[32] For a similar interpretation, see also Lipiński (2001: 244), who assumes that Proto-Semitic could create external plurals either by the lengthening of the singular vowel or by particular suffixes such as *-ān* and *-āt*. The analysis of *-ān* as an independent collective/plural suffix is found in Brockelmann 1908: 451 and Kuryłowicz 1973: 140. The suffix *-an/-ān* is also a common plural marker in Cushitic (Zaborski 1986: 295), which might be a reason why its use expanded in Geʿez, although this point requires further study.

[33] For a detailed investigation of the Egyptian plural markers, see Schenkel 1983: 173–209 and, based on Schenkel, Zeidler 1992.

[34] Petráček considers the masculine plural morpheme as having an "agglutinating" character (Petráček 1965: 227).

[35] Zaborski quotes the plural markers *-w-*, *-aw-*, and *-iw* for the masculine plural and feminine plural in Berber, and *-ūwa* and *-wā* for Chadic (Zaborski 1976: 3–6). For the attestations in Cushitic, see Zaborski 1986.

[36] Voigt reconstructs the masculine plural with final /t/ as well, that is, as **-uutV*, which corresponds to the feminine plural **-aatV*. This reconstruction applies to both the nominal and verbal system, which Voigt considers to have been morphologically identical at the earliest stages of Semitic (Voigt 1999: 12 and 1987: 11).

[37] The semivowel + vowel contractions assumed for this derivation are also known from other environments in Semitic, such as roots II-*w/y*, in which a similar development occurred probably as early as Proto-Semitic: **yaqwumu > *yaqūmu*, *yaḥwafu > yaḥāfu*, etc. Exceptions like Classical Arabic *'iḥwat-un* 'brothers' where the syllable initial /w/ is preserved word-internally are rare in Semitic.

masculine nominative *malk-w-u > *malkū	feminine nominative *malk-w-atu > *malkātu
masculine genitive *malk-w-i > *malkī	feminine genitive *malk-w-ati > *malkāti
masculine accusative **malk-w-a > **malkā	feminine accusative **malk-w-ata > **malkāta

Although the underlying phonological process is the same in the masculine and feminine in this reconstruction, the diptotic case system, again, remains unexplained. Furthermore, this derivation primarily rests on the assumption that the Egyptian and other Afroasiatic external plurals with /w/ are related to the external plural markers -ū/-ī and -āt in Semitic.[38]

Although there is no doubt that Afroasiatic had a plural marking morpheme {w} or {u}, it is nevertheless questionable if it underlies the Semitic external plural markers -ū, -ī, and -āt. The problem with a reconstruction as suggested by Petráček, Voigt, and Tropper is that when /w/ is attested as part of an internal plural or external plural marker, it is primarily found in post-vocalic position. This is also true for Egyptian when the /w/ is taken as a consonant. Although this observation does not necessarily invalidate Voigt's and Tropper's reconstruction, it is nevertheless important.

If the /w/ originally occurred after the singular vowel, the reconstructed forms would be as follows:

masculine nominative	*kalbu-w > *kalbū
masculine genitive	*kalbi-w > *kalbī
masculine accusative	*kalba-w > *kalbaw

The nominative and genitive plural would be the same as in the previously discussed derivations, while the accusative plural differs — although the hypothetical form is at least attested as a marker of the masculine plural in Semitic. When we assume the same reconstruction for the feminine plural, the resulting form is not reconcilable with the feminine plural markers attested in Semitic:

feminine plural	**malkawtV

Thus, the feminine plural cannot be derived by this type of /w/-insertion. This observation conforms to Schenkel's suggestion that the feminine plural forms in -wt in Egyptian are a secondary development caused by an analogy with the masculine form -(a)w.

Another phonological derivation has been suggested by Vycichl, who reconstructs an original nominative/locative marker -u and a genitive/accusative marker -i; the latter was attached to both the plural and dual. In Arabic, the original dual form *āji would have developed into ay (Vycichl 1958: 176). Furthermore, Vycichl assumes that a similar form -aj- underlies the verbal dual and reconstructs it as *yaqtul-aj-u-ni, which presumably contracted to yaqtulāni (Vycichl 1958: 177). This type of contraction is rather unlikely.

The derivation of the external plural markers by the various phonological processes discussed so far have all encountered several problems, especially when we try to apply the same basic development to both masculine and feminine nouns. Although it is theoretically possible to assume different underlying processes for masculine and feminine plurals, the greatest obstacle encountered in all these reconstructions is the absence of any explanation how the diptotic case system in the plural developed. Consequently, none of these phonologically motivated reconstructions is very convincing.

---

[38] As mentioned in section 8.2 above, the phonological realization of the /w/-external plurals in Egyptian is not certain. Schenkel suggested that it was similar to the plural marker -aw in Ge'ez, at least for certain noun types. He reconstructs four different nominal types depending on the quality of their linking vowel in the masculine singular. These linking vowels are *Ø, *a, *i, and *u, to which a masculine ending *-u presumably was attached, resulting in the masculine singular forms -Ø (< *Øu), -aw, -ī, and -ū (Schenkel 1983: 203). The plural of these singular bases was produced by the lengthening of the final *-u, resulting ultimately in the forms -w < *-Øū, -aw(w) < *-aū, -iw(w) < *-iū, and -uw(w) from < *-uū in Old Egyptian, which then became -aw, -ī, and -ū in Middle Egyptian (Schenkel 1983: 203; Zeidler 1992: 197). Allen assumes only one masculine plural marker, -w, for Middle Egyptian that was attached to every masculine singular noun, although the -w was not always written because it was a weak consonant (Allen 2000: 18, 36). The feminine -wt, which, according to Schenkel, is a less frequent biform of a more common feminine plural marker -t, probably formed by analogy with the masculine and is not original (Schenkel 1983: 209). Again, Allen posits only one feminine plural marker, -wt, for Middle Egyptian (2000: 36).

The third method to derive external plural markers is, as mentioned above, from various suffixes that originally functioned to mark feminine, abstract, and/or collective nouns. This derivation was, for example, proposed by Brockelmann, who states that one of the primary means to express nominal plurality is by the same marker that is used for the indication of the feminine singular, -(a)t, which can also mark abstracts and collectives (Brockelmann 1908: 426–27).[39] Other external plural markers presumably originate in abstract/collective endings as well, such as the masculine plural -ū and -ī, which Brockelmann derives from the abstract endings *-ūt and *-īt (Brockelmann 1908: 452).[40] The same basic principle of derivation would be true for the dual markers *-ā and *-ay. Brockelmann assumes different abstract/collective endings for most of the external plural and dual markers,[41] and, thus, avoids the phonological difficulties encountered in the previous reconstructions.[42] The derivation of -ū and -ī from the original abstract endings -ūt and -īt faces a different phonological problem, though. It is unclear why the assumed /t/ should have been lost. Such a loss of final /t/ is unparalleled in Proto- or early Semitic.

Kuryłowicz follows the same semantic development from *abstract > collective > plural* (Kuryłowicz 1973: 39).[43] He further argues that Arabic originally had three grammatical genders, masculine, feminine, and impersonal. The impersonal plurals that take complements in the feminine singular reflect the development of *collective > plural*, while the introduction of the plural morphemes -ūna and -āt for attributes were motivated by personal plurals.[44] The feminine plural -āt presumably constitutes the oldest morpheme of nominal plurality. Originally, it was gender neutral and acquired its feminine status as a result of polarization (Kuryłowicz 1973: 138–39).[45] Although Kuryłowicz suggested the threefold gender distinction primarily for Arabic, this type of reconstruction has interesting implications for the reconstruction and development of external plurals in Semitic in general.

---

[39] The expression of abstracts and collectives by the feminine singular marker -(a)t is common in Semitic languages, as, for example, in Classical Arabic raġbat-un 'wish' from the verbal root rġb (Fischer 1987: §75a); Akkadian damiqt-um 'goodness' and kitt-um 'truth' (von Soden 1995: §60); Hebrew nəqāmā 'vengeance', gədūlā 'greatness', and yōšébet 'population' (Gesenius et al. 1910: §122q); and also generally by adding the feminine ending to adjective endings in Geʿez (Dillmann et al. 2003: §120).

[40] The abstract ending -ūt is frequently used in Semitic languages, as in Aramaic malkūtā' (emphatic state) 'kingdom', rəbūtā' 'greatness' (see Bauer and Leander 1962: 197 for biblical Aramaic; Nöldeke 2001: §138 for Syriac), Hebrew yaldūt 'youth' (Gesenius et al. 1910: §86k), and Akkadian abbūt-um 'fatherhood' and meṭlūt-um 'manhood' (von Soden 1995: §56s). This abstract ending is only rarely found in Geʿez, for example, gʷəḥlut 'fraud' (Dillmann et al. 2003: §120) and only used in Aramaic loans in Classical Arabic, as in malakūt-un 'kingdom' (Fischer 1987: §65c). The abstract ending -īt is used less frequently than -ūt in Semitic. It is attested in Hebrew šə'ērīt 'remainder' and rē(')šīt 'beginning' (Gesenius et al. 1910: §86k), Geʿez nafāṣit 'remnant' (Dillmann et al. 2003: §120), and Aramaic 'aḥᵃrīt 'end' (Bauer and Leander 1962: 197) and mardītā' 'journey' (Nöldeke 2001: §75). In Akkadian, -īt is only used as the feminine form of masculine nouns ending in -ī (von Soden 1995: §56o and 56q). Bauer and Leander suggested that -ūt derives from *-uw plus feminine ending and -īt from *-ī plus feminine ending (Bauer and Leander 1962: 197). This derivation is based on the fact that the absolute forms of the abstracts in -ūtā' do not contain /t/ in Aramaic, as in malkū, rəbū. This suggestion, in connection with the aforementioned fact that Akkadian only knows the ending -īt as a feminine form of -ī, might have interesting implications for the derivation of these abstract endings. It is possible that the abstract endings -ūt and -īt constitute a combination of the original plural endings -ū and -ī and the feminine marker -t that was added secondarily. The marking of abstracts by the masculine plural is rare in Semitic, but it does occur occasionally, as in Hebrew zəqūnîm 'old age' and bəśārîm 'fleshliness', and Syriac ḥayyē 'life' and raḥmē 'compassion'. It is also possible that -ūt was an original abstract ending in Semitic and -īt developed secondarily by analogy with -ūt.

[41] The feminine plural marker -āt is an exception since it is presumably derived by the lengthening of the singular vowel /a/ (Brockelmann 1908: 441). The ending -ay is still occasionally found as feminine/abstract suffix, as in Hebrew śāray 'princess' and maybe also 'eśrē < *-ay 'ten' (Gesenius et al. 1910: §80l), Geʿez radʾēt 'help' < *radʾayt (Dillmann et al. 2003: §120), Syriac salway 'quails', kawkəbay 'kind of bird', ṭûʿyay 'error' (Nöldeke 2001: §83), and probably Classical Arabic -ā ('alif maqṣūra) ḏikrā 'memory' and daʿwā 'call/demand' (Fischer 1987: §75b). In Akkadian, the ending -āy is only used in the same function as the Nisbe-ending -ī (von Soden 1995: §56p).

[42] A similar reconstruction was proposed by O'Leary, who assumed that the endings -t, -at, and -y — originally used for the feminine and abstracts — developed into the attested external plural markers. The ending -y underlies the oblique plural -ī (O'Leary 1969: 192–93).

[43] The feminine singular ending -at would originally have been a derivative to form abstracts from adjectives (Kuryłowicz 1973: 145).

[44] This assumption would fit well into the "Animacy Hierarchy" that underlies the marking of plurality. The hierarchy goes from *speaker > addressee > third person > kin > human > animate > inanimate*. If a singular ~ plural distinction exists in a language, it must affect the top segment of this hierarchy, although it can break up at any point after that. This means, if inanimate nouns form plurals in a given language, all other categories preceding it in the animacy hierarchy must have equivalent plural formations, although a language that has animate plurals does not necessarily have to have the same construction for inanimate nouns. Agreement in number must follow this hierarchy as well (Corbett 2000: 56). Consequently, the hierarchy breaks up after the category "animate" in Classical Arabic.

[45] If I understand Kuryłowicz's theory correctly, it seems that he nevertheless assumes that the long /ā/ in -āt is the result of the lengthening of the /a/ in -at, which occurred to differentiate the functions collective ~ feminine (1973: 145). The assumption that -āt is the most original external plural marker is widespread since it is the only plural morpheme that is attested in all Semitic languages (see, e.g., Retsö 1997: 273).

Originally, there most likely did not exist any marked distinction of gender and number, at least not for impersonal nouns. Consequently, the notion that some of the external plural markers developed from *abstracts > collectives > plurals*, where this development is primarily assumed for impersonal nouns, is quite convincing. The gender dependent plurals, *-āt* and *-ū*, would then be the result of a different development originally based on the verbal system or predicative construction that had no inherent connection to nominal plurals and only got associated with nominal plurality through an expansion of external plural marking.[46]

The derivation of external plural markers from original abstract/collective endings includes, as mentioned above, the morphemes of the dual as well. Advocates of this reconstruction assume that the dual oblique marker reflects the original feminine/abstract ending **-ay*, which either acquired its dualic function by having been employed for natural occurring pairs or by a process of restriction. The same original plural *-ay presumably underlies the masculine constructs in Hebrew and Aramaic and the Old Akkadian and Assyrian oblique plural *-ē* (e.g., Retsö 1997: 275; Cross 2003: 356).

Although the general development from *feminine/abstract > collective > plural* is widely accepted, it has been argued that not all external plural markers can be identified with morphemes that originally marked the feminine singular or abstracts and collectives (Moscati 1954b: 175; Nöldeke 1982: 51 regarding the ending *-ay). This criticism is certainly true for the masculine plural markers *-ū* and *-ī* and the feminine plural *-āt*.[47] Furthermore, the diptotic system of the external plural and dual markers remains, yet again, unexplained. If we want to reconstruct the development of the external plural markers in Semitic, we need to find a derivation that can account for the diptotic case system of these morphemes.

8.4. Reconstruction of the External Plural Markers in Semitic

As we have seen in the previous sections, Afroasiatic had a common set of morphemes that could be used for marking plurality, all of which are attested in Semitic. Some of these morphemes can be connected to original feminine, abstract, and/or collective endings, such as *-ān, *-at, and probably *-ay, while others have to be derived differently.

In Semitic, the various external plural markers behave differently concerning the marking of case and gender. There are two distinct groups of external plural markers regarding case: (1) those that are case dependent, that is, the plural markers vary depending on syntactic context — these include the masculine plural *-ū and *-ī and its allomorph *-ay and the dual markers *-ā and *-ay — and (2) those that are used independent of case and are only secondarily marked thus, such as *-āt*, *-ān*, and *-(a)w*. Furthermore, only *-āt* and *-ū/-ī* seem to be genuinely gender-dependent, at least in most Semitic languages. All other external plural markers are not particularly indexed for grammatical gender — the restrictive use of *-ān* for the masculine plural in Geʿez is probably secondary. These two differences have important implications for the derivation of the plural morphemes.

In order to understand the derivation of the external plural markers on nouns, we also have to look at non-nominal forms that use external plural markers. These include the prefix conjugations and the predicative adjective (= stative).

The Proto-Semitic forms of the masculine plural of the prefix conjugation can be reconstructed as:[48]

    Third-person masculine plural   **yaqtulū±na*
    Second-person masculine plural   **taqtulū±na*

The distribution of the forms with and without *-na* has no immediate significance for the present study. The important form in our context is the final *-ū*. This final *-ū* is the plural morpheme for all three relevant types of prefix conjugations that can be reconstructed for Proto-Semitic, that is, **yaqtul*, **yaqtulu*, and **yaqtula* (Moscati 1964: 135). Since this plural has the same form as the masculine plural nominative *-ū* on nouns, it is likely that these two forms reflect the same underlying morpheme. If we were to derive this *-ū* in the verbal system by

---

[46] For the suggestion that the origin of the external plural markers should be sought in the predicative adjective, see Huehnergard 2004: 149.

[47] The morpheme *-āt* is not usually found among those morphemes that mark abstract nouns. Thus, an abstract derivation cannot account for the long vowel of this morpheme.

[48] For a different reconstruction, see Voigt 1987 and 1997, who assumes that both the nominal and verbal plural had a final /t/, that is, masculine plural **-uutV* and feminine plural **-aatV*.

insertion of a /w/ or simple lengthening of the singular vowel, we would obviously not arrive at the regular *-ū* morpheme that is attested throughout Semitic, except in the singular base *yaqtulu*. Unless we assume an early leveling of the *yaqtulū* < **yaqtulu* plural, the derivation of the plural /ū/ by insertion of a plural morpheme /w/ or lengthening of the singular vowel is not possible in the prefix conjugations.

The same *-ū* is regularly found in the predicative adjective, which should be reconstructed as **qatalū* for the third-person masculine plural with a singular base **qatala*. Again, the derivation by lengthening of the singular vowel or the insertion of a /w/ before or after the base vowel does not yield the attested forms. It is therefore highly unlikely that the masculine plural *-ū* in the verbal system and the predicative adjective derive from any such process. It seems, rather, that the *-ū* is monomorphemic and cannot be split up into any further constituents, at least not on the basis of our evidence. It could be suggested that the verbal system and predicative adjective took over the masculine plural *-ū* and feminine plural *-ā* from the nominal system, but, in my opinion, this is unlikely. On the contrary, the usage of /ū/ in the verbal system and on the predicative adjective seems to be more original than the use of *-ū* as masculine plural marker on nouns, a point that hopefully becomes clear in the discussion of the feminine plural below. Thus, if we assume that the *-ū* on the predicative adjective is an original and undividable morpheme, the same should be true for the masculine external plural marker. The expansion of the predicative *-ū* for the nominative plural is not surprising since the predicative adjective is by definition used in the nominative.

Before looking at the derivation of the masculine oblique, let us first consider the feminine plural marker *-āt*. The external feminine plural marker most likely had its origin in the same predicative form as the masculine plural, for which it is reconstructed as **qatalā* (e.g., Bauer and Leander 1991: § 63h) with a singular base **qatalat*. The reconstruction of the feminine plural of the prefix conjugation is disputed. Huehnergard assumes a Proto-Semitic form **yaqtulna* (2004: 151), while others reconstruct the same suffix as for the predicative adjective, that is, **yaqtulā*.[49] Note that whatever form might underlie the feminine plural prefix conjugation, none of the suggested reconstructions has the same ending *-āt* as the external feminine plural on nouns.[50] Thus, the derivation of the external feminine plural differs from the derivation of the masculine plural. Another difference between the masculine plural and feminine plural is the aforementioned lack of genuine case distinction in *-āt*. This morpheme is only secondarily marked for case by the addition of the masculine plural case vowels, while the masculine plural *-ū* in the nominal system seems to be connected to a specific case from its earliest attestations in Semitic. If the derivation of the nominal external feminine plural were exactly parallel to the masculine plural, we would expect a form *-ā*, which is indeed attested, although not in the function of the feminine plural, but as a nominative (masculine + feminine) dual.

The nominal feminine plural *-āt* can nevertheless be derived from the predicative feminine plural *-ā* by suffixation of the feminine singular marker *-t*. That is, once the element *-t* was interpreted as primarily being a feminine ending, it was added to all nominal feminine forms independent of number, including the original feminine plural ending *-ā* derived from the predicative adjective, resulting in **-ā-t*.[51] Subsequently, case endings were added in parallelism with the vowels attested in the masculine plural, /u/ and /i/, although these vowels were treated like the short case vowels of the singular since they did not represent the primary plural markers in the feminine plural. This secondary addition of the feminine marker /t/ explains why the masculine plural and feminine plural seem to behave differently with regard to inherent case marking. The original feminine plural **-ā* was attributed a secondary function as marker of duality, according to Kuryłowicz's fourth law of analogy.[52] If this interpretation is correct, it explains why paired body parts are generally treated as feminine in Semitic. The ending

---

[49] Most prominently, it was Hetzron who assumed a Proto-Semitic form with final *-ā* (Hetzron 1973/4: 35 and 1976: 103).

[50] Since it is beyond the scope of this article to discuss the Proto-Semitic feminine plural of the prefix conjugation, the current investigation focuses on the plural of the predicative adjective. This restriction does not have any significant impact on the derivation suggested here.

[51] Bauer and Leander already suggested this derivation (1991: § 63h). Note that the original feminine ending that is derived from the predicative verbal adjective was most likely *-t*, not *-at*, since the contrast between the masculine and feminine singular was **qatala ~ *qatala-t*, not **qatala ~ **qatal-at*, which consolidates the derivation for the feminine plural suggested here.

[52] Kuryłowicz's fourth law of analogy states: "Quand à la suite d'une transformation morphologique une forme subit la différenciation, la forme nouvelle correspond à sa fonction primaire (de fondation), la forme ancienne est réservée pour la fonction secondaire (fondée)" (Kuryłowicz 1945–49: 30). Retsö made a similar suggestion with regard to the morpheme *-ay*, which, according to him, was an abstract/collective ending primarily used for countable parts of the body, time units, etc. (Retsö 1997: 278).

-*ā*, first still with an inherent feminine notion, was used for expressing plurality of paired body parts. From this restricted function it acquired dualic status and was then interpreted as the general nominative dual marker. The secondary character of the dual markers can also be deduced by the fact that these markers, *-ā* for the nominative and *-ay* for the oblique, are suffixed to the nominal base, no matter whether it is masculine or feminine, without being marked for gender themselves. This can be illustrated by Classical Arabic *malik-* 'king' (masculine singular) > *malik-ā* (nominative), *malik-at-* 'queen' (feminine singular) > *malik-at-ā* (nominative), and *bin-t-* 'girl' (feminine singular) > *bin-t-ā* (nominative). Although the masculine dual seems to be formed in a similar manner as the masculine plural, that is, by suffixing a particular morpheme to the nominal base, the formation of the feminine differs significantly from both the masculine and feminine external plural markers. Thus, the rather particular position of the dual marker *after* the feminine nominal base might confirm the assumption that the dual marker *-ā* and its oblique counterpart *-ay* are the result of a secondary development. This assumption does not imply that they could not have been Proto-Semitic or even part of an earlier stage of Afroasiatic.

To summarize the investigation thus far, the nominative external plural and dual markers *-ū*, *-ā*, and *-āt* can be derived from the verbal system and the predicative adjective. The masculine plural *-ū* is the common masculine plural marker found on verbs and predicative constructions, *-ā* is the original feminine plural which was attributed a secondary and restricted function after the reinterpretation of /t/ as a general feminine marker that was also added to the original feminine plural *-ā*, resulting in *-āt*. Thus, these nominative plural markers have no connection to abstract morphemes but are derived from the verbal system and predicative constructions. Especially the feminine plural marker *-āt* confirms the priority of predicative plural markers over external noun plurals with long vowels.

The next question is how to derive the masculine oblique plural and dual forms *-ī* and *-ay*. The case distinction in the feminine plural and dual is, as mentioned above, the result of an analogy with the masculine. A direct derivation from the verbal system or predicative adjective is not possible in these cases since there is no plural marking *-ī* in any verbal or predicative form.[53]

In order to find the origin of the masculine plural /ī/, it is helpful to look at broken plural patterns in Semitic and other Afroasiatic sub-branches. The long vowels of external plural markers, /ū/, /ā/, and /ī/, all have parallels in broken plural formations. This does not necessarily indicate that the long vowels of internal plural patterns and those of external plural markers had the same origin, but the occurrence of all three long vowels in both plural formations is nevertheless interesting.

The vowel /ā/ is the most frequently occurring vowel in internal plural formations. In Classical Arabic, it is attested in the patterns *ʾaCCāC, CiCāC, CuCāC, CuCCāC, CaCāʾiC*, and for the plural of quadriliterals *CaCāCiC*.[54] Old South Arabian probably has the pattern *ʾaCCāC* as well, although this assumption cannot be verified because of the absence of vowel indication in the orthography. Tigre has similar patterns as Classical Arabic, such as *ʾaCCāC, CəCāC, CaCāCəC*, and *CāCāC*.[55] Patterns based on /ā/ are also attested in Modern South Arabian.[56] Internal plural formations with /ā/ are also known from other Afroasiatic languages. Tuareg has a frequently occurring plural with /â/, as in *edäbir* 'male dove' which has a plural *idbâr* (Ratcliffe 1998: 102). A similar insertion of /ā/ is attested in Hausa, as in *birnī* 'city', plural *birānē*, *kulkī* 'cudgel', plural *kulākē*, and in Afar, where we find forms like *deber* 'hobbling rope', plural *debāre* (Ratcliffe 1998: 106, 113).

The vowel /ū/ is commonly used in broken plural formations as well, although it does not occur in as many patterns as /ā/. In Semitic, /ū/ is attested in the Classical Arabic pattern *CuCūC*, a pattern that most likely also underlies Harsusi *CeCewweC*, and in Geʿez and Tigre *ʾaCCūC*.[57] Again, plural formations with long /ū/ are also found in other Afroasiatic languages. In Hausa, /ū/ can be used together with reduplication of the final root radical and addition of an external plural marker when the noun is biconsonantal in the singular, as in *ʾabu* 'thing', plural

---

[53] There is, of course, the feminine singular *taqtulī-*, but, in my opinion, it is unlikely that this feminine /ī/ is the source of the masculine oblique plural.

[54] Examples include *ʾayyām-un* 'days', *riğāl-un* 'men', *ruʿāʾ-un* 'shepherds', *kuttāb-un* 'scribes', and *ʿarāʾis-u* 'brides'.

[55] For example, *ʾaklāb* 'dogs', *qərāb* 'skins', *ʿālāb* 'numbers', *kanāfər* 'lips'; see Raz 1983: 19–22 for more examples and variations of these patterns.

[56] For a thorough investigation of these plural patterns, see Ratcliffe 1998: 87–92.

[57] See Ratcliffe 1998: 87–94. Examples include Classical Arabic *buyūt* 'houses', Geʿez *ʾahgur* 'cities', and Tigre *ʾadkul* 'masts'. Hebrew probably also has remnants of an original broken plural pattern *CuCūC* that underlies forms like *zəḵûr* 'men' and *gəḇûrā* 'heroes'.

'abūbuwā and garī 'town', plural garūruwā. In Afar, plurals can likewise be expressed by a lengthened internal vowel, as in rakub 'camel', plural rakūba (for the attestations in Hausa and Afar, see Ratcliffe 1998: 108, 112).

The vowel /ī/ is less frequently used in internal plurals than /ā/ and /ū/. In Classical Arabic, it is primarily attested in the broken plurals of certain quadriliteral nouns CaCāCīC, as in yanābīʿ-u 'wells', but also occasionally in the pattern CaCīC, as in ʿabīd- 'slaves' and ḥamīr- 'donkeys'. Hebrew also seems to preserve vestiges of an original plural pattern CVCīC, as in the word pəsîl-îm 'idols' from the singular pésel, to which the external plural marker -îm was added secondarily. Geʿez does not have an internal plural pattern with */ī/, but the same quadriliteral pattern as in Arabic is attested in Tigre.[58] To my knowledge, no internal plural pattern containing /ī/ is attested in either Berber or Chadic, but the Cushitic language Afar can form the plural of a noun with a singular base vowel /i/ in the last syllable by the lengthening of this vowel, as in ʾalib 'tendon', plural ʾalība, or by insertion of /ī/ in CiCC bases, as in birta 'metal', plural birīta (Ratcliffe 1998: 113).

These comparisons with internal plural patterns show that there is a clear association of the long vowels /ā/, /ī/, and /ū/ with plurality not only in Semitic, but in Afroasiatic in general. As mentioned before, it is not clear whether the long vowels of broken plurals and those of external plurals are necessarily derived from the same source. It is nevertheless clear that these vowels do function as (parts of) plural markers throughout Afroasiatic, although not necessarily for the same underlying syntactical functions. As shown in section 8.2, singular nouns ending in -ā in Hausa, which are associated with the feminine, change their vowel to either /ī/ or /ū/ in the plural, which would be corresponding to the masculine plural in Semitic. Furthermore, Hausa has the aforementioned -ī ~ -ai ablaut between the dual (-ī) and the plural (-ai), both of which are also used in Semitic, but in the opposite distribution, that is, -ī would be the masculine plural and -ai the dual. Although it is, of course, difficult to establish the etymologies of the plural and dual morphemes in Hausa and their relationship to the Semitic plural and dual markers, the phonological similarity between these morphemes is nevertheless striking. If they are indeed related, it would confirm the assumption that the basic external plural and dual morphemes of Semitic languages, -ū, -ī, -ā, and -ay, are of common Afroasiatic stock, although they do not seem to have been functionally bound in the same way as in Semitic. This suggests that the grammatical environments and distribution of these morphemes attested in Semitic is most likely a Semitic innovation and redistribution of previously un- or differently conditioned plural markers.[59]

The distribution of the external plural markers in Semitic can be reconstructed as follows. Originally, there was a set of three long vowels that could be used to mark plurality both in internal and external plurals. Two of these long vowels were also connected to the verbal system and the predicative adjective, from which they acquired their association with certain genders, that is, -ū for the masculine and -ā for the feminine. As mentioned above, the feminine plural was subsequently expanded by the /t/ of the feminine singular, while the original -ā was restricted in usage, first for paired body parts and then for the dual in general. Because the singular had a triptotic case system, the plural likewise had to be marked for case. This was achieved by substituting the nominative -ū in the masculine with the only plural vowel that was not yet functionally bound, -ī. In other words, the vocalic plural markers that Semitic inherited from Afroasiatic were functionally redistributed in Semitic. Thus, the diptotic case system in the plural was the result of a redistribution and restriction of the three original vocalic plural morphemes.

The Semitic oblique dual marker -ay also belongs to the common Afroasiatic stock of morphemes that was used to mark plurality. Interestingly, -ay and its component /y/ are never part of internal plural formations. They are exclusively attested in external plural markers. This suggests that -ay was derived differently than the long plural vowels /ā/, /ī/, and /ū/. It is likely that this plural marker originated in the feminine/abstract ending

---

[58] As in ǧanābil 'baskets'. Tigre /i/ corresponds to original *ī; for more examples, see Raz 1983: 20. Whether the Old South Arabian broken plural written CCyC reflects long /ī/ or consonantal /y/ is not certain (Ratcliffe 1998: 90).

[59] It is also possible that Semitic preserves the more original situation and that we have redistributions in the rest of Afroasiatic, but at least the common usage of /ā/, /ī/, and /ū/ in internal plural patterns throughout Afroasiatic, that is, the association of plurality with long vowels, seems to be common Afroasiatic heritage. The origin of these long vowel plural markers is impossible to determine. We could hypothesize that they result from the lengthening of corresponding short vowels, but a simple association of plurality with vowel length is equally likely. This would then parallel the connection of plurality with consonantal gemination and reduplication. Consonantal gemination for plurals is, for example, known from Akkadian, as in abum 'father' (singular), abbū (plural), aḫum 'brother', plural aḫḫū.

-*ay*, although its pluralic function must have developed very early on since it is found in various sub-branches of Afroasiatic. In Semitic, it underwent a similar process of restriction as the vocalic plural markers and was associated with the oblique dual. Why it was chosen for this particular function is difficult to say. It is possible that its phonetic compounds, /a/ and /y/, were associated with the nominative dual /ā/ and the masculine oblique marker /ī/, but this has to remain speculative. The association of the nominal ending -*ay* with duality is an inner Semitic and secondary development. This is shown by the fact that -*ay* could also act as oblique plural marker, as in Old Akkadian and Assyrian, which seems to be a vestige of its original pluralic function. The masculine plural construct forms in Hebrew and Aramaic should, therefore, be interpreted as vestiges of the original plural function of -*ay* and not as the result of an analogy with the dual.

8.5. Conclusion

We can distinguish two different sets of plural markers in Afroasiatic languages. The first set consists of three original long vowels, /ā/, /ī/, and /ū/, that were associated with plurality and used for both internal and external plural formations. Which of the two usages, internal or external, is more original, is impossible to determine, but Afroasiatic probably had both possibilities from very early on. These long vowels also underlie the plural markers in the verbal system and the predicative adjective, from which they acquired their status as person and gender-bound plurals. The derivation of the long vowels from a short vowel by addition of a glide cannot be proven with certainty and is, in my opinion, not likely. All derivations including a glide face phonological problems when we try to apply them systematically and are, thus, unconvincing. It is more likely that these vocalic morphemes simply were original long vowels. Whether these vowels are related to original singular case vowels or nominal stem vowels is not determinable with our evidence. In Semitic, these vocalic plural markers were functionally redistributed on the basis of their use in the verbal system and predicative adjective. Thus, -*ū* was interpreted as masculine plural nominative, while -*ā*, the original feminine ending, was restricted in use to paired body parts and then the nominative dual in general. The replacement of -*ā* was caused by the introduction of a new feminine plural morpheme -*āt* that developed through the spread of the /t/ from the feminine singular after it was interpreted as a general feminine marker. The original plural marker -*ī* was attributed the function as masculine plural oblique. Thus, the diptotic case system of the external plural markers is the result of the functional redistribution of original vocalic plural morphemes and is not connected to the occasional diptotic system found in the singular in Classical Arabic and in Ugaritic. As has been argued above, the vocalic plural markers are not connected to abstract endings.

The external and internal plural component /w/ and its various realizations, specifically -*aw*, was most likely originally restricted to biconsonantal roots to make these fit into the more common triradical pattern. This assumption is consolidated by the fact that -*(a)w* is still primarily used for biconsonantal nouns in Semitic and other Afroasiatic languages, although its use spread to triradical nouns as well. Thus, the plural marker /w/ and its various compounds is not originally connected to abstract formations either.

The second set of plural markers includes certain abstract endings that could be used to indicate plurality, but only in the function of external plural markers. The semantic development of these morphemes was from *abstract > collective > plural*. These abstract endings include -*(a)t*, -*ān*, and -*ay*, which are attested in Semitic languages to various degrees. These abstract endings were employed to mark specific plural categories, such as particularizing and individualizing plurals (-*ān*) and impersonal plurals (-*at*). The oblique dual marker in Semitic most likely had its origin in the original abstract/feminine ending -*ay*. It acquired its association with the dual in Semitic by the same process of functional restriction as the vocalic plural morpheme. Vestiges of its original plural function can still be traced in Old Akkadian and in the construct state in Hebrew and Aramaic.

Bibliography

Allen, James P.
 2000 *Middle Egyptian: An Introduction to the Language and Culture of Hieroglyphs*. New York: Cambridge University Press.

Bauer, Hans, and Pontus Leander
 1962 *Grammatik des Biblisch-Aramäischen*. Hildesheim: Georg Olms. Reprint, 1927.
 1991 *Historische Grammatik der hebräischen Sprache des Alten Testamentes*. Hildesheim: Georg Olms. Reprint, 1922.

Beeston, Alfred F. L.
 1984 *Sabaic Grammar*. Manchester: University of Manchester Press.

Bloch, A.
 1989 "Plurals of Multiplication, Plurals of Division." *Jerusalem Studies in Arabic and Islam* 12: 118–34.

Brockelmann, Carl
 1908 *Grundriss der vergleichenden Grammatik der semitischen Sprachen*, Vol. 1. Berlin: von Reuther und Reichard.

Corbett, Greville G.
 2000 *Number*. Cambridge Textbooks in Linguistics. Cambridge: Cambridge University Press.

Cross, Frank M.
 2003 "Some Problems in Old Hebrew Orthography with Special Attention to the Third Person Masculine Singular Suffix on Plural Nouns [-âw]." In *Leaves from an Epigrapher's Notebook: Collected Papers in Hebrew and West Semitic Paleography and Epigraphy*, edited by Frank M. Cross, pp. 351–56. Harvard Semitic Studies 51. Winona Lake: Eisenbrauns.

Diakonoff, I. M.
 1965 *Semito-Hamitic Languages: An Essay in Classification*. Languages of Asia and Africa. Moscow: Nauka.
 1988 *Afrasian Languages*. Languages of Asia and Africa. Moscow: Nauka.

Dillmann, A.; Carl Bezold; and James A. Crichton
 2003 *Ethiopic Grammar*. Second edition. Eugene: Wipf and Stock.

Fassberg, S. E.
 1990 *A Grammar of the Palestinian Targum Fragments from the Cairo Genizah*. Harvard Semitic Studies 38. Atlanta: Scholars Press.

Fischer, W.
 1987 *Grammatik des klassischen Arabisch*. Porta Linguarum Orientalium, neue Serie, 11. Wiesbaden: Harrassowitz.

Gesenius, W., et al.
 1910 *Gesenius' Hebrew Grammar*. Oxford: Clarendon.

Gray, L. H.
 1934 *Introduction to Semitic Comparative Linguistics*. New York: Columbia University Press.

Hetzron, R.
 1973/4 "The Vocalization of Prefixes in Semitic Active and Passive Verbs." *Mélanges de l'Université Saint-Joseph* 48: 35–48.
 1976 "Two Principles of Genetic Reconstruction." *Lingua* 38: 89–108.

Huehnergard, J.
 1998 *A Grammar of Akkadian*. Harvard Semitic Studies 45. Atlanta: Scholars.
 2004 Afro-Asiatic. In *The Cambridge Encyclopedia of the World's Ancient Languages*, edited by R. D. Woodard, pp. 138–59. Cambridge: Cambridge University Press.

Johnstone, T. M.
    1975   "The Modern South Arabian Languages." *Afroasiatic Linguistics* 1: 1–29.

Kienast, B.; E. Graefe; and Gene B. Gragg
    2001   *Historische semitische Sprachwissenschaft*. Wiesbaden: Harrassowitz.

Kuryłowicz, J.
    1945–49 "La nature des procès dits 'analogiques.'" *Acta Linguistica* 5: 15–37.
    1973   *Studies in Semitic Grammar and Metrics*. Prace Jezykoznawcze 67. London: Curzon.

Lambdin, T. O.
    1978   *Introduction to Classical Ethiopic (Geʿez)*. Atlanta: Scholars.

Lipiński, Edward
    2001   *Semitic Languages: Outline of a Comparative Grammar*. Second edition. Leuven: Peters.

Macdonald, M. C. A.
    2004   "Ancient North Arabian." In *The Cambridge Encyclopedia of the World's Ancient Languages*, edited by R. D. Woodard, pp. 488–533. Cambridge: Cambridge University Press.

Macuch, R.
    1982   *Grammatik des samaritanischen Aramäisch*. Studia Samaritana 4. Berlin: de Gruyter.

Moscati, S.
    1954a   "Il plurale esterno maschile nelle lingue semitiche." *Rivista degli Studi Orientali* 29: 28–52.
    1954b   "Sulla flessione nominale dell'Arabico classico." *Rivista degli Studi Orientali* 29: 171–82.
    1964   *An Introduction to the Comparative Grammar of the Semitic Languages: Phonology and Morphology*. Porta Linguarum Orientalium, neue Serie, 6. Wiesbaden: Harrassowitz.

Muraoka, T., and B. Porten
    2003   *A Grammar of Egyptian Aramaic*. Second revised edition. Handbuch der Orientalistik 1; Nahe und der Mittlere Osten 32. Leiden: Brill.

Nebes, N., and P. Stein
    2004   "Ancient South Arabian." In *The Cambridge Encyclopedia of the World's Ancient Languages*, edited by R. D. Woodard, pp. 454–87. Cambridge: Cambridge University Press.

Newman, Paul
    1990   *Nominal and Verbal Plurality in Chadic*. Publications in African Languages and Linguistics 12. Dordrecht: Foris.

Nöldeke, Theodor
    1875   *Mandäische Grammatik*. Halle: Verlag der Buchhandlung des Waisenhauses.
    1982   "Zur Bildung des Plurals beim aramäischen Nomen." In *Beiträge und neue Beiträge zur semitischen Sprachwissenschaft: Achtzehn Aufsätze und Studien*, edited by T. Nöldeke and C. Snouch Hurgronje, pp. 48–62. Amsterdam: APA-Philo Press. Reprint, 1904.
    2001   *Compendious Syriac Grammar*. Winona Lake: Eisenbrauns. Reprint, 1904.

O'Leary, de Lacy
    1969   *Comparative Grammar of the Semitic Languages*. Amsterdam: Philo.

Petráček, K.
    1965   "Die Isomorphie im System der arabischen Pluralbildung." In *Symbolae Linguisticae in Honorem Georgii Kuryłowicz*, edited by W. Taszyczi, pp. 227–29. Prace Komisji Jeykoznawstwa 5. Krakow: Polskiej Akademii Nauk.

Ratcliffe, R. R.
    1998   "Defining Morphological Isoglosses: The 'Broken' Plural and Semitic Subclassification." *Journal of Near Eastern Studies* 57: 81–123.

Raz, Shlomo
  1983 *Tigre Grammar and Texts.* Afroasiatic Dialects 4. Malibu: Undena.

Retsö, Jan
  1997 "State and Plural Marking in Semitic." In *Built on Solid Rock: Studies in Honour of Professor Ebbe Egede Knudsen on the Occasion of His 65th Birthday April 11th 1997*, edited by E. Wardini, pp. 268–82. Serie B-Skrifter 98. Oslo: Novus.

Schenkel, Wolfgang
  1983 *Aus der Arbeit an einer Konkordanz zu den altägyptischen Sargtexten.* Göttingen Orientforschungen 12. Wiesbaden: Harrassowitz.

von Soden, Wolfram
  1995 *Grundriss der akkadischen Grammatik.* Third edition. Analecta Orientalia 33. Rome: Pontificio Istituto Biblico.

Streck, M. P.
  2000 *Das amurritische Onomastikon der altbabylonischen Zeit*, Band 1: *Die Amurriter.* Alter Orient und Altes Testament 271. Münster: Ugarit-Verlag.

Tropper, J.
  2004 "Gedanken zum Pluralmarker {ū} im Semitischen." *Journal of Semitic Studies* 49: 199–213.

Voigt, R. M.
  1987 "The Classification of Central Semitic." *Journal of Semitic Studies* 32: 1–21.
  1997 "Zur Nominal- und Verbalnasalierung im Semitischen." *Wiener Zeitschrift für die Kunde des Morgenlandes* 87: 207–30.
  1999 "Nominal (and Verbal) Nasalization and the Nominal Plural Morphemes in Semitohamitic." In *Afroasiatica Tergestina* (Papers from the Ninth Italian Meeting of Afro-Asiatic [Hamito-Semitic] Linguistics, Trieste, April 23–24, 1998), edited by M. Lamberti and Livia Tonelli, pp. 11–22. Padova: Unipress.

Vycichl, Werner
  1958 "Numerus und Kasus im Klassischen Arabisch." *Rivista degli Studi Orientali* 33: 175–79.

Wright, William
  2002 *Lectures on the Comparative Grammar of the Semitic Languages.* Gorgias Reprint Series 28. Piscataway, New Jersey: Georgias. Reprint, 1890.

Zaborski, Andrzej
  1976 "The Semitic External Plural in an Afroasiatic Perspective." *Afroasiatic Linguistics* 3: 1–9.
  1986 *The Morphology of Nominal Plural in the Cushitic Languages.* Veröffenlichungen der Institut für Afrikanistik und Ägyptologie der Universität Wien 39. Wien: AFRO-PUB.

Zeidler, J.
  1992 "Altägyptisch und Hamitosemitisch. Bemerkungen zu den *Vergleichenden Studien* von Karel Petráček." *Lingua Aegyptia* 2: 189–222.

9. SEMITIC TRIRADICALITY OR PROSODIC MINIMALITY? EVIDENCE FROM SOUND CHANGE[1]

Robert D. Hoberman

9.1. Introduction

The idea that words in Semitic languages are built on roots which predominantly consist of three consonants is a theory that was conceived about twelve hundred years ago. Students of Semitic languages find the concept of the root so convenient and useful that one finds it hard to think about Semitic morphology without it. Yet occasionally during the past century and increasingly in recent years thoughtful investigators have expressed doubt as to whether roots really function in the mental processing of Semitic languages by native speakers and even as to whether roots are theoretically appropriate entities for the description of Semitic morphology. Evidence on both sides of the question is collected in Shimron 2003. In his introduction Shimron observes that among the contributors to the volume all the psycholinguists support the validity of roots, while all or nearly all the "straight" linguists argue against roots. In this paper I examine a sound change in Aramaic that previous scholars have sought to account for in terms of root structure. I argue that prosodic structure, and not root structure, is what played the crucial role in this historical change. That is not to say that roots play no role in other historical or synchronic phenomena.

Northeastern Neo-Aramaic has a set of words that reflect the change exemplified by *šə́mma* 'name' from Earlier Aramaic *šma:*.[2] Table 9.1 lists all the words that I have been able to identify with confidence as belonging to this set.[3] We can ask what caused this change, but this really consists of two distinct questions: What changed in the sound pattern of Aramaic when *šma:* shifted to *šə́mma* (section 9.2)? And what motivated, or set off, the historical change (section 9.3)?

Table 9.1. Words Exhibiting the *šma:* > *šəmma* Change

Gloss	Syriac	Pre-NENA*	Turoyo	Aradhin	Urmi	Azerbaijan	Hertevin	ZJ-group
'name'	šma:	—	ʔəšmo	šumma	šimma	šimma	šemma	šəmma
'blood'	dma:	—	ʔadmo	dəmma	dimma	dimma	demma	dəmma
'years'	(šnayya:)	*šne:	ʔəšne	šinne	šinni	šinne	šenne	šənne
'sky'	šmayya:	—	šma:yo	šmayya	šmajja	—	šmaya	—
	—	*šme:	—	—	—	šimme	—	šimme

---

[1] Versions of this paper were presented at the North American Conference on Afroasiatic Linguistics, Cambridge, Massachusetts, in 1992, and the Annual Meeting of the Linguistic Society of America, Boston, 2004. I am grateful to members of those audiences and to several participants in the symposium honoring Gene Gragg for their helpful comments, to my Stony Brook colleagues Christina Bethin, Ellen Broselow, and Lori Repetti for helping me think about some of the theoretical issues, to Adam Ussishkin and Adamantios Gafos for useful suggestions, and to Yona Sabar for help with the Zakho and Nerwa data.

[2] Northeastern Neo-Aramaic is a group of languages and dialects spoken by somewhere between two-hundred thousand and two million people in Iraq, Iran, Syria, Turkey, and a large diaspora. Northeastern Neo-Aramaic is one branch of Central Aramaic, the other being the Turoyo group. (The term Central Aramaic was proposed in Jastrow 1990.) By "Earlier Aramaic" I mean whatever relatively conservative Aramaic varieties of the first millennium were fairly similar to both classical Syriac and proto-Central Aramaic. Proto-Central Aramaic was a close sister of Syriac, so I generally cite classical Syriac forms to represent Earlier Aramaic, without intending to imply that Northeastern Neo-Aramaic is a daughter of Syriac.

My sources for Classical Syriac are Brockelmann 1928, 1968, and Nöldeke and Euting 1898; for the Urmi Christian dialect of Aramaic, Maclean 1895, 1901, Marogulov 1976, Oraham 1943, Polotsky 1967; for the Jewish dialects of northwestern Iraq (the "Zakho-Jewish group," including Zakho itself, Amadiya, and the Nerwa manuscripts edited by Sabar) Polotsky 1967, Sabar 1976, 1984, 2002; for Turoyo, see Jastrow 1985. Other sources are indicated where relevant.

[3] Transcriptions of Aramaic data obtained from published sources have been changed only as much as necessary to eliminate insignificant diversity of symbols and make cross-dialectal comparison easier. For the Urmi Christian and Azerbaijan Jewish dialects I use the symbol ° to indicate pharyngealized (or velarized, "flat") words. Stress in modern Aramaic words is penultimate unless indicated otherwise, except for the Jewish Azerbaijan dialect, in which stress is generally on the final syllable. The symbol ˣ marks forms that were ungrammatical, or non-existent, at the relevant historical stage, while * marks reconstructed forms that are presumed to have been grammatical.

Table 9.1. Words Exhibiting the *šma: > šəmma* Change (*cont.*)

Gloss	Syriac	Pre-NENA*	Turoyo	Aradhin	Urmi	Azerbaijan	Hertevin	ZJ-group
'yesterday'	(eθma:l)	*tma:l	—	tummil	timmal	timmal	ʔetmal	təmmal
'snake'	(ḥewya:)	*ḥwe:[4] (absolute)	—	xuwwe	xuvvi, -a	xuje	ḥowwe	xuwwe, xu:we
'what-you-may-call-it'	hna:	—	hno	—	hinna	—	—	hənna
'three' (feminine)	tlaθ	—	—	təlləθ	—	—	ṭellad-	ṭəllas-
'bottom'	ešta:	—	—	šitta	(išta)	—	šetta	—
'ten' (feminine)	ʕsar	—	—	əssar	—	—	—	—
'-teen'	ʕsar	—	-ḥṣar	-əssər	-°(s)sar	-ssar	-ʔessar	-ʔsar

*If different from Syriac form.

9.2. Question 1: What changed in Aramaic phonology when Earlier Aramaic *šma:* shifted to Northeastern Neo-Aramaic *šə́mma*?

9.2.1. Some Answers that Don't Work

Before proposing an answer to this question, I survey some answers that have been offered by other scholars of Neo-Aramaic. To be fair, none seems to have given more than brief, passing attention to the question, and their proposals are more in the nature of tentative suggestions than fully thought-out analyses. Three proposals can easily be shown to fail upon closer analysis.

9.2.1.1. Epenthesis

One hypothesis leaps to the mind of any Semitist (for instance, Sabar 1976: 39 n. 25) aware that ancient Semitic languages and Proto-Semitic, as it is generally reconstructed, as well as Classical Arabic, do not allow initial consonant clusters: perhaps forms like *šma:* changed to forms like *šəmma* in order to open the initial consonant clusters. The need to avoid clusters would motivate epenthesis, initiating this chain of developments: *šmá: > šəmá: > šə́ma(:) > šə́mma*. Notice that in most of the words that underwent the *šəmma* shift the second consonant is a sonorant. It might be suggested that epenthesis in Aramaic applied specifically in initial obstruent-sonorant clusters, and this proposal gains plausibility from the fact that such a conditioning of epenthesis has been observed in several languages (for Winnebago this is known as Dorsey's Law). However, as an explanation of the change from the original *šma:* the epenthesis theory runs into a serious difficulty: we have no reason, other than the very change we are trying to explain, to believe that initial clusters were problematic in Earlier Aramaic varieties like Classical Syriac and the ancestor of Central Neo-Aramaic.

The evidence regarding initial clusters in the Earlier Aramaic ancestor of Northeastern Neo-Aramaic deserves re-examination. The main reason to think that in Earlier Aramaic there was a schwa-like vowel between an initial consonant and the following one is that the second consonant, if it is one of the set susceptible to spirantization, is spirantized. However, the spirantization of the second consonant in words like Syriac *kθav* 'he wrote' does not prove that it was actually pronounced ˣ[kəθav] in Earlier Aramaic. There is no doubt that when spirantization first applied, during the first millennium B.C.E., there was a vowel there, and the word was something like *katab*. Subsequently, when the first vowel was lost, spirantization would naturally have been preserved. There is no reason for *kθav* to be replaced by ˣ*ktav* because the sequence *kθav* is privileged over *ktav* in terms of the cross-linguistic tendency for syllables to be structured in such a way that sonority increases from the peripheries of syllables to their nuclei. Because θ is higher in sonority than *t*, *kθav* is to be expected, rather than ˣ*ktav*. At this stage spirantization was no longer an automatic process, and in fact *t* and θ were separate phonemes (e.g., Syriac

---

[4] The Northeastern Neo-Aramaic word probably derives from the Earlier Aramaic absolute state, as suggested by Maclean 1895: 27. The Jewish Arbel form is *xiwwa* (Khan 1999: 585).

ḥzi:θ 'I saw' versus ḥzi:t 'you saw'). Therefore spirantization is no proof of the existence of schwa vowels in initial consonant clusters. On the contrary: we know that Earlier Aramaic tolerated initial consonant clusters in at least some words. For instance, the etymon of Earlier Aramaic *tre:n* 'two' had an initial consonant cluster in Proto-Semitic (something like **θnayn*), in the earliest Aramaic (conditioning the change from **θnayn* or **tnayn* to **trayn*), and in nearly all modern Central Aramaic dialects (*tre:*), and likewise *šta:* 'six' and *šti:* 'drink' had initial clusters in older Aramaic (Testen 1985; Hoberman 1989). The simplest explanation for the facts is that these words had initial clusters continuously from the most ancient Semitic stage until today. Furthermore, the epenthesis in Turoyo *ʔəšmo* 'name', *ʔadmo* 'blood', *ʔəšne* 'years', *ʔabro* 'son', *ʔabne* 'sons' make sense only if earlier forms were pronounced with initial consonant clusters, as *šma:*, *dma:*, *šne*, *bra:*, *bne:*, rather than **šəma:*, etc. The common ancestor of a pair of cognates like Turoyo *ʔəšmo* and Northeastern Neo-Aramaic *šəmma* can only be one with an initial cluster: *šma:*. (This is another word that we should reconstruct as having an initial cluster in Proto-Semitic, something like **šm-V*, on the basis of the Arabic form of the word.) Many modern Central Aramaic dialects allow an almost unlimited range of initial clusters both with and without sonorants: *šmá:ʔa* 'hear', *ptá:xa* 'open', *rtá:xa* 'boil' (these forms are from the Jewish dialect of Amadiya [Hoberman 1997a], but similar examples are found in most dialects [Odisho 1988; Sara 1974; Jastrow 1985: 25]).[5] If the change to *šəmma* were motivated by a structural requirement to break up initial clusters, this requirement must have come into effect later than the period of proto-Central Neo-Aramaic, the common ancestor of Turoyo and Northeastern Neo-Aramaic, and then become defunct before the stage of the modern dialects. This is less likely than the alternative, that initial consonant clusters were pronounced throughout this period. In terms of its initial cluster, then, there would have been nothing wrong with the pronunciation *šma:*, and we have no explanation for the hypothetical epenthesis that would have set off this chain of developments.

There is another fact that is not accounted for by epenthesis, and it leads us in the right direction. It is not only the words in table 9.1 that gained bulk between Earlier Aramaic and Northeastern Neo-Aramaic; *all* short words did (leaving the term "short" undefined for the moment). The standard grammars of Syriac, the best-documented of all pre-modern Aramaic languages, include a breakdown of nouns by stem shape, making it easy to search the relevant sections of Nöldeke and Euting 1898 and Brockelmann 1968 to produce a list of the short words in the language, a nearly complete list if not a complete one. Checking this list against Northeastern Neo-Aramaic dictionaries (Maclean 1901; Oraham 1943; Sabar 2002) shows the following: Some of the short words do not survive into Northeastern Neo-Aramaic (*zna:* 'kind, species' and *tda:* 'breast' are among those that have been lost), but those that did survive have *all* lengthened, and they lengthened by diverse mechanisms. Here are some examples:

(1)

Gloss	Earlier Aramaic	Northeastern Neo-Aramaic	Mechanism
'mill'	*rḥe:	ʔərxe	epenthesis
'son'	bra:	bró:na	suffixation (*-o:n-* diminutive)
'father-in-law'	ḥma:	xəmyá:na	epenthesis and suffixation (*-a:n-* agent)
'brother'	ʔaḥa:	ʔá:xa, ʔaxó:na	vowel lengthening or suffixation
'hand'	yða:	ʔí:ða	glide vocalization and vowel lengthening

Earlier Aramaic *bra:* 'son' has acquired a diminutive-forming suffix, taking the form *bro:na* or the like in most Northeastern Neo-Aramaic dialects. An exception is the Hertevin form *ʔebra*, lacking the suffix but gaining length with an epenthetic initial syllable (as in Turoyo *ʔabro*). (This incidentally is further evidence that the form in proto-Central Neo-Aramaic was [bra:], not ˣ[bəra:].) Similarly, *ʔaḥa:* 'brother' has changed in two ways in different dialects: the Amadiya Jewish dialect shows lengthening of the first vowel, *ʔa:xa*, while the very similar Zakho Jewish dialect has the diminutive suffix in *ʔaxo:na*; both types are widespread in Northeastern Neo-Aramaic. The former is similar to a change evidenced as early as classical Syriac in *ʔi:ða:* < *iða:* < *yða:* 'hand'.

---

[5] Speakers of modern Aramaic reciting Classical Syriac pronounce initial clusters without epenthesis (Hoberman 1997b). This is no doubt a product of their vernacular speech pattern, but it also happens to coincide with what Syriac must have originally sounded like in this respect.

Syriac has a set of words that form plurals with the older Aramaic suffix *-ayya:* rather than the *-e:* which replaced it generally, and nearly all these are short words (Nöldeke and Euting 1898: §72). If *-ayya:* had been replaced by *-e:* in these plurals they would have been short. For example, Syriac has *šnayya:* 'years', not the expected ˣ*šne:*, and *šma:he:* 'names', not ˣ*šme:*. Three of the five short words with Syriac plurals in *-ayya:* survive in Northeastern Neo-Aramaic: 'son', 'year', and 'sky'.[6] The plural 'sons', *bnayya:* in Syriac, has acquired the diminutive suffix in most Northeastern Neo-Aramaic dialects, along with the singular, yielding forms like *bno:ne*. Northeastern Neo-Aramaic *šənne* 'years' derives not from Syriac *šnayya:* but from a form like **šne:*, just as Northeastern Neo-Aramaic *šəmme* 'sky' derives not from Syriac *šmayya:* but from **šme:*, and these two, being short, underwent the *šəmma* change. Forms of 'sky' with *-ay(y)a* exist in several Christian dialects (Aradhin, Urmi, Hertevin, as well as Turoyo), but this is evidently a borrowing from classical Syriac, as it is not found in Jewish dialects, where *šəmme* is homonymously both 'sky' < **šme:* < *šmayya:* and 'names' < **šme:* < *šma:he:*.

Other short words in Syriac were lengthened in different ways. For 'father-in-law' Syriac had both the short *ḥma:* and the long *ḥemya:na:*, but only the long form has survived into Northeastern Neo-Aramaic. *ʔava:* 'father' has been replaced by loanwords. In some dialects the short numerals 'one' and 'two' were lengthened when they serve as nouns.

Another older Aramaic short word that survives in Northeastern Neo-Aramaic is 'mill', Hertevin *ʔerḥe*, Aradhin *arxe*, Zakho Jewish *ʔərxe*, Urmi *irxi*, which derives not from the determinate state, Syriac *raḥya:* 'mill(stone)' (whence Turoyo *rəḥyo*), but from the old absolute state **rḥe:*, not attested in classical Syriac (Maclean 1895: 26), which, as Krotkoff (1985: 128) suggested, may have survived "due to the association of the *-e* with the plural because ... the mill is an assembly of two millstones."[7] In **rḥe:* > Hertevin *ʔerḥe*, Aradhin *arxe*, epenthesis took place, probably because of the high sonority of *r*, precluding the *šəmma* change (Maclean 1895: 26).[8]

I have been able to identify only four other short nouns or adjectives in Syriac, *zna:* 'kind', *qwe:* 'woven fabric', *tða:* 'breast', and *teða:* (<**teðʔa:*) 'grass', none of which has survived into Northeastern Neo-Aramaic. Thus all short Aramaic words that survive in Northeastern Neo-Aramaic have been lengthened in one way or another. An adequate explanation for the *šəmma* shift should at the same time explain why no short words survive as such. Three have been proposed.

9.2.1.2. Penultimate Stress

Werner Arnold (personal communication) has suggested that "When in the Neoaramaic dialects stress shifted from the ultima to the penultima, monosyllabic words need an additional syllable." That is, if stress is to be on the penultimate syllable, a word clearly must have at least two syllables. But the fact that the penultimate syllable is the normal position for stress in a language does not necessarily mean that all words must have at least two syllables. Polish is a language with penultimate stress, much more uniformly so than modern Aramaic, but Polish has many monosyllables; this means that the Aramaic penultimate stress pattern is no explanation for the change in syllable structure we are concerned with.

---

[6] In addition to these, there is *ʔi:ða* 'hand', which is not short in Syriac although the still earlier Aramaic form *yða:* is, and consequently in Syriac there are two plural forms, *ʔi:ðayya:* and *ʔi:ðe:*, neither of which is short. In Northeastern Neo-Aramaic the plural is generally a reflex of *ʔi:ða:θa*, never of **ʔi:ðayya*.

[7] Jastrow's suggestion (1988: 84) that rather than seeing this as an old absolute state "kann man *ʔerḥe* als ursprünglichen Plural erklären" pushes Krotkoff's idea a bit too far, in view of the fact that the Earlier Aramaic plural form (Syriac *rḥawwa:θa:*) was not replaced by **rḥe* but survives as the Northeastern Neo-Aramaic plural: Urmi *irxavati*, Hertevin *ʔerḥa:ta*, Aradhin *arxa:θa*, Zakho Jewish *ʔərxa:θa*.

[8] There is support for a reconstructed form **rḥe:* in the Azerbaijan and Arbel Jewish forms, respectively *irxel*, *ʔirxel* (presumably [ʔərxé:l], with phonetics deduced from Garbell 1965: 25, 36; Khan 1999: 49–53, 70–71), which suggest that the word was stressed on its final vowel — its only vowel if the reconstruction as **rḥe:* is correct — even before the general shift of stress to the final syllable in Azerbaijan and Arbel. A similar development is reflected in Syriac *ḥarya:* /*ḥerya:* 'excrement', Arbel *xre*, Urmi *ixri*, Aradhin *axri*; the final *-i* in Urmi is identical to the plural ending (< *-e:*) but the final *-i* in Aradhin is puzzling.

9.2.1.3. Absorption into the Pattern CeCCa

Otto Jastrow (1988: 9) points out in his grammar of the Hertevin dialect that the change from *šma:* to *šəmma* has the result of assimilating this word to the class of nouns of the form *CeCCa* (pronounced [CəCCa]), such as *lebba* 'heart' and *qenna* 'nest'. True enough, and we might add that the *lebba* set has gained other members, such as *pemma* 'mouth'. However, this fact cannot be the motivation for the *šəmma* change because in modern Aramaic there are numerous words, mainly borrowings but also some native items, that do not fit any inherited Aramaic canonical shape. In fact, the general trend in modern Aramaic seems to be not toward *reduction* of the number of stem shapes in the vocabulary as a whole but toward an *increase* in variety. So we still lack an explanation of why words like *šma:* changed their form while words of other shapes did not.

9.2.2. Canonical Stem Shape

An explanation of an entirely different sort was proposed by Nöldeke (1868: 86), who said that the words *dəmma* and *šəmma* "sind in die Categorie der dreiradicaligen übergegangen" ("have gone over into the category of triradicals"). Sachau (1895: 19) states this theory in more detail, listing the word *šəmma* among examples demonstrating the "strenuous efforts" which the language has made to satisfy the demands of a "law of triradicality": "Um nun den Anforderungen dieses Gesetzes [scil. "die Triradicalität"] zu genügen, machen jene zweiconsonantigen Wörter gewaltsame Anstrengungen, indem sie durch Anfügung eines Alef, Je, Wau, oder He oder auch durch Verdoppelung des zweiten Consonanten es auf die erforderliche Dreizahl zu bringen suchen: Bildungsweisen, die sich als Nothbehelfe, als nicht organisch erwachsen, als einer jüngeren Periode angehörig unschwer zu erkennen geben" ("In order to satisfy the demands of this law, such biconsonantal words make strenuous efforts to meet the requisite number of three, by adding an alef, ya, waw, or ha [that is, respectively ʔ or a:, y or i:, w or u:, or h or a:] or by doubling the second consonant, developments which are easy to recognize as expedients, as having grown inorganically, as belonging to a more recent period").

I believe that Nöldeke and Sachau were on the right track in suggesting that there is some minimal structure or bulk that every word in this language must have. Conventional linguistic terminology calls such a requirement "minimality." The changes that produced Northeastern Neo-Aramaic *bro:na*, *bno:ne*, *ʔa:xa*, *ʔaxo:na*, *xəmya:na*, *treʔe*, *ʔərxe*, and Hertevin *ʔebra*, in addition to the *šəmma* set would be isolated, idiosyncratic, inexplicable changes if they are not seen as part of the general movement toward meeting a requirement of word-length. These changes seen together prove that the Northeastern Neo-Aramaic minimality requirement was operative in the historical development of this language. The purpose of this paper is to determine more precisely the nature of the minimality requirement that was met by the change from *šma:* to *šəmma*.

9.2.2.1. The Root-based Approach to Semitic Morphology

Words in Semitic languages strikingly conform to a relatively small set of canonical forms. There are two main approaches to delineating these forms, and each approach would provide a different answer to question 1. One approach traditionally defines patterns in terms of roots consisting typically of three consonants.[9] For example, Arabic *maktab* 'office' is said to be composed of a root *k-t-b* meaning 'write' and a pattern *maCCaC* meaning 'place'. On this approach, the answer to question 1 would be that *šma:* shifted to *šémma* to match the canonical triconsonantal-root structure, in this case *š-m-m*. This is the answer offered by Nöldeke and Sachau.

9.2.2.2. The Prosodic Approach to Semitic Morphology

The second approach defines Semitic canonical stem shapes in terms of prosodic templates. Research on the phonologies of many languages has shown that the prosodic structure of words, including accentual patterns

---

[9] It makes more sense to view stem shapes as being defined in terms of templates (patterns), each of which has three slots, where each slot can be occupied by one or more segment (Goldenberg 1994). For our purposes this is not different from the triconsonantal-root approach.

and templatic morphology, is best understood not in terms of consonant and vowel segments but in terms of metrical units like foot, syllable, and mora. A mora is a measure of syllable weight which can be defined for our purposes as follows: a short vowel is one mora, a long vowel is two moras, a syllable-final consonant is one mora. Syllable-initial consonants in most languages do not constitute moras because they are usually irrelevant in such phenomena as stress assignment and poetic meter.[10] On this approach Arabic *maktab* might be said to be one foot consisting of two syllables, each syllable with two moras. The form [maktab] is the simplest way to pronounce the combination of consonants and vowels consisting of a prefix *ma-* (or *m-*) which forms nouns, a vocalism *a* (or *a-a*), and the lexical material from a more basic word, perhaps *uktub* 'write', or *kitaab* 'book', or *kaatib* 'clerk'. (The indeterminacy of the base for this derivational process, as for many other derivational processes in analyses of this type, is an important weakness of this approach, but we will ignore that here.) On this approach, the answer to question 1 is that *šma:* shifted to *šəmma* in order to meet minimal-word requirements defined in terms of the prosodic elements mora, syllable, and foot.

Which of the two approaches to Semitic morphology is more enlightening for our problem? I assume that there was a synchronic minimality constraint at the time that forms like *šəmma* originated and that its synchronic analog in the modern language will be very similar. Sachau proposes that the requirement is "Triradicalität": the stem must contain at least three "Radicale oder Consonanten." (I say "stem" because Sachau does not begin using the word "Wurzel" until the next section, "Nomina von dreiradicaligen Wurzeln"; the section with which we are concerned is called "Zweiradicalige Nomina.") However, the requirement cannot in fact be specifically three *consonants* because many of Sachau's own examples do not have three consonants, even counting *y*, *w*, and *ʔ* as consonants: *a:wa* 'father', *ħa:θa* 'sister', *i:da* 'hand', *ka:ka* 'tooth', *pa:θa* 'face', *ša:qa* 'leg', *ma:ya* 'water', *še:ta* 'year', *ya:ma* 'sea', *ka:we* 'window', *ma:θa* 'village'. Of course it would be possible to analyze these words as containing additional abstract root consonants in their underlying representations, so that, for instance, *i:da* might be said to contain a root *ʔ-y-d* (and proto-Northeastern Neo-Aramaic *ʔi:ða* contained a root *ʔ-y-ð*). But there is no reason to treat *ʔi:ða* 'hand' as if it contained a root *ʔ-y-ð* because the language has no words other than *ʔi:ða* itself that would contain the same root. A root is an abstraction, an element in a theory (though a very valuable theory). If the only motivation for such an analysis is to save the theory that words must contain three consonants, the analysis can carry no weight; it begs the question. Furthermore, in many Northeastern Neo-Aramaic dialects, for instance, Aradhin (Krotkoff 1982), the general direction of change is the loss of *ʔ*, *ʕ*, *y*, and *w*, so that many words that historically had roots of three segments now appear without them, as *xa:la* 'eat' (historically *ʔxa:la*), *θe:(-le)* 'he came' (< *ʔθe:-*), *ur* 'enter' (imperative; < *ʕvor*), *ara* 'earth' (< *ʔarʕa:*). It is hard to see how one could formulate the idea that a different, contrary change (*šma:* > *šəmma*) is motivated by some need to have roots of three consonants or segments.

9.2.3. A Prosodic Approach to Word Minimality in Northeastern Neo-Aramaic

9.2.3.1. Some Data

So what is the minimal legitimate word in modern Northeastern Neo-Aramaic? In order to determine this I examined all the attested nouns, adjectives, and verbs in two Northeastern Neo-Aramaic dialects, Hertevin (Jastrow 1988) and Aradhin (Krotkoff 1982), collecting all the "short" items.[11] Words of the shapes CVCCV(C) and CV:CV(C), and longer words that end in those sequences, are plentiful, so I defined "short" words as shorter than those shapes: short words are those which are either monosyllables or disyllables of which the first syllable is light (an open syllable with a short vowel), that is CVCV(:)(C). I examined only nouns, adjectives, and verbs

---

[10] For surveys of the reasoning and evidence behind this approach, see the articles in Goldsmith 1995 by Broselow, Perlmutter, and McCarthy and Prince.

[11] These two glossaries were chosen because of their size: they are not too large to be examined completely yet large enough to be statistically representative of the vocabulary as a whole and to be likely to include all the most frequent words. They also have the advantages of being documented with phonetic precision, including explicit marking of vowel quantity, which is essential to our topic, and of being based on colloquial, vernacular speech, rather than literary texts that contain numerous borrowings from Classical Syriac. Sabar's dictionary (2002) is much larger than Krotkoff's and Jastrow's glossaries and would be most appropriate for this investigation. I did not search it comprehensively because of its size, but a relatively brief examination shows that Sabar's vocabulary does not differ from Krotkoff's and Jastrow's in ways that relate to our topic.

because in Aramaic, as in many languages, function words such as prepositions, pronouns, adverbs, etc., are often shorter than the minimum length of the major lexical categories and have atypical sound patterns in other respects as well.[12]

9.2.3.1.a. Theme I Monosyllabic Imperatives and Perfects

Hertevin and Aradhin, as well as other dialects including Zakho/Amadiya Jewish, have productive categories of short words. In all three the (singular) imperative of verbs of Theme I (pʕal) is a monosyllable: Hertevin *ploṭ* 'go out', Aradhin *pḷoṭ*, Zakho Jewish/Amadiya *pḷo:ṭ*. In Hertevin and Zakho/Amadiya, Theme I verbs have another monosyllabic form, which functions in Hertevin as a perfect and in Zakho as a preterite: Hertevin *pleṭ* 'gone out', Zakho *šqi:l* 'took'. I postpone discussion of these productive types and first take up short words of non-productive categories.

9.2.3.1.b. Hertevin

The Hertevin glossary contains about 1,300 lexical items. Looking first at native Aramaic words, only a small handful are short as defined above: *ma:* 'hundred', *mare* 'possessor of', *ṭo:* 'better', a few relic absolute state forms appearing in *yo:m b-yo:m* 'day by day', *koš-šet* 'every year', and *koy-yom* 'every day', and the shortened first part of *palg-ú:-palga:* 'half-and-half'. Each of these is in one way or another outside of the canonical vocabulary in terms of meaning or function.

As for borrowed words (mostly from Kurdish, or from Arabic or Turkish borrowed via Kurdish), there are three monosyllables with short vowels and single final consonants (*ber* 'awareness', *čaṭ* [name of a village], *ħas* 'command') and forty-three monosyllables with long vowels or final consonant clusters (e.g., *te:r* 'sufficient quantity', *ʔahl* 'people'); none have the shapes CV: or CV. There are fifteen disyllables with light penultimates, such as *pare:* 'money', *kadi:* 'tame', *xari:b* 'foreign' (intriguingly, the first vowel is *a* in all but one, *geleh* 'complaint'). There are also a few trisyllabic words with light penultimate syllables, such as *ʔo:dawe:* 'whey' and *ṭarbela:* 'perplexed'.

The borrowed vocabulary is marked by several other departures from the normal phonological structure of the dialect, such as stress on a final or antepenultimate syllable, short vowels in open syllables, and long vowels in closed syllables, so borrowed words are not representative of the sound patterns of the inherited Aramaic component. We conclude that native words of the major lexical classes may not be short as defined above.

9.2.3.1.c. Aradhin

Krotkoff's glossary of the Aradhin dialect contains about 1,700 lexical items, including just fifty-three short words, of which only ten are native Aramaic. As in Hertevin, the borrowed portion of the vocabulary includes a significant number (forty-three) of short lexical items, and they are not limited in function or type. Of these, nine are monosyllables with a long vowel (e.g., *čo:l* 'wilderness'), ten are monosyllables with a final consonant cluster (e.g., *drist* 'straight', *zerq* 'small, white grapes'), and twenty-one are disyllables in which the first syllable is light (*gira* 'hill', *paqo* 'whole grain wheat', *saʕa* 'hour'). There are no monosyllables with the shapes CVC, CV:, or CV. In addition there are seven trisyllabic words with light penultimate syllables, all of them borrowed (e.g., *kalapuš* 'the dried greens of a plant', *másʔala* 'matter, problem', *sarača* 'furuncle', *sílsila* 'descendants'). As for the native items, in four an original *ʔ* had been deleted, producing a short open syllable where a closed syllable existed previously: *ara* 'earth' < **arʔa* (< Earlier Aramaic *ʔarʕa:*), *kibe* or *gəbe* 'he wants' < **k-bʔe* (< **k-bʕe:*), *mara* 'illness' < **marʔa* (< Earlier Aramaic *marʕa:*), *nara* 'ax' < **narʔa* (< Earlier Aramaic *na:rya:*). Another

---

[12] Thus in Aradhin the numerals 'one' (masculine and feminine) and 'two' are *xa, ða, tre* (< Earlier Aramaic *ħað, ħða:, tre:n*) when they occur before a noun, that is, when they are dependent, but are extended to *xaʔa, ðaʔa, treʔe* when they stand alone as the independent head of a noun phrase (Krotkoff 1982: 46). A similar extension occurs in the dialect of Tisqopa (Rubba 1993: 21) and in the Zakho and Amadiya Jewish dialects.

three are bound forms, which from the historical point of view are relics of older Aramaic construct state forms and in the modern language occur only as components of personal names and are probably not to be considered full words at all: *bi:* 'house of', *bar* 'son of', and *mar* 'honorific title before the name of a bishop' (Krotkoff 1982: 134). Two are "allegro forms" of the "emphatic copula" (37): *hon* < *howin* 'I am', *hule* 'he is'. The remaining item is *yaʔr* or *yaʔar* 'May'.

All these are either relatively recently formed (some Northeastern Neo-Aramaic dialects, among them Jewish Zakho and Amadiya, do not have the regular deletion of *ʔ* that Aradhin does) or outside the system of the major, open lexical classes of nouns, adjectives, and verbs. Furthermore, underlying long vowels are shortened before *ʔ*, producing many superficially short words, most of them infinitives like *plaʔa* 'divide'; otherwise infinitives have long *a* (*dma:xa* 'sleep'), so a word like *plaʔa* is underlyingly /pla:ʔa/. We may say, then, that in a relatively recent ancestor of the Aradhin dialect short words do not exist within the native Aramaic vocabulary.

To summarize, in Hertevin, Aradhin, and Zakho/Amadiya, native Aramaic words of the productive, major lexical classes (still postponing discussion of the short imperatives and perfects/preterites) are minimally of the shapes CVCCV(C) or CV:CV(C), that is, disyllables with heavy penults. Borrowed words may in addition be heavy monosyllables (CV:C or CVCC), disyllables with light penults (CVCV, CVCVC, CVCVCC, or CVCV:C), or trisyllables with light penults. How should these observations be formalized?

9.2.3.2. Binarity

It has been observed cross-linguistically that minimal words must be prosodically binary, having either two moras or two syllables. In languages with phonemic vowel length ("quantity-sensitive" languages), the binarity is usually moraic (words must contain two moras), while in quantity-insensitive languages the binarity is usually syllabic (words must contain two syllables; McCarthy and Prince 1995). Northeastern Neo-Aramaic has phonemic vowel quantity, so we should expect binarity to be moraic. However, vowel quantity in Northeastern Neo-Aramaic has little functional load, as vowel length is predictable in most cases (Jastrow 1988: 10, 14–15; Hoberman 1997a). Furthermore, unlike the pattern in typical quantity-sensitive languages like Latin and Arabic, stress placement in Northeastern Neo-Aramaic does not depend on syllable weight. Thus Northeastern Neo-Aramaic behaves mainly as a quantity-insensitive language, which would lead us to expect that the minimal word would be disyllabic. In fact the language vacillates between the two: in the native vocabulary words must be disyllabic, while the borrowed vocabulary contains bimoraic monosyllables.

(2) Syllabic binarity: A word must be at least disyllabic.
(3) Moraic binarity: A word must be at least bimoraic.

Syllabic binarity motivates the shifts *šm-a:* > *šə́(m)ma*, *rħ-e:* > *ʔə́rħ-e*, and *br-a:* > *br-o:n-a*. It is violated, however, by numerous loanwords (e.g., *zerk* 'small, white grapes', *čo:l* 'wilderness', and *gə́ra* 'hill' (from Kurdish *gir*), which has acquired the Aramaic word-marking suffix *-a*. In nearly all loanwords, including *zerq*, *čo:l*, and *gəra*, however, moraic binarity holds.

9.2.3.3. Stress-to-Weight

In most Northeastern Neo-Aramaic dialects, including the phonologically conservative dialects, word stress is penultimate. Furthermore, there is a strong tendency for stressed syllables to be heavy, either CVC or CV:, a fact which was first observed by Rubba (1989, 1993: 17–25). Synchronic effects of this are evident in many Northeastern Neo-Aramaic dialects. Short vowels are often lengthened when they fall in the penultimate, and therefore stressed, syllables. Thus in Hertevin there are alternations like *ka:la*, plural *kala:ta* 'bride', *da:da*, plural *dadawa:ta* 'mother', *ga:re*, plural *garawa:ta* 'roof'; these stems have underlying short vowels, /kal-a, dad-a, gar-e/, which lengthen when stressed. Similar facts exist in most other Northeastern Neo-Aramaic dialects. The short vowels in words like *kala:ta* and nominal patterns like *CaCa:Ca*, *CaCi:Ca*, *CaCo:Ca*, and *CaCu:Ca* have been seen by most scholars of modern Aramaic as *exceptions* to a putative generalization that vowels in open syllables are long (Jastrow 1988, 14–15, 91). However, this generalization, though statistically true (Hoberman

1997a), misses the point. The correct principle, as Rubba has argued, is that *vowels in open syllables are long if the syllable is stressed*. Vowels in unstressed syllables, like the first vowel in *kala:ta* and the many words with the patterns CaCa:Ca, CaCi:Ca, CaCo:Ca, CaCu:Ca, and others, are in general short. The exceptions — long vowels in unstressed syllables — always have some separate, specific raison d'être. This is accounted for by another type of constraint:

(4) Stress-to-weight. If a syllable is stressed, it must be heavy (CV: or CVC; cf. Kager 1999: 268).

In view of the fact that the default position for stress is on the penultimate syllable (in words of more than one syllable), the minimal word is determined by the interaction of two constraints, both of them widely known cross-linguistically. Together with the stress-to-weight constraint, the minimality restrictions specified above will give the correct results. If a word consists of two or more syllables, as (2) stipulates, stress will be on the penultimate syllable, which will therefore be heavy to satisfy (4) as well. Constraint (3) is not superfluous, however, but necessary to explain why there are many loanwords of the shapes CV:C and CVCC but few if any of the bimoraic or monomoraic shapes CVC, CV:, or CV in Northeastern Neo-Aramaic dialects, though in Kurdish and Turkish, the chief sources of loanwords in Northeastern Neo-Aramaic, they are plentiful.

This analysis accounts for *ʔaħa:* > *ʔá:xa* 'brother'. Still, *ʔa:xa* has an short vowel in its underlying form, /ʔax-a/, as we can see from the alternative singular *ʔaxó:na* and the plural *ʔaxawá:θa*. It would account for hypothetical **šə́ma* > *šə́mma*. Kapeliuk (1992) points out that in the Northeastern Neo-Aramaic dialect of Urmi an intervocalic consonant that follows a stressed short vowel is often geminated. This takes place in both nouns and verbs of some productive types, such as *malximma* 'fit (feminine)' < *malxəma* (cf. masculine *malxim*), and serves to bring such words in line with the general pattern of the language, in which stressed syllables must be heavy (either closed or containing a long vowel). Kapeliuk includes among the examples of this phenomenon the word *imma* 'one hundred', which I take to be possibly an instance of the *šə́mma* change. Kapeliuk's observation could provide an explanation for the final step in the chain of developments beginning with epenthesis, *šə́ma* > *šə́mma*.

9.2.3.4. Does Binarity Apply to Stems or to Full Words?

One way of resolving the difference between minimality in native words and in loanwords might be to postulate that the moraic binarity constraint applies to stems rather than full words (cf. McCarthy and Prince 1995: 323–25). Native Aramaic nouns have a class-marking suffix *-a* or *-e* (*kalb-a* 'dog', *ga:r-e* 'roof'). The stems of minimal words, excluding the class-markers, are identical in prosodic shape to most short loanwords. Thus **zerk** 'small, white grapes' parallels native **kalb**+*a* 'dog', and **čo:l** 'wilderness' parallels native **gó:r**+*a* 'man'.

Unfortunately, this resolution of the contradiction is insufficient. To see why, we must now turn to the productive categories of short words, which we postponed earlier. These are the (singular) imperative of verbs of Theme I (pʕal), Hertevin *plot̠* 'go out', Aradhin *pl̠ot̠*, Zakho Jewish/Amadiya *pl̠o:t̠*, and another monosyllabic form of Theme I verbs, which functions in Hertevin as a perfect and in Zakho as a preterite: Hertevin *plet̠* 'gone out', Zakho *šqi:l* 'took'.[13] These clearly violate syllabic binarity (2). Here are two typical Theme I verbs, with a Theme II verb for comparison (Amadiya Jewish examples):

(5)

	Theme I		Theme II
	'open'	'see'	'send'
Gerund/Progressive	ptá:xa	xzá:ya	mšadó:re
Present (< Earlier Aramaic active participle)	pá:tǝx	xá:ze	mšá:dǝr
Imperative	pto:x	xzi:	mšá:dǝr
Preterite (< Earlier Aramaic passive participle)	pti:x	xze:	mšó:dǝr

Forms like *pto:x, pti:x, xzi:, xze:* comply with moraic binarity (3) but violate syllabic binarity (2).

---

[13] The stem vowels are basically long in Hertevin and Aradhin, as well as in Zakho/Amadiya, as the suffixed forms show: plural Hertevin *pl̠u:t̠en*, Aradhin *pl̠u:t̠u*, third-person feminine singular Hertevin *pli:t̠a*. The long vowel shortens in the unsuffixed forms through the quite general process of shortening in closed syllables (Jastrow 1988: 10, 13–14).

These two subminimal, monosyllabic forms are frequently lengthened, in some dialects, by the addition of a meaningless suffix. In Hertevin it is *-ek*, as in *ptoħ* ≈ *ptoħħek* 'open' (imperative), *pteħ* ≈ *pteħek* (perfect; Jastrow 1988: 53). A variety of other monosyllabic forms have similar free variants that are not short, including the irregular *(b)zaħ* ≈ *(b)zaħħek* 'let's go' ('we will go'), *ʔet* ≈ *ʔettek* 'there is', *let* ≈ *lettek* 'there isn't', *bass* ≈ *bassek* 'it's enough', *hwen* (ibid., p. 211) ≈ *hwennek* (ibid., p. 53) 'I have become'. The suffixation of *-ek* can even be fed by phonological processes that have the effect of creating a short form. Thus the Theme I verb *k-l-y* 'stop, remain standing' has the regular imperative singular *kli:*, plural *klo:wen* (ibid., p. 39), but for this particular verb (of which the imperative is presumably used especially frequently) the imperative plural may be contracted to *klo:n*, a subminimal form to which *-ek* may be added creating the lengthened form *klo:nnek* (ibid., p. 53). There is no *-ek* in the imperatives and perfects of verbs of Themes II and III, which are disyllabic (e.g., *maħlop* 'exchange').

In the Jewish dialects of northwestern Iraq (Zakho, Amadiya, etc.) a different meaningless suffix, *-ən*, has a similar function:[14]

(6) Imperative singular   *pto:x* ≈ *ptó:xən*
    Preterite masculine singular   *ptí:x* ≈ *ptí:xən*

The dummy suffix *-ən* appears also in *ʔi:θ* ≈ *ʔí:θən* 'there is' and second-person singular verb forms like *pátxət* ≈ *patxé:tən* 'you (singular masculine, feminine) open' (< Earlier Aramaic *pa:tx* + *att*). There is no dummy suffix in feminine or plural:

(7) Imperative plural   *ptó:xun*
    Preterite feminine singular   *ptí:x-a*
    Plural   *ptí:x-i*

The feminine and plural forms, and the masculine singular when supplemented by *-ek* or *-ən*, comply with syllabic binarity. The unsuffixed masculine singular does not, but, like many loanwords, it complies with moraic binarity. The affixation of *-ek* in Hertevin and *-ən* in Zakho/Amadiya, which "repairs" short forms by making them longer, proves that short words violate a general pattern of the language, the requirement for words to exceed some minimum length. Imperatives and perfects may be viewed as meeting the requirement in their underlying forms, which contain long vowels, but as being subminimal in their actual pronunciation. Furthermore, the affixation of these dummy suffixes demonstrates that the minimality constraint applies not at the level of stems, but at the level of whole words because while a form like *pti:xa* is fine, *pti:x* is only partially good; it conforms to moraic binarity but not to syllabic binarity, which is precisely why it is extended to *pti:xən*. Therefore the major constraint that applies to native Aramaic words must be disyllabicity, applying to the whole inflected word.

The major conclusions so far are these:

(8) a. Northeastern Neo-Aramaic vacillates between quantity-sensitivity and -insensitivity, with concomitant vacillation between moraic and syllabic application of foot-binarity and word minimality.
    b. For the native vocabulary in general, syllabic binarity applies.
    c. In the imperative and preterite and in loanwords, bimoraicity is sufficient.
    d. Just as there is vacillation between quantity-sensitivity and -insensitivity, there is vacillation on the application of minimality to certain categories of words, reflected in the affixation of the dummy suffixes, optionally in most cases.

9.2.3.5. C$_2$ is Sonorant

In nearly all the words exhibiting the *šəmma* change (table 9.1) the second consonant, the one which is geminated, is a sonorant (*m, n, w,* or *l*). This suggests that the phonetic mechanism of the change may have

---

[14] In the dialect of the seventeenth-century Nerwa manuscripts, Sabar has discerned some syntactic/semantic relevance of this *-ən* (Sabar 1976: xxxiv, 40 n. 34).

commenced with syllabification of the sonorant consonant (e.g., *šma:* > *šmaː*). The same mechanism may have operated in the items in table 9.2.[15] In most of Northeastern Neo-Aramaic the numeral 'one hundred' is *ʔəmma* or the like, but the pronunciation of this word at an earlier period is unclear. In Syriac it is spelled <mʔʔ>, but vocalized *maː*. Is the first <ʔ> merely a historical spelling, based on an earlier **mʔaː*? Oddly, before this word the conjunction *w-* and prepositions *b-, l-* take an epenthetic *a*, suggesting a pronunciation like *wamʔaː* or *wammaː* in Syriac (Nöldeke and Euting 1898: §43E, though Nöldeke suggests a pronunciation "*wamā*"). If in pre-Northeastern Neo-Aramaic the word was **mʔaː*, which is the expected descendent of Proto-Semitic **miʔat-* and would coincide with the Syriac facts, then this **mʔaː* could have metathesized to *ʔmaː* and then undergone the *šəmma* change, producing the Northeastern Neo-Aramaic form *ʔəmma*. Alternatively, the expected *mʔaː* could have become something like *mmaː* or *m̥maː*, yielding *əmma* through vocalization of the initial sonorant consonant. The remaining items in table 9.2, the prepositions *b-* and *l-* when suffixed, have forms like *ʔəbb-e* 'in him', *ʔəll-e* 'to him', resembling words like *šəmma, ʔəmma*, but the mechanism of the change is unclear. The corresponding Turoyo forms *ʔeːl-e, ʔeːb-e* would follow by the regular sound changes from proto-Central Neo-Aramaic forms **ʔəbb-, *ʔəll-* (cf. Turoyo *leːbo* < *ləbbaː* 'heart' and many similar items). If so these would not coincide temporally with the *šəmma* change, which took place in Northeastern Neo-Aramaic but not in Turoyo, therefore after the split of Central Neo-Aramaic into the two branches.

Table 9.2. Northeastern Neo-Aramaic Words Exhibiting Changes Similar to the *šmaː* > *šəmma* Change

Gloss	Syriac, Pre-NENA	Turoyo	Aradhin	Urmi	Azerbaijan	Hertevin	ZJ-group
'hundred'	maː (=[mmaː] or [mʔaː]?)	mo (tremo, tloθomo)	imma	imma	imma	ma (-ʔma)[16]	ʔəmma
'in' (suffixed)	b-	ʔeb-	əbb-	—	ibb-	-b-	ʔəbb-
'to' (suffixed)	l-	ʔel-	əll-	ill-	ill-	lal-	ʔəll-

9.2.3.6. Feminine Numerals

Several Northeastern Neo-Aramaic dialects maintain distinct masculine and feminine numerals from 'one' to 'ten'. The feminine numeral 'three' (Aradhin *ṭiḷḷiθ*, attested also in Hertevin *ṭelladma* and Zakho Jewish *ṭallasma* 'three hundred') is a case of the *šəmma* sound change, but it also contributes to a paradigmatic change in the feminine numerals. All the feminine numerals from 'two' to 'nine' and, in most dialects, '-teen' (from the feminine form of 'ten') have become disyllabic (table 9.3). The phonetic changes by which they have become disyllabic are diverse and in some cases resemble processes we have discussed above, but I would not assume that Aradhin *tišša* 'nine' (feminine; < Earlier Aramaic *tšaʕ*) is an instance of the *šəmma* change, but rather that it is due to paradigmatic pressure.

Table 9.3. The Feminine Numerals

Gloss	Syriac, Pre-NENA	Turoyo[17]	Aradhin	Mangesh	Hertevin	ZJ-group
'one'	ħða:	ħðo	ða(ʔa)	xða	ħda	(xədda?[18])
'two'	tarteːn	tarteː	tərte	tətta	(treːma)	tarteʔ-ma
'three'	tlaːθ	tloːθ	ṭiḷḷiθ	ṭəllaθ	ṭellad-ma	ṭa/ṭəllas-ma

---

[15] There are few more possible examples that are still more uncertain or doubtful. Azerbaijan has *kimma* 'how much', from Earlier Aramaic *kmaː*, but all other dialects known to me have *kma* and the like. Aradhin has *šowwaṭ* 'February' (Syriac *švaːṭ*). For 'someone, so-and-so' (Earlier Aramaic *plaːn*) the form is unclear. Maclean (1901) writes the Urmi word <pelān> 'someone, so-and-so' (transliterated here from Syriac script), which, together with his transcription 'pilân', would indicate [pilan] from an earlier **pillan*, ultimately from Earlier Aramaic *plaːn*. Maclean (1895: 282–83) lists a few other words that might be considered here but probably do not represent the same phenomenon.

[16] Note the *ʔ* in *tmaneʔma* 'eight hundred'; is this by analogy with *ʔarbeʔma, šawweʔma, ʔeččeʔma*, or an indication of original **ʔmaː*?

[17] Jastrow 1998: 358.

[18] Sabar (1976: 39 n. 25) records *xədda* as the colloquial Jewish Amadiya form, but I have not heard it from speakers from that community; it may have become obsolete under pressure from the influential Zakho dialect. Otherwise the dialects of the Zakho-Jewish group have *xa* for both masculine and feminine.

Table 9.3. The Feminine Numerals (*cont.*)

Gloss	Syriac, Pre-NENA	Turoyo	Aradhin	Mangesh	Hertevin	ZJ-group
'four'	ʔarbaʕ	ʔarbaʕ	ʔärbe	ʔarbə	ʔarbeʔ-ma	ʔarbeʔ-ma
'five'	ħa(m)meš	ħamməš	xamməš	xamməš	ħammeš-ma	xamməš-ma
'six'	še:θ	še:θ	iššit	ʔəššət	ʔeššet-ma	ʔəššət-ma
'seven'	švaʕ	švaʕ	išwa	ʔəšwa	šawweʔ-ma	(ʔə)šwaʔ-ma, šowaʔ-ma
'eight'	tma:ne:	tmo:ne:	tma:ne	tmanə	tma:neʔ-ma	(tmanya ʔimmaye)
'nine'	tšaʕ	čaʕ	tišša	təšə	ʔeččeʔ-ma	ʔiččaʔ-ma
'ten'	ʕsar	ḥsa:r	əssər	—	—	—
'-teen'	-ʕsar	-ḥsar	-əssər	-ssar	-ʔessar	-ʔsar, -ʔəssar

9.2.3.7. Nöldeke's Zweiradikalige Substantive

The classic treatment of short words in Semitic is Nöldeke's 1910 article "Zweiradikalige Substantive," which discusses most of the items I have examined here, among others. Nöldeke demonstrates that short word stems often lengthen *necessarily*, as he says, when new words are derived from them through the characteristically Semitic templatic morphology. He adds that even those short words that are basic, not derived, sometimes lengthen, though there is no necessity for such because no derivational template is involved.[19] Many of Nöldeke's observations about developments in ancient Semitic languages are not accounted for by the analysis presented here for Northeastern Neo-Aramaic. It has been the purpose of the present work to show just what "necessity" it was that compelled these words to lengthen in modern Aramaic.

9.3. Question 2: What motivated the historical change in Aramaic phonology?

Up to this point we have shown *how* the *šma:* > *šə́mma* change is embodied in the phonology of Aramaic. We have not addressed the question of *why* — what set off the change? In other words, what caused the disyllabicity constraint to come to the fore? Constraint (2) was not active in Earlier Aramaic, which had not only many monosyllabic basic words but also several productive morphological templates that produced monosyllabic words. The constraint became active as a consequence of morphosyntactic changes: the loss of the only two Earlier Aramaic morphological categories in which the basic form of a word (the citation form) can be monosyllabic and unsuffixed, namely, the perfect tense of verbs and the absolute state of nouns and adjectives. The historical impetus for the modern Aramaic disyllabic minimality is thus morphological, not phonological. The absence of short words (of major lexical classes) in Northeastern Neo-Aramaic is a consequence of the loss of two important morphological categories of Earlier Aramaic nominals and verbs in which monosyllabic stems can appear unsuffixed: the absolute state of nouns and adjectives and the perfect tense of verbs. Only a few relic forms of these categories survive in the modern language. The other productive categories that had unsuffixed stems in older Aramaic are the Theme I (pʕal) active participle, which was and remains disyllabic (e.g., Syriac *ša:qəl*), satisfying the minimal template; and the Theme I passive/perfect participle and imperative, which remain as the anomalies that we have discussed above. I suggest that the requirement for words to have at least two syllables is an epiphenomenon, a mere side effect of the loss of the older Aramaic absolute state and perfect tense on one hand and, on the other, of the general sound changes which produced long vowels in stressed open syllables (as in *ʔa:xa* < *ʔaḥa:* 'brother', *ʔi:ða* < *yða:* 'hand', and the like).

---

[19] "Bildete man aber weitere Ableitungen von solchen Wörtern, so mußte man in vielen Fällen notwendig einen dritten Radikal annehmen; ... Und auch ohne Not wandelten namentlich jüngere Dialekte manchmal die bilitteralen Formen in trilitterale der üblichen Weise um. Gerade aber darin, daß die Verstärkung bei mehreren dieser Wörter auf ganz verschiedene Art geschieht, zeigt sich wieder, daß die einfache bilitterale Form die ursprüngliche ist" (Nöldeke 1910: 111) ("But when further derivations have been built from such words, in many cases it was necessary to add a third radical.... And even without necessity younger dialects, especially, often reshaped the biliteral forms to triliteral in the usual way. But the very fact that the strengthening in some of these words happened in entirely different manners shows that the simple biliteral form is the original one" [translation by RDH]).

In the Earlier Aramaic perfect paradigm, many of the forms are monosyllabic (some with disyllabic alternatives). They are highlighted in the following table:

(9) The Syriac Perfect Tense

	Singular		Plural	
	'kiss'	'see'	'kiss'	'see'
Third-person masculine	**nšaq**	**ħzi:**	**nšaq**(u:n)	**ħzi:w**
Third-person feminine	nešqaθ	ħezyaθ	**nšaq**(e:n)	**ħzi:**
Second-person masculine	**nšaqt**	**ħzi:t**	nšaqto:n	ħzi:to:n
Second-person feminine	**nšaqt**	**ħzi:t**	nšaqte:n	ħzi:te:n
First-person	nešqe:θ	**ħzi:θ**	**nšaqn**(an)	**ħzi:n**

The absolute and construct states of nouns and adjectives are often monosyllabic too. In older Aramaic the basic form of a noun is the absolute state, and the determinate state marks syntactic-semantic definiteness. In Syriac and Eastern Aramaic, the basic form of a noun is the determinate state, which is suffixed. The absolute state appears only with quantifiers and in some idioms and is not attested for all nouns in Syriac; it is thus on a trajectory of obsolescence. Still in Syriac the absolute state is normal for predicate adjectives.

(10) The Syriac Nominal States

Nouns	Determinate State	Absolute State	Construct State
'house'	bayta:	**bay**	**be:θ**
'year'	šatta: (< *šanta:)	**šna:**	**šnaθ**
'head'	re:ša	**re:š**	**re:š**
'name'	**šma:**	šem	šem
'son'	**bra:**	bar	bar
'hand'	ʔi:ða: (< *yða:)	yað	yað, ʔi:ð

Adjective 'good'			
masculine singular	ṭa:va:	**ṭa:v**	**ṭa:v**
feminine singular	ṭa:vθa:	ṭa:va:	ṭa:vaθ
masculine plural	ṭa:ve:	ṭa:vi:n	ṭa:vay
feminine plural	ṭa:va:θa:	ṭa:va:n	ṭa:va:θa:

The absolute state has been lost in Northeastern Neo-Aramaic (except for a few fossils). The construct state survives and is productive, but is phonologically and syntactically bound (though it may be stressed): *bé:θa* 'house', *bé:θ ħakó:ma* 'king's house, palace', *bé: ħakó:ma* 'royal family'.

With the extinction of the perfect tense and the absolute state in Central Neo-Aramaic, the monosyllabic forms of a huge number of nouns, verbs, and adjectives were replaced, as the basic, lexical, or citation form, by disyllables. Thereupon the language became intolerant of monosyllables.

This is an instance of a class of phenomena known as "the emergence of the unmarked" (Kager 1999: 215–16). There is a perennial conflict between the pressure to simplify pronunciation to a relatively easy form (represented in Optimality Theory as markedness constraints, like binarity and stress-to-weight) and the pressure to preserve lexical and morphological information (faithfulness constraints). In Earlier Aramaic there were numerous monosyllabic words, corresponding to a mental grammar in which faithfulness constraints, mandating the preservation of monosyllabic morphological-lexical forms, dominated the universal syllabic binarity (markedness) constraint, rendering it powerless. When the perfect tense and absolute state became obsolete, nearly all monosyllabic forms of nouns, adjectives, and verbs disappeared from the language. Children acquiring Aramaic as their native language no longer had evidence to pronounce monosyllables, and the universal disyllabic binarity (a markedness constaint) could assert itself. The effect was that all the few surviving monosyllables grew longer, in one way or another. Thus the *šma:* > *šə́mma* shift is a case of phonological change driven by prior morphological change. Morphological change instigated by sound change is a commonplace of historical linguistics, but the contrary is not so well known.

Abbreviations

ˣ	forms that were ungrammatical, or non-existent, at the relevant historical stage
*	reconstructed forms that are presumed to have been grammatical
NENA	Northeastern Neo-Aramaic
ZJ	Zakho-Jewish dialect group

Bibliography

Brockelmann, Carl
- 1928 *Lexicon Syriacum*. Hildesheim: Georg Olms.
- 1968 *Syrische Grammatik: Mit Paradigmen, Literatur, Chrestomathie und Glossar*. Leipzig: VEB Verlag Enzyklopädie.

Broselow, Ellen
- 1995 "Skeletal Positions and Moras." In *The Handbook of Phonological Theory*, edited by John A. Goldsmith, pp. 175–205. Blackwell Handbooks in Linguistics 1. Oxford: Blackwell.

Garbell, Irene
- 1965 *The Jewish Neo-Aramaic Dialect of Persian Azerbaijan: Linguistic Analysis and Folkloristic Texts*. Janua Linguarum 3. The Hague: Mouton.

Goldenberg, Gideon
- 1994 "Principles of Semitic Word-structure." In *Semitic and Cushitic Studies*, edited by Gideon Goldenberg and Shlomo Raz, pp. 29–64. Wiesbaden: Harrassowitz.

Goldsmith, John A.
- 1995 *The Handbook of Phonological Theory*. Blackwell Handbooks in Linguistics 1. Oxford: Blackwell.

Hoberman, Robert D.
- 1989 "Initial Consonant Clusters in Hebrew and Aramaic." *Journal of Near Eastern Studies* 48: 25–29.
- 1997a "Modern Aramaic Phonology." In *Phonologies of Asia and Africa (Including the Caucasus)*, edited by Alan S. Kaye and Peter T. Daniels, pp. 313–35. Winona Lake: Eisenbrauns.
- 1997b "The Modern Chaldean Pronunciation of Classical Syriac." In *Humanism, Culture, and Language in the Near East: Studies in Honor of Georg Krotkoff*, edited by Asma Afsaruddin and A. H. Mathias Zahniser, pp. 253–65. Winona Lake: Eisenbrauns.

Jastrow, Otto
- 1985 *Laut- und Formenlehre des neuaramäischen Dialekts von Mīdin im Ṭūr ʿAbdīn*. Wiesbaden: Harrassowitz.
- 1988 *Der neuaramäische Dialekt von Hertevin (Provinz Siirt)*. Semitica Viva 3. Wiesbaden: Harrassowitz.
- 1990 "Personal and Demonstrative Pronouns in Central Neo-Aramaic." In *Studies in Neo-Aramaic*, edited by Wolfhart Heinrichs, pp. 89–103. Harvard Semitic Studies 36. Atlanta: Scholars Press.
- 1998 "The Neo-Aramaic Languages." In *The Semitic Languages*, edited by Robert Hetzron, pp. 334–77. New York: Routledge.

Kager, René
- 1999 *Optimality Theory*. Cambridge Textbooks in Linguistics. Cambridge: Cambridge University Press.

Kapeliuk, Olga
- 1992 "Miscellanea Neo-Syriaca." *Jerusalem Studies in Arabic and Islam* 15: 60–73.

Khan, Geoffrey
- 1999 *A Grammar of Neo-Aramaic: The Dialect of the Jews of Arbel.* Handbuch der Orientalistik, Abteilung 1, Band 47. Leiden: Brill.

Krotkoff, Georg
- 1982 *A Neo-Aramaic Dialect of Kurdistan: Texts, Grammar, and Vocabulary.* American Oriental Series 64. New Haven: American Oriental Society.
- 1985 "Studies in Neo-Aramaic Lexicology." In *Biblical and Related Studies Presented to Samuel Iwry*, edited by Ann Kort and Scott Morschauser, pp. 123–34. Winona Lake: Eisenbrauns.

Maclean, Arthur John
- 1895 *Grammar of the Dialects of Vernacular Syriac.* Cambridge: Cambridge University Press. Reprint, Amsterdam: Philo, 1971.
- 1901 *Dictionary of the Dialects of Vernacular Syriac.* Oxford: Clarendon. Reprint, Amsterdam: Philo, 1972.

Marogulov, Q. I.
- 1976 *Grammaire néo-syriaque pour écoles d'adultes (dialecte d'Urmia)*, translated by Olga Kapeliuk. Comptes rendus du G.L.E.C.S, Supplément 5. Paris: Geuthner.

McCarthy, John J., and Alan S. Prince
- 1995 "Prosodic Morphology." In The *Handbook of Phonological Theory*, edited by John A. Goldsmith, pp. 318–66. Oxford: Blackwell.

Nöldeke, Theodor
- 1868 *Grammatik der neusyrischen Sprache am Urmia-See und in Kurdistan.* Leipzig: Weigel.
- 1910 "'Zweiradikalige Substantive." In *Neue Beiträge zur semitischen Sprachwissenschaft*, by Theodor Nöldeke. Strassburg: K. J. Trübner. Reprinted in *Beiträge und neue Beiträge zur semitischen Sprachwissenschaft*, Vol. 2, pp. 109–78. Amsterdam: APA-Philo Press, 1982.

Nöldeke, Theodor, and Julius Euting
- 1898 *Kurzgefasste syrische Grammatik.* Leipzig: C. H. Touchnitz. Reprinted in *Compendious Syriac Grammar*, translated by James A. Crichton. London: Williams & Norgate, 1904.

Odisho, Edward Y.
- 1988 *The Sound System of Modern Assyrian (Neo-Aramaic).* Semitica Viva 2. Wiesbaden: Harrassowitz.

Oraham, Alexander Joseph
- 1943 *Oraham's Dictionary of the Stabilized and Enriched Assyrian Language and English.* Chicago: Consolidated Press (Assyrian Press of America).

Perlmutter, David
- 1995 "Phonological Quantity and Multiple Association." In *The Handbook of Phonological Theory*, edited by John A. Goldsmith, pp. 307–17. Oxford: Blackwell.

Polotsky, Hans Jacob
- 1967 "Eastern Neo-Aramaic." In *An Aramaic Handbook*, Part II/2, edited by Franz Rosenthal, pp. 97–111. Porta Linguarum Orientalium, neue Serie, 10. Wiesbaden: Harrassowitz.

Rubba, Johanna
- 1989 "Prosodic Conditions on Vowel Length in Neo-Aramaic." n.p.
- 1993 Discontinuous Morphology in Modern Aramaic. Ph.D. dissertation, University of California, San Diego.

Sabar, Yona
- 1976 *Pəšaṭ Wayəhî Bəšallaḥ: A Neo-Aramaic Midrash on Beshallaḥ (Exodus).* Wiesbaden: Harrassowitz.
- 1984 *Midrashim ba-'Aramit Yehude Kurdisṭa'n la-parashiyot Vayehi, Beshallaḥ, ye-Yitro* (*Homilies in the Neo-Aramaic of the Kurdistani Jews on the parashot Wayḥi, Beshallaḥ, and Yitro*). Jerusalem: Israel Academy of Sciences and Humanities [in Neo-Aramaic and Hebrew].
- 2002 *A Jewish Neo-Aramaic Dictionary: Dialects of Amidya, Dihok, Nerwa and Zakho, Northwestern Iraq.* Semitica Viva 28. Wiesbaden: Harrassowitz.

Sachau, Eduard
  1895 *Skizze des Fellichi-Dialekts von Mosul*. Berlin: Akademie der Wissenschaften in Commission bei Georg Reimer.

Sara, Solomon I.
  1974 *A Description of Modern Chaldean*. Janua Linguarum 213. The Hague: Mouton.

Shimron, Joseph
  2003 *Language Processing and Acquisition in Languages of Semitic, Root-based Morphology*. Language Acquisition and Language Disorders 28. Amsterdam and Philadelphia: Benjamins.

Testen, David
  1985 "The Significance of Aramaic $r < {*}n$." *Journal of Near Eastern Studies* 44: 143–46.

10. AKKADIAN-EGYPTIAN LEXICAL MATCHES[1]

Alexander Militarev

10.1. Introduction

There are a number of lexical matches between Akkadian and Egyptian, at least some of which the present author regards as loanwords. Most of the examples analyzed below have been adduced in previous studies (especially in *HSED*), but almost none of them was treated as borrowing. Some of the examples were postulated as probable loans in Militarev 1984, but the publication was in Russian and remains unnoticed.

The examples discussed below can be conventionally divided into two broad groups — isolated matches in Akkadian and Egyptian and matches in Akkadian and Egyptian with Afrasian parallels. The former group can be subdivided according to the direction of influence — presumed Akkadian loans into Egyptian, presumed Egyptian loans into Akkadian, instances of borrowing with unclear direction, and uncertain cases.

10.2. Isolated Matches in Akkadian and Egyptian

10.2.1. Presumed Akkadian Loans into Egyptian

10.2.1.1. Akkadian [Old Babylonian] *nemsētu* 'washbowl' (*CAD* N/2 165), *namsû* 'washbowl' (*CAD* N/2 245) < *mesû* 'to wash, to clean' [Old Babylonian] (*CAD* M/2 30) < Semitic **msw* 'melt, dissolve, flood' (*HALOT* 604; Leslau 1987: 368).

Egyptian [Pyramid text] *nms.t* 'Art Krug' (*Wb.* 2.269); compared to "babylon. *namša*" (*Wb.* 2.269).

A deverbal origin of the Akkadian term implies an Akkadian loan into early Egyptian.

10.2.1.2. Akkadian [Old Babylonian on] *šappu* '(a container)'; Sumerian loanword written syllabically and as (DUG.)ŠAB (*CAD* Š/1 479); otherwise related to Semitic **šap-* 'basket' (< **špy* 'weave, sew'?): Arabic *saff-at-* 'panier, corbeille, etc., fait de feuilles de palmier' (Biberstein-Kazimirski 1860: 1.1096); Tigrinya *safi* 'flat basket' (Kane 2000: 792), *säfʔi* 'kind of sieve' (ibid., p. 798), Tigrinya *säfəʔ*, Amharic *səfe-t*, Gurage *säf* 'wicker basket' (Leslau 1979: 537); Soqotri *m-séfi* 'panier' (Leslau 1938: 289).

Egyptian [Eighteenth Dynasty] *sp.t* 'ein Gerät aus Gold' (*Wb.* 4.97).

There are no visible parallels for the Egyptian term besides the Akkadian one, and the former's relatively late attestation speaks against its genuine origin. The Akkadian term, on the contrary, is attested in the early period of Akkadian and is either a Sumerian loan or an inherited Semitic word; in any case, it is etymologically motivated. Unless a chance look-alike, the present example represents an Akkadian loan into Egyptian.

10.2.1.3. Akkadian [Old Akkadian] *ḫubšašû* '(a bottle or cup)' (*CAD* Ḫ 215).

Egyptian [Greek period] *ḫbs* 'Art Krüge für Myrrhe' (*Wb.* 3.257).

Compared as cognates < Afrasian **ḫubVs-* 'vessel' (*HSED* no. 1366).

The precise correspondence of the triradical roots in both languages makes the possibility of a chance look-alike very low. In addition, the lack of parallels in other Afrasian languages and the late attestation of the Egyptian term as opposed to the early attestation of the Akkadian term suggest an Akkadian loan into Egyptian.

---

[1] This study was carried out within the framework of projects supported by the Russian Foundation for the Sciences ("Biblical Etymologies"), the Russian Foundation for the Humanities ("Semitic Etymological Dictionary"), the Santa Fe Institute ("Evolution of Human Languages"), and the Russian Jewish Congress ("Tower of Babel"). I also express my gratitude to the Oriental Institute for the opportunity to participate in the symposium in honor of my good friend, Gene Gragg.

10.2.1.4. Akkadian [Old Babylonian] *makurru* (*makkūru, magurru*) 'deep-going boat'; Sumerian loanword; written syllabically and as (GIŠ)MÁ.GUR₈ (*CAD* M/1 141). An alternative interpretation of the Akkadian noun is its secondary formation with *ma-* prefixed, compare *kāru* 'embankment, quay-wall, mooring place, harbor' [Old Akkadian on] (*CAD* K 231); compare also Geʕez *kawra* 'steer a ship' (Leslau 1987: 300) and Arabic (South Arabia) *kawwara* 'place a boat in the water' (ibid.; regrettably, Leslau does not specify the dialect and source).

Egyptian [Twenty-second Dynasty] *mkr* 'Art Schiff' (*Wb.* 2.163).

This is a very likely Akkadian loan (of Sumerian or Semitic origin?) into Egyptian.

10.2.1.5. Akkadian [Old Akkadian on] *kirû* (*kiriu*) 'garden, orchard, palm grove' (*CAD* K 411); < Sumerian KIRIFL (*AHw* 485).

Egyptian [Middle Kingdom; Late Egyptian] *kꜣri* 'Gärtner' (*Wb.* 5.108).

Is this an Akkadian term of Sumerian origin borrowed into Egyptian? Otherwise both derived from Afrasian *kwr ~ *ʔkr 'to cultivate', *kiry- ~ *kVw/ʔVr- 'garden, cultivated field' (Militarev 2002).

10.2.1.6. Akkadian [Old Babylonian on] *umāmu*, auch *emammu, emāmu* 'Tiere, Getier' (*AHw* 1412).

Egyptian [Medical texts] *ʕmʕmw* 'ein vierfüssiges Tier' (*Wb.* 1.186).

This is a special case, which does not entirely fit into this section. The Akkadian forms, compared to the Egyptian word in *HSED* no. 1122 as cognate < Afrasian *ʕum-ʕam- 'animal', are more likely to continue Semitic *hVm/wām- 'large wild feline' (cf. also *ūmu* 'ein Mytischer Löwe' [*AHw* 1420]); see Militarev and Kogan 2005: Arabic *hawwām-* 'lion' (Biberstein-Kazimirski 1860: 2.1460), Tigrinya *həmmäm* 'leopard' (Littmann and Höfner 1956: 7); compare also North Cushitic: Beja *hiam* 'cheetah' (Hudson 1996), *yĭham* 'leopard' (ibid.). In this case only the Egyptian term is to be treated as an isolated form. A semantic and structural affinity between Akkadian and Egyptian is too strong to be accidental. Is this an Akkadian loan in Egyptian with Akkadian *h- > 0 rendered as ʕ- in Egyptian?

10.2.2. Presumed Egyptian Loans in Akkadian

10.2.2.1. Akkadian [Lexical lists] *dišarru* '(wild growing cereals)' (*CAD* D 160).

Egyptian [Old Kingdom, Middle Kingdom] *dšr* 'Körner (roter Farbe?)' (*Wb.* 5.491; likely < *dšr* 'red').

These words are compared in *HSED* no. 720 with a note that it may be "a cultural loanword." Unless a chance coincidence, the Akkadian term is a loanword from Egyptian.

10.2.2.2. Akkadian [Old Babylonian, Mari, Standard Babylonian] *ašaḫḫu* 'storehouse' (*CAD* A/2 411]; 'eine Art Speicher in *bīt a.*' (*AHw* 78).

Egyptian *wsḫ.t* (1) 'Transportschiff für Lasten' [Old Kingdom, Middle Kingdom] (*Wb.* 1.366); (2) 'Halle, Hof (Raum im Palast, Tempel)' [Pyramid text] (ibid.); probably < *wsḫ* 'weit sein, weit' (*Wb.* 1.364).

Akkadian *ašaḫḫu* and Egyptian *wsḫ.t* 'hall', *sḫ.w* 'wide space, yard' are compared, together with West Chadic Kirfi *šoko* 'house', as cognate forms < Afrasian *saq- 'house' in *HSED* no. 2200 (note that the very reconstruction of the Afrasian affricate *q and its reflexes in various Afrasian languages are so highly hypothetical that the Kirfi example may be disregarded). The Egyptian nouns are likely of deverbal origin from *wsḫ* '(to be) wide' with the meaning 'spacious (ship, premises)', in which case the Akkadian term is a tenable loan from Egyptian.

10.2.2.3. Akkadian [Ur III, Standard Babylonian] *ḫawû* (*ḫabû, ḫaʔû*; a kind of cloth); Akkadian loanword into Sumerian; the *ḫ.*-cloth is used as a seat cover for thrones (*CAD* Ḫ 162–63).

Egyptian [Pyramid text] *ḥꜣw.t* 'Platte mit Untersatz, Opferplatte; Altar' (*Wb.* 3.226); *ḥꜣy.t* 'Art Altar' [Middle Kingdom; Eighteenth Dynasty] (*Wb.* 3.224).

Akkadian *ḫaʔu* is compared to Egyptian *ḥꜣw.t* in *HSED* no. 1308 as cognates < Afrasian *ḫaʔ-/*ḫaw- 'altar, throne'; however, such a meaning (and the corresponding object) could hardly exist in the tenth millennium, to which I date the common Afrasian language. Unless a chance look-alike, perhaps a somewhat earlier Egyptian term with a broader meaning was borrowed into Akkadian.

10.2.3. Tenable Borrowings with Unclear Direction

10.2.3.1. Akkadian [Old Babylonian, Mari] *šurāmu* '(a container)' (*CAD* Š/3 339).
   Egyptian [Old Kingdom] *šȝm.w* 'Art grosser Krug' (*Wb.* 4.411), possibly <*čVrVm-*.
   HSED no. 574: "Probably, a *Wanderwort*."
   The lack of other Afrasian parallels makes a common Afrasian origin unlikely, while the correspondence of the triconsonantal root skeletons speaks against a chance look-alike. Hence, a loan hypothesis is more tenable, though an early attestation in both languages gives no hint as to the direction of borrowing.

10.2.3.2. Akkadian [Neo-Assyrian] *pagalu* 'a libation vessel' (*AHw* 808).
   Egyptian [Middle Kingdom] *pgȝ* 'Schale, Napf' (*Wb.* 1.563), possibly <*pVgVl-*.
   These words were compared in *HSED* no. 1922 as cognates < Afrasian **pagal-* 'vessel'.
   This example is similar to the previous one, the only difference being an earlier attestation of the Egyptian term as an indirect argument for borrowing from Egyptian into Akkadian.

10.2.3.3. Akkadian [Neo-Babylonian] *šiddatu* '(a stand for a large vat)' (*CAD* Š/2 402); 'ein Behälter', Late Babylonian 'ein Holzgefäss' (*AHw* 1230); compared (ibid.) to Mishnaic Hebrew *šiddā*, Jewish Aramaic *šiddətā-* 'Kiste', Syriac *šeddətā* 'Kruguntersatz' (West Semitic forms are likely Akkadisms).
   Egyptian [Medical texts, Middle Kingdom] *šdi* 'Art Behälter' (*Wb.* 4.568).
   These words are compared in *HSED* no. 553 as cognates < Afrasian **čid-* 'vessel'. However, the lack of available parallels in other Afrasian languages speaks against the common Afrasian status of the Akkadian-Egyptian terms.

10.2.4. Less Certain Cases (loans or look-alikes equally possible)

10.2.4.1. Akkadian *inimmû* 'a cup' (synonym list: *i-nim-mu-u* = *ka-a-su*; *CAD* I 148).
   Egyptian [New Kingdom] *nm* 'grosses Gefäss (*Wb.* 2.264).
   These words are compared in *HSED* no. 1875 as cognates < Afrasian **nim-* 'vessel'. No other Afrasian parallels are adduced. However, there is only a partial coincidence in the root composition (note that Egyptian *n-* may reflect **n-* or **l-*) and meaning; the Akkadian term attested in a synonym list alone is not quite reliable.

10.2.4.2. Akkadian [Old Babylonian] *suādu, suʔādu, sumādu, sumandu, ṣumādu* (an aromatic plant, probably *Cyperus esculentus*; *CAD* S 338).
   Egyptian [Book of the Dead, Middle Kingdom] *išd.t* 'Art heiliger Baum in Heliopolis' (*Wb.* 1.136).
   A partial coincidence in the root composition if *suʔādu* is the main Akkadian protoform (note also that Akkadian *s* continues Semitic **s* < Afrasian **c* while Egyptian *š* reflects Afrasian lateral **č-*). The fact that the meanings are not well specified does not completely rule out a possibility of a common areal term, but rather speaks for a chance look-alike.

10.2.4.3. Akkadian [Middle Babylonian, Standard Babylonian, Middle Assyrian] *lammu* 'almond tree; sapling'; Sumerian loanword GIŠ.LAM (*CAD* L 67).
   Egyptian [Pyramid text] *imȝ* 'ein Fruchtbaum: die männliche Dattelpalme?' (*Wb.* 1.79).
   Unless a chance look-alike, the Egyptian word can be an Akkadian loan, if the underlying form in Egyptian is **lVm-* (which is only one of several opportunities) and the Akkadian term is indeed a Sumerism.

10.2.4.4. Akkadian [Standard Babylonian] *šallapānu* (*šallabānu*) '(a plant)' (*CAD* Š/1 247); [Middle/Young Babylonian Lexical list] 'ein Sumpfgrass?' (*AHw* 1148).

Egyptian [Middle Kingdom] *sʒp.t* 'Lotusblatt' (*Wb.* 4.18), [New Kingdom] *srp.t* (*Wb.* 4.195), can go back to **sVlVp-* or **sVrVp-*.

These words are compared as cognates < Afrasian **salap-* 'plant' in *HSED* no. 2183. This comparison is questionable because of more than one possibility for reconstructing the underlying form of both terms, as well as the fact that the meaning in Akkadian is not well defined. Compare Arabic *salab-* 'écorce de l'arbre ou du roseau; fibres d'un arbre particulier à l'Yémen dont on tresse des cordes' (Biberstein-Kazimirski 1860: 1.1118), which, if related to the Akkadian term, points to *šallabānu* hardly being comparable with the Egyptian example. If, however, the correct reading in Akkadian is *šallapānu* and *-ʒ-* in the Egyptian form reflects *-l-*, then it is more likely an areal term, with the direction of borrowing unclear.

10.2.4.5. Akkadian [Old Akkadian on] *nāḫu* 'lard' (*CAD* N 142).

Egyptian [New Kingdom] *nḥḥ* 'Öl' (*Wb.* 2.302).

These words are compared in *HSED* no. 1836 with the note "a cultural word?" As for consonantal correspondences, note that Egyptian *ḥ* reflects Afrasian *ḥ, which is considered to regularly yield *0* in Akkadian but in quite a few cases also yields *ḫ*. On the other hand, the two terms may have a different origin. To Akkadian *nāḫu*, *nuḫḫu* compare Arabic *nuḫḫ-*, *naḫāḫat-* 'moelle' (Biberstein-Kazimirski 1860: 2.1219), and to Egyptian *nḥḥ* compare Arabic *nḥy* 'agiter le lait dans un vase pour en faire du beurre' (Biberstein-Kazimirski 1860: 2.1218). The possibility of an Akkadian loan into later Egyptian cannot be ruled out completely.

10.3. Matches in Akkadian and Egyptian having Afrasian Parallels

There are cases of Akkadian-Egyptian matches having parallels in other Afrasian languages which are likely to be treated as cognates going back to a common Afrasian protoform. However, in view of a series of obvious Akkadian-Egyptian cultural isoglosses (above), inter-borrowing even in such cases is possible. A few examples follow.

10.3.1. Akkadian [Old Akkadian, Standard Babylonian] *buʔdu* (*būdu*, or *puʔdu*, *pūdu*; an implement; *CAD* B 303: "If the OIP 14 52 ref. is to be connected with the lexical and bilingual evidence, the meaning may be narrowed down to a spatula or a spoon"); *būdu*, *buʔdu* 'ein Gerät aus Holz u Metall' (*AHw* 135).

Egyptian [Medical texts] *bʒd.t* 'Schopflöffel (zum Schöpfen von Öl)' (*Wb.* 1.432). Among other possibilities, the word may reflect *bʔd.

These words are compared as cognates in *HSED* no. 299 under the reconstructed protoform **boʔVd-*, together with East Chadic: Mokilko *boode*, Bidiya *booda* 'gourd'. Compare also Berber: Qabyle *a-buyeddu* 'pot spécial pour servir le bouillon de couscous (et le beurre fondu)' (Takács 1999: 106 after Dallet 1982).

The connection of the Akkadian and Egyptian terms as cognates in *HSED* was criticized in Takács 1999: 105 ("The common origin … is more than dubious. The meaning of the Akkadian word is obscure"). However, the comparison seems to me not unlikely.

Though both Akkadian and Egyptian terms may, together with Mokilko *boode*, Bidiya *booda*, and Qabyle *a-buyeddu*, continue Afrasian **buʔd-*, a specific meaning 'spoon/dipper' of the Egyptian and probably of the Akkadian term is better explained as borrowing of one of the forms from the other, any of which may well be inherited from the Afrasian protoform. The direction of borrowing is a tangled issue: on the one hand, the Akkadian term is isolated in Semitic, which makes its priority problematic; on the other hand, it is attested since a much earlier period than the Egyptian one.

10.3.2. Akkadian [Old Babylonian, Ras Shamra, el-Amarna, Nuzi, Neo-Assyrian, Neo-Babylonian] *dūd-* 'kettle' (*CAD* D 170); Ugaritic *dd* 'medida de capacidad; recipiente' (*DLU* 129); Hebrew *dūd* 'cooking pot; basket' (*HALOT* 215); Syriac *dūdā* 'olla' (Brockelmann 1928: 144), Jewish Aramaic *dūdā* 'boiler, caldron, pot' (Jastrow

1950: 283), Mandaic *duda* 'cauldron' (Drower and Macuch 1963: 104); Goggot *duddiyä* 'kind of jar' (according to Leslau 1979: 199, < Somali *diddo*; rather an inherited Semitic word).

Egyptian [Old Kingdom] *dd.t* 'Schale; Topf für Bier, Salbe' (*Wb.* 5.501).

West Chadic: Angas *dadūt* 'a small bottle-shaped calabash' (Foulkes 1915).

These words are compared as related forms in *HCVA* 5: 13. Either the words are common Afrasian or the Akkadian word was borrowed into Egyptian.

10.3.3. Akkadian [Middle Babylonian] *rību* '(a vessel)' (*CAD* R 323).

Egyptian [late] *rb* 'Art Topf (aus Kupfer)' (*Wb.* 2.414) <**rVb-* or **lVb-*.

Central Chadic: Zime-Batna *ruḫu* (Sachnine 1982), Mada *érḫe-ŝ* (Barreteau and Brunet 2000), Mofu *rəḫa-ŝ* (Barreteau and Bléis 1990) 'pottery clay' (-*š*- suffixed in Mada and Mofu?).

In *HSED* no. 2110, Akkadian, Egyptian and Central Chadic Margi *řřba* are compared as cognates < Afrasian **rib-* 'vessel'. One wonders whether the Akkadian and Egyptian words are Common Afrasian or a chance look-alike, or the late Egyptian is an Akkadian loan.

10.3.4. Akkadian [Standard Babylonian, Lexical list] *ubbuntu, uppuntu* 'a vessel' (*AHw* 1400).

Egyptian [Old Kingdom] *hbn.t* 'Art grosser Krug' (*Wb.* 2.487).

West Chadic **HVbyan-*/**bVHyan-*: Mupun *ḫéèn* 'bottle gourd', Sura *ḫéɛn* 'gourd' (*HSED* no. 1205).

East Chadic **bVn-* 'pumpkin': Gabri *ti-bini*, Kabalai *tə-bəni*, Kwang *bone* < Afrasian **hVben-* (ibid.).

In *HSED* no. 1121, the Akkadian form *uppunu* is compared to Egyptian [Greek period] *ʕfn* 'ein Gefäss' (*Wb.* 1.183) and West Chadic: Ngizim *fənà* 'calabash', Central Chadic: Tera *fènan* 'calabash', Mbara *fánáy* 'pot'. All are treated as cognates < Afrasian **ʕufan-* 'vessel'. This comparison is problematic not only because in the Akkadian term, **ʕ-* in the Anlaut and *-pp-* in the Inlaut, corresponding to *ʕ-* and *-f-* in the Egyptian match, represent only one of the possibilities (my comparison faces the same difficulty), but also because the Chadic forms hardly go back to **ʕufan-* as they are expected to preserve some traces, at least vocalic, of the initial **ʕ-*. At the same time, Egyptian *hbn.t* is compared (in *HSED* no. 1205) with Akkadian *ḫabannatu* '(a container)' [occurring in Mari, el-Amarna, Standard Babylonian, and as an Akkadian loanword in Hittite] (*CAD* Ḫ 7), West Chadic **HVbyan-*/**bVHyan-*: Mupun *ḫéèn* 'bottle gourd', Sura *ḫéɛn* 'gourd', and East Chadic **bVn-* 'pumpkin': Gabri *ti-bini*, Kabalai *tə-bəni*, Kwang *bone* < Afrasian **hVben-*. However, it is Akkadian *ubbuntu* (but not *uppuntu*) which exactly corresponds to Egyptian *hbn.t* and the latter Chadic forms, unlike Akkadian *ḫabannatu* with *ḫ*- reflecting **ḫ-* or even **ḥ-* but not **h-*.

If the reading of the Akkadian word as *ubbuntu* is the correct one, a common origin of the quoted Akkadian, Egyptian, and Chadic forms from Afrasian **hVbVn-* is quite tenable, though a borrowing of the later Akkadian term (isolated in Semitic, at that) from Egyptian cannot be ruled out.

10.3.5. Akkadian [Babylonian Lexical lists] *tannu* 'wooden bowl' (*AHw* 1391).

Egyptian [Greek period] *tn.w* 'Korb (aus Binsen)' (*Wb.* 5.310).

West Chadic: Polchi *táŋ* 'water pot'.

These words are compared in *HSED* no. 2368 as cognates < Afrasian **tan-* 'container'. An isolated Chadic form does not seem sufficient to grade this root as Common Afrasian. It may well be an Akkadian loan into late Egyptian.

10.3.6. Akkadian *šaduppu* (a basket) < Sumerian DUB + *ṭuppu*; lex. *ša-du-ub* = GÁ×DUB *ša-du-up-pu* Ea IV 286. Variant of *pisanduppu* (*CAD* Š/1 61).

Egyptian [New Kingdom] *sdf* 'Art Mass für Feigen' (*Wb.* 4.370).

Central Chadic: Mofu *šidɛf* 'pot' (*HSED* no. 2161).

These words are compared as cognates < Afrasian **saduf-*/**siduf-* 'container' in *HSED* no. 2161. It appears to be an Akkadian loan (< Sumerian) in late Egyptian (then borrowed into Mofu?).

10.3.7. Akkadian [Old Babylonian on] *šaššūgu* (*šuššūgu*, *šuššūqu*) '(a tree)' (as wood used for frames, doors, wheel rims, etc.; *CAD* Š/2 176).

Egyptian [Pyramid text] *ssḏ* 'Art kostbares Holz (aus Syrien), als Material für Geräte (Möbel u.ä.)' (*Wb.* 4.279).

These words are compared in *HSED* no. 2204 as cognates < Afrasian **sasog-* 'tree', redupl. < **sog-* 'tree, wood' (*HSED* no. 2269): Central Chadic: Mafa *soegwe* 'firewood'; East Cushitic: Somali *sogsog* 'kind of acacia' ('Acacia Etbaica' Abraham 1962: 226).

The Akkadian, Mafa, and Somali forms are likely <**sag^w(sag^w)-*, while the Egyptian term (costly wood from Syria!) looks like a loan from Akkadian.

10.3.8. Akkadian [Neo-Babylonian] *ḫallimu* 'a k. of raft' (only plural *ḫallimānu*; *CAD* Ḫ 45).

Egyptian [Old Kingdom, Middle Kingdom, Eighteenth Dynasty] *ḥmn.ty* 'Art Schiff' (*Wb.* 3.283), metathesis < **ḥVmVl-*?

Central Chadic **ḥ/hulum-* 'boat': Mbara *hùlùm* (Tourneux et al. 1986), Musgu *hɔlúm*, *hullum* (Lukas 1941).

Is this a common Afrasian or an areal term?

10.3.9. Akkadian *kukkû* 'darkness (as a name for the netherworld)' lex. < Sumerian (prob. KU$_{10}$.KU$_{10}$; *CAD* K 498).

Egyptian [Pyramid text] *kk* 'dunkel sein', *kkw* 'Finsternis, Dunkel; von der Dunkelheit der Unterwelt' (*Wb.* 5.142–43).

West Chadic **kuwi-*: Mupun *kūo kūo* (Frajzyngier 1991), Sura *kòo* (Jungraithmayr 1963–64), Ankwe *kwo* 'darkness' (Kraft 1981), Angas *kukwi* 'absolutely dark' (Foulkes 1915), Bokkos *kìkyaw* 'became black' (Jungraithmayr 1970).

This is a most entangled case. There is an obvious cultural influence reflected in a specific meaning related to the netherworld. One wonders whether it can be an inherited Egyptian term (cognate to Chadic) borrowed into Akkadian (whence into Sumerian)?

10.4. Conclusions

A relevantly large number of specific Akkadian-Egyptian lexical isoglosses listed and discussed above can hardly be a result of chance coincidence. Since most of them can neither be well explained as Afrasian terms of common origin, inter-borrowing is the most plausible explanation. In most cases, the direction of borrowing seems to be from Akkadian into Egyptian, though there are several cases of presumably the reverse direction. The above presumptions, if true, testify to cultural contacts between the Akkadian-speaking area and Egypt starting from the earliest written period, and not only in the first millennium before the common era. In terms of semantics it is worth mentioning that out of twenty-six presumed Akkadian-Egyptian contact terms, thirteen (50%) refer to vessel names, and five (almost 25%) to plant names.

It would not be prudent for a linguist to speculate about extra-linguistic issues such as the significance of this or that semantic class of linguistic borrowing for elucidating cultural influences or about historical periods, concrete events, and locations that may have served as the historical background for the assemblage of data adduced in the present study, especially when the history of both parties of the claimed contacts has already been studied adequately. In presenting instances of possible cultural contact between ancient cultures, my goal is to direct the attention of the historians of the ancient Near East to this linguistic phenomenon.

As for comparative Afrasian linguistics, distinguishing between inherited and borrowed lexical items is one of the most sophisticated and delicate problems. It is sufficient to mention cases of generally accepted Sumerian loanwords in Akkadian whence they are thought to spread in other Semitic languages, some of which, on closer analysis, turn out to be Akkadisms in Sumerian, supported by reliable Semitic and even Afrasian cognates. There are other cases of seemingly well-established Cushitic loanwords in Ethiopian Semitic, to which reliable Arabic and other Semitic parallels happen to be found thus posing the question: are they, on the contrary, Semitisms in Cushitic or should they be treated as common Afrasian lexemes? The established Egyptian-Semitic inter-borrowings, besides several isolated Egyptian loans in Ugaritic, Aramaic, Arabic, Neo-Babylonian, and Neo-Assyrian, are mostly limited to a three dozen well-adapted Egyptian loans in biblical Hebrew pointing to rather early close contacts between Egypt and the Canaanite populations and several hundred lexical items of presumably West Semitic origin attested in Egyptian literature of the New Kingdom, with a small group of still earlier loans from what seems to be the West Semitic language area. If the data adduced in the present contribution (dedicated to my good old friend Professor Gene Gragg, with his unusually wide scope of linguistic interests), and their interpretations by the author hold water, the long-lasting Akkadian-Egyptian lexical contacts will add new dabs to that picture.

Bibliographic Abbreviations

AHw W. von Soden. *Akkadisches Handwörterbuch: Unter Benutzung de lexikalischen Nachlasses von Bruno Meissner (1868–1947)*. Wiesbaden: Otto Harrassowitz, 1965–1981.

CAD A. Leo Oppenheim et al., editors. *The Assyrian Dictionary of the Oriental Institute of the University of Chicago*. Chicago: The Oriental Institute, 1956–.

DLU G. Del Olmo Lete and J. Sanmartín. *Diccionario de la lengua ugarítica,* Volumes 1–2. Aula Orientalis 7. Barcelona: Editorial AUSA, 1996–2000.

HALOT L. Koehler and W. Baumgartner. *The Hebrew and Aramaic Lexicon of the Old Testament,* Volumes 1–6, edited and translated by M. E. J. Richardson, W. Baumgartner, and Johann Jakob Stamm. Leiden: Brill, 1994–2000.

HCVA I. A. Diakonoff, A. Belova, A. Militarev, and V. Porkhomovsky. "Historical Comparative Vocabulary of Afrasian." *St. Petersburg Journal of African Studies* 3 (1995): 5–26; 5: 4–32.

HSED V. E. Orel and O. V. Stolbova. *Hamito-Semitic Etymological Dictionary: Materials for a Reconstruction*. Handbuch der Orientalistik 1; Nahe und Mittlere Osten 18. Leiden: Brill, 1995.

Wb. A. Erman and H. Grapow. *Wörterbuch der ägyptischen Sprache*. Seven volumes. Berlin: Akademie Verlag, 1971.

Bibliography

Abraham, Roy Clive
    1962   *Somali-English Dictionary*. London: University of London Press.

Barreteau, Daniel, and Yves Le Bléis
    1990   *Lexique mafa: Langue de la famille tchadique parlée au Cameroun*. Paris: ORSTOM, Librairie Orientaliste Paul Geuthner.

Barreteau, Daniel, and André Brunet
    2000   *Dictionnaire Mada: Langue de la famille tchadique parlée dans l'extrême-nord du Cameroun*. Berlin: Dietrich Riemer Verlag.

Biberstein-Kazimirski, Albert de
    1860   *Dictionnaire arabe-français*. Paris: Maison-neuve et cie.

Brockelmann, Carl
    1928   *Lexicon Syriacum*. Halle: Max Niemeyer.

Dallet, Jean-Marie
- 1982 *Dictionnaire kabyle-français: Parler des At Mangellat (Algérie)*. Études ethno-linguistiques Maghreb-Sahara 1. Paris: Société d'études linguistiques et anthropologiques de France.

Drower, Ethel Stefana, and R. Macuch
- 1963 *A Mandaic Dictionary*. Oxford: Clarendon Press.

Faulkner, Raymond Oliver
- 1962 *A Concise Dictionary of Middle Egyptian*. Oxford: Clarendon Press.

Foulkes, H. D.
- 1915 *Angass Manual: Grammar and Vocabulary*. London: Kegan Paul, Trench, Trübner and Co.

Frajzyngier, Zygmunt
- 1985 *A Pero-English and English-Pero Vocabulary*. Marburger Studien zur Afrika und Asien Kunde; Serie A; Afrika 38. Berlin: Dietrich Reimer Verlag.
- 1991 *A Dictionary of Mupun*. Sprache und Oralität in Afrika 11. Berlin: Dietrich Reimer Verlag.

Hudson, R. A.
- 1996 *A Dictionary of Beja*. n.p.

Jastrow, Marcus
- 1950 *A Dictionary of the Targumim, the Talmud Babli and Yerushalmi, and the Midrashic Literature*. New York: Pardes.

Jungraithmayr, Herrmann
- 1963/64 "Die Sprache der Sura (Maghavul) in Nord-Nigerien." *Afrika und Übersee* 47: 8–59, 204–20.
- 1970 *Die Ron-Sprachen: Tschadohamitische Studien in Nordnigerien*. Glückstadt: J. J. Augustin.

Kane, Thomas Leiper
- 2000 *Tigrinya-English Dictionary*. Two volumes. Springfield: Dunwoody Press.

Kraft, Charles H.
- 1981 *Chadic Wordlists*. Three volumes. Marburger Studien zur Afrika und Asien Kunde; Serie A; Afrika 23–25. Berlin: Dietrich Reimer Verlag.

Leslau, Wolf
- 1938 *Lexique Soqoṭri (Sudarabique moderne) avec comparaisons et explications étymologiques*. Collection Linguistique 41. Paris: Librairie C. Klincksieck.
- 1979 *Etymological Dictionary of Gurage (Ethiopic)*, Volume 3. Wiesbaden: Harrassowitz.
- 1987 *Comparative Dictionary of Geʕez (Classical Ethiopic)*. Wiesbaden: Harrassowitz.

Littmann, Enno, and Maria Höfner
- 1956 *Wörterbuch der Tigre-Sprache. Tigre-Deutsch-Englisch*. Wiesbaden: F. Steiner.

Lukas, Johannes
- 1941 *Deutsche Quellen zur Sprache der Musgu in Kamerun*. Beihefte zur Zeitschrift für Eingeborenen-Sprachen 24. Berlin: Dietrich Reimer Verlag.

Militarev, Alexander
- 1984 "What Contribution to Historical Science Can Be Made by the Comparative and Historical Afrasian Linguistics of Today?" *Linguistic Reconstruction and Prehistory of the East*, Part 3: *Summaries and Papers for the Conference*, edited by Institut Vostokovedeniia, pp. 14–17. Moscow: Nauka Publishing House [in Russian].
- 2002 "The Prehistory of a Dispersal: The Proto-Afrasian (Afroasiatic) Farming Lexicon." In *Examining the Farming/Language Dispersal Hypothesis*, edited by Peter Bellwood and Colin Renfrew, pp. 135–50. McDonald Institute Monographs 1363–1349. Cambridge: The McDonald Institute for Archaeological Research.

Militarev, Alexander, and Leonid Kogan
- 2005 *Semitic Etymological Dictionary*, Volume 2: *Animal Names*. Münster: Ugarit-Verlag.

Sachnine, Michka
- 1982 *Le Lamé (Nord-Cameroun)*, Volume 2: *Dictionnaire lamé-français, Lexique français-lamé*. Langues et cultures africaines 1. Paris: Société d'études linguistiques et anthropologiques de France.

Stolbova, O.
- 1996 *Studies in Chadic Comparative Phonology*. Moscow: Diaphragma Publishers.

Takács, Gábor
- 1999 *Etymological Dictionary of Egyptian*, Volume 1: *A Phonological Introduction*. Boston: Brill.

Tourneux, H.; C. Seignobos; and F. Lafarge
- 1986 *Les Mbara et leur langue (Tchad)*. Langues et cultures africaines 6. Paris: Société d'études linguistiques et anthropologies de France.

11. CONSTRAINTS ON ELLIPSIS IN BIBLICAL HEBREW[1]

Cynthia L. Miller

11.1. Introduction

From a linguistic point of view, there is a strange notion that is current among Hebraists and biblicists, namely, that ellipsis in biblical poetry operates without restrictions. Anything, it is assumed, can be deleted anywhere so long as it is possible to make sense out of the verse. As a result, ellipsis is sometimes used as a wild card for reading a bicolon with textual or lexical difficulties, with the interpreter understanding a word or even an affix from one line as performing "double-duty" in an adjacent line.[2] Underlying this assumption is the correct observation that the syntax of biblical poetry differs from that of biblical prose (see Sappan 1981). But the otherness of biblical poetry is often incorrectly understood to imply that no syntactic constraints operate in biblical poetry at all.

In specifying the constraints on ellipsis in modern languages, linguists are interested in determining the nature of the formal representations by which "speakers of a language are able to systematically generate appropriate meanings" for elided structures with incomplete constituents (Lappin 1996: 145). But examining ellipsis in an ancient language requires that we understand how ellipsis operates in two additional, and more preliminary, respects. First, we must be able to recognize that ellipsis has occurred and that the surface syntax is indeed fragmented.[3] This task is not always straightforward. For example, because verbless predications are fully grammatical in Hebrew, we must consider whether ellipsis of the verb has occurred or whether the sentence is simply a structurally complete verbless clause (e.g., Psalm 49:4 and Proverbs 13:1; see Miller 2003). Second, we must be able to interpret the fragmented structure correctly; that is, we must know what structure to assign to the sentence fragments and what should be restored in the ellipsis site. In this paper, I provide an overview of some of the conditions governing ellipsis in biblical Hebrew.[4] I am particularly interested in exploring four problems relating to ellipsis of the verb: (1) the semantic relations between non-deleted constituents and the constituents that correspond to them in the antecedent clause; (2) content identity between the deleted verb and its antecedent; (3) context identity between coordinated conjuncts; and (4) locality conditions on the antecedent conjunct.[5] In applying linguistic theory and method to ancient Hebrew, I hope to follow in the steps of my teacher who brought linguistics to bear on other ancient Near Eastern languages in insightful ways.

---

[1] The research in this paper was supported by the Graduate School of the University of Wisconsin-Madison, the Memorial Foundation for Jewish Culture, and the Ettinger Family Foundation. I am grateful to W. Randall Garr for comments on the final draft, and to the participants of the Gragg Symposium for stimulating discussions on the topic.

The abbreviations used to indicate Hebrew morphology are found at the end of the article. Punctuation is as follows: hyphens divide separable morphemes; colons divide inseparable morphemes. Slashes divide conjuncts rather than poetic lines. In translations of biblical examples involving ellipsis, underlining indicates the antecedent(s); material that has been deleted by ellipsis is italicized and enclosed in square brackets.

[2] The term "double-duty" originated with Dahood (1965: §13.44a and 1970: 429–44). A similar approach to ellipsis was followed by some medieval Hebrew grammarians who described elliptical constructions in terms of one item "standing for" or "serving for" an item that is deleted; see, for example, Chomsky 1952: 356–58; Khan 2000: 128–31.

[3] In viewing ellipsis as a syntactical process that fragments the surface syntax, I exclude a number of situations that have been broadly considered "elliptical" by biblical scholars: (1) sentences that are contextually incomplete and require the hearer/reader to supply information contextually or pragmatically (see Lyons 1971: 174–75; Halliday and Hasan 1976: 142–46); (2) bicola in which the second line is appositional to the final constituent of the first line (e.g., "the remnant of Israel" is appositional to "your people" in Jeremiah 31:7); (3) optional constituents that appear in one line but are absent from a parallel line (e.g., the prepositional adjunct *bəśimḥâ* 'with joy' in Psalm 100:2, *pace* Watson 1984: 305); and (4) a constituent that heads an embedded coordinate structure (e.g., the interrogative *maddûa* 'why' in Isaiah 50:2, *pace* Rosenbaum 1997: 160).

[4] For previous analyses of ellipsis in biblical poetry, see Geller 1979: 299–317; O'Connor 1980: 122–29, 401–7; Watson 1984: 303–6; Dion 1992: 14–16; Rosenbaum 1997: 158–70; Miller 2003.

[5] Two constraints on ellipsis are not discussed in detail here. One is the Major Constituent Constraint, which claims that the remnants of gapping will be "major constituents" (as described by Hartmann 2000: 147). Biblical Hebrew follows the Major Constituent Constraint. The other is the Head Condition, which states that forward-deleted material may not be syntactically subordinate to an overt (non-deleted) head (Hartmann 2000: 40). The evidence for biblical Hebrew is not clear on this latter point. On the one hand, the sentence fragments in question-answer pairs follow the head constraint. On the other hand, interrogatives, complementizers, etc., should all go in a head that would c-command anything deleted under them. While usually the overt head occurs before the first conjunct, there are examples with repetition of the head in both lines, which would seem to violate the condition.

11.2. Preliminaries

11.2.1. Coordinate Structures

Before examining the conditions involving verbal ellipsis in biblical Hebrew, some preliminaries are in order.[6] First, ellipsis takes place out of coordinate structures, as illustrated in (1).

(1) Isaiah 1:27

ṣîyôn	bə-mišpāṭ tippādeh	/ wəšābê-hā	bi-ṣdāqâ	Ø
Zion:F	by-justice redeem:IMPF:PS:3FS	and-return:ActPTC:MP-3FS	by-righteousness	

[CONJUNCT1] Zion by justice shall be redeemed (*tippādeh*) /
CORRESPONDENT1 CORRESPONDENT2 ANTECEDENT

[CONJUNCT2] and her repentant ones by righteousness [shall be redeemed (*yippādû*)].
REMNANT1 REMNANT2 ELLIPSIS SITE/ELIDED CONSTITUENT

Each conjunct comprises an independent clause. The elided constituent, the verb, has been deleted from the second conjunct to leave two remnant constituents, the subject noun phrase *šābêhā* 'her repentant ones' and the prepositional phrase *biṣdāqâ* 'by righteousness'. The first conjunct has two constituents corresponding to the remnants of the second, *ṣîyôn* 'Zion' and *bəmišpāṭ* 'by justice'. By contrast, ellipsis involving the verb does not occur between an independent clause and a subordinate clause. As a result, sentences such as (2) are unattested:

(2) Unattested sentence (ellipsis from main clause to subordinate clause):

Zion by justice shall be redeemed (*tippādeh*), /
so that (*ləma'an*) her repentant ones by righteousness [shall be redeemed (*yippādû*)]

The requirement that conjuncts must be coordinate relates to syntactic structure and not to the presence of an overt marker of coordination. Although the conjunction *waw* is quite common between conjuncts exhibiting ellipsis, it is not required.[7] In example (3) *waw* coordinates the conjuncts:

(3) Psalm 88:13

hă-yiwwāda'	ba-ḥōšek	pil'ekā	/ wə-ṣidqātə-kā	bə-'ereṣ	nəšîyâ	Ø
INTERR-know:IMPF:PS:3MS	in-darkness	wonder-2MS	and-righteousness-2MS	in-land.of	forgetfulness	

Is your wonder made known in darkness, /
and your righteousness _____ in the land of oblivion?

However, in the syntactically identical verse in (4), *waw* does not occur. Instead, the lines are asyndetically coordinate; that is, they are coordinate without an overt conjunction.

(4) Psalm 88:12

ha-yəsuppar	baq-qeber	ḥasde-kā	/ 'emûnātə-kā	bā-'ăbaddôn	Ø
INTERR-tell:PS:3MS	in:the-grave	faithfulness-2MS	constancy-2MS	in:the-Abaddon	

Is your faithfulness recounted in the grave, /
your constancy _____ in Abaddon?

The statistically prominent use of explicit coordination between conjuncts often seems to relate to the need to demarcate their boundaries, as in (5):

---

[6] I assume a binary branching structure for coordination but do not develop this idea. I also assume that small conjuncts are necessary in accounting for conjoined DPs (determiner phrases) as subject (Wilder 1997: 64). Elsewhere, I assume a Large Conjunct (rather than Small Conjunct) Hypothesis. The biblical Hebrew data do not require a shared structures approach (as advocated, e.g., by Lin 2002) because biblical Hebrew does not allow asymmetrical readings of constructions in which the verb has been gapped.

[7] See McShane (2005: 141–42) for a comparison of explicit coordination with verb gapping in English and Russian.

(5) Isaiah 1:3

yādaʿ	šôr	qōnē-hû	/wa-Ø-ḥămôr	ʾēbûs	bəʿāl-āyw
know:PF:3MS	ox	owner-3MS	and-donkey	manger:of	master:P-3MS

The ox <u>knows</u> its owner, /
and the donkey ____ its master's manger.

Because the objects in the two clauses are not explicitly marked with the definite object marker *ʾet*, the conjunction breaks up four adjacent noun phrases and thus helps to indicate where the second conjunct begins. Contrastively, in (6) the object noun phrases are marked with *ʾet* and no coordinating conjunction appears:[8]

(6) Isaiah 41:7

wayḥazzēq		ḥārāš	ʾet	ṣōrēp	/
encourage:IMPFCONS:3MS		artisan	ACC	smith:PTC:MS	
Ø maḥălîq		paṭṭîš	ʾet	hôlem	pāʿam
smooth:CS:PTC:MS		hammer	ACC	strike:PTC: MS	anvil

The artisan <u>encourages</u> the goldsmith, /
the one who smoothes with the hammer ___ the one who strikes the anvil.

In specifying that verbs elide out of conjoined clauses, I understand interrogatives to occur at a higher level — in (3) and (4) the interrogative in the first line governs both conjuncts. Similarly, subordinating conjunctions (e.g., *kî*), sentence adverbials (e.g., *ʾākēn*), and the presentative *hinnēh* occur at a higher level than the clause. Vocatives also stand outside of the clause proper:

(7) Psalm 114:7

mil-lipnê	ʾādôn	ḥûlî	ʾāreṣ	/ mil-lipnê	ʾĕlôah	yaʿăqōb	Ø
from-before	lord	writhe: IMV:FS	earth:F	from-before	god.of	Jacob	

Before the Lord, <u>writhe</u>, O earth, /
Before the God of Jacob ____.

The unmarked vocative noun phrase, 'O earth', stands between the two conjuncts, with the result that the antecedent verb is in final position in the first conjunct. For the purposes of ellipsis, the vocative does not count as a clausal constituent.[9]

The condition that ellipsis of the verb occurs out of coordinate structures is not controversial from a linguistic point of view, but it has not generally been recognized by biblical scholars, who instead view the poetic bicolon as the relevant context. What is less clear is the relationship between this syntactic condition on coordinate structures and poetic lineation, a question that we revisit in section 11.6 below. For the moment, we can observe that parallel lines sometimes provide the appropriate syntactic conditions for ellipsis — ellipsis is possible when each line comprises a conjunct and the two lines together form a coordinate structure, as in the examples we have seen thus far. But verbal ellipsis may also occur out of coordinate structures that are smaller or larger than the bicolon. In the examples that follow, I divide verses according to their coordinate conjuncts rather than their poetic lines.

11.2.2. Linear Order and Direction of Deletion

A second general condition on ellipsis involving clausal constituents relates to linear order and the direction of ellipsis. Ordinarily, the clausal constituents are in precisely the same order. In (1) above, the order of constituents in each conjunct is subject, prepositional phrase, verb. In (6) above, the order of constituents is verb, subject, object.

---

[8] The absence of *waw* before the second conjunct is not related to the presence of the *waw* consecutive imperfect verb in the first conjunct. For an example where a *waw* consecutive imperfect verb is gapped from the first line and the conjunction *waw* appears before the second conjunct, see 1 Kings 20:32: 'They put (*wayyaḥgərû*) sackcloth on their loins and Ø ropes on their heads'.

[9] Similarly, O'Connor considers the vocative to be "extraneous" to the clause (1980: 79–81). McCawley views the vocative as "extrasentential"; that is, it is not a syntactic constituent of the host sentence (1988: 2: 763–64).

If the constituents are not in identical order, they are in chiastic (or, mirror) order. In (3) above, the order of constituents in the first conjunct is verb, prepositional phrase, subject. In the second conjunct, the remaining constituents are chiastic with the constituents to which they correspond — subject, prepositional phrase. I therefore assume that the position of the elided verb is also chiastic in relation to its antecedent.[10]

The direction of ellipsis is usually forwards. Forwards ellipsis of any clausal constituent may occur when the ellipsis site is initial, medial, or final in the clause. Forwards ellipsis of the verb from initial position occurs in (5) and (6). Forwards ellipsis of the verb from final position occurs in (1) and (7). Forwards ellipsis from medial position is illustrated in (8), where the verb is flanked by its subject and object:

(8) Isaiah 60:2

kî	hinnēh	ha-ḥōšek	yəkasseh	'ereṣ /	wa-'ărāpel	Ø	lə'ummîm
for	behold	the-darkness	cover:IMPF:3MS	earth	and-thick.darkness		people:P

For behold, darkness <u>will cover</u> the earth, /
and thick darkness ____ the peoples.

Backwards ellipsis is highly constrained in two ways.[11] First, it never occurs in prose. Second, it occurs in poetry only when the constituent is final in the conjunct:[12]

(9) Psalm 94:3

'ad	mātay	rəšā'îm	Ø	YHWH /	'ad	mātay	rəšā'îm	ya'ălōzû
until	when	wicked:MP		YHWH	until	when	wicked:MP	exult:IMPF:3MP

How long [*will*] the wicked [*exult*], O LORD, /
How long <u>will</u> the wicked <u>exult</u>?

The constraint on backwards ellipsis accords with what we know about backwards ellipsis in general — it only occurs when the ellipsis site is right peripheral (i.e., in final position in its conjunct). In Russian, for example, both forwards and backwards gapping of verbs is possible, but backwards gapping occurs only when the verb is final in the clause.[13]

11.3. Semantic Relations Between Remnants and Corresponding Constituents

The first problematic area relates to the semantic relations between remnants and their corresponding constituents. Verb gapping in English results in specific semantic relationships between these pairs of constituents (see the discussion in Prince 1988). Consider the English sentence in (10a). The final (rightmost) constituent of each conjunct (here, the objects) will be tonically stressed:

---

[10] Verb gapping out of chiastic constituents is not limited to poetry. See Judges 6:37 (example [11]) for a prose example within direct speech.

[11] I consider examples like (16) below to exhibit backwards ellipsis (gapping) of the verb and not right node raising. (Right node raising refers to a coordinate construction in which the conjuncts share elements that appear only at the end of the final conjunct, as exemplified in the following English sentence: *Peter tried ____ and John succeeded in running the triathlon.*) Right node raising may have as its target portions of constituents; backwards ellipsis in biblical Hebrew only involves major constituents. Furthermore, backwards ellipsis in biblical Hebrew does not operate on the basis of phonological form, but rather (like forwards ellipsis) on the basis of morpho-syntax (see discussion below). On the distinctions between right node raising and gapping, see Hartman 2000: 53–58.

[12] Three purported instances of backwards ellipsis from medial position can be mentioned briefly. In Proverbs 13:1, the first conjunct should be understood as a verbless clause; see the discussion in Miller 2003. A second example is suggested by Dahood (1970: 435) for Psalm 91:9: *kî- 'attâ YHWH maḥsî 'elyôn śamtā mə'ônekā*. His translation, however, requires emending the pronominal suffix in the first line from first to second person: 'If you consider Yahweh himself your refuge, // the Most High your mainstay'. (Note that his translation moves the overt verb from the second conjunct to the first conjunct.) However, the verse can be understood without ellipsis, following the NJPS: 'Because you took the LORD — my refuge, the Most High — as your haven', rather than as an instance of medial backwards ellipsis. A third purported instance occurs in Zechariah 9:17, where the verb *yənôbēb* in the second conjunct should be understood as embedded within an unmarked relative clause rather than as the antecedent of medial backwards ellipsis (following the analysis of Arnold B. Ehrlich, *Randglossen zur Hebräischen Bibel* [reprint 1968] 5: 344).

[13] Compare the following Russian examples of verb gapping: (a) forwards gapping: *Ja čitaju naučnuju statju, a on ____ detektiv* 'I read a scientific article, and he ____ a detective novel' or *Ja naučnuju stat'ju čitaju, a on detektiv ____* 'I a scientific article read, and he a detective novel ____'; (b) backwards gapping: *Ja naučnuju statju ____, a on detektiv čitaet* 'I a scientific article ____, and he a detective novel read' (van Oirsouw 1987: 122). Japanese, by contrast exhibits only backwards gapping of verbs, and verbs are always final in the clause: *John-ga raisu-o ____ Bill-ga sushi-o tabeta* 'John rice ____ and Bill sushi ate' (ibid., p. 134).

(10) a. John writes nóvels; /my brother ___ biógraphies.
   b. *I write nóvels; /I ___ biógraphies.

From a semantic point of view, the paired constituents must be in a disjoint set relation — they are not coreferential. Thus, the sentence in (10a) is not grammatical if *John* is understood to be the same individual as *my brother*. Likewise, the sentence in (10b) is ungrammatical, unless the conjuncts are spoken by two different individuals in a conversation. Similarly, the final constituents in (10a) are not coreferential — the *novels* do not refer to the same literature as *biographies*, for example, as biographical novels. Instead, the first two paired constituents (*John, my brother*) refer to two individuals who are writers; the second set of paired constituents (*novels, biographies*) refers to their respective literary productions. Furthermore, the first set of paired constituents follow what Hartmann (2000: 162–66) calls the Maximal Contrast Principle — they must stand in a semantic relation of contrast.

In biblical prose, where verb gapping is extremely rare, remnants and their corresponding constituents form a disjoint set in this way:

(11) Judges 6:37

Behold, I am going to lay a fleece of wool on the threshing floor.

... ʾim	ṭal	yihyeh	ʿal	hag-gizzâ	ləbaddāh	/ wə-ʿal	kol	hā-ʾāreṣ	Ø	ḥōreb ...
if	dew	be:IMPF:3MS	upon	the-fleece	to:alone:3FS	and-upon	all.of	the-earth		dryness

If dew <u>will be</u> upon the fleece alone /
and upon all the ground ___ dryness,

then I will know that you will deliver Israel by my hand, as you have said.

The first pair of constituents ('dew' and 'dryness') is not coreferential but comprises a contrastive semantic set. The second pair of constituents ('upon the fleece' and 'upon the ground') also is not coreferential but describes contrastive locations.

Biblical poetry, however, differs. Usually the paired constituents are coreferential:

(12) Numbers 23:7

min	ʾărām	yanḥēnî	bālāq /	melek	môʾāb	Ø	mē-harrê	qedem
from	Aram	lead:IMPF:CS:3MS:1S	Balaq	king.of	Moab		from-mountain:P.of	East

From Aram, Balaq <u>led me</u>, /
the king of Moab ___ from the eastern mountains.

Balaq and the king of Moab are coreferential, as are Aram and the eastern mountains. Together, the two conjuncts describe only one event.

When the paired constituents are not strictly speaking coreferential, the two lines still do not necessarily express contrast. In (13), for example, 'kings' and 'their queens' are not coreferential, nor are 'foster fathers' and 'nursing mothers'. But there is no contrast between the conjuncts; instead, the two sentences describe a single situation:

(13) Isaiah 49:23

wə-hāyû	məlākîm	ʾōmənayik	/ wə-Ø	śārôtêhem	mênîqōtayik
and-be:PFCONS:3MP	king:P	support:PTC:MP:2FS	and-	princess: P:3MP	nurse:PTC:FP:2FS

Kings <u>shall be</u> your foster fathers, /
and their queens ___ your nursing mothers.

In (14), however, the paired constituents are not coreferential, and the two conjuncts do refer to two separate events by which Jael grasps the implements used to kill Sisera (Greenstein 1983: 64–65):

(14) Judges 5:26

yād-āh	lay-yātēd	tišlaḥnā	/ wîmîn-āh	ləhalmût	ʿămēlîm	Ø
hand-3FS	to:the-tentpen	send:IMPF:3FP[14]	and:right.hand-3FS	to-mallet.of	worker:P	

---

[14] Although the verb is pointed by the Masoretes as a third-person feminine plural imperfect, it probably should be understood as a third-person feminine singular energic form. See Waltke and O'Connor 1990: 517 n. 63.

Her hand to the tent pin <u>she extends</u>, /
and her right hand to the workmen's mallet ____.

Rarely in biblical poetry, non-coreferential paired constituents are truly contrastive. One example, involving ellipsis of the entire verb phrase instead of just the verb, is found in (15):

(15) Isaiah 1:21

ṣedeq	yālîn	bāh	/ wə-'attâ	məraṣṣəḥîm	∅
righteousness	lodge:IMPF:3MS	in:3FS	and-now	murder:PTC:MP	

Righteousness <u>was dwelling in her</u> /
but now murderers _____.

Here the paired items ('righteousness' and 'murderers') are contrastive in several ways. The noun *ṣedeq* describes an abstract quality, which is personified, as opposed to the participle *məraṣṣəḥîm*, which describes human agency and is concrete. By placing these two nouns in an elliptical structure, the poet explicitly contrasts the righteous, ethical inhabitants of the past, with the wicked, murderous inhabitants of the present.[15]

When the paired constituents are truly contrastive, backwards ellipsis is more frequent than forwards ellipsis:[16]

(16) Psalm 20:8

'ēlleh	bā-rekeb	∅ / wə-'ēlleh	bas-sûsîm	∅ / wa-'ănaḥnû	bə-šēm	YHWH	'ĕlōhênû	nazkîr
these	in:the-chariot	and-these	in:the-horse:P	and-we	in-name.of	YHWH	god:1P	remember:IMPF:CS:1P

Some on chariotry ____, /
and some on horses ____, /
but we on the name of the LORD our God <u>we will call</u>.[17]

The subject constituents in the first two conjuncts provide a contrast with the psalmist and his fellow-worshipers. The prepositional phrases contrast military equipment with God's presence.

We have seen that the semantic relations between remnants and their corresponding constituents in biblical prose follow the constraint of maximal contrast. In biblical poetry, this constraint is relaxed. Paired constituents are usually coreferential; when they are not, contrastive focus is rare but possible.

11.4. Content-identity

A second problematic area involves content-identity, the requirement that the deleted constituent and the antecedent must be identical. In ellipsis involving the verb, content-identity minimally involves the lexical verb, but other features related to verbal forms must also be specified.

In biblical Hebrew, an important restriction concerning content-identity is that the two verbs must agree with respect to derivational verbal stem (or, *binyan*). For example, it would be impossible for ellipsis to occur with an active *qal* form of the verb in one conjunct and a causative *hiphil* in the other.[18]

Assuming that the verbs agree lexically and with respect to stem, it has long been noted (Greenstein 1983: 46–47) that they need not be identical with respect to gender or number, as illustrated in (17), repeated here from (1):

---

[15] Some recent commentators consider the words *wə'attâ məraṣṣəḥîm* to be a gloss on the basis that its style differs from the surrounding lines (Blenkinsopp 2000: 180) or for reasons of meter (Wildberger 1991: 60).

[16] See also Psalm 115:1.

[17] The *hiphil* of *zkr* usually means 'to mention', 'to make known', 'to profess, praise' (Koehler and Baumgartner 1994–2000: 1:270). In this verse, the verb has been translated 'call' (e.g., NJPS, NJB) or 'trust' (e.g., KJV, NIV). Other translations follow the Septuagint μεγαλυνθησόμεθα and translate 'boast' (RSV) or 'take pride' (NRSV). The lexical semantics of *nazkîr* do not affect the syntactic analysis.

[18] As Berlin notes, it is not unusual in biblical poetry for parallel lines to have the same lexical verb in different stems. For example, Job 22:30 pairs a form of the verb *mlṭ* in the *piel* with a form in the *niphal*: 'He will deliver (*piel*) the unclean; /and he will be delivered (*niphal*) through the purity of your hands' (Berlin 1985: 38; see also the examples on 36–40). But ellipsis involving the verb in lines such as these is not possible.

(17) Isaiah 1:27

ṣîyôn	bə-mišpāṭ	tippādeh	/ wə-šābê-hā	bi-ṣdāqâ	Ø
Zion:FS	by-justice	redeem:IMPF:PS:3FS	and-return:APTC:MP-3FS	by-righteousness	

Zion (feminine singular) by justice <u>shall be redeemed</u>, /

and her repentant ones (masculine plural) by righteousness [*shall be redeemed*].

'Zion' is construed as feminine singular, whereas 'her repentant ones' is grammatically masculine plural.

Along with gender and number, the verbs need not be identical with respect to person, as illustrated in a question-answer sequence from prose, in (18):[19]

(18) Genesis 42:7

He (Joseph) said to them (his brothers),

... mē-'ayin	bā'tem ...
from-where	come:PF:2MP

"From where <u>have you come</u> (2MP)?"

They said,

Ø	mē-'ereṣ	kənaʿan	li-šbor	'ōkel
	from-land.of	Canaan	to-buy:INF	food

"[*We have come* (1P)] from the land of Canaan to buy food."

A more interesting question involves the question of verbal form. In English, the elided verb and its antecedent must agree in tense, as illustrated in the ungrammatical example in (19), taken from Wilder 1997: 72:

(19) *John <u>arrives</u> today and Mary ____ yesterday

In biblical Hebrew, verbs must be identical in tense/aspect and modality. In other words, a perfect cannot serve as the antecedent for an imperfect, nor an imperfect for an infinitive. However, instances in which either the ellipsis site or the antecedent is negated provide an interesting window into verb forms that "count as" identical for purposes of ellipsis.

(20) Genesis 27:12

Perhaps my father will feel me (imperfect) and then I will be (perfect consecutive) in his eyes as one mocking him,

... wə-hēbē'tî	'ālay	qəlālâ /	wə-lō'	Ø	bərākâ
and-come:PFCONS:CS:1s	upon-1S	curse	and-not		blessing

and <u>I will bring</u> (perfect consecutive) <u>upon myself</u> a curse /

and not ____ a blessing.

In (20), the antecedent is a so-called perfect consecutive verb. In this sentence, it expresses irreal modality as part of the apodosis of a hypothetical sentence. Since the perfect consecutive cannot be negated, the elided verb must be the imperfect 'ābî', also expressing irreal modality.[20]

A similar example appears in (21):

(21) Psalm 115:1

lō'	lānû	Ø	YHWH /	lō'	lānû	Ø	/ kî	lə-šim-kā	tēn	kābôd
not	to:1P		YHWH	not	to:1P		CONJ	to-name-2MS	give:IMV:MS	glory

   a. Not to us [*give glory*], O LORD, /

   b. not to us [*give glory*], /

   c. but to your name <u>give glory</u>.

---

[19] For a similar question-answer pair involving ellipsis within poetry, see Psalm 121:1–2: mē'ayin yābō' 'ezrî / 'ezrî Ø mē'im YHWH 'ōśê šāmayim wā'āreṣ 'From where <u>does</u> my help <u>come</u>? My help ____ from the LORD, maker of heaven and earth'.

[20] I assume that because the first verb in the apodosis is imperfect, the elided verb should be imperfect also. See, for example, Exodus 19:5. Perfect verbs can also occur in the apodosis of conditions (Waltke and O'Connor 1990: 530–34).

The verbal antecedent in line (c) is an imperative.[21] The deleted verbs in lines (a) and (b), which are negated, must be the imperfect *tittēn*, expressing deontic modality.[22]

Examples (20) and (21) are important for two reasons. First, they tell us that content-identity of deleted forms must agree with respect to type of modality, even though they do not agree in form. Second, example (21) is interesting in that it demonstrates that backwards deletion in biblical Hebrew operates in the same way as forwards deletion with respect to content-identity. By contrast, backwards deletion in English has been argued to differ from forwards deletion with respect to content-identity.[23]

11.5. Context-identity

A third problematic area involves context-identity, that is, the ways in which the two conjuncts must match in order for verbal ellipsis to take place. As a first approximation, we can say that the clausal constituents match at the level of the clause, as we have seen in each example thus far. However, the internal structures of clausal constituents are not relevant to ellipsis. In (22), for example, the constituent structures match at the level of the clause — both conjuncts have the shape of negative existential predicate plus a noun phrase:

(22) Micah 7:1

'ên   'eškôl   le-'ĕkôl   / Ø   bikkûrâ   'iwwətâ   napš-î
NEG.EXIST cluster   to-eat:INF   ripe.fig   desire:PF:3FS soul-1S

There is no grape cluster to eat /
___ ripe fig (which) my soul desires.

The internal structures of the noun phrases are not identical. In the first conjunct, the noun phrase contains an embedded infinitival clause. The second conjunct contains an unmarked relative clause.

Because constituents that are in final position within the conjunct may delete either backwards or forwards, the ends of the conjoined conjuncts may have constituents that superficially appear as if they have "swapped" places:[24]

(23) Psalm 48:7 (from Greenstein 1983: 46)

rə'ādâ   'ăḥāzāt-am   šām   Ø / ḥîl   Ø   kay-yôlēdâ
trembling:F   seize:PF:3FS-3MP there   writhing:M   like:the-birth:PTC:FS

Trembling has seized them there [*like a birthing woman*] /
Writhing [*has seized them there*] like a birthing woman.

The verb plus object and the adverb *šām* have been deleted forwards from the first conjunct. The prepositional phrase *kayyôlēdâ* has been deleted backwards from the second conjunct. The two lines match, not because the adverb *šām* and the prepositional phrase *kayyôlēdā* correspond to one another, but because the linear arrangement of constituents at the ends of the conjuncts allows the adverb to delete forwards and the prepositional phrase to delete backwards.

---

[21] The conjoined prepositional phrases at the end of the verse (*'al ḥasdə-kā 'al 'ămittekā*) should probably be understood as part of the preceding clause. In that case, they should be considered to have elided backwards along with the verb and object ('Do not to *us* [give glory on account of your lovingkindness and faithfulness], but rather *to your name* give glory on account of your lovingkindness and faithfulness').

[22] Although it is unusual for the psalmist to use *lō'* ('not') with the imperfect in a command addressed to God, the same construction occurs in Psalm 40:12: 'You, O LORD, must not withhold (*lō'-tiklā'* [imperfect]) your mercies from me'.

[23] Wilder (1997: 88–101), for example, argues that forwards deletion occurs at logical form; backwards deletion occurs at phonological form.

That is, verb forms in backwards deletion agree in phonological form, but morpho-syntactic identity is not required:

  a. *John said that I [**am** *the best swimmer*] and Mary said that she **is** the best swimmer.

  b. John said that I [**was** *the best swimmer*] and Mary said that she **was** the best swimmer.

In contrast, verb forms in forwards deletion need not agree in phonological form:

  a. I **am** a great swimmer and Mary [*is*] a great golfer.

[24] See Wilder 1997: 59–60 for examples of "swapping" in English, though he does not use the term.

Conjuncts whose clausal constituents do not match may count as having identical structures for the purposes of ellipsis, if the paired constituents bear the same semantic roles within their respective conjuncts. In (24), the adverb *yômām* 'daily' corresponds to the prepositional phrase *ballāyəlâ* 'in the night' in the second conjunct.

(24) Psalm 121:6

yôm-ām	*haš-šemeš*	*lō'*	*yakke-kkâ*	/ *wə-Ø*	*yārēaḥ*	*bal-lāyəlâ*
day-ADV	the-sun	not	strike:IMPF:3MS-2MS	and-	moon	in:the-night

Daily (adverb) the sun <u>will not strike you</u> /
and the moon [*will not strike you*] in the night (prepositional phrase).

Ellipsis is possible because the paired constituents have the same semantic relation to the predicate.[25] Recognition of this feature of context identity means that there are far fewer instances of the ellipsis of a bare preposition across clausal conjuncts than posited by most biblical scholars. Take, for example, (25):

(25) Psalm 114:8

ha-hōpəkî	*haṣ-ṣûr*	*'ăgam*	*māyim*	/ Ø	*hal-lāmîš*	*lə-ma'yənô*	*māyim*
the-turn:PTC:MS	the-rock	pool.of	water		the-flint	to-spring.of	water

<u>the one who turns</u> the rock (into) a pool of water, /
[*the one who turns*] flint <u>into</u> a spring of water.

In this example, we can clearly see that the two conjuncts are identical because deletion of the verb (here the participle *hōpəkî*) has occurred. The question is: has the preposition *l-* been deleted backwards from the second conjunct to the first? The answer is no. The verb *hpk* may mark its two objects using two accusative noun phrases (as in the first conjunct) or using an accusative noun phrase and a prepositional phrase headed by *l-* (as in the second conjunct).[26] Ellipsis of the participle has occurred; ellipsis of a bare preposition has not.[27]

Up to this point, we could argue that context identity does not require syntactic identity, but rather that the semantic roles of non-verbal constituents be identical. However, there are a few cases in which the syntax is precisely identical and yet the semantic relations between paired constituents are not:

(26) Isaiah 59:10

kāšalnû	*baṣ-ṣohŏrayim*	*kan-nešep*	/ Ø	*bā-'ašmannîm*	*kam-mētîm*
stumble:PF:1P	in:the-noon	as:the-twilight		in:the-vigorous	as:the-dead:P

<u>We stumble</u>   at (*b-*) noon   as (*k-*) at twilight, /
_____   among (*b-*) the vigorous   like (*k-*) dead men.

Here the non-verbal constituents in each conjunct are syntactically identical — a prepositional phrase headed with the preposition *b-* followed by another prepositional phrase headed with the preposition *k-*. We can maintain that semantic roles are most important only if we claim that the semantic roles in (26) are broadly identical.[28] In that case, the prepositional phrases headed by *b-* serve to locate the action or event — in the first conjunct, the location is temporal; in the second conjunct the location is social — and the prepositional phrases headed with *k-* provide the manner of the action.[29] However, it is not entirely clear whether syntax or semantic roles is the determining condition.

---

[25] For another example, see Proverbs 18:3: *bəbô' rāšā' bā' gam bûz / wə'im qālôn Ø ḥerpâ* 'Comes the wicked man comes derision, / And with the rogue, contempt' (NJPS). The infinitival phrase *bəbô' rāšā'* ('when the wicked person comes') must be understood as a prepositional phrase (and thus as one constituent for purposes of gapping), just like *'im qālôn* ('with the rogue').

[26] For evidence of the first configuration of objects with *hpk* (two accusative noun phrases), see Leviticus 13:10, 25 (cf. vv. 16, 17 with the *niphal* form of the verb, in which the preposition is found, presumably because the *niphal* can only take one argument associated with it). This evidence was collected in Greenstein 1978. For examples of verb gapping involving the second configuration of objects with *hpk* (an accusative noun phrase and a prepositional phrase), see Amos 5:7, 6:12, 8:10.

[27] Similarly, in Psalm 105:10 (//1 Chronicles 16:17), the bicolon pairs two syntactic variations — verb + object + prepositional phrase with *l-* and verb + object + adverbial accusative (the prepositional phrases 'to Jacob'/ 'to Israel' indicate the recipients of the verbal action and are not arguments of the verb). No bare preposition ellipsis has occurred.

[28] For an example where the conjuncts match in this way (without ellipsis), see Psalm 49:5 (Berlin 1985: 62–63).

[29] It is possible that ellipsis involving comparatives (including the preposition *k-*) operates differently.

In a very rare case, there appears to be no syntactically matching expression that can serve as an antecedent of the elided verb:

(27) Psalm 123:1–2

a 'ēlêkā   nāśā'tî   'et   'ên-ay   hay-yōšəbî   baš-šāmāyim
   to:you   lift:PF:1S   ACC   eye:D-1S   the-dwell:PTC:MS   in:the-heaven:P

b hinnēh   kə-'ênê   'ăbādîm   Ø   'el   yad   'ădônê-hem
   behold   as-eye:D.of servant:MP   to   hand.of   master:P-3MP

c kə-'ênê   šipḥâ   Ø   'el   yad   gəbirt-āh
   as-eye:D.of maidservant   to   hand.of   mistress-3FS

d kēn   'ênê-nû   Ø   'el   YHWH   'ĕlōhê-nû ...
   thus   eye:D.of-1P   to   YHWH   god-1P

a To you I lift up my eyes, O dweller in the heavens,
b Behold, as the eyes of male-servants [*lift up] to the hand of their masters,
c as the eyes of a female-servant [*lift up] to the hand of her mistress,
d thus our eyes [*lift up] to the LORD our God until he should pity us.

In (a), the verb *nāśā'tî* takes as its object the noun phrase *'et 'ênay* 'my eyes'. In (b), (c), and (d), however, the noun phrases containing the word 'eyes' cannot be construed as either the object or the subject of *nāśā'tî*. Furthermore, we cannot understand the deleted verb as a passive (*niphal*), to read 'the eyes of male servants are lifted up', although this approach has been followed by some scholars,[30] because this expression never appears in the Bible.[31]

There seem to be three options for restoring the fragmented clauses. The first option is to understand the verb *nāśā'tî* as the antecedent. Linguists have noted a possibly similar situation involving verb phrase ellipsis in English, as illustrated in (28):

(28) Harry used to be a great speaker, but he can't Ø [*be a great speaker/speak] any more because he lost his voice (from Hardt 1993: 34)

The second conjunct must be restored as *he can't speak any more*, for which there is no syntactic antecedent, and not *but he can't be a great speaker anymore*, for which there is. Explaining precisely how speakers interpret the sentence fragment is debated. One approach is that of Lappin who argues that hearers infer *Harry used to speak* from *Harry used to be a great speaker*.[32] In other words, hearers infer that the construction *NP is an N* implies that *NP V's* where N is a deverbal noun and V is the verb that corresponds to the N (Lappin 1996: 158). Similarly, in (27), we could posit that readers infer that the construct phrase (composed of a noun in the construct state followed by a noun in the absolute state) implies that the absolute noun refers to the agent who affects the item referred to by the construct noun.[33] That is, a reader cognitively interprets the fragmented structures as illustrated in (29):

(29) a To you I lift up my eyes, O dweller in the heavens,
     b Behold, as male-servants [*lift up*] their eyes to the hand of their masters,
     c as a female-servant [*lifts up*] her eyes to the hand of her mistress,
     d thus [*we lift up*] our eyes to the LORD our God

---

[30] Briggs and Briggs (1906–1907: 2:450–51) acknowledge that a verb is missing in lines (b)–(c). They restore the *niphal* of *nś'* and translate: 'Lo! as the eyes of menservants (are lifted up) to the hand of their lords; (Lo!) as the eyes of a maidservant (are lifted up) to the hand of her lady'. In (d), however, they seemingly understand a verbless clause and translate: 'So our eyes are unto Yahweh, our God, until He be gracious to us'.

[31] In Proverbs 30:13, the word 'eyelids' is the subject of the *niphal* of *nś'*: 'There is a generation — how high are their eyes/and their eyelids are lifted up (*yinnāśē'û*)'. But the expression as a whole ('the eyelids are lifted up') refers to haughty, arrogant behavior and is therefore unlike the meaning in Psalm 123:1–2.

[32] Kempson et al. 1999 argue for a semantic/pragmatic approach to ellipsis resolution. Similarly, Hardt 1992.

[33] See Waltke and O'Connor 1990: 143–46 for a discussion of the so-called "subjective genitive."

The second option would be to restore the elided verb semantically on the basis of the common expression: 'to lift up the eyes and look'.³⁴ The fragmented structures would then be restored as in (30):

(30) a To you I lift up (*nāśā'tî*) my eyes, O dweller in the heavens,
 b Behold, as the eyes of male-servants [*look* (*rā'û*)] to the hand of their masters,
 c as the eyes of a female-servant [*look*] to the hand of her mistress,
 d thus our eyes [*look*] to the LORD our God until he should pity us.

Restoring the fragmented clauses with a form of *r'h* produces an appropriate expression, as illustrated in (31):³⁵

(31) Isaiah 17:7

wə-'ênāyw	*'el qədôš*	*yiśrā'ēl*	*tir'ênâ*
and-eye:D-3MS	to holy.one.of	Israel	see:IMPF:3FP

And his eyes will look to the Holy One of Israel.

A final option, proposed by Dahood (1966: 3:209), understands verbless clauses rather than elliptical ones in conjuncts (b) through (d):³⁶

(32) a To you I lift up my eyes, O dweller in the heavens,
 b Behold, as the eyes of male-servants (are) on the hand of their masters,
 c as the eyes of a female-servant (are) on the hand of her mistress,
 d thus our eyes (are) on the LORD our God …

However, this interpretation does not seem likely. The use of the preposition *'el* as the predicate of a verbless clause is unusual.³⁷

Example (27) is a stark reminder that sometimes we are unable to determine whether ellipsis has occurred or, if it has, precisely how to restore the fragmented structure. We have seen that syntactic constraints are central to the ways in which conjuncts match, but understanding those constraints does not always assist us in knowing how they should be applied.

11.6. Local Proximity

A final condition on verbal ellipsis involves local proximity. In general, an ellipsis site must find its antecedent in the nearest conjunct which meets the other conditions for ellipsis. For example, in (33a), the elliptical conjunct will normally be interpreted as (c), rather than as (b).

(33) a John bought stocks, Mary sold bonds, and Chris ___ real estate.
 b *John bought stocks, Mary sold bonds, and Chris [*bought*] real estate.
 c John bought stocks, Mary sold bonds, and Chris [*sold*] real estate.

In other words, although the first conjunct (*John bought stocks*) fulfills the other requirements for ellipsis in English, it is not the nearest conjunct to the ellipsis site. English speakers ordinarily interpret the ellipsis site on the basis of the immediately preceding antecedent.³⁸

---

³⁴ The expression occurs thirty-five times in the Bible (Genesis 13:10, 13:14, 18:2, 22:4, 22:13, 24:63; 24:64; 31:10, 31:12, 33:1, 33:5, 37:25, 43:29; Numbers 24:2; Deuteronomy 3:27, 4:19; Joshua 5:13; Judges 19:17; 1 Samuel 6:13; 2 Samuel 13:34, 18:24; Isaiah 40:26, 49:18, 60:4; Jeremiah 3:2, 13:20; Zechariah 2:1, 2:5, 5:1, 5:5, 5:9, 6:1; Daniel 8:3, 10:5; 1 Chronicles 21:16).

³⁵ Compare Isaiah 37:23, which has the same collocation of subject, verb and prepositional phrase, except for the addition of the adverbial noun phrase *mārōm* 'haughtily'.

³⁶ Dahood adduces KTU 1.6:28–30 as an Ugaritic parallel for his translation: "Like the heart of a wild cow for her calf, like the heart of a wild ewe for her lamb, so was the heart of Anath for Baal."

³⁷ As possible analogous examples in which a prepositional phrase headed with *'el* serves as the predicate of a verbless clause, see Genesis 3:16, 4:17; Exodus 37:9, and Joshua 8:33. In some other potential cases, the preposition has a different meaning; see, for example, Isaiah 3:8, where the sense of the preposition is 'against', rather than 'on' or 'towards': *kî ləšônām ûma'allēhem 'el YHWH lamrôt 'ēnê kəbôdô*. The NRSV translates: "… because their speech and their deeds are against the LORD, defying his glorious presence."

³⁸ But note the example cited by Kempson et al. 1999: 229, example 9: *John thinks he's clever. Bill does too. John's wife, however, certainly does not.* The second clause can be construed as *Bill thinks that Bill is clever* or as *Bill thinks that John is clever*. The third clause can also be construed with the first clause as antecedent: *John's wife does not think that John is clever*.

In most instances of ellipsis in biblical poetry, the antecedent will be the nearest clause that meets the other requirements for ellipsis. However, the antecedent need not be the immediately preceding clause, as in (34):

(34) Psalm 18:42

yəšawwə'û	/ *wə-'ên*	*môšîa'*	/ Ø *'al*	YHWH	/ *wəlō'*	*'ān-ām*
cry:IMPF:3MP	and-NEGEXIST	rescue:CAUS:PTC:MS	to	YHWH	and-not	answer:PF:3MS-3MP

   a They cried out /
   b and there was no rescuer /
   c ____ to the LORD /
   d and he did not answer them.

The missing verb in (c) must find its antecedent in (a) since the clause in (b) is not an appropriate antecedent. Ellipsis takes place across a clause boundary, but the antecedent is found in the nearest clause that meets the other conditions on ellipsis.[39]

In some cases, however, two preceding clauses could equally serve as the antecedent conjunct on syntactic terms, as in (35):

(35) Zechariah 9:5

(a) *tēre'*	*'ašqəlôn*	/ (b) *wə-tîrā'*	/ (c) *wə-* Ø *'azzā*	/ (d) *wə-tāḥîl*	*mə'ōd*
see:IMPF:3FS	Ashkelon	and-fear:IMPF:3FS	and-Gaza	and-writhe:IMPF:3FS	exceedingly

(e) *wə-* Ø *'eqrôn kî*	*hōbîš*	*mebbāṭ-āh*
and- Ekron because/that	wither:PF:3MS	hope-3FS

   a Ashkelon sees
   b and is afraid
   c and Gaza [*is afraid/sees*]
   d and writhes exceedingly
   e and Ekron [*writhes exceedingly/*is afraid*] because/[*sees*] that its hope has withered.

From a purely linguistic point of view, we would expect that the elided verb in (c) should be restored from the nearest preceding conjunct in (b) and read 'Gaza is afraid'. Similarly, the elided verb in (e) should be restored from the immediately preceding conjunct in (d) to read 'Ekron writhes exceedingly'. However, from the point of view of poetic parallelism, the antecedent of (c) is more likely the verb *tēre'* in (a). In the same way that Ashkelon sees and is afraid, Gaza sees and writhes. However, the antecedent of (e) is more difficult to determine because the line about Ekron is not precisely parallel to those involving Ashkelon and Gaza. If the statement about Ekron is viewed as parallel to that of Ashkelon and Gaza, then the missing verb in (e) is *tēre'* and *kî* is a complementizer: 'Ekron sees that its hope has withered'. If the missing verb in (e) is the immediately preceding verb from (d), then *kî* introduces the reason: 'Ekron writhes exceedingly because its hope has withered'. In this verse, it is not entirely clear whether the sentence fragment in (e) should be restored on the basis of (a) or (d). Perhaps the poetic shaped the lines with this linguistic ambiguity in order to allow for multiple readings.

In another poetic construction, two adjacent clauses can equally serve as the antecedent for ellipsis. In other words, the locality constraint, which specifies that ellipsis occurs with the nearest acceptable antecedent, is relaxed. The construction is one in which four lines appear together — two independent clauses, followed by two dependent clauses. O'Connor (1980: 421–22) refers to this construction as "mixing." An example of the construction (without ellipsis) appears in (36):

(36) 2 Samuel 1:20

'al taggîdû	*bə-gat*	/ *'al təbaśśərû*	*bə-ḥûṣōt*	*'ašqəlôn* /
not declare:JUSS:2MP	in-Gath	not tell.news:JUSS:2MP	in-street:P.of	Ashkelon

pen tiśmaḥnâ	*bənôt*	*pəlištîm* /	*pen ta'ălōznâ*	*bənôt*	*hā-'ărēlîm*
lest rejoice:IMPF:3FP	daughter:P.of	Philistine:P	lest exult:IMPF:3FP	daughter:P.of	the-uncircumcised:P

---

[39] Another example of ellipsis (both of the negative and of the subject of the verbless clause) across clause boundaries is found in Numbers 23:19: *lō' 'îš 'ēl / wîkazzēb / û-*Ø *ben 'ādām* Ø */ wəyitneḥām* 'God is not a man so that he should lie and [not] a human [is God] that he should repent'.

a Do not announce in Gath,
b Do not tell the news in the streets of Ashkelon,
c Lest the daughters of the Philistines rejoice,
d Lest the daughters of the uncircumcised exult.

The lines in (a) and (b) are identical in syntactic structure (negative, verb, prepositional phrase) and synonymous in parallelism. The lines in (c) and (d) are identical in syntactic structure (conjunction, verb, prepositional phrase) and synonymous in parallelism. It is impossible to know whether (c) and (d) are subordinate to (a) or (b), respectively, or to both (a) and (b).

When ellipsis appears in the two dependent clauses, either or both of the two main clauses could serve as the antecedent:

(37) Isaiah 45:13

hû'yibneh   'îr-î   / wə-gālût-î yəšallēaḥ   / lō' Ø bi-mḥîr / wəlō' Ø bə-šōḥad
he build:IMPF:3MS city-1S   and-exile-1S send.out:(D):IMPF:3MS not in-price and-not in-payment

a he will build my city
b and my exiles he will release
c not for a price [*he will build my city/he will release my exiles*]
d and not for a payment [*he will build my city/he will release my exiles*]

In this example, the (c) and (d) lines exhibit stripping (or, bare argument deletion) in which all of the antecedent sentence has been deleted except for one constituent, the prepositional phrase.[40] The remnant constituents could relate to either (a) or (b).

Conditions on local proximity, then, appear to take into account poetic features such as the semantic parallelism of poetic lines. While parallel poetic lines do not provide the determining context within which ellipsis takes place, poetic structure may encourage the reader to accept a distant antecedent instead of a closer one or to accept two antecedents for a single ellipsis site.

11.7. Conclusions

We have seen that verbal ellipsis in biblical Hebrew follows constraints related to coordination, linear order, the direction of deletion, the semantic relations of non-gapped constituents, content identity, context identity, and locality.

Biblical poetry differs from biblical prose in two ways. First, poetry exhibits a vastly greater quantity of ellipsis; and second, poetry relaxes only three of the constraints on verbal ellipsis: (1) the direction of deletion (poetry allows backwards ellipsis from final ellipsis sites), (2) the semantic relations of non-gapped constituents (poetry allows non-contrastive, coreferential constituents), and (3) locality (poetry allows a non-local antecedent). Of these three relaxed constraints, only the first (backwards ellipsis) is unexpected. The second and third (coreferential constituents and non-local antecedents) directly result from the most prominent feature of biblical poetry, parallelism.

---

[40] For evidence that conjuncts (c) and (d) must involve deletion of a verb (even though in English we translate 'without'), see Isaiah 55:1: 'Ho, all who are thirsty, come to the water/and whoever does not have money, /come, buy and eat/come! buy without silver (*bəlô' kesep*) and without price (*bəlô' məḥîr*) wine and milk'. The negative is within the prepositional phrase headed with the preposition *b-*, not outside it, as is the case in Isaiah 45:13.

Abbreviations

ACC	accusative marker
Act	active
ADV	adverbial
CS	causative stem (e.g., Hiphil, Hophal)
D	dual
F	feminine
IMPF	imperfect
IMPFCONS	imperfect consecutive
IMV	imperative
INF	infinitive
INTERR	interrogative marker
JUSS	jussive
KJV	King James Version
M	masculine
NIV	New International Version
NJB	New Jerusalem Bible
NJPS	New Jewish Publication Society
NRSV	New Revised Standard Version
NEG.EXIST	negative existential
P	plural
PF	perfect
PFCONS	perfect consecutive
PS	passive
PTC	participle
RSV	Revised Standard Version
S	singular

Bibliography

Berlin, Adele
    1985   *The Dynamics of Biblical Parallelism*. Bloomington: Indiana University Press.

Blenkinsopp, Joseph
    2000   *Isaiah: A New Translation with Introduction and Commentary*, Volume 1. Anchor Bible 19. New York: Doubleday.

Briggs, Charles Augustus, and Emilie Grace Briggs
    1906–1907   *A Critical and Exegetical Commentary on the Book of Psalms*. Two volumes. International Critical Commentary. New York: Scribner's.

Chomsky, William
    1952   *David Kimḥi's Hebrew Grammar [Mikhlol]*. New York: Bloch.

Dahood, Mitchell
    1965   *Ugaritic-Hebrew Philology: Marginal Notes on Recent Publications*. Biblica et Orientalia 17. Rome: Pontifical Biblical Institute.
    1966   *Psalms 1: 1–50*. Anchor Bible 16. Garden City: Doubleday.
    1970   *Psalms 3: 101–150*. Anchor Bible 17a. Garden City: Doubleday.

Dion, Paul E.
> 1992 *Hebrew Poetics*. Second edition. Mississauga: Benben Publications.

Ehrlich, Arnold B.
> 1968 *Randglossen zur Hebräischen Bibel: Text Kritisches, Sprachliches und Sachliches*. Hildesheim: Olms.

Geller, Stephen A.
> 1979 *Parallelism in Early Biblical Poetry*. Harvard Semitic Monographs 20. Missoula: Scholars Press.

Greenstein, Edward L.
> 1978 "The Study of Deletion (double-duty) Phenomena in Ugaritic and Biblical Hebrew." (Paper presented to the American Oriental Society). n.p.
> 1983 "How Does Parallelism Mean?" In *A Sense of Text: The Art of Language in the Study of Biblical Literature (*Papers from a Symposium at the Dropsie College for Hebrew and Cognate Learning, May 11, 1982), edited by Stephen A Geller, Edward L. Greenstein, and Adele Berlin, pp. 41–70. Jewish Quarterly Review Supplement. Winona Lake: Eisenbrauns.

Halliday, M. A. K., and Ruqaiya Hasan
> 1976 *Cohesion in English*. English Languages Series 9. London: Longman.

Hardt, D.
> 1992 "VP Ellipsis and Semantic Identity." In *Proceedings of the Stuttgart Ellipsis Workshop*, edited by S. Berman and A. Hestvik. Arbeitspapiere des Sonderforschungsbereichs 340; Sprachtheoretische Grundlagen für die Computerlinguistik 29. Stuttgart: Universitäten Stuttgart und Tübingen.
> 1993 Verb Phrase Ellipsis: Form, Meaning, and Processing. Ph.D. dissertation, University of Pennsylvania.

Hartmann, Katharina
> 2000 *Right Node Raising and Gapping: Interface Conditions on Prosodic Deletion*. Amsterdam: Benjamins.

Kempson, Ruth; Wilfried Meyer-Viol; and Dov Gabbay
> 1999 "VP Ellipsis: Toward a Dynamic, Structural Account." In *Fragments: Studies in Ellipsis and Gapping*, edited by Shalom Lappin and Elabbas Benmamoun, pp. 227–89. New York: Oxford University Press.

Khan, Geoffrey
> 2000 *The Early Karaite Tradition of Hebrew Grammatical Thought: Including a Critical Edition, Translation and Analysis of the* Diqduq *of ʾAbū Yaʿqūb Yūsuf ibn Nūḥ on the Hagiographa*. Studies in Semitic Languages and Linguistics 32. Leiden: Brill.

Koehler, Ludwig, and Walter Baumgartner
> 1994–2000 *The Hebrew and Aramaic Lexicon of the Old Testament*. Five volumes. Translated and edited by M. E. J. Richardson, Walter Baumgartner, and Johann Jakob Stamm. Leiden: Brill.

Lappin, Shalom
> 1996 "The Interpretation of Ellipsis." In *The Handbook of Contemporary Semantic Theory*, edited by Shalom Lappin, pp. 145–75. Blackwell Handbooks in Linguistics. Oxford: Blackwell.

Lin, Vivian I-Wen
> 2002 Coordination and Sharing at the Interfaces. Ph.D. dissertation, Massachusetts Institute of Technology.

Lyons, John
> 1971 *Introduction to Theoretical Linguistics*. Cambridge: Cambridge University Press.

McCawley, James D.
> 1988 *The Syntactic Phenomena of English*. Two volumes. Chicago: University of Chicago Press.

McShane, Marjorie J.
　2005　　*A Theory of Ellipsis*. Oxford: Oxford University Press.

Miller, Cynthia L.
　2003　　"A Linguistic Approach to Ellipsis in Biblical Poetry: Or, What to Do When Exegesis of What Is There Depends on What Isn't." *Bulletin of Biblical Research* 13: 251–70.

O'Connor, M.
　1980　　*Hebrew Verse Structure*. Winona Lake: Eisenbrauns.

Prince, Ellen F.
　1988　　"Discourse Analysis: A Part of the Study of Linguistic Competence." In *Linguistics: The Cambridge Survey*, Volume 2: *Linguistic Theory: Extensions and Implications,* edited by Frederick J. Newmeyer, pp. 164–82. Cambridge: Cambridge University Press.

Rosenbaum, Michael
　1997　　*Word-order Variation in Isaiah 40–55: A Functional Perspective*. Studia Semitica Neerlandica 36. Assen: Van Gorcum.

Sappan, Raphael
　1981　　*The Typical Features of the Syntax of Biblical Poetry in the Classical Period*. Jerusalem: Kiryat-Sefer [in Hebrew].

van Oirsouw, Robert R.
　1987　　*The Syntax of Coordination*. Croom Helm Linguistics Series. London: Croom Helm.

Waltke, Bruce K., and M. O'Connor
　1990　　*An Introduction to Biblical Hebrew Syntax*. Winona Lake: Eisenbrauns.

Watson, Wilfred G. E.
　1984　　*Classical Hebrew Poetry: A Guide to Its Techniques*. Journal for the Old Testament Supplement 26. Sheffield: Journal for the Old Testament Press.

Wildberger, Hans
　1991　　*Isaiah: A Commentary*, Volume 1. Translated by H. Trapp. Continental Commentaries. Minneapolis: Fortress.

Wilder, Chris
　1997　　"Some Properties of Ellipsis in Coordination." In *Studies on Universal Grammar and Typological Variation*, edited by Artemis Alexiadou and T. Alan Hall, pp. 59–107. Linguistik Aktuell 13. Amsterdam: Benjamins.

12. THE UGARITIC ALPHABETIC CUNEIFORM WRITING SYSTEM IN THE CONTEXT OF OTHER ALPHABETIC SYSTEMS[1]

Dennis Pardee

For the last three-quarters of a century, the archaeological site of Ras Shamra on the north Syrian coast, where a Late Bronze Age city bearing the name of "Ugarit" was located, has provided innumerable treasures that allow us bit by bit to understand how life was lived on the Levantine coast three thousand years ago.[2] The palace of the king has been released from the dust of the millennia, as have many private dwellings, both great and small, the streets and paths that crisscrossed the town, the temples and sanctuaries where the many gods of the pantheon received their offerings, the ceremonial entrance to the city on its western side, and all kinds of smaller objects.[3] Among the latter, a special place must be reserved for the approximately 4,500 objects bearing texts which have added the words of the men and women of the time to the mute testimony of the uninscribed objects.[4] Most of the texts were inscribed on clay tablets and more than half of these documents were couched in a writing system and a language that was already well known in 1929 when the first tablets began appearing: I refer to Akkadian, the Semitic language of Mesopotamia which had become by the middle of the second millennium B.C.E. the *lingua franca* of the entire Near East, from Iran to Egypt and including Anatolia and Syria. But alongside these texts which could be read immediately by the Assyriologists, tablets inscribed with an unknown system were a part of the very earliest tablet discoveries in May of 1929 (Schaeffer 1956). It was well known at the time that the Mesopotamian system, which had been invented to write Sumerian, had subsequently been adapted for the setting down of texts in languages linguistically unrelated to Sumerian, first Akkadian, then Hittite, Elamite, Hurrian, and Urartian. What the archaeologists had uncovered at Ras Shamra, however, was something very different: a new cuneiform system that had nothing in common with the Mesopotamian system but the fact that the signs were formed by pressing a stylus into clay.

Because the writing system was new, it had to be deciphered, which was basically accomplished within a year by three scholars working more or less independently, two French and one German. They had noticed very early on that what appeared to be individual words were set off one from another by a small vertical wedge and that the words thus set off were usually made up of from one to five signs; this observation led to the hypothesis that the language being represented might belong to the western Semitic group of which the principal representatives are Arabic, Aramaic, and Hebrew. To test this hypothesis, they attempted to identify words known from these languages in the new texts. At first working by trial and error, they had succeeded by the end of the first year in identifying correctly about one-half of the new signs with graphemes representing consonantal phonemes in the other languages. The basic hypothesis thus appeared to be well on its way to being proved, and the three pioneers rapidly published their results and continued their research with the purpose of a full decipherment; from this stage on, the results attained plus the possibility of comparing one's own work with that of colleagues had a snowball effect and within another year almost all the signs of the new writing system were identified to the satisfaction of the Semitists working on these texts. Because of scribal variation in the production of individual signs, some ambiguities remained and others arose with the passage of time and the discovery of new texts, but the pioneering work of C. Virolleaud, E. Dhorme, and H. Bauer[5] permitted the tablets to be read and launched the process of

---

[1] A preliminary version of this article intended for the French-speaking general public has appeared in Pardee 2004. This version contains the gist of my argument and some of the illustrations but only a few footnotes and is considerably simplified.

[2] From the immense bibliography on things Ugaritic, practical considerations permit the mention of only a few recent items that may be considered both basic and informative for readers unacquainted with the field: Yon 1997b; Pardee 1997c, 1997d; and Watson and Wyatt 1999.

[3] The most up-to-date presentation of the sectors of the city and of a small selection of the artifacts discovered there is by Yon (1997a), now available in English translation (Yon 2006).

[4] All inscribed objects discovered through the 1988 campaign were catalogued by Bordreuil et al. (1989). The statistics extractable therefrom have been altered by the continued discovery of tablets in the "House of Urtenu," where some 500 additional tablets and fragments have been discovered from 1992 through the last major campaign in 2002.

[5] See the very detailed study of the historical process of decipherment by Day (2002).

understanding those upon which the initial research was carried out and those that were to continue coming to light with virtually every new digging campaign.

Thus a new branch of ancient history was born, based on a body of texts that were inscribed in the thirteenth century B.C.E. and which included myths, ritual texts, letters, treaties and contracts, medical texts, economic texts, and even, as we shall see, scribal exercises. These new data permit a better understanding of the first-millennium textual corpora, whether Aramaic, Hebrew, or Phoenician. The study of the Hebrew Bible, for example, acquired a new facet, for the earlier texts from Ugarit provided a hitherto unknown background for the biblical texts: details of Canaanite religion known only by allusions in the biblical text were now fleshed out by myths, ritual texts, and lists of divine names.[6]

My intention here is not, however, to discuss Ugaritic literature, but the Ugaritic writing system and its place in the larger picture of alphabetic writing systems.

It is important to make two aspects of the latter question clear from the beginning: the present state of epigraphic discovery in the Near East obliges us to accept that the system of writing known from the Ugaritic texts must have been invented at Ugarit — because that is the only place yet uncovered where significant numbers of texts inscribed by means of that system have been found — but there can be no doubt that the alphabet itself had been invented some centuries earlier. Two other groups of inscriptions, poorly understood but certainly alphabetic, exist; these are known by their place of origin as "Proto-Sinaitic" — because found primarily in the Sinai — and "Proto-Canaanite" — because found in Canaan.[7] The recent discovery of inscriptions of the Proto-Sinaitic type in the western desert of Egypt shows that the use of alphabetic writing was not limited to the Sinai.[8] Egyptologists are not in agreement on the dating of these texts because they were not found in stratified contexts, but no one to my knowledge dates them any later than the fifteenth century and some date them as early as the nineteenth century (Middle Kingdom), a date which some now believe to be corroborated by the Wadi el-Hol discoveries. On the other hand, some of the Proto-Canaanite inscriptions were discovered in stratified contexts and the oldest appear to go back to the seventeenth century. It appears clear, therefore, that the alphabetic principle was known and that a system of alphabetic writing was actually in use in northern Egypt and in Canaan during the first half of the second millennium B.C.E. An overly enthusiastic view of the Ugaritic alphabetic writing system as representing the invention of the alphabet — a view that I have set up as a straw man but which one actually encounters occasionally — must therefore be rejected.

Now, what about alphabetic cuneiform? I first discuss the characteristics of the system then offer some thoughts on dating its inception.

The decipherment of the new system of writing which I have just described would have gone more rapidly if a discovery of the twelfth campaign had taken place during the first. I refer to the first abecedary recognized as such by C. Virolleaud, principal epigrapher for the Mission de Ras Shamra:[9] it was discovered in 1948 during the first campaign at Ras Shamra after World War II and it bears the excavation number RS 12.063 (fig. 12.1).[10] "Abecedary" is the term used for an inscription consisting of the letters of the alphabet in the order conventionally adopted for learning purposes by the scribes of a given culture. This particular example by its perfect state of preservation not only eliminated any residual doubt regarding the number of signs of which the Ugaritic system

---

[6] An expert comparison of Ugarit and the Bible has not appeared in English in recent years, although several of the articles in the *Handbook of Ugaritic Studies* (Watson and Wyatt 1999) are relevant. In German, see Loretz 1990.

[7] I have provided a brief *status questionis* with bibliography on these two groups of inscriptions; see Pardee 1997a, 1997b.

[8] One may find various views on these inscriptions by entering "Wadi el-Hol" in any Internet search engine. For a published "first try" at decipherment, see Wimmer and Wimmer-Dweikat 2001. For the finder's first published statement (of which I am aware) on the implications of these inscriptions for the history of the alphabet, see Darnell 2003.

[9] At least two other partial abecedaries had been discovered in earlier campaigns, but because of their state of preservation, they were not recognized immediately as such by Virolleaud: RS 10.081, published as an enigmatic text (Virolleaud 1940–41: 34) but soon recognized by him to be a partial abecedary in 1948–1949 (see Virolleaud 1951: 23), and RS 5.274, published three times as an enigmatic text (Herdner 1963: 290, text 215; Dietrich et al. 1976: 424, text 7.54; idem 1995: 526, text 7.54) and recognized only in 1999 by my then-student Robert C. Hawley as a fragment of an abecedary.

[10] It was published in Virolleaud 1951: 22–23 just before the re-publication of RS 10.081 as an abecedary. Because of its state of preservation and landmark status in the history of the alphabet, this abecedary has become an icon in Syria, where it is rightly considered a national treasure and has been reproduced innumerable times in various formats, in particular on the five-hundred pound bank note.

was made up but it also demonstrated the extremely close relationship that existed between this cuneiform system and the linear writing used to inscribe the first-millennium inscriptions. "Linear writing" as used here refers to writing effected on a hard surface, whether by pen and ink or by inscribing stone or metal, and reflecting one of the stages of the alphabet evolved from the original pseudo-pictographic sign forms. The close relationship between this cuneiform writing and the linear system is assured by the fact that the conventional order was essentially identical at Ugarit and in first-millennium Syria-Palestine.

The table in figure 12.2 shows the signs of the Ugaritic alphabet, based on the inscribed version of RS 12.063, and it allows an immediate comparison with the alphabet in which the first-millennium texts were inscribed, that is, the Phoenician alphabet that was borrowed by speakers of Aramaic and Hebrew for the purpose of writing texts in their languages. The first thing to note is that the Ugaritic abecedary consists of thirty signs whereas the Phoenician/Hebrew repertory includes only twenty-two signs. (Hebraists will remember, however, that there are indications that the number of consonantal phonemes in Hebrew was greater and that the Hebrew phonetic system must originally have differed from that of the Phoenicians from whom Hebrew speakers borrowed the alphabet; see, for example, the methodologically rigorous study of Blau 1982.) In the history of the study of Ugaritic, it took a while for the nature of the last three signs to become clear, that is, that they express variants of phonemes represented by preceding signs rather than independent phonemes. Thus the phonemic inventory represented by this abecedary numbered twenty-seven rather than thirty. Signs #28 and #29 are variants of the first sign, that which corresponds to *aleph* in Hebrew. The reigning hypothesis today regarding these signs is that they all consist of the glottal stop that is represented by *aleph* alone in the other West Semitic languages and that the variants represent this consonantal character plus a vocalic variation: /ʼ/ + /a/ for the first (#1 — as a grapheme corresponding to a pure consonant, this was the first sign of the old linear alphabet), /ʼ/ + /i/ for the second (#28), and /ʼ/ + /u/ for the third (#29). It appears likely that the extra *aleph*s were invented for the purposes of writing other languages where a syllable can begin with a vowel, for example, Akkadian or Hurrian, something that cannot occur in the ancient West Semitic languages. It is no less the case, however, that the signs are used with some consistency as syllabograms when the language inscribed is Ugaritic. The most plausible explanation of #30 is that it actually represents a phonetic evolution of another phoneme, #19 corresponding to *samekh* in Hebrew, which according to this theory would have expressed an affricate when *samekh* itself had become, or was becoming, a fricative (Tropper 1995: 505–28). One will note immediately that these explanations of the extra signs imply that the order of the alphabet was considered fixed and invariable at the point when they were added.

The basic repertory of consonantal phonemes expressed by the Ugaritic writing system was thus twenty-seven, two fewer than in Old South Arabian, the writing system of which constitutes a one-to-one representation of the most complete system of consonantal phonemes attested for a Semitic language: twenty-nine graphemes for twenty-nine consonantal phonemes. Ugaritic has no sign for what in Hebrew is known as *śin* (specialists of Old South Arabian represent it as s^2) — this phoneme had fused with *šin* whereas in Hebrew it is *šin* that fused with *ṯa* — and no sign for what in Arabic is known as *ḍād* — this phoneme disappeared from all the Northwest Semitic languages. The tradition of alphabetic learning is established at Ugarit by well over a dozen abecedaries, all of which show the same order.[11] It is nevertheless the case that there exist clear indications that the writing system did not correspond perfectly to the phonetic system of the language: {ḏ}, for example, #16, is used relatively rarely, most commonly in proper nouns of non-Semitic origin, and the historical phoneme that it represents is usually rendered by {d} (#5), as in Aramaic (cf. the relative/determinative pronoun written {d} which corresponds to /dū/ in Arabic and to /dᵊ/ or /dīʸ/ in Aramaic but to /zeʰ/ in Hebrew). The phoneme /ẓ/ (#18) appears also to be on its way out, for it is represented frequently by {ṣ} (#22), sometimes by {ġ} (#26). These facts may be interpreted in one of two ways: either the Ugaritic alphabet was already ancient when the texts we know were written, and the language would have evolved while the graphic system retained its ancient form; or else the alphabet borrowed

---

[11] In Dietrich et al. 1995: 490–97, fourteen tablets are transcribed that include one or more alphabetic sequences, partial or whole, in various states of preservation. To this number are to be added RS 5.274 (see n. 8) and RS 94.2440 (see below). On the special case of the *halaḥam* abecedary, see below.

by the Ugaritians would have been borrowed from another people who spoke a language that was similar but not identical to Ugaritic. In favor of a borrowing, one may cite the existence of signs ##28–30, for these were clearly added to a pre-existing graphic inventory.

When the Ugaritic consonantal inventory and the order in which the scribes learned the alphabet are compared with Hebrew/Phoenician, the conclusion is unavoidable that the order of the elements of the two systems was identical and that the distribution of the five extra signs in the Ugaritic system was in some sense random. Rather, however, than considering that the Ugaritians borrowed the alphabet from a twenty-two grapheme tradition and then simply inserted the five signs randomly to express additional consonantal phonemes, a more likely hypothesis is that the alphabet was invented for a particular West Semitic language of which the inventory of consonantal phonemes numbered at least twenty-seven and that the Phoenician twenty-two sign alphabet represents a phonetic simplification of an older system (where {ḫ} #4 has fused with {ḥ} #9, {š} #13 with {ṯ} #25, {ḏ} #16 with {z} #8, {ẓ} #18 with {ṣ} #22, and {ġ} #26 with {ʿ} #20). This distribution of the consonants according to the older order attested by Ugaritic indicates that the Phoenician system represents the reduction of an older system; if the Ugaritic system were secondary to a system like the Phoenician one, it appears that the five extra signs would have been tacked on at the end as was the case with the manifestly secondary signs, ##28–30, and as was the case with the signs added after *tau* by the Greeks when they adapted the Phoenician writing system to their own needs (see Baurain et al. 1991, esp. Brixhe 1991 and Piérart 1991).

In summary to this point, the examination of a Ugaritic abecedary shows that the Ugaritic graphic system represents an older system made up of at least the twenty-seven elements known from the first twenty-seven signs of the Ugaritic system. This graphic inventory may have been borrowed relatively late from an alphabetic tradition that made use of twenty-seven signs or it may represent a local usage that goes back several centuries.

Before discussing in more detail these questions of origin and dating, it may be instructive to take a quick look at the various forms taken by the Ugaritic abecedaries which, it may be added here, provide the broadest range of these scribal exercises known for a given language or writing tradition of the ancient Near East. RS 12.063 consisted, as we have seen, of a single sequence of the thirty signs used by the scribes of Ugarit and it was written by a single scribe who already had a reasonably well-practiced hand. RS 24.281 (fig. 12.3), on the other hand, bears two abecedaries, the first on the top part of the tablet, the second under this one. Each clearly reflects the hand of a different scribe and the top example appears to represent the better hand. One may conclude that a teacher wrote out the top version while the lower is the work of an apprentice scribe. Note that the student faithfully placed each sign directly under the model inscribed by the master, but that he started writing along the bottom edge of the tablet, which forced him to place the last eight signs, when he got around to writing them, above the beginning of the alphabet. One may also note that the student's wedges tend to be broader than the master's and that he has difficulty organizing the wedges of the complex signs ({d} #5, {r} #24, {i} #28, and {ś} #30).

RS 94.2440 (fig. 12.4) also bears two abecedaries, but here the signs of the second were not placed directly under the corresponding signs of the first and, moreover, four additional lines of writing are found here, each bearing one or two geographical names *ʾAtalligu, Mulukku, ʾAru, Ḫalbu Rapši,* and *Ḫalbu Karradi,* with all but the first of these additional lines placed upside-down from the perspective of the abecedaries. There are awkwardly made signs throughout this exercise, which appears to be from the hand of a single apprentice scribe. There is also what can only be described as a repeated mistake since the phenomenon is unattested elsewhere: each instance of {r} in lines 4, 5, and 6, as well as the {r} in the first abecedary, contains six wedges instead of the canonical five (one extra at the right).

RS 16.265 (fig. 12.5) attests to a much more complicated set of exercises: on the *recto* there is a letter, on the *verso* a series of disparate words, and on the right, upper, and left edges the initial signs only of three abecedaries, in two cases through sign #11 {y} and once only through sign #5 {d}. This latter version is very awkwardly inscribed and one of the five forms is incorrect (the {b} #2 is actually a {d} #5). The hand of the letter is firm and professional, but its content leaves no doubt that we are dealing with a bit of scribal humor:

1.	[t]ḫm iṯtl	[Me]ssage of ʾIṯtēlu
2.	l mnn . ilm	to MNN: May the gods
3.	tǵrk . tšlmk	guard you, may they keep you well,
4.	tʿzzk . ảlp ym	may they strengthen you, for a thousand days
5.	w rbt . šnt	and ten thousand years,
6.	b ʿd ʿlm ****[12]	through the endless reaches of time.
7.	iršt . ȧršt	A request I would make
8.	l ảḫy . l rʿy	of my brother, my friend,
9.	w ytnnn	and may he grant it
10.	l ảḫh . l rʿh	to his brother, his friend,
11.	rʿ ʿlm . ******	(his) friend forever:
12.	ttn . w tn	May you give, and give!,
13.	w l ttn	and may you indeed give,
14.	w ȧl ttn	and will you not certainly give?,
	Lower Edge	
15.	tn ks yn	give (me) a cup of wine
16.	w ištn	that I might drink!

The awkward writing of the abecedaries, in particular the one on the upper edge, shows them to be by another hand. The writing on the left edge (fig. 12.6) is also very different from that of the main text; in particular the {d} of which the lower wedges, usually horizontals, are virtually verticals with the head down.

A final peculiarity of the alphabetic cuneiform writing system at Ugarit is that it appears in two fundamentally different forms, the long form consisting of thirty elements of which I have spoken to this point and a short form.[13] The short form is not yet illustrated by an abecedary and its precise configuration is for that reason uncertain. It is attested by a small number of texts that can only be interpreted by recourse to the theory of a writing system consisting of fewer elements than are to be found in the standard system, for certain sequences of signs may only be interpreted as meaningful words if it is assumed that a single sign in this system may represent two graphemes in the standard writing system. Moreover, these texts were inscribed from right to left, as is the case with the first-millennium Northwest Semitic inscriptions, rather than from left to right as is normally the case with Ugaritic. Several of these texts were found outside the borders of the kingdom of Ugarit and one of them, the jar-handle inscription from Sarepta, has been identified as expressing a brief text in the Phoenician language (Greenstein 1976; Bordreuil 1979). Indeed, none of the texts in the short alphabet discovered at Ugarit is long enough or detailed enough to determine whether the language is Ugaritic or Phoenician. It is thus a distinct possibility that the short alphabet was created by reducing the number of elements of the regular Ugaritic alphabet for the purpose of writing Phoenician — which could mean, of course, that the consonantal phonetic inventory of Phoenician had already been reduced to twenty-two by the end of the Late Bronze Age.

This overview of the alphabets and abecedaries discovered at Ras Shamra would be incomplete without the mention of an abecedary discovered in 1988 which belongs neither to the tradition represented by the other abecedaries known to date nor to the tradition represented by the texts written in the so-called short alphabet. The text in question is RS 88.2215 (fig. 12.7),[14] an abecedary consisting of twenty-seven elements but arranged in the order adopted by the scribes in the South Semitic tradition known as the "halaḥam" tradition because the first four signs are {h, l, ḥ, m}. It appears clear, however, that the purpose of this abecedary was not simply to set down the Ugaritic alphabet in another order, for several of the signs show forms that either result from a 90° rotation to the

---

[12] The asterisks here and in line 11 represent the cuneiform "doodles" visible on the tablet after these lines.

[13] The most complete presentation of the data on the short alphabet is by Dietrich and Loretz (1988). See also Bordreuil's (1981) epigraphic study of the best preserved of the texts written in the short alphabet.

[14] *Editio princeps* by Bordreuil and Pardee (2001: 341–48, text 32).

left (e.g., {š}, the fourth sign in line 2, or {z}, the second sign in the last line, which by this rotation has taken the form of {à} in the standard system) or else are simply very different from the standard form (e.g., {ṭ}, the first sign in line 4). It appears equally clear that the purpose of the abecedary was not simply to set down the graphemes of the South Arabian tradition, for, half a millennium later, the graphemic inventory of the earliest datable Old South Arabian texts clearly numbered twenty-nine, not twenty-seven.[15] The tradition represented by this abecedary did not arrive at Ugarit without leaving traces elsewhere, though, for a similar version was found at Beth-Shemesh in Palestine in the 1930s (Bordreuil and Pardee 2001: 342, bibliography in n. 3), also in cuneiform script on clay but written from right to left in the form of a circle around the outer edge of flattened ball of clay. To date no inscription in a South Arabian language has been discovered at Ugarit and no inscription at all, other than this abecedary and its counterpart from Beth-Shemesh,[16] is attested that would represent the language that this twenty-seven element system was used to set down in writing. Other discoveries are awaited that would allow us to go beyond pure speculation in attempting to explain why this abecedary was inscribed at or found its way to Ugarit.[17]

We may now take up the question of dating the invention of the alphabetic cuneiform writing system at Ugarit. Because the Akkadian texts from Ras Shamra refer to a king Niqmaddu, who would have been on the throne early in the second half of the fourteenth century B.C.E., and because the most famous scribe in the Ugaritic tradition, a certain Ilimilku, described himself as the servant of a king named Niqmaddu, it was long believed that the Ugaritic writing system could not have been invented any later than about 1350 B.C.E. I, like most of my colleagues, believed it necessary to say that the Ugaritic writing system must have been in use for a period of approximately two centuries, from the first half of the fourteenth century down to the destruction of Ugarit sometime in the second decade of the twelfth century. And I hasten to add that there does not yet exist any certain proof that this tableau is not the correct one. But a tablet discovered in 1992 has made us reconsider the pros and the cons of that hypothesis. I refer to RS 92.2016 (fig. 12.8),[18] which bears a badly preserved text with mythological motifs but, perhaps more importantly, a colophon (line 40′) belonging to the series of colophons inscribed by Ilimilku in which he identifies himself as the scribe of the text in question. In these colophons, he names his hometown as Šubannu and states that he was a student of ʾAtanu the divining-priest. On the new text, the name of the scribe has broken off at the left, but the two other elements are present, the name of the town and the name of the teacher (fig. 12.8), and it thus appears 99% sure that Ilimilku was the scribe of this text. Now, virtually all the texts from the archive where this text was found date from the last decades of the thirteenth century. The tablets belonged to the archives of an important personage name Urtenu. In the texts, the kings Ammistamru, Ibiranu, Niqmaddu, and Ammurapi are named, the last kings of Ugarit who occupied the throne from about 1260 to about 1185 B.C.E. So if this new Ilimilku text was inscribed in the fourteenth century, Urtenu must have inherited it from his ancestors. That is, of course, not impossible, but it cannot be judged a certainty, either. To some of us, it even appears more plausible that the Niqmaddu under whom he served was the last to bear this name, the one who reigned near the end of the thirteenth century rather than the one who reigned around the middle of the fourteenth century. An examination of the archive known as the Library of the High Priest, where the other texts bearing a colophon of Ilimilku were found, has led to the conclusion that those texts also belong to the end of the Late Bronze Age, rather than a century and a half earlier (Dalix 1997a).

---

[15] For a recent overview of the situation in Old South Arabian epigraphy, see Nebes and Stein 2004.

[16] The tablet bearing the Beth-Shemesh version is rather badly damaged and the precise order and number of signs is for this reason uncertain. There are clearly, however, two principal differences between that version and RS 88.2215: {b} (#9 in RS 88.2215 and in the traditional South Arabian order) appears to have been omitted entirely and {d} (#11 in RS 88.2215) appears to have been located near the end of the abecedary (where the South Arabian tradition places it). For a detailed comparison of the two abecedaries, see Bordreuil and Pardee 2001: 345–48.

[17] As is well known today, two ostraca bearing signs that resemble linear Old South Arabian signs were discovered in 1968 in a Late Bronze Age stratum at Kamid el-Loz in Lebanon (Mansfeld 1969). Dietrich and Loretz 1988: 63 refer to these as "Das *missing link* zwischen der nördlichen und südlichen Alphabettradition" and in the course of their study took them as the theoretical basis for interpreting certain Ugaritic sign forms as reflecting the Old South Arabian form rather than the Canaanite linear form (see ibid., pp. 101–27). I have never considered it plausible that the inventor of the Ugaritic cuneiform alphabet would have borrowed his base forms willy-nilly from two alphabetic traditions, but because the cuneiform rendition represents such an abstraction of the original (to the point that not everyone believes that the cuneiform alphabet is in fact a direct representation of linear forms), there are few hard data by which to judge. On the cases of {g} and {ś}, see further discussion below.

[18] *Editio princeps* by A. Caquot and A.-S. Dalix (2001, text 53).

What other proofs are cited in favor of the hypothesis that the Ugaritic alphabet would already have been in use in the fourteenth century? Two are commonly cited, the Ugaritic version of a treaty between a Hittite sovereign named Shuppiluliuma and a king of Ugarit named Niqmaddu (RS 11.772+) and a letter where it is claimed that Amenhotep III of Egypt is mentioned by his cognomen Nimuria (RS 18.113A).

Parallels between the Ugaritic treaty, RS 11.772+, and a series of Akkadian texts that go back to as early as the time of Shuppiluliuma I, king of Hatti around the middle of the fourteenth century, have led to a virtual unanimity among historians in identifying the Ugaritic text as the version in the local language of one of these texts from the time of Shuppiluliuma I.[19] Recently, however, A.-S. Dalix (1998) published a study of the archive where the Ugaritic text was discovered, the so-called Western Palace Archive, and she concluded that most of these texts date to the late thirteenth to early twelfth century (cf. Dalix 1997b)[20] — just like the texts from the Library of the High Priest. In my new study of the Ugaritic treaty just cited (Pardee 2001), I claim (1) that there are no archaic epigraphic features present, and (2) that the differences between this text and the Akkadian texts are important enough to preclude seeing the Ugaritic text as a simple translation of one of the known Akkadian texts. The hypothesis according to which the Ugaritic treaty is to be dated to the time of Shuppiluliuma II and the last Niqmaddu requires, of course, accepting that the relations between those kings would have been similar to those between their ancestors a century and a half earlier and that these relations would have been set down in a text that was very similar to the Akkadian texts dating to the fourteenth century; such a text has not been discovered in any other language, Akkadian or Hittite, and many historians doubt that the situations could have been so similar.[21] On the other hand, I know of no data that would directly rule out this historical reconstruction, but I am not a historian and certainly not a Hittitologist.[22] Yet another hypothesis exists to explain the apparently late Ugaritic version: it would represent a late Ugaritic translation of one of the fourteenth-century Akkadian documents. This is certainly a possible explanation — I cannot say how plausible but certainly possible — but it requires this qualification: the Akkadian text that would have been translated according to this hypothesis certainly is not one that survived the destruction of the city of Ugarit for, as I have already said, the differences between the Ugaritic text and the known Akkadian texts are too great to allow the late-translation hypothesis to be based on any known Akkadian text.

The other textual indication of the antiquity of the Ugaritic writing system would date somewhat earlier than the one just discussed, for Amenhotep III was on the throne of Egypt a few years before Shuppiluliuma I and RS 18.113A would be even older than the treaty document just discussed. As early as 1974, however, A. F. Rainey (1974: 188) proposed that the word *nmry* in line 9, which the editor of the text interpreted as the proper name Nimuria, was in fact a Semitic word meaning 'splendor', an interpretation accepted since by other scholars (van Soldt 1983: col. 693; idem 1990: 345 n. 164; idem 1991: 88; Dijkstra 1999: 158; Singer 1999: 678; see also p. 623 n. 67, and p. 631 n. 87).[23] This interpretation appears perfectly plausible to me, for Rainey's suggestion was based on the appearance of a very similar word, one ending in {t} rather than {y}, in a Ugaritic text discovered in 1961 and published in 1968 (RS 24.252: 23') where it can only refer to the splendor characteristic of royalty.[24] A masculine form with enclitic -*y* could easily be a variant of *nmrt* with a similar meaning.[25] Moreover, the meaning

---

[19] The relevant bibliography is indicated in my recent re-study of this text (Pardee 2001).

[20] W. H. van Soldt had already come to the conclusion of a late dating of the Western Archive (1991: 57–58), but he considered RS 11.772+ to be an exception to the generality.

[21] One of my French colleagues, J. Freu, had the kindness to send me the manuscript of an article before its publication in which he utterly rejects the hypothesis that RS 11.772+ could represent a treaty dating to the late thirteenth century (Freu 2004).

[22] While it does not appear to me to be out of the question that the Ugaritic text could represent a treaty between Niqmaddu III and Shuppiluliuma II near the end of the thirteenth century, Dalix's suggestion to re-date the known Akkadian texts to these two rulers (1997b: 824; 1998: 14 n. 54) must be judged completely out of the question — so out of the question that I did not even address it in my article on RS 11.772+ (Pardee 2001). Just to leave no doubt in anyone's mind, however, refuting this suggestion is the principal burden of Freu's article (2004).

[23] As early as 1962, M. Liverani expressed doubt about the identification with Amenhotep III (1962: 28 n. 6), but in 1979 he described the identification as "probable" (col. 1298).

[24] *Editio princeps* by C. Virolleaud (1968: 551–57). See my re-edition of this text (Pardee 1988: 75–118), especially the discussion of *nmrt* on p. 115.

[25] Because of the /m/ in both forms, both would have to be loanwords from Akkadian, for the root is NWR 'to be light, bright; to burn', and word-internal /W/ may go to /M/ in Akkadian but does so in none of the old West Semitic languages. Though the fact of the loan may be considered hypothetical, the existence of real corresponding words in Akkadian is not: *nmrt* could correspond either to *namirtu* or to *namurratu*, both denoting 'brightness', particularly that of divinity or royalty, while *nmry* would correspond to a formally masculine form to which the Ugaritic enclitic morpheme -*y* has been attached (*namirrū*, a *plurale tantum* meaning 'supernatural, awe-inspiring luminosity' is the best-attested such form in Akkadian, but a direct loan of that particular word into Ugaritic would be expected to be written {nmrr}).

of the passage where this word is found goes against the Egyptian interpretation, for it speaks of gods worshipped in the kingdom of Ugarit and refers explicitly to "all the gods of Alashia," that is, of Cyprus. In grammatical terms, *nmry* would be the direct object of the verb *rgmt* in line 6 and the literal translation of the phrase would be "I pronounce to the gods the splendor of eternal kingship," that is, that of the king to whom the letter is addressed, apparently the king of Ugarit to whom an underling is writing from Cyprus.

What, then, are the oldest certainly datable examples of the Ugaritic script? There are in fact several, all dating to the reign of Ammistamru II, who may have taken the throne around 1260 B.C.E. and died about a quarter of a century later.[26] His personal seal, inscribed in Ugaritic, is known from two sources, the first a double impression on the tablet RS 16.270 (fig. 12.9), a contract in the Akkadian language dating to the time of Ammistamru II; the second a triple impression on a bulla discovered at the neighboring site of Ras Ibn Hani in 1983 (RIH 83/21; fig. 12.10). The seal was inscribed so as to be read from the seal itself, not from the impression as is usually the case; the impressions appear, therefore, in mirror-image with the text running from right to left. The text, which reads *mišmn ʿmyḏtmr mlk ủgrt* 'Seal of ʿAmmīyiḏtamru, king of Ugarit', shows two important peculiarities: the archaic form of the royal name and the archaic form of one of the signs.

The standard Akkadian writing of the royal name reflects a pronunciation *Ammistamru* while the normal Ugaritic writing, {ʿmṯtr} for ʿAmmiṯtamru, reflects only the frequent correspondence of Ugaritic {ṯ} to Akkadian /s/. But here the form is {ʿmyḏtmr}, to be pronounced something like /ʿammīyiḏtamru/ in the cased form or /ʿammīyiḏtamir/ in the absolute form. This writing reveals that the name is based on the root ḎMR 'to guard, to care for'. The commonly attested form ʿAmmiṯtamru thus shows reduction of the triphthong /īyi/ and devoicing of the /ḏ/ in contact with the /t/.[27] Because only the contracted form of the name appears in all the other documents of the fourteenth and thirteenth centuries, that is, for both Ammistamru I and Ammistamru II, there are no data on the chain of tradition that allowed the king or a scholar of his court to be aware of the older form of the name. It does appear legitimate to say, however, that it was the king himself who wanted the archaic form of his name to appear on his personal seal.

The archaic sign-form on the seal is the {g} in line 3 (second sign of the place name *ủgrt* — visible on both impressions on RS 16.270 and on two of the three on RIH 83/21). It was carved in the stone of the seal by the scribe in the form of two wedges whereas the more commonly attested form is that of a single vertical wedge. A two-wedged form is attested in various clay-inscribed texts, for example, in RS 15.111: 4 (fig. 12.11), also dated to the time of Ammistamru II, though here and in most of the examples in clay the upper horizontal wedge is not nearly so large as is the vertical wedge. Several examples of this form in texts discovered at Ras Ibn Hani, most of which appear to date to the time of Ammistamru II, may be taken as confirming that the two-wedged form is archaic. Observing that the {g} in the first-millennium linear scripts is made with two strokes, one is tempted to posit that the original Ugaritic form consisted of two wedges, though it would have evolved fairly rapidly to a form produced by simply pivoting the stylus to the right when incising the vertical wedge and finally to the commonly attested form consisting of a simple vertical wedge. Positing that the original form of the {g} had two wedges leads to the further hypothesis that the cuneiform signs were imitations of the linear forms that were current when the cuneiform alphabet was invented, for the first-millennium linear {g} is made with two strokes. Such direct imitation of a linear form is absolutely clear for only one other sign, {s̀} (#30), one of the additional signs that is indubitably an imitation of the Phoenician *samekh*, which consists of three horizontal strokes crossing a vertical. The imitative form of {s̀} that consists of just four wedges, though comparatively rare in the scribal hands of Ugaritic, is clear in RS 94.2440 (fig. 12.12) — more commonly, the long cross-strokes are broken down into sets of three oblique wedges placed on each side of the vertical, as in RS 12.063 (figs. 12.1–2). One might argue that the clearly supplementary nature of this sign rules out using it to prove that the original cuneiform

---

[26] The precise chronology of the kings of Ugarit is unknown because of the absence of good synchronisms with other royal figures for the chronology of whose reigns more numerous data are available. J. Freu (1998: 37) dates the reign of Ammistamru II to 1260–1230 B.C.E., Singer (1999: fold-out after p. 732) to 1260–1235 B.C.E.

[27] For the publication of the bulla from Ras Ibn Hani and this explanation of the full form of the name, see Bordreuil and Pardee 1984. Because of the damage suffered by the impressions on RS 16.270 (see fig. 12.9), the precise reading of the seal based on those impressions had been debated before the discovery of RIH 83/21 and the unambiguous data which became available with these impressions.

alphabet was based directly on the linear alphabet. A counter-argument might say that the process of rendering linear forms into various combinations of triangular impressions in clay involved a level of abstraction that makes most identifications difficult to establish and hence that it is legitimate to exploit the rare clear examples in favor of the hypothesis — one of these is {g}, the third sign of the basic graphemic inventory.

Some brief conclusions, which must begin, "nothing is certain, but...." The most recent discoveries compared with the data known for some time lead me to prefer the hypothesis according to which the alphabet would have been invented in the thirteenth century, perhaps during or shortly before the reign of Ammistamru II, rather than a century or more earlier. I would go so far as to say that until a text which may certainly be dated to an earlier king is attested, the presently attested data allow for no other conclusion, albeit a provisional one that is subject to revision at any time.[28] The combinations of wedges forming these signs would have been in imitation of a linear alphabet used in the region and the repertory of consonantal phonemes in the language represented by that script would have numbered twenty-seven. For absence of data, it is presently impossible to say whether this linear alphabet was actually used at Ugarit before the invention of the cuneiform alphabet or whether this invention represents the borrowing of a neighbor's writing system and its adaptation to the cuneiform principle. If, however, the Ugaritians were previously writing their language by means of a linear script, for example, with pen and ink on papyrus, an explanation is required for why such a light and supple material would have been abandoned in favor of writing on clay.

---

[28] Benjamin Sass was kind enough to show me his article in advance that has since appeared as Saas 2004–5 in which he argues that all the evidence commonly adduced for dating the Proto-Sinaitic and Proto-Canaanite inscriptions earlier than the fourteenth century may be called into question. If his assessment proves to be correct, the time between the invention of the linear alphabet and its adaptation to wedged forms would be in the range of a century rather than half a millennium or more.

On another matter even more relevant to the topic treated in my study, Dr. Sass tells me that he sees no reason to change his views (1988: 165–66) regarding the implausibility of an early dating of one of the Kamid el-Loz sherds bearing an inscription in alphabetic cuneiform. Two such sherds were discovered at this site, one dated securely to the end of the Late Bronze Age, the other at an unrecorded level in an area where materials from both the Middle Bronze Age and Late Bronze Age were discovered.

190   DENNIS PARDEE

Figure 12.1. Ras Shamra Tablet RS 12.063

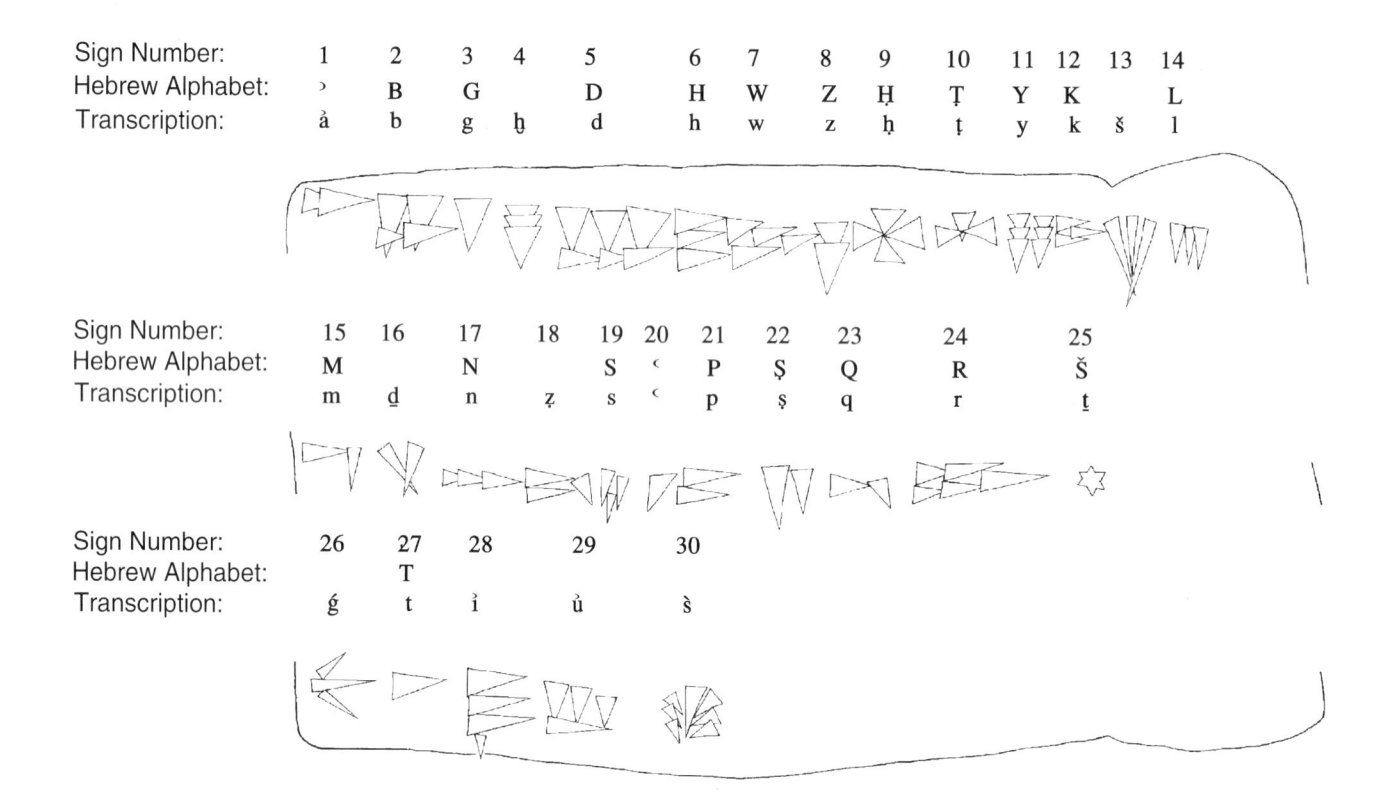

Sign Number:	1	2	3	4	5	6	7	8	9	10	11	12	13	14
Hebrew Alphabet:	ʾ	B	G		D	H	W	Z	Ḥ	Ṭ	Y	K		L
Transcription:	å	b	g	ḫ	d	h	w	z	ḥ	ṭ	y	k	š	l

Sign Number:	15	16	17	18	19	20	21	22	23	24	25
Hebrew Alphabet:	M		N		S	ʿ	P	Ṣ	Q	R	Š
Transcription:	m	ḏ	n	ẓ	s	ʿ	p	ṣ	q	r	ṯ

Sign Number:	26	27	28	29	30
Hebrew Alphabet:		T			
Transcription:	ġ	t	i̓	u̓	ś

Figure 12.2. Ugaritic Alphabet: Comparison with Hebrew Alphabet (Abecedary RS 12.063)

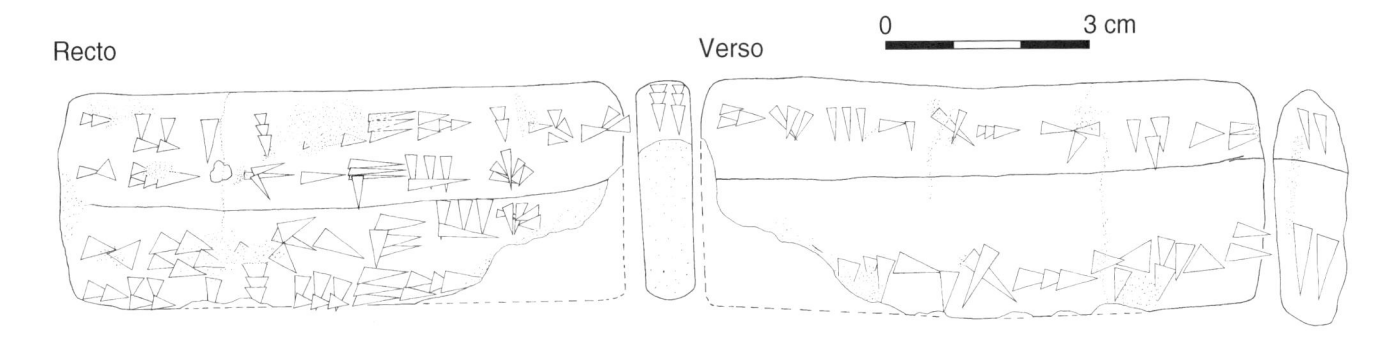

12. UGARITIC ALPHABETIC CUNEIFORM IN THE CONTEXT OF OTHER ALPHABETIC SYSTEMS   191

Figure 12.3. Ras Shamra Text RS 24.281

Figure 12.4. Ras Shamra Text RS 94.2440

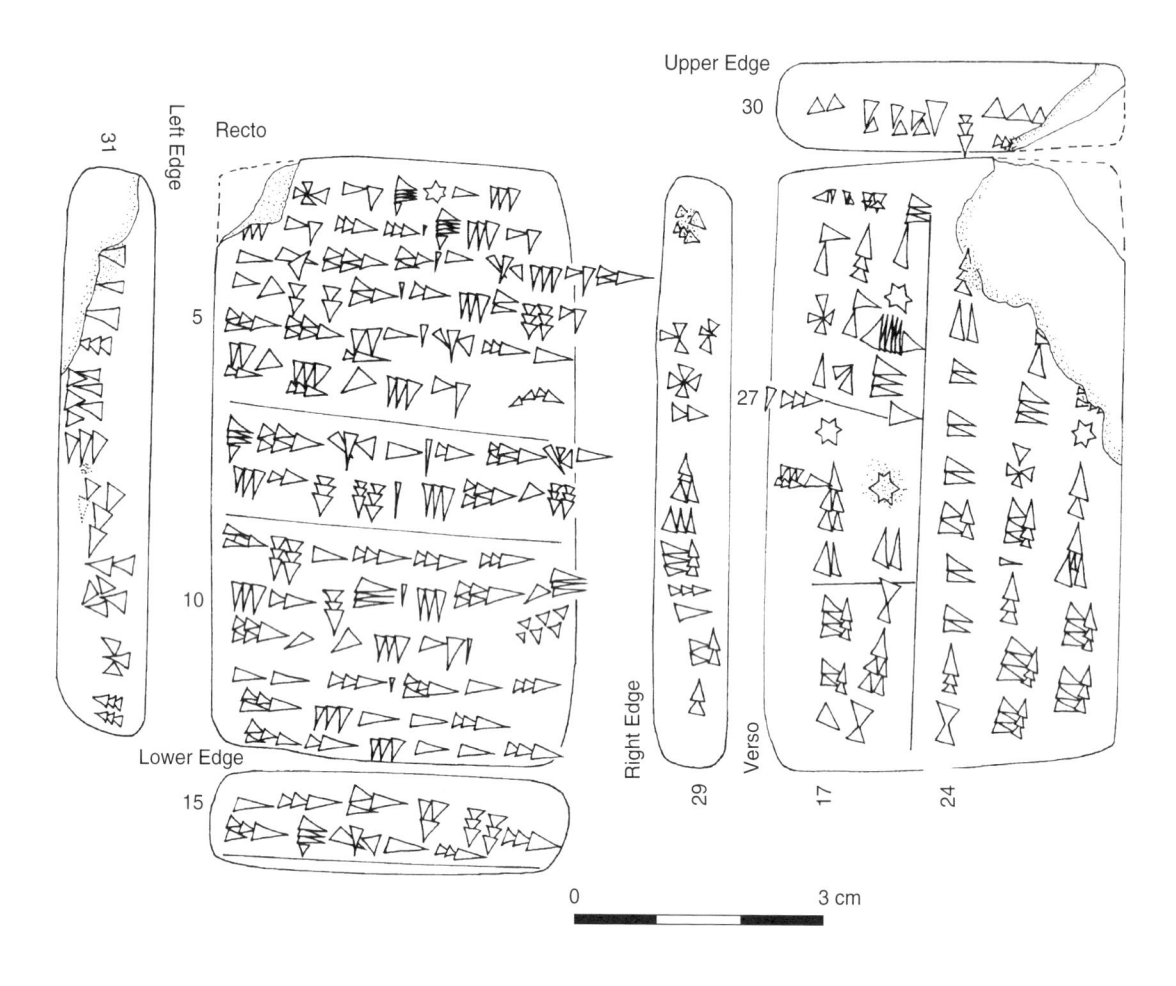

Figure 12.5. Ras Shamra Text RS 16.265

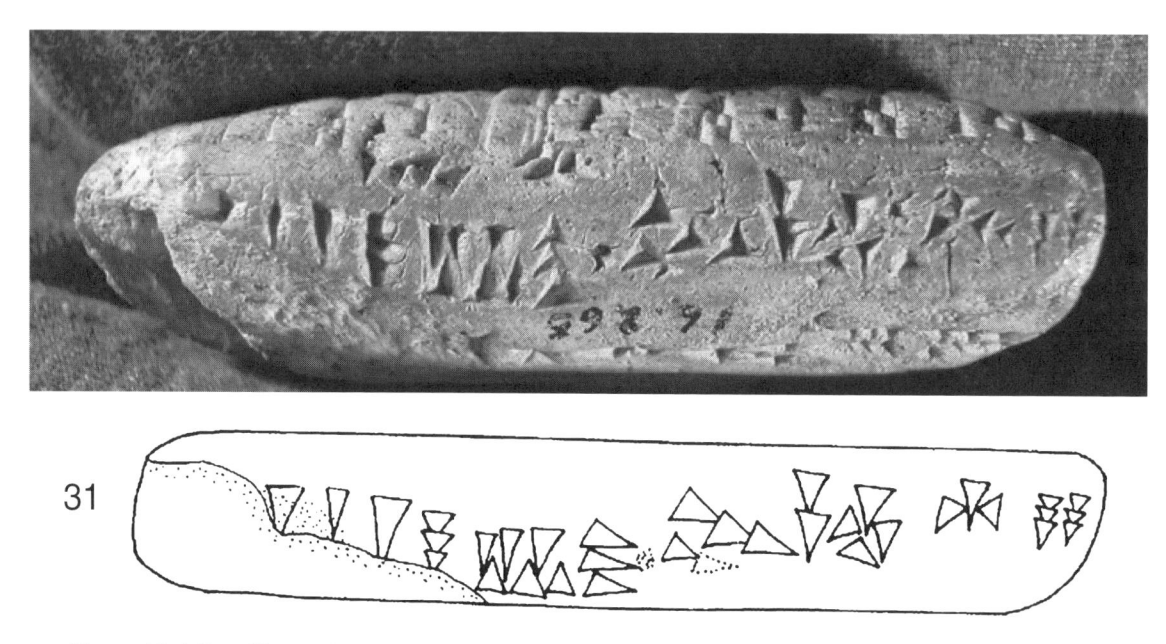

Figure 12.6. Ras Shamra Text RS 16.265 Left Edge showing Different Hand from That of Main Text

12. UGARITIC ALPHABETIC CUNEIFORM IN THE CONTEXT OF OTHER ALPHABETIC SYSTEMS   193

1. h l ḥ m q w ṯ r
2. b t ḏ š k n ḫ ṣ
3. s p ʾ ʿ ḍ g d ġ
4. ṭ z y

Figure 12.7. Ras Shamra Text RS 88.2215

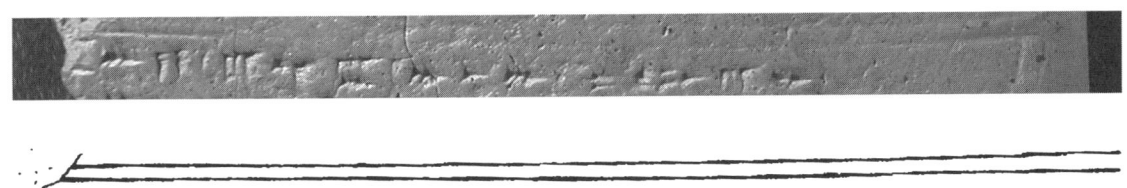

[spr . ỉlmlk . š]ᵣbᵢny . lmd . atn . prln

Scribe: Ilimilku the Shubbanite, student of Atanu the Diviner

Figure 12.8. Ras Shamra Text RS 92.2016, Line 40

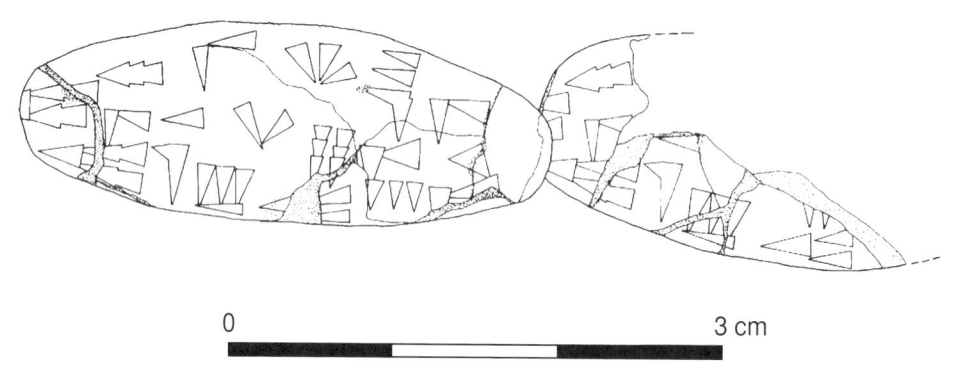

Figure 12.9. Ras Shamra Text RS 16.270 Bearing Double Impression of Personal Seal of Ammistamru II

12. UGARITIC ALPHABETIC CUNEIFORM IN THE CONTEXT OF OTHER ALPHABETIC SYSTEMS

Upper Surface

Long Side

Short Side

0   3 cm

Figure 12.10. Ras Ibn Hani Bulla RIH 83/21 Bearing Triple Impression of Personal Seal of Ammistamru II

Figure 12.11. Ras Shamra Text RS 15.111, Line 4, Showing Two-wedged Archaic Form of {g} in {u̇grt}

a

b

Figure 12.12. Ras Shamra Text RS 94.2440 Showing Imitative, Four-wedged Form of {ṡ}; (*a*) First Abecedary and (*b*) Second Abecedary

Abbreviations

RIH Ras Ibn Hani
RS   Ras Shamra

Bibliography

Baurain, Claude; Corinne Bonnet; and Véronique Krings, editors
    1991   *Phoinikeia grammata: Lire et écrire en Méditerranée* (Actes du Colloque de Liège, 15–18 novembre 1989). Collection d'Études Classiques 6. Namur: Société des Études Classiques.

Blau, Joshua
    1982   *On Polyphony in Biblical Hebrew*. Proceedings of the Israel Academy of Sciences and Humanities 6. Jerusalem: Israel Academy of Sciences and Humanities.

Bordreuil, Pierre
    1979   "L'inscription phénicienne de Sarafand en cunéiformes alphabétiques." *Ugarit-Forschungen* 11: 63–68.
    1981   "Cunéiformes alphabétiques non canoniques. 1) La tablette alphabétique sénestroverse RS 22.03." *Syria* 58: 301–10.

Bordreuil, Pierre, and Dennis Pardee
    1984   "Le sceau nominal de ʿammīyiḏtamrou, roi d'Ougarit." *Syria* 61: 11–14.
    1989   *La trouvaille épigraphique de l'Ougarit*, Volume 1: *Concordance*. Ras Shamra-Ougarit V. Paris: Éditions Recherche sur les Civilisations.
    2001   "Textes alphabétiques en ougaritique." In *Études ougaritiques*, Volume 1: *Travaux 1985–1995*, edited by M. Yon and D. Arnaud, pp. 341–92, 411–14. Ras Shamra-Ougarit XXIV. Paris: Éditions Recherche sur les Civilisations.

Brixhe, C.
    1991   "De la phonologie à l'écriture: Quelques aspects de l'adaptation de l'alphabet cananéen au grec." In *Phoinikeia grammata: Lire et écrire en Méditerranée* (Actes du Colloque de Liège, 15–18 novembre 1989), edited by Claude Baurain, Corinne Bonnet, and Véronique Krings, pp. 313–56. Collection d'Études Classiques 6. Namur: Société des Études Classiques.

Caquot, A., and A.-S. Dalix
    2001   "Un texte mythico-magique." In *Études ougaritiques*, Volume 1: *Travaux 1985–1995*, edited by M. Yon and D. Arnaud, pp. 393–405. Ras Shamra-Ougarit XXIV. Paris: Éditions Recherche sur les Civilisations.

Dalix, A.-S.
    1997a   Iloumilkou, scribe d'Ougarit au XIIIe siècle avant J. C. Ph.D. dissertation, Institut Catholique de Paris et Université de Paris.
    1997b   "Ougarit au XIIIe siècle av. J.-C.: Nouvelles perspectives historiques," *Académie des Inscriptions et Belles-Lettres: Comptes Rendus*, pp. 819–24.
    1998   "Šuppiluliuma (II ?) dans un texte alphabétique d'Ugarit et la date d'apparition de l'alphabet cunéiforme. Nouvelle proposition de datation des 'Archives Ouest.'" *Semitica* 48: 5–15.

Darnell, J. C.

2003 "Die frühalphabetischen Inschriften im Wadi el-Hôl." In *Der Turmbau zu Babel: Ursprung und Vielfalt von Sprache und Schrift: Eine Ausstellung des Kunsthistorischen Museums Wien für die Europäische Kulturhauptstadt Graz 2003. Schloss Eggenberg, Graz 5. April bis 5. Oktober 2003*, Volume 3A, edited by W. Seipel, pp. 165–71. Vienna: Kunsthistorisches Museum; Milan: Skira.

Day, P.

2002 "*Dies diem docet:* The Decipherment of Ugaritic." *Studi Epigrafici e Linguistici* 19: 37–57.

Dietrich, M., and O. Loretz

1988 *Die Keilalphabete: Die phönizisch-kanaanäischen und altarabischen Alphabete in Ugarit.* Abhandlungen zur Literatur Alt-Syrien-Palästinas und Mesopotamiens 1. Münster: Ugarit-Verlag.

Dietrich, M.; O. Loretz; and J. Sanmartín

1976 *Die keilalphabetischen Texte aus Ugarit.* Alter Orient und Altes Testament 24. Kevelaer: Butzon & Bercker; Neukirchen-Vluyn: Neukirchener Verlag.

1995 *The Cuneiform Alphabetic Texts from Ugarit, Ras Ibn Hani and Other Places (KTU).* Second edition. Abhandlungen zur Literatur Alt-Syrien-Palästinas und Mesopotamiens 8. Münster: Ugarit-Verlag.

Dijkstra, M.

1999 "Ugaritic Prose." In *Handbook of Ugaritic Studies*, edited by W. G. E. Watson and Nicolas Wyatt, pp. 140–64. Handbuch der Orientalistik 1; Der Nahe und Mittlere Osten 39. Leiden: Brill.

Freu, J.

1998 "La fin d'Ugarit et de l'Empire hittite. Données nouvelles et chronologie." *Semitica* 48: 17–39.

2004 "Šuppiluliuma I ou Šuppiluliyama (II)?" *Res Antiquae* 1: 111–24.

Greenstein, E. L.

1976 "A Phoenician Inscription in Ugaritic Script?" *Journal of the Ancient Near Eastern Society of Columbia University* 8: 49–57.

Herdner, A.

1963 *Corpus des tablettes en cunéiformes alphabétiques découvertes à Ras Shamra-Ugarit de 1929 à 1939.* Mission de Ras Shamra 10; Bibliothèque Archéologique et Historique 79. Paris: P. Geuthner.

Liverani, M.

1962 *Storia di Ugarit nell'età degli archivi politici.* Studi Semitici 6. Rome: Università di Roma.

1979 *Supplément au Dictionnaire de la Bible*, Volume 9. Paris: Letouzey et Ané.

Loretz, O.

1990 *Ugarit und die Bibel: Kanaanäische Götter und Religion im Alten Testament.* Darmstadt: Wissenschafliche Buchgesellschaft.

Mansfeld, G.

1969 "Deux 'ostrakons' incisés à l'écriture paléo-canaanéene du tell de Kāmid el-Lōz." *Bulletin du Musée de Beyrouth* 22: 67–75.

Nebes, N., and P. Stein

2004 "Ancient South Arabian." In *The Cambridge Encyclopedia of the World's Ancient Languages*, edited by R. D. Woodard, pp. 454–87. Cambridge: Cambridge University Press.

Pardee, Dennis

1988 *Les textes para-mythologiques de la 24ᵉ campagne (1961).* Ras Shamra-Ougarit IV. Paris: Éditions Recherche sur les Civilisations.

1997a   "Proto-Canaanite." In *The Oxford Encyclopedia of Archaeology in the Near East*, Volume 4, edited by Eric M. Meyers, pp. 252–54. New York: Oxford University Press.

1997b   "Proto-Sinaitic." In *The Oxford Encyclopedia of Archaeology in the Near East*, Volume 4, edited by Eric M. Meyers, pp. 354–55. New York: Oxford University Press.

1997c   "Ugaritic." In *The Oxford Encyclopedia of Archaeology in the Near East*, Volume 5, edited by Eric M. Meyers, pp. 262–64. New York: Oxford University Press.

1997d   "Ugarit Inscriptions." In *The Oxford Encyclopedia of Archaeology in the Near East*, Volume 5, edited by Eric M. Meyers, pp. 264–66. New York: Oxford University Press.

2001   "Le traité d'alliance RS 11.772+." *Semitica* 51: 5–31.

2004   "Aux origines de l'alphabet." *Dossiers d'Archéolgie*, hors série 10: 34–39.

Piérart, M.
1991   "Écriture et identité culturelle: Les cités du Péloponnèse nord-oriental." In *Phoinikeia grammata: Lire et écrire en Méditerranée* (Actes du Colloque de Liège, 15–18 novembre 1989), edited by Claude Baurain, Corinne Bonnet, and Véronique Krings, pp. 565–76. Collection d'Études Classiques 6. Namur: Société des Études Classiques.

Rainey, A. F.
1974   "The Ugaritic Texts in Ugaritica 5." *Journal of the American Oriental Society* 94: 184–94.

Sass, Benjamin
1988   *The Genesis of the Alphabet and Its Development in the Second Millennium B.C.* Ägypten und Altes Testament 13. Wiesbaden: Harrassowitz.

2004–5   "The Genesis of the Alphabet and Its Development in the Second Millennium B.C. — Twenty Years Later." *De Kêmi à Birīt Nāri. Revue Internationale de l'Orient Ancien* 2: 147–66.

Schaeffer, C. F. A.
1956   "La première tablette." *Syria* 33: 161–68.

Singer, I.
1999   "A Political History of Ugarit." In *Handbook of Ugaritic Studies*, edited by W. G. E. Watson and Nicolas Wyatt, pp. 603–733. Handbuch der Orientalistik 1; Der Nahe und Mittlere Osten 39. Leiden: Brill.

van Soldt, W. H.
1983   Review of *Ugarit in Retrospect: 50 Years of Ugarit and Ugaritic*, edited by Gordon Douglas Young. *Bibliotheca Orientalis* 40: cols. 692–99.

1990   "Fabrics and Dyes at Ugarit." *Ugarit-Forschungen* 22: 321–57.

1991   *Studies in the Akkadian of Ugarit, Dating and Grammar*. Alter Orient und Altes Testament 40. Kevelaer: Butzon & Bercker; Neukirchen-Vluyn: Neukirchener Verlag.

Tropper, J.
1995   "Die letzte Zeichen des ugaritischen Alphabets." *Ugarit-Forschungen* 27: 505–28.

Virolleaud, C.
1940–41   "Textes administratifs de Ras Shamra en cunéiforme alphabétique." *Revue d'Assyriologie* 37: 11–44.

1951   "Les nouvelles tablettes de Ras Shamra (1948–1949)." *Syria* 28: 22–56.

1968   "Les nouveaux textes mythologiques et liturgiques de Ras Shamra (XXIVe Campagne, 1961)." In *Ugaritica* V, edited by Claude F.-A. Schaeffer, pp. 545–95. Mission de Ras Shamra 16; Bibliothèque Archéologique et Historique 80. Paris: P. Guethner.

Watson, W. G. E., and Nicolas Wyatt
1999   *Handbook of Ugaritic Studies*. Handbuch der Orientalistik 1; Der Nahe und Mittlere Osten 39. Leiden: Brill.

Wimmer, S. J., and S. Wimmer-Dweikat
    2001   "The Alphabet from Wadi el-Hôl: A First Try." *Göttinger Miszellen* 180: 107–11.

Yon, M.
    1997a   *La cité d'Ougarit sur le tell de Ras Shamra*. Guides Archéologiques de l'Institut Français d'Archéologie du Proche-Orient 2. Paris: Éditions Recherche sur les Civilisations.
    1997b   "Ugarit." in *The Oxford Encyclopedia of Archaeology in the Near East*, Volume 5, edited by Eric M. Meyers, pp. 255–62. New York: Oxford University Press.
    2006   *The City of Ugarit at Tell Ras Shamra*. Winona Lake: Eisenbrauns.

13. WEST SEMITIC PERSPECTIVES ON THE AKKADIAN VETITIVE

David Testen

13.1. Introduction: The Expression of Negative Wishes in Semitic

As a rule, the Semitic languages do not show a direct negative counterpart to the imperative stem (e.g., Akkadian *šiber*, Hebrew *šəbor*, Arabic (*'u*)*θbur*, Amharic *səbär*, etc., 'break!'). What one finds instead for the expression of negative commands is a fully inflected finite verb (often in a modally marked shape) to which one or another of the negating particles has been prefixed. Such constructions are typically employed in these languages not only to form negative commands — that is, the speaker's injunction that the addressee not carry out a given action — but also more generally to express any wish or desire that a given event or situation not come about, regardless of whether it falls under the control of the addressee or not. These constructions thus serve as negative counterparts not only to the imperative but to wish-forms in general, particularly those morphologically reflected in many of the Semitic languages by the jussive verbal mood. Compare the literary Arabic paradigms listed in table 13.1.

Table 13.1. Literary Arabic Paradigms: The Imperative, the Negative Jussive, and the Jussive

	Imperative 'ruin!'	*Negative Jussive 'may X not ruin!'*	*Jussive 'may X ruin!'*
First-person singular	—	lā 'aθbur	li-'aθbur
First-person plural	—	lā naθbur	li-naθbur
Second-person masculine singular	('u)θbur	lā taθbur	li-taθbur
Second-person feminine singular	('u)θbur-ī	lā taθbur-ī	li-taθbur-ī
Second-person dual	('u)θbur-ā	lā taθbur-ā	li-taθbur-ā
Second-person masculine plural	('u)θbur-ū	lā taθbur-ū	li-taθbur-ū
Second-person feminine plural	('u)θbur-na	lā taθbur-na	li-taθbur-na
Third-person masculine singular	—	lā yaθbur	li-yaθbur
Third-person feminine singular	—	lā taθbur	li-taθbur
Second-person dual	—	lā yaθbur-ā	li-yaθbur-ā
Third-person masculine plural	—	lā yaθbur-ū	li-yaθbur-ū
Third-person feminine plural	—	lā yaθbur-na	li-yaθbur-na

In the case of literary Arabic, the morphological distinction between the negative of the jussive form ('may you not break, do not break!') and the negative of the indicative non-past ('you are not breaking, you do not break, you shall not break') resides in the modal ending of the verb — compare jussive *lā taθbur* to indicative *lā taθburu*. For a good many Semitic languages, on the other hand, the principal locus of the distinction lies in the nature of the negating particle — compare, for example, Hebrew *lo tišbar* 'you shall not break' to *'al tišbar* 'do not break'. However, while we find clear agreement across the Semitic family supporting the basic reconstructability of the negative wish-formation, we find a considerable amount of disagreement across the various languages as to the identity of the negating particle serving in this function.

(a) In certain languages (e.g., Arabic, cf. table 13.1), the negator employed in negative jussive formations is the language's "all-purpose," default negative particle.

(b) In certain others, negative jussive structures are marked by a single negating particle (Amharic *ay-yəsbär* 'may he not break!') in contrast to indicative structures, which feature a bipartite circumfixed structure (Amharic *al-säbbärä-m* 'he did not break', *ay-(yə)säbr-əm* 'he does not break').

(c) In still other languages, the negating elements used in indicative and jussive situations are entirely distinct — the Canaanite languages, Ugaritic, and early Aramaic, for example, employ a special jussive negator * 'al (cf. Hebrew 'al, Phoenician 'l, Ugaritic al) in contrast to a more general negator used with the indicative.

13.2. Negative Wish-formations in Akkadian

Negative wish-formations in Akkadian are of this last type. There are in fact two distinct syntactic formations in Akkadian which serve to express negative wishes, each distinguished by its negating particle. The first of these, known in the Assyriological literature as the "prohibitive," is formed by adding the particle *lā* in front of a finite verb showing the normal inflection of the present/future tense-shape. The resulting formation (*lā tešebber* 'may you not break') is thus distinguished from its indicative-mood counterpart (*ul tešebber* 'you do not break, will not break') solely by the presence of the *lā* rather than the general negator *ul*.

It is with the second Akkadian structure marking negative wishes and commands, known as the "vetitive" construction, that the present investigation is concerned. In contrast to the prohibitive, the core of which is a finite verb inflected in the non-past shape (*tešebber*), the vetitive is built around a finite verb showing the morphology of the preterite (*tešber* 'you [masculine singular] broke'). In this, the vetitive formation agrees with what we find in its affirmative counterpart, the precative. Note the paradigms in table 13.2, in which the preterite, precative, and vetitive shapes of Old Babylonian are juxtaposed.

Table 13.2. Old Babylonian Paradigms: The Preterite, the Precative, and the Vetitive[1]

	Preterite	*Precative*	*Vetitive*
First-person singular	ešber	lu-šber	ajj-ešber
Second-person masculine singular	tešber	(lu tešber)	e tešber
Second-person feminine singular	tešberi	(lu tešberi)	e tešberi
Third-person singular	išber	l-išber	ajj-išber
[First-person plural]	nišber	i nišber	(*e nišber?)
Second-person plural	tešbera	(lu tešbera)	e tešbera
Third-person masculine plural	išberu	l-išberu	ajj-išberu
Third-person feminine plural	išbera	l-išbera	ajj-išbera

While it might appear somewhat curious to find that Akkadian used the same conjugation-form on the one hand to narrate real situations which obtained in the past (e.g., '[It came about that] you sent the letter' or '... you did not send the letter') and on the other hand to express the speaker's personal commitment to *irrealis* propositions still hovering in the potential future ('I urge/command you to send the letter', 'not to send the letter'), it is well known that the same functional pairing is to be found among the West Semitic languages. Biblical Hebrew, for example, employed its jussive (i.e., the formal counterpart to the Akkadian preterite verb-form) for both the narrative tense (in the so-called "waw-consecutive" construction) and wishes — compare *way-yəhī* '(and) it was' alongside *yəhī* 'let there be!', both of these being distinct from the indicative non-past *yihyɛ* '(he) is, will be'. The literary Arabic jussive is likewise encountered in both wishes and past-tense clauses (*li-yakun* 'may he be!', *lam yakun* 'he was not').[2] It is not difficult to reconcile the function of 'wish' with 'past' if we posit that the original "jussive/preterite" formation was centered on the perfective aspect, with tense and mood left unspecified. Several of the descendant languages have independently introduced secondary formal distinctions to distinguish

---

[1] Note that the second-person forms of the precative are infrequent, their role being more typically filled by the imperative. The first-person plural of the vetitive has not been identified for Old Babylonian.

[2] An analogous duality of function is found in the early Indo-Iranian languages, where the so-called "injunctive" verbal formation, which is used as one of the means of expressing wishes and commands, is distinguished from the indicative past-tense form (aorist or imperfect) solely by the addition of a prefixed vowel (the "augment") in the latter form. Compare examples such as the following, from Gatha Avestan and Vedic, respectively: *at tūm mōi dāiš ašəm* '*may you show* (*dāiš*, second-person singular aorist stem = injunctive) me Righteousness' (Yasna 43.10), *mā no dīrghā abhi naśan tamisrāḥ* '*let the long dark nights not come upon* (mā neg. + *naśan*, third-person plural imperfect stem = injunctive) us' (RV.2.27.14).

these functions by grammaticalizing reflexes of the "emphatic" particle *l- into syntagms encoding one or another of these two functions — hence in historical Akkadian the preterite *išber* '(he) broke' is distinguished from *l-išber* 'may (he) break', Arabic (*li-*)*yaθbur* 'may (he) ruin' is distinct from *lam yaθbur* 'he did not ruin', and biblical Hebrew *yəhī* 'may (he) be' is distinct from *w-ay-yəhī* '(and) (he) was'.[3]

There is, in short, nothing particularly surprising in the presence of what appears to be a "preterite" verb-form at the heart of the Akkadian vetitive construction. The problem arises when we consider the particle preposed to the verb in this formation. The negating particle in question manifests itself in two systematically related allomorphs.

(a) For the third person, the various dialects of early Babylonian availed themselves of a wide range of spelling conventions in the attempt to render the initial syllable of the vetitive.

šumam A *ušarši* ... zēr awēlūtim A *ibni* '*may he not allow him to acquire* a name, *may he not produce* offspring' (Codex Hammurapi xliv 46 ff.)
ina rīšika A-IA *ipparkû* '*may he not depart* from your side' (PBS 7 105)
A-WA-*di-in* '(he) *is not to give*' (ARM 6 50: 15)

In addition to A, A-IA, and A-WA (the last of these being limited to texts from Mari), the spellings found expressing the opening syllable of the vetitive in the various periods of Babylonian include A-I, A-A, and IA. For our present purposes we leave aside the details of this array of graphic complexities, merely noting that Assyriologists take these to be attempts at rendering a sequence composed of (1) the vowel *a-*, (2) the geminate semivowel *-jj-*, and (3) the preradical vowel of the "preterite" verb at the heart of the construction (*ajj-išber* 'let him/her not break', *ajj-išberu* 'let them [masculine] not break', *ajj-išbera* 'let them [feminine] not break', compare the preterite *išber, išberu, išbera*); *mutatis mutandis*, the same structure *ajj-* is believed to reside in the corresponding first-person singular formations (*ajj-ešber* 'may (I) break'; cf. *ešber* '(I) broke'), although fewer examples of the first person are attested.

mūtam ša attanaddaru A-IA-*āmur* '*may I not see* (*ajjāmur*) the death which I constantly dread' (Gilg. M. ii 13)

In both the third-person and the first-person singular structures, it is noted, the vetitive is built around core verbal formations which are vowel-initial (*išber-, ešber*).

(b) In the remainder of the vetitive paradigm (i.e., in those elements of the paradigm which feature a consonant-initial subject-prefix) the vetitive particle systematically displays the shape *e-* rather than *ajj-* (*e-tešber, e-tešberi, e-tešbera* 'may you [masculine singular, feminine singular, common plural] not break; do not break!')

ṭeḫi E *tādur* 'approach, do not be afraid' (Gilg. Y. 147)

(c) A comparable prefixed *e-* dominates the paradigm of the vetitive in the Old Assyrian dialect, regardless of the character of the verb's subject-marker.

E-*nibāš* 'Let-Us-Not-Be-Shamed' (PN; Stamm 1939: 175)
libbaka E *iprid* '*may* your heart *not fear*' (KTS 17: 6)
ana maknākim ša ekallim ekallam E *īterrišu* '*he is not to make demands* of the palace regarding the palace's sealed room' (*CCT* 4 7c: 6)
ana qaqqadija E *aplaḫ* '... *lest I be afraid*' (*CCT* 1 50: 13 ff.)

Not surprisingly, it has long been assumed that the two allomorphs of the vetitive particle (*ajj-* and *e-*) represent differing manifestations of what was originally a single entity. How, however, are we to reconstruct this entity? In principle, it might certainly be possible to assume as the starting point the shape which the particle assumes before a following vowel (*ajj-*) and thereby arrive at an early Semitic proto-shape *'*ayy* or *hayy*.

---

[3] Akkadian has thus grammaticalized the *l*-prefixed shape to form the modal "precative" paradigm (*l-išber, lu tešber*), leaving the simpler verb-form as the preterite (*išber, tešber*). Although the literary Arabic wish-construction typically contains a prefixed *li-* (the so-called *lām al-'amr*), in early texts this *li-* was optional. For an etymological analysis tracing the Arabic negative past-tense particle *lam* back to a compound of the emphatic marker **la-* + the negative *mā*, see Testen 1998a: 201 ff.; for an analysis of the Hebrew "waw-consecutive" marker *waC-* (as in *way-yišbar, wat-tišbar* '[and] he, she broke') as **wa-aC-*, where *-aC-* is interpreted as the Hebrew reflex of the emphatic **l*-particle, see Testen ibid. pp. 193 ff.

Would, however, regular sound change lead to the development of *-*ayy* > *e*- in the environment of a directly following consonant? While such a development — presumably through a simplification of the geminate *-*yy* in preconsonantal sandhi-position (* ʾ/*hayy t*- > *(ʾ/*h*)*ay*(*y*) *t*- > *e t*-) — cannot be ruled out, it is not supported by any direct evidence from outside of the vetitive paradigm. Buccellati (1996: 183f.), on the other hand, has posited that the vetitive particle originally contained a simple diphthong *-*ai* and ascribes the geminated shape *ajj*- to an assimilation of the underlying subject-markers *ʾ- and *y- to the closing component of the preceding diphthong.[4]

Third-person singular (/plural)	*ʾay-y-aprús	>	ʾayy-iprús
First-person singular	*ʾay-ʾ-aprús	>	ʾayy-aprús
Second-person singular (/plural)	*ʾê-t-aprús	>	ʾêt-aprús

Since there is no clear parallel to the phonological reconstruction which this reconstruction demands, however, it is not clear that the assumed assimilation *-*y*ʾ- > *-*yy*- is independently justifiable.

13.3. The Vetitive Particle as a Comparative Semitic Problem

13.3.1. Phoenician, North Ethiopic, and Arabic Comparanda

For the most part, the reconstruction of the vetitive marker has typically been treated as an inter-Akkadian issue and thus handled as a problem of internal reconstruction. Since, however, the investigation of the prehistory of Akkadian is at the same time the investigation of the prehistory of all the languages of the Semitic family, it is worth examining the issue of the vetitive from a comparative perspective. To be sure, there is no other Semitic language which shows a special negative-wish marker with the shape *ʾ/*hayy* or *ʾ/*hai*. There are, however, languages that employ elements with quite similar shapes which serve other negating functions, and it behooves us to consider the possibility that the Proto-Semitic ancestor of the vetitive particle might have originally served as a more general negative but has survived in East Semitic only in the context of wish-constructions.

Two areas within the Semitic realm — the northern area of Syro-Palestine and the northern area of Ethiopia — provide us with data relevant to this issue. While in Hebrew and the neighboring Canaanite languages the general negator is the particle reconstructable as *lā (cf. Hebrew *lo*(ʾ)), in Phoenician we find an element spelled ʾy or ʾ(y)- (presumably representing a syllable ʾī or ʾe) serving this function, either alone or compounded with another negative particle, *bl*.

ʾl ybqš bn mnm k ʾy šm bn mnm 'let him not seek anything in it, for *there is not anything placed* in it' (KAI 14: 5)[5]

[k]l mšʾt ʾš ʾybl št bps z 'every payment that *is not* entered in this tablet' (KAI 69: 18)

wʾm ʾbl tšt šm ʾtk 'and if *you do not put* my name alongside yourself' (KAI 10: 13)

Among the Ethiosemitic languages, the languages of the northern branch of the family show a negator with the shape ʾi- (in Gəʿəz and Tigre) or ʾay (in Tigrinya). Both of these seem to be distinct from the form *al*-, which predominates among the southern Ethiopic languages (with assimilation of the -*l* to a directly following consonant in many situations).[6]

---

[4] "...The form ʾ*ayyiprus* is the only instance in Babylonian where *y* is preserved as the overt marker of the third person in verbal external inflection..." (Buccellati 1996: 184). Buccellati follows Hetzron in assuming that there were originally two "jussives" in Proto-Semitic (viz., a volitional *ʾaprús and a preterite *ʾáprus), distinguished accentually.

[5] In the absence of written vowels we cannot tell with certainty, of course, whether to read ʾy šm ... mnm here with a participial reading of šm ('not placed [is] anything'), as has been done in the translation here, or with a finite verb ('[they] did not place anything, anything was not placed').

[6] As Hudson (2003) observes, the phonological behavior of the Ethiopic negative particle(s) is eccentric. The fact that the subject-markers of the negated verbs in Southern Ethiopic routinely appear as simple consonants, rather than the geminates which one might expect from an assimilation of *al-C- (thus Amharic *aysäbrəm*, *atsäbrəm* 'he, she does not break' rather than *ay-yəsäbr-əm, *at-təsäbr-əm) is indeed noteworthy, but I am not certain that assuming the underlying negator must have been *ay- rather than *al- can fully account for the incongruity — in any event, the first-person singular *alsäbrəm* is surely more efficiently derived from an earlier *(ʾ)al-(ʾ)əsäbər-əm than from a proto-shape with *ay-. Leaving aside the quantity seen in the subject-marking consonants, complete assimilation to a following consonant does not seem to have been a regular feature of early Ethiopic *l, but it is nonetheless routinely encountered in reflexes of the negative particle — compare, in addition to Southern Ethiopic negated verbs such as *aysäbrəm*, the Gəʿəz particle ʾ*akko* 'not'. I have suggested elsewhere (Testen 1998a: 177ff.) the possibility that the unorthodox assimilatory properties of the */l* of the negator reflect the original syllabic */l̥*, which I reconstruct for this word (i.e., Proto-Semitic *ʾ/l̥ > Northwest Semitic ʾ*al*, Ethiopic ʾ*al* [ʾ*aC*- in close juncture], Akkadian *ul*), and I find it quite conceivable that this original */l̥* is likewise responsible for the apparent discrepancies in the quantity of the Southern Ethiopic subject-markers.

Gəʿəz	ʾi-təfrāh naši'ot la-Māryām fəxərtəka 'do not fear to take Mary as your fiancée' (Matthew 1:20)
	ʾi-yətxaddag zəyya ʾəbn diba ʾəbn 'one stone will not be left on another here' (Matthew 24:2)
Tigre	ʾawtobus ʾi ʿala, ʾəbbəlli sabab ʾəlli ʾagid ʾi-maṣʾako 'there was no bus because of this I have not come sooner'
Tigrinya	nəḥna mənəm ḥadä nägär ʾay-gäbärna-n 'we did not do anything'

In addition, traces of a counterpart to the Northern Ethiopic negative particle ʾi are found among the Southern Ethiopic negative forms of the verb of existence. The underlying construction on which the latter verbs are based consisted of the Southern Ethiopic cognate to Gəʿəz *hallawa* '(he) exists', to which the negative particle *(ʾ)i-* has been prefixed — Early Ethiopic *ʾi-halla(wa)* > early Southern Ethiopic *i-(h)ällä* > *y-ällä* > Amharic *yällä*, Argobba *(y)ellaw*, Soddo *yellä*, Zay *il(l)o, ilä*, Muher *yännä*, Chaha *enä*, Inor *enä* (Hudson 2003: 214f.).[7]

Is it possible to relate these Phoenician and Ethiopic negators to the vetitive *ayy-/e-* of Akkadian? The Northern Ethiopic negative *ʾi-/ʾay-* has been described as a reflex of the familar *ʾal*, which is well attested in Southern Ethiopic, and indeed in many Ethiosemitic languages the palatalization of *l > y* is a familiar development — compare, for example, Amharic *bäl, bäy* 'say (masculine singular, feminine singular)' (the latter < *bäl-i*) and *bəl-ʷall* 'he has said' to *bəy-yeyalläh*ʷ 'I have said' (< *bəl-ye-*). Gəʿəz is not one of the languages that shows the effects of this shift, however, and it would thus be necessary to assume that a palatalization took place in the prehistory of Gəʿəz which subsequently vanished, leaving no trace beyond the putative development of *ʾi < *ʾal*. Moreover, even if we assume that the existence of Northern Ethiopic *ʾi* and *ʾay* can be correctly attributed to such a secondary palatalization, this analysis presupposes an unmotivated analogical leveling which would have arbitrarily generalized the palatalized variant at the expense of the basic shape *ʾal*. In light of the existence of Phoenician *ʾy*, I find it simpler to assume that the *ʾi* and *ʾay* of North Ethiopic are not reflexes of the same negator which yielded the South Ethiopic *al*.

There is more to the issue than linking North Ethiopic *ʾi-/ʾay* and Phoenician *ʾy*, however, since the forms in question seem clearly to be akin to the largely synonymous particles of the type of Hebrew *ʾên*.

wə-*ʾên* ʾīš meʾanšê habbayit šăm babbayit 'but *there is no* man of the men of the house there in the house' (Genesis 39:11)

ʾên-kåmôkå båʾɛlohīm '*there is no* (one) like you among the gods' (Psalms 86:8)

This element may be traced back to a Pre-Hebrew * *ʾayn-* (see below). Clearly related to Hebrew *ʾên* is the Ugaritic particle spelled *in*, presumably to be read as either *ʾin* or *ʾen*.

d-*in* bn lh km aḫh w šrš km aryh 'for whom *there is no* son like his brother, (nor) offspring like his kinsman' (2 Aqht i 19f.)

Is it not in fact possible that both of these negating elements — namely * *ʾī*/ * *ʾay* (> Phoenician *ʾy*, Ethiopic *ʾi/ ʾay*) and * *ʾayn* (> Hebrew *ʾên*, Ugaritic *in*, Moabite *ʾn*) — are in fact reflexes of a single ancestral proto-element? A judicious application of Ockham's principle suggests that we should be reluctant to assume the presence of two discrete elements (Pre-Phoenician * *ʾVy-* and Pre-Hebrew * *ʾayn-*) so close to one another in form and function. Conflating the two elements by assuming that the Phoenician negator represents a truncated manifestation of the same particle which gave rise to *ʾên* would enable us to reduce the size of the set of negating particles for early Semitic. The shape of Phoenician *ʾy* would be quite consistent with the Hebrew particle (* *ʾayn-*), assuming that it is possible to account for the absence of the final *-n* in some manner.

To be sure, there is a syntactic distinction between *ʾy* and *ʾên* which merits remark: the Hebrew and Ugaritic particles are specifically associated with predicating "non-existence" (e.g., *ʾên ʾīš* 'there is no man'), whereas

---

[7] On the other hand, it is less clear that the *ay-* of Amharic *aydäll-äm* '(he) is not (X)' is to be linked with the negative *ʾay-* of Tigrinya, as Hudson suggests (2003: 213f.). I find it more likely that the stem *aydäll-* reflects a frozen third-person prefixed verb *a(y)-yədäbəl-* to which the suffixed subject-marker set has been appended — that is, *a(y)-yədäll-əm > aydäll-ä-m* '(he) is not', whence *aydäll-äh-əm* '(you masculine singular) are not', *aydäll-ähu-m* '[I am not]', in all likelihood under the influence of *yäll-ä-m, yäll-äh-əm, yäll-ähu-m*. For parallels to the use of an inflected third-person form as the basis for the construction of a new paradigm for "be," compare the third-person singular forms of "be" in Persian (*hast*, whence first-person singular *hast-am*, second-person singular *hast-i*) and Polish (*jest*, whence first-person singular *jest-em*, second-person singular *jest-esz*).

the Phoenician and Ethiopic particles which we have examined above function as more general negators of predicates.

The bridge which allows us to reconstruct a common forerunner underlying this array of negating element(s) lies, I suggest, in Classical Arabic. Arabic has extensively revamped the set of Semitic negators, having, for example, lost all trace of the negating *'l and having acquired a new negating *mā*.[8] Nevertheless, early Classical Arabic still made use of an element which was in all likelihood the formal counterpart of Hebrew *'ên*. This was the particle known to the medieval grammarians as the "negating *'in*" (*'in al-nāfiya*). Although this particle had the same shape as two other particles (namely, the conditional particle *'in* 'if' and the *'in* which reflected the "lightened" [*muxaffafa*] manifestation of the presentation particle *'inna*[9]), on syntactic and semantic grounds it was patently a distinct entity. This third *'in* was described as the equivalent of the negative *mā* (alongside which it is not infrequently encountered) and most routinely occurred in conjunction with *'illā* 'except for'.

    'in ʿindakum min sulṭānin bihāḏā 'There is no proof of this in your possession' (Sura 10:69, 72:26)
    'in 'aradnā *'illā* l-ḥusnā 'We desired *nothing but* the best things' (Sura 9:108)

Historians of Arabic have long debated the negative *'in*, some assuming that it resulted from a regrammaticalization of one of the other two *'in*s, while others trace it back to the rhetorical use of an alternative form of the question word 'where?' (Arabic *'ayna*); several have remarked on its general similarity to the Hebrew negator *'ên*, which in turn has also been taken to reflect the interrogative 'where?' ("*Where is X?' > 'There is no X!').[10]

For the moment we shall simply take note of the close match in function between Arabic *'in* and Hebrew *'ên* and its ilk and the possibility of an acceptable match in terms of historical phonology. It is clear from the various shapes through which the Hebrew element is manifested that we are obliged to reconstruct an early diphthong *-ay-* at the heart of this form (thus *'ayn-*) — this is most clear, of course, from the tonic shape *'áyin*, which matches exactly what we expect to find from a "segholate"-type stem containing a medial *-ay-* (cf., e.g., Hebrew *báyit* 'house' < *bayt-*). The remaining Northwest Semitic forms (Moabite *'n*, Ugaritic *in*) may thus be viewed as reflections of a monophthongization which has shifted the original *-ay-* into a front vowel (most probably *-ē-*), a monophthongization which was entirely regular for these languages.

What Arabic *'in* contributes to the discussion is the fact that it indicates that the *-n* of the negator originally stood in word-final position. Had there been any syllabic material following the underlying *-n* we would expect to find it surviving in Arabic. This leads us to reconstruct the negative particle in question as *#'ayn#* (where "#" represents an early word boundary).

Since we are thus dealing with a rather highly marked phonological situation — that is, an early Semitic diphthong embedded within a closed syllable in a monosyllabic word — we must be wary about claiming that we can readily predict the ultimate outcome of this form for the various descendant languages. I would like to suggest that we should at least entertain the possibility that some or all the forms which we have examined above constitute the regular reflexes of the reconstruction *#'ayn#*. It is not surprising, for example, to find that a word-final *-n* has not survived in several of the languages in question (Phoenician and Northern Ethiopic) — note that in these languages the original word-final nasal ending of the substantive has likewise not survived (cf. e.g., Phoenician *b'l* 'lord' vs. Arabic *baʿl-un* and early Akkadian *bēl-um*). It is also not surprising to find that in several cases the diphthong has been monophthongized (and in some cases shortened) in what had originally been a closed syllable (Arabic *'in* [cf. Fischer 2002: 30] and Gǝʿǝz/Tigre *'i* < *'ī(n)*).

To be sure, we should note that it is quite likely that the stem in question (*'ayn*) seems also to have been capable of appearing in situations in which the *-n* was not word-final but rather was followed either by some

---

[8] I am treating negative *mā* here as an Arabic innovation rather than as an Afroasiatic survival, as Faber (1991) does. I suspect that it arose from the grammaticalization of the pronominal *mā* within negating complexes such as the antecedent of Amharic *al-säbbärä-m, a-ysäbr-ǝm* '(he) didn't, doesn't break' (based, I suspect, on an earlier '*[he] didn't, doesn't break anything'). Colloquial Arabic formations such as Cairene *ma-ruḥt-iš, ma-barūḥ-š* '(I) didn't, don't go' may well preserve this earlier structure in an altered form, with *mā* promoted to the role of principal negating element (as in Classical Arabic) and *-š* (< *šayʾan*

'[a] thing') introduced to fill the slot formerly occupied by the earlier indefinite pronominal.
[9] While the conditional *'in* (e.g., *'in raʾaytuhu qultu lahu* 'if I see him I shall say to him …') is very familiar to students of Arabic, the *'in al-muxaffafa min al-θaqīla* is typical of the earliest strata of the literary language — compare such Qurʾanic examples as *wa-'in kādū la-yaftinūnaka* [= *wa-'innahum…*] 'and verily they almost seduced you', which corresponds in sense to *wa-'innahum la-kādū yaftinūnaka*.
[10] See the discussion of the literature in Leslau 1992.

manner of inflectional ending or by a pronominal suffix. There seems in fact to have been a bifurcation of the reflexes of this element which roughly correlates with a split in function, with reflexes of the endingless *ˀayn# serving as negators of predicates (Arabic ˀin, Phoenician ˀy, and Northern Ethiopic ˀi/ ˀay), while the suffixed manifestation of this element (*ˀayn-X-) gave rise to markers of non-existence in various languages (cf. Hebrew ˀên [and ˀên-ɛnnû 'he is not'], Akkadian jan-u).

13.3.2. *ˀayn and the Akkadian Vetitive

Having drawn up as our reconstruction the sequence *#ˀayn(-), let us now return to the question of the allomorphs of the Babylonian vetitive marker. As has been noted above, these have been identified as ajj- before a vowel and e- before a consonant, apparently leaving us a choice of *ˀai- or *ˀajj- as the proto-form. I would like to suggest a third option, however, in that an equally plausible candidate for the proto-shape is a disyllabic *ˀaji. From such a starting point, it would be a fairly simple task to derive either of the two observed vetitive allomorphs.

(a) The simple intervocalic -j- would necessarily have been lost, leading, we may presume, to the regular contraction of the now adjacent vowels *-a- and *-i- (*ˀa(j)i- > *(ˀ)ai- > e-).

(b) In close juncture with a directly following vowel, however, it is easy to imagine that the second vowel of *ˀaji- could have become desyllabified. The result of this desyllabification would have been, for all practical purposes, the equivalent of a second *-j-, and the resulting sequence of the original semivocalic *-j- and the secondarily non-vocalic *-i- should have been sufficient to prevent the contraction which would have befallen a simple *-j- (ˀaji-ˀaprus > *aji-aprus > ajj-aprus).

As it happens, this hypothetical pre-Akkadian *ˀaji- is entirely consistent with the reconstructed *ˀayn which we posited above as the early West Semitic forerunner of Hebrew ˀáyin and Arabic ˀin. We need only posit that in the early East Semitic counterpart to the Proto-Semitic *ˀayn the *-n, located as it was between the *i-component of the preceding diphthong and the end of the word, came to act as a syllable in its own right. There are a considerable number of situations throughout Akkadian in which we find a high vowel (typically -i-, but under certain circumstances -u-) in places where we would reconstruct on comparative Semitic grounds an *-n-. In all the situations in question, we are able to reconstruct an *-n- with no directly adjacent vowel (see table 13.3).[11]

Table 13.3. Akkadian High Vowels as Reflexes of Proto-Semitic *n

IMPERATIVE G I-N

idin 'give!'	< *n̥din	Compare Arabic (ˀi)ntij 'produce!'
ubuḫ 'bark!'	< *n̥bux	(ˀu)nθur 'observe!'

UNPREFIXED GT I-N (INFINITIVE, IMPERATIVE, VERBAL ADJECTIVE)

itaṭl-um (Old Assyrian)	< *itaṭul- < *n̥taṭul-	Compare Arabic (ˀi)ntiḏār
'to look at one another (infinitive)'		'waiting (verbal noun)'

UNPREFIXED GTN I-N (INFINITIVE, IMPERATIVE, VERBAL ADJECTIVE)

itattuk-a 'drip (plural)!'	< *n̥tantuk-

UNPREFIXED NTN (INFINITIVE, IMPERATIVE, VERBAL ADJECTIVE)

itaplas 'keep looking at!'	< *n̥ta(n)plas-

---

[11] On the development of the various unprefixed verbal formations and the "cohorative" particle, see Testen 1993; the conjugation of Akkadian "to have" is discussed in Testen 2000 and the plural pronominals in Testen 1995. The presence of -s- in the Modern South Arabian words for "shoulder, back" rather than the expected *š, *θ, or *ś is curious. A roughly similar phenomenon is found in the Modern South Arabian terms for "nine" (Mehri sɛ, Jibbali soˤ, etc.), which I have suggested ascribing to an early loss of the *i of the original *tišˤ- (thus *tišˤ- > *t(V)š- > *tš- > s-; Testen 1998b). Is it possible that a comparable development took place in the term for "shoulder, back," perhaps via an epenthetic dental inserted between the *-n- and the following *-š- (i.e., *kn̥šād- > *k(V)nᵗšVd- > Jibbali kensed)?

Table 13.3. Akkadian High Vowels as Reflexes of Proto-Semitic *n (cont.)

IRREGULAR VERB 'TO HAVE'

iši 'I have'	< *'-nśi'	'*I (have) picked up'
t-iši- 'you have'	< *t-nśi'-	'*you (have) picked up'
iši- 'he has'	< *y-nśi'-	'*he (has) picked up'
n-iši 'we have'	< *n-nśi'-	'*we (have) picked up'

PLURAL PRONOMINAL ENDINGS

Second-person feminine *attina*	< *'antnna	[Arabic *'antunna*]
Third-person feminine *šina*	< *šnna	[Arabic *hunna*]
Third-person masculine *šunu*	< *šnnū	[rebuilt from feminine (Testen 2005)]

PREPOSITION 'IN, FROM'

ina	< *nna < *mna	[Arabic *min*, Gəʿəz *'əmna*]

COHORTATIVE PARTICLE

i (*nišber*) 'let's (break)!'	< *n̥- < *l̥- before n-	Compare *l-išber, lu tešber* 'may he, you break!'; Arabic *wa-l-naθbur* 'and let's ruin!'

PERHAPS…

kišād-um 'neck'	< *knSʔād- ?	Compare Mehri *kənsîd*, Jibbali *kensed* 'shoulder'
kipr-um 'edge, shore'	< *knp(V)r- ?	Compare Gəʿəz *kanfar* 'lip, edge'?

We may take cases such as those listed in table 13.3 as evidence that there was a pre-Akkadian sound change which replaced Proto-Semitic *n with a high vowel in such situations, in a manner analogous to what we find in the prehistory of Greek and Indo-Iranian, where the Indo-European nasals *n and *m are changed to the vowel *a* whenever the phonological environment obliged the nasal to serve as a syllabic.[12]

In other words, there is no phonological problem with tracing both shapes of the Akkadian vetitive particle, *ajj-* and *e-*, back to a disyllabic *aji, which in turn may be traced back to a pre-Akkadian sequence * 'ayn̥. This matches quite closely the shape which we have reconstructed above for the early precursor of Hebrew *'ayin* and Arabic *'in*, and which we have regarded as a plausible potential starting point for the development of a set of negating particles of Northern Canaanite and Northern Ethiopic (namely, Phoenician *'y/ '(y)-*, Gəʿəz and Tigre *'i*, and Tigrinya *'ay*).[13]

13.3.3. The West Gurage Prohibitive

The aim of the preceding paragraphs was to indicate that there is no compelling evidence in support of the existence of a negative element * 'ayy in early Semitic distinct from * 'ayn. The assumption of the former on the part of some researchers has been prompted by a set of surface shapes (Phoenician *'y*, North Ethiopic *'i / 'ay*, and Akkadian *ajj*) which are actually just as consistent with the reconstructed * 'ayn which underlies Hebrew *'ên* and Arabic *'in*.

A comparison linking the Akkadian vetitive marker *ajj-/e-* with the other putative reflexes of * 'ayn cited above faces one potential complication in that none of the other forms which we have seen are associated with specifically modal situations in the way that Akkadian *aji- is. Arabic *'in* seems in fact to have been restricted to non-modal situations and while Ethiopic *'i* and *'ay* do occur in modally marked situations (e.g., in wish/command

---

[12] For example, Greek (*he*)*katon*, Sanskrit *śatam*, Avestan *satəm* 'hundred' < Indo-European *kṃtom — compare Latin *centum*, Lithuanian *šimtas*, English *hund-red*.

[13] It may indeed be possible to trace others of the set of proposed cognates back to the same disyllabic * 'ayn which has been proposed above as the starting point for pre-Akkadian *aji. Thus, for example,

Arabic *'in* might in principle reflect an earlier * 'ayin < an original * 'ayn — thus * 'ayn > * 'ayin > * 'a(y)in > *'in* in a closed syllable (cf. *mit-tu* '[I] died' < *ma(w)it-tu). For Arabic *-in-* < Semitic *-n̥-*, compare *bint-un* 'daughter', *θint-āni* 'two (feminine)' [by-forms of (*'i*)*bnat-un*, (*'i*)*θnat-āni*] < *bn̥-t-um, *θn̥-t-ā- [= bn-at-um, θn-at-ā-] (Testen 1985).

constructions containing the jussive — Gəʿəz ʾi-yəsbər 'may he not break'), it is significant that for these languages the particle in question functions as the unmarked negative marker, and hence its appearance in wish-constructions can hardly be ascribed any great significance.

We might thus be tempted to conclude that Akkadian *aji is isolated among the reflexes of Semitic *ʾayn as the sole instance in which a reflex of this particle serves specifically to mark wishes. There is, however, one further instance of a probable reflex of *ʾayn which is of direct relevance to the question of the Akkadian vetitive. Interestingly, a match for the vetitive particle of Akkadian is found in one of the "youngest" of the Semitic languages (i.e., those which have only comparatively recently come to the attention of scholars of Semitic).[14] Leslau has found that the western languages of the Gurage cluster of southern Ethiopia employ two discrete formations for the expression of negative commands. In addition to showing a reflex of the familiar negated jussive construction which we have been examining above — for example, Inor (Ennemor) a-ykəft 'may he not open', a-tkəft 'may you (masculine singular) not open' (< *al-yəkfət, *al-təkfət), directly comparable to Amharic ay-yəkfät, at-təkfät — these languages also form negative commands by prefixing the syllable ən- to the past-tense verbal form. Compare the paradigms from Chaha and Inor in table 13.4.

Table 13.4. Past, Negated Past, and "Prohibitive" Formations in Chaha and Inor

	Past		Negated Past		"Prohibition"	
Chaha						
Second-person singular	käfätxäm		an-käfätxä	'you	ən-käfätxä	
Second-person feminine singular	käfätx'im	'you	an-käfätx'	did	ən-käfätx'	'don't
Second-person masculine plural	käfätxum	opened'	an-käfätxu	not	ən-käfätxu	open'
Second-person feminine plural	käfätxəmam		an-käfätxəma	open'	ən-käfätxəma	
Inor						
Second-person singular	käfädxä		an-käfädxä-da	'you	ən-käfädxä	
Second-person feminine singular	käfädšəm	'you	an-käfädåuwa-ta	did	ən-käfädš	'don't
Second-person masculine plural	käfädxum	opened'	an-käfädxuwa-ta	not	ən-käfädxuwa	open'
Second-person feminine plural	käfädxäm		an-käfädxä-ta	open'	ən-käfädxä	

By regular phonological development, the Semitic sonorants *n, *l, and *r have fallen together in West Gurage as either n or r, depending upon the environment.[15] The negating an- of the indicative negative (e.g., Chaha an-käfätxä) is thus clearly the West Gurage reflex of the negative al- which prevails throughout Southern Ethiopic (cf. Amharic al-käffätxä-m). Given the divergent vowel in ən-, however, we must look elsewhere in order to establish the source of the negative marker of the West Gurage prohibitive construction. On comparative-Ethiopic grounds, Leslau concludes that the most likely early Ethiopic source for ən- is a pre-form containing an *n — compare Gəʿəz ʾən-dā ʿī 'I don't know', and ʾəmbi 'no' — and Leslau's comparison extends further afield to encompass the negators ʾin of Arabic and ʾên of Hebrew.

To find a clear functional counterpart to the ən- of the West Gurage prohibitive formation, however, we must return to ancient Mesopotamia. The Akkadian vetitive and the West Gurage prohibitive may both be characterized, *mutatis mutandis*, by using the same morphosyntactic formula: "add the reflex of *ʾayn (Akkadian *aji-, West Gurage ən-) at the beginning of the inflected past-tense verbal form." The inflected verbal form differs, of course, between these two sets of data (prefixed preterite/jussive in Akkadian vs. suffixed "perfective" in West Gurage), but the agreement found in the prohibition-marking prefixes is nonetheless striking. Note that early Arabic provides a potential bridge between the two in that, like the West Gurage languages, it is capable of using the past-

---

[14] Ironically, of course, the "younger" a language is — that is, the more recent the onset of its period of documentation — the "older" it is in the sense of being further removed from the the original common ancestor.

[15] Compare, for example, Chaha and Inor enä '(he) is not' < *ʾi-halla(wa), cited above (contrast Amharic yällä, Soddo yellä, etc.).

tense form of the verb as a means of expressing wishes, especially formulaic blessings and curses (*laʿana-ka llāhu* 'God curse [lit. 'cursed'] you!', *lā faḍḍa fāka* 'may He not break your face!').[16]

13.4. Much Ado about '*Nothing'

Given that we are capable of reconstructing a shape *ʾayn* and that it seems to have occurred routinely in negative situations, how are we to understand the nature of the lexical entity *ʾayn* itself? As we have seen above, the etymologies of several researchers have concluded that it should be interpreted as the interrogative word 'where?' Such a conjecture cannot be ruled out, of course, but textual evidence from the Bible suggests that at its heart Hebrew *ʾáyin* was actually a substantive meaning essentially 'nothing'. Its syntactic role is most clearly seen in examples such as the following passages, in which *ʾáyin* is found governed by a prefixed preposition.

kål haggôyim kə- ʾáyin nɛgdô 'all the nations are *like nothing* before Him' (Isaiah 40:17)
hannôten rôzənīm lə- ʾáyin 'he who brings princes *to nothing*' (Isaiah 40:23)
hen- ʾattɛm me- ʾayin 'Behold, you are (less) *than nothing*' (Isaiah 41:24)
kī gåḏôl hayyôm hahû' me- ʾayin kåmohû 'for great will be that day, *there will be none* like it' (Jeremiah 30:7)

If we posit that the original Semitic precursor of Hebrew had roughly the same value ('*nothing', '*not anything'), it is not difficult to imagine how it might have come to be grammaticalized on the one hand as an index of non-existence ('there does not exist ...') and on the other as a sentential negator ('not').

(1) When the element *ʾayn '*nothing' was employed in the role of a predicate to a subject noun-phrase, it would have presumably functioned to qualify the subject as a "non-existent" thing — that is, '*A house is nothing with respect to him' — and hence could easily have developed ultimately into an explicit marker of non-existence of the type of Hebrew *ʾên* and its relatives — 'No house exists to him', 'He has no house' (Hebrew *ʾên báyiṯ lô*).

(2) As long as Proto-Semitic *ʾayn was a noun phrase in syntactic terms, there should be no reason that it could not have also occurred as an argument within verbal clauses (e.g., '*he sees nothing'). From such a starting point — that is, a sentential structure which is negative in function even though it contains no negated verb — it would not be difficult to reach a secondary stage in which the argument *nothing has been bleached and grammaticalized into a simple marker of negation ('*he does not see ...'). Once such a stage was reached, of course, the *ʾayn would no longer have been an argument, and it would become possible to insert any desired noun phrase into the syntactic slot formerly occupied by *ʾayn. From the etymological point of view, a sentence like Gəʿəz *ʾi-yəreʾʾi nəguśa* 'he does not see the king' might thus be thought of as possessing two objects ('**Nothing (he) sees (the) king'), but this should be no more disconcerting than what we find in the grammaticalized negative constructions of such familiar languages as the colloquial Arabic of Cairo (*mā-byišūf-iš il-malik* 'he does not see the king', *mā-byišūf-iš* < **mā (bi-)yišūf(u) šayʾan* '*he does not see (a) thing') or modern French (*il ne voit pas le roi* (*ne voit pas* < **non videt passum*) '*does not see (a) "step"'); indeed, the prehistorical development that we are envisioning for early Semitic is quite close to what has happened within the history of English, the negator *not* of which results from the grammaticalization of an indefinite negative pronominal construction underlying the modern (if, in American English, infrequent) *naught* (hence *I haven't a clue* < *I have not* < *I have "naught"*).[17]

13.5. Conclusion

In short, I would like to suggest that, although the structure of the Akkadian vetitive lacks an exact parallel in West Semitic, we nonetheless find clear analogues to its key constituents in one manifestation or another. As an exercise in comparative linguistics, the question of the vetitive is quite instructive in that no single West Semitic language provides us with the sum total of the information necessary to achieve a complete analysis of the vetitive.

---

[16] This negative wish-formation with *lā* contrasts with the negative indicative, which features the negator *mā* (*mā faḍḍa* 'he did not break ...').

[17] I presume that ultimately the negative indefinite pronominal *ʾayn is in one manner or another to be regarded as a manifestation of the pronominal stem *ʾayy- 'which'. The formal relation between *ʾayn and *ʾayy- is reminiscent of what is seen in the Arabic interrogatives *man* 'who' and *mā* 'what'. Might there perhaps have been an early Semitic formant *-n which produced secondary (perhaps indefinite?) pronominals out of interrogative bases?

From biblical Hebrew we learn that the prehistorical precursor of the vetitive particle is to be reconstructed with a diphthong *-ay- (hence Proto-Semitic *'ayn-), while from Arabic we acquire the key detail that the *n of the reconstructed proto-form stood (at least in certain key constructions) in word-final position (*'ayn#), and finally from modern West Gurage we find a semantic/functional parallel which justifies us in positing that the reconstructed proto-particle in question could routinely serve as a formant in wishes and commands.

If we are correct in juxtaposing the Akkadian vetitive and the prohibitive construction of West Gurage, it is worth considering the ramifications of this for the general picture of the Semitic family. *Ceteris paribus*, this geographically peripheral distribution suggests that we may well be in the presence of a quite archaic — indeed, Common Semitic — linguistic feature. At the same time we should note that, if *'ayn as a negating particle is in fact to be traced back to a grammaticalized pronominal *'ayn '*nothing', that grammaticalization must in all likelihood have taken place prior to the breakup of the ancestral language.

Of the four principal sub-areas of which the Semitic language-family is composed — namely East Semitic, Northwest Semitic, Southwest Semitic, and Arabic — the use of a reflex of *'ayn in the expression of negative wishes is shared by members of the easternmost and westernmost branches (East Semitic and Southwest Semitic). Of the two remaining branches, early Northwest Semitic seems to have consistently used a reflex of *'l in the same function. Interestingly, the two branches that retain traces of the volitional *'ayn share a tendency to employ the local counterpart to this *'l (namely Akkadian *ul* and Southern Ethiopic *al-*) as a general negative. Perhaps there is a causal connection relating these facts — one might imagine, for example, that the prehistorical precursor of Northwest Semitic systematically replaced an original volitional negation *'ayn using its reflex of the general negator *'l (hence early Semitic *'ayn tVθbir '*may you not break' > early Northwest Semitic *'al taθbir). In the process of making this substitution, the Northwest Semitic branch seems to have discarded whatever non-volitional functions the particle *'l may have had, reassigning these to the reflex of either *'ayn (hence Phoenician (*) 'y tšbr 'you do/will not break') or *lā (Hebrew *lo tišbor*). In pre-Arabic, similarly, the reflex of *'ayn survived in non-volitional situations — 'in fa'ala '(he) did not do' — at least in the earlier phases of the documented language, while as a marker of wishes/commands *'ayn has given way to *lā* — compare *lā yaf'al* and (obsolescent) *lā fa'ala* 'may he not do'.[18]

To be sure, it is possible to draw other conclusions on the relation of the various negative and volitional structures we have examined and the prehistorical developments underlying this array of forms. What this investigation has attempted to demonstrate is that we are entitled to reconstruct a pre-Akkadian particle *ayi, which in turn may be traced back to an early Semitic element *'ayn(-) with the ultimate meaning '*nothing'. Following the trail of this particle has led us from ancient Mesopotamia to modern Ethiopia, and the span of historical time and the range of geographical space which the examination of this problem have involved underscore the broad scope which comparative-linguistic research frequently entails. I am grateful for the opportunity to present this study in honor of Gene Gragg as a token of my appreciation both for the insights which he has made available to the field of Near Eastern historical linguistics and for the model which he has provided for generations of young scholars at the University of Chicago.

---

[18] In light of the replacement of pre-Arabic *'in (< *'ayn) by *lā* which is posited here, it may be of relevance that *lā* also serves as the literary Arabic counterpart to the Hebrew marker of non-existence *'ên* — for example, *lā 'ilāha 'illā llāhu* 'there is no god but God'.

Abbreviations

2 Aqht	Cyrus Gordon. *Ugaritic Textbook: Grammar, Texts in Translation, Cuneiform Selections, Glosary, Indices.* Analecta Orientalia 38. Rome: Pontifical Biblical Institute, 1965.
ARM 6	Jean-Robert Kupper. *Correspondance de Bahdi-Lim Prefét du Palais de Mari.* Archives Royales de Mari 6. Paris: Imprimerie nationale, 1954.
CCT 1	Sidney Smith. *Cuneiform Texts from Cappadocian Tablets in the British Museum, London*, Part 1. London: The British Museum, 1921.
CCT 4	Sidney Smith. *Cuneiform Texts from Cappadocian Tablets in the British Museum, London*, Part 4. London: The British Museum, 1927.
Gilg.	R. C. Thompson. *The Epic of Gilgamish. Text, Transliteration, and Notes.* Oxford: Clarendon Press, 1930.
KAI	Herbert Donner and Wolfgang Röllig. *Kanaanäische und aramäische Inschriften.* Wiesbaden: Harrassowitz, 1962–1964.
KTS	Julius Lewy. *Die altassyrischen Texte vom Kültepe bei Kaisarije.* Keilschrifttexte in den Antiken-Museen zu Stambul. Constantinople: Selbstverlag der Antikenmuseen, 1926.
PBS 7	Arthur Ungnad. *Babylonian Letters of the Hammurapi Period.* Publications of the Babylonian Section, University Museum, University of Pennsylvania. Philadelphia: University Museum, 1915.
PN	Personal name
RV	Rg-Veda

Bibliography

Buccellati, Giorgio

1996   *A Structural Grammar of Babylonian.* Wiesbaden: Harrassowitz.

Faber, Alice

1991   "The Diachronic Relationship Between Negative and Interrogative Markers in Semitic." In *Semitic Studies in Honor of Wolf Leslau on the Occasion of his Eighty-fifth Birthday, November Fourteenth 1991,* edited by A. S. Kaye, pp. 411–29. Wiesbaden: Harrassowitz.

Fischer, Wolfdietrich

2002   *A Grammar of Classical Arabic*, translated by Jonathan Rodgers. Third revised edition. Yale Language Series. New Haven: Yale University Press.

Hetzron, Robert, editor

1997   *The Semitic Languages.* Routledge Language Family Descriptions. London: Routledge.

Hudson, Grover

2003   "Ethio-Semitic Negative Non-Past." In *Selected Comparative-Historical Afrasian Linguistic Studies in Memory of Igor M. Diakonoff,* edited by M. Lionel Bender, Gábor Takács, and David L. Appleyard, pp. 209–18. Lincom Studies in Afroasiatic Linguistics 14. Munich: Lincom Europa.

Leslau, Wolf

    1992   "The Negative Particle ʾin in Arabic and (ʾ)ən in Ethiopic." In *Gurage Studies: Collected Articles*, edited by Wolf Leslau, pp. 660–68. Wiesbaden: Harrassowitz.

Raz, Shlomo

    1997   "Tigré." In *The Semitic Languages*, edited by R. Hetzron, pp. 446–56. London: Routledge.

Stamm, Johann Jakob

    1939   *Die akkadische Namengebung*. Mitteilungen der Vorderasiatisch-aegyptischen Gesellschaft 44. Leipzig: J. C. Hinrichs.

Sivan, Daniel

    1997   *A Grammar of the Ugaritic Language*. Handbuch der Orientalistik, Abteilung 1, Nahe und der Mittlere Osten 28. Leiden: Brill.

Testen, David

    1985   "The Significance of Aramaic r < *n." *Journal of Near Eastern Studies* 44: 143–46.

    1993   "The East Semitic Precative Paradigm." *Journal of Semitic Studies* 38: 1–13.

    1995   "Secondary Vowels in Semitic and the Plural Pronominal Endings." In *Kurylowicz Memorial Volume*, Part 1, edited by Wojciech Smoczynski, pp. 543–51. Analecta Indoeuropaea Cracoviensia 2. Krakow: Universitas.

    1998a   *Parallels in Semitic Linguistics: The Development of Arabic la- and Related Semitic Particles*. Studies in Semitic Languages and Linguistics 26. Leiden: Brill.

    1998b   "Modern South Arabian 'nine.'" *Bulletin of the School of Oriental and African Studies* 61: 314–17.

    2000   "Conjugating the 'Prefixed Stative' Verbs of Akkadian." *Journal of Near Eastern Studies* 59: 81–92.

    2005   "The Akkadian Demonstrative *ammiu*." In *Studia Semitica et Semitohamitica: Festschrift für Rainer Voigt anläßlich seines 60. Geburtstages am 17. Januar 2004*, edited by Bogdan Burtea, Josef Tropper, and Helen Younansardaroud, pp. 405–16. Alter Orient und Altes Testament 317. Münster: Ugarit-Verlag.

CONTRIBUTORS

M. Lionel Bender
401 S. Emerald Lane
Carbondale, IL 62901
eswg@siu.edu

Stuart Creason
Department of Near Eastern Languages and Civilizations
The Oriental Institute
The University of Chicago
1155 E. 58th Street
Chicago, IL 60637
s-creason@uchicago.edu

Joseph L. Daniels II
Department of Near Eastern Languages and Civilizations
The Oriental Institute
The University of Chicago
1155 E. 58th Street
Chicago, IL 60637
jldaniels@sjprep.org

Peter T. Daniels
254 Palisade Avenue
Jersey City, NJ 07907
grammatim@verizon.net

Samuel Ethan Fox
2809 W. Greenleaf
Chicago, IL 60645
sfox29@earthlink.net

W. Randall Garr
Department of Religious Studies
University of California, Santa Barbara
Santa Barbara, CA 93106
wrgarr@religion.ucsb.edu

Richard L. Goerwitz III
Carleton College
1 North College Street
Northfield, MN 55057
rgoerwit@carleton.edu

Rebecca Hasselbach
Department of Near Eastern Languages and Civilizations
The Oriental Institute
The University of Chicago
1155 E. 58th Street
Chicago, IL 60637
hasselb@uchicago.edu

Robert D. Hoberman
Department of Linguistics
Stony Brook University
Stony Brook, NY 11794-4376
robert.hoberman@stonybrook.edu

Charles E. Jones
Blegen Library
The American School of Classical Studies
54 Souidias Street
10676 Athens
Greece
ce-jones@ascsa.edu.gr / cejo@midway.uchicago.edu

Alexander Militarev
19 Nikulinskaya Str., app. 127
Moscow 119602
Russia
alex.mil@jum.ru

Cynthia L. Miller
Department of Hebrew and Semitic Studies
University of Wisconsin–Madison
1220 Linden Drive
1344 Van Hise Hall
Madison, WI 53706
clmiller2@wisc.edu

Dennis Pardee
Department of Near Eastern Languages and Civilizations
The Oriental Institute
The University of Chicago
1155 E. 58th Street
Chicago, IL 60637
d-pardee@uchicago.edu

David Testen
11741 North Shore Drive
Reston, VA 20190
dtesten@alumni.uchicago.edu / tesxd@earthlink.net

INDEX

abjad — 56, 59–60
abugida — 56, 60, 62
accents — 111–20
accentual parsing — 113
adaptive reuse — 58–59, 63
Afar — 124, 133–34
Afrasian — 1–25, 155–60
    see also Afroasiatic
Afroasiatic — 6, 53, 61, 123–27, 129, 131, 133–35, 139, 206
    Proto-Afroasiatic — 128
    see also Afrasian
Agew — 1–3, 5–7, 9–13, 15–16, 18–19, 21
Akhmimic — 59
Akkadian — 2–3, 43, 46, 50, 55, 60, 81–84, 87–88, 90, 97–98, 123–28, 130, 134, 155–61, 181, 183, 186–88, 201–11
    Babylonian Akkadian — 87, 98
    Old Akkadian — 125, 131, 135, 155–56, 158
alphabet — 2, 53, 55–62, 182–90
alphabetic cuneiform — 181, 185, 189
    see also Ugaritic script
Altaic — 57, 61
Amadiya — 139, 141, 145–49
Amharic — 5, 10, 19, 21–22, 24, 45, 155, 201, 204–6, 209
Angas — 159–60
Ankwe — 160
aphel — 85–86, 94–96
Arabian
    Ancient North Arabian — 124
    Epigraphic South Arabian — 43–46, 48–50
    Modern South Arabian — 43, 45–46, 48, 207
    Old South Arabian — 123–24, 133–34, 183, 186
    South Arabian — 53, 62, 186
Arabic — 3, 43–44, 46, 54, 56, 58–60, 62, 71, 88, 123–25, 127–30, 133–35, 140–41, 143–46, 155–56, 158, 160–61, 181, 183, 201–4, 206–11
Aradhin — 139–40, 142, 144–47, 149–50
Aramaic
    Babylonian Jewish Aramaic — 71, 90
    Biblical Aramaic — 82, 92, 125–26, 130
    Central Neo-Aramaic — 139–41, 149, 151
    Imperial Aramaic — 81–83, 87–91, 94, 96–98
    Jewish Babylonian Aramaic — 82
    Judean Aramaic — 90
    Late Aramaic — 81–82, 97
    Middle Aramaic — 70, 72, 78, 81–82, 90–92, 95, 97–99
    Neo-Aramaic — 69, 71, 73
    Northeastern Neo-Aramaic — 69, 71–72, 139–44, 146–52
    Old Aramaic — 81–82, 88–89
    Qumran Aramaic — 84, 94
    Samaritan Aramaic — 125
Argobba — 205
Armenian — 53–55, 59, 69, 73
Aroid — 2–7
assimilation — 81, 90, 96, 204
Assyrian — 62, 69, 125, 131, 135, 157
    Neo-Assyrian — 157–58, 161
    Old Assyrian — 203, 207
Avestan — 208

Babylonian — 87, 91, 97, 99, 157, 159, 203–4, 207
    Middle Babylonian — 81, 157–59
    Neo-Babylonian — 157–78, 160–61
    Old Babylonian — 81, 125, 155–58, 160, 202
    paleo-Babylonian — 55
    Standard Babylonian — 81, 156–59
Beja — 1–7, 16, 19, 156
Berber — 1, 4, 6, 123–24, 126, 128, 134, 158
bicolon — 165, 167, 173
Bidiya — 158
binarity — 146–48, 151, 166
Bohairic — 59
Bohtan — 69–73
Bokkos — 160
borrowing — 58–60, 142–44, 155–61, 184, 189
    see also loanword
Burman — 60
Buryat Mongolian — 58

Cairene — 206
Canaanite — 59–60, 161, 182, 186, 202, 204, 208
    Proto-Canaanite — 60, 182, 189, 199
case system — 123–24, 127, 129, 131, 134–35
Chadic — 1–25, 123, 126, 128, 134, 159–60
    Central Chadic — 2, 159–60
    East Chadic — 2, 158–59
    West Chadic — 2, 156, 159–60
Chaha — 205, 209
Chinese — 53–55, 57, 62
cognate — 3, 5–6, 71, 90, 93, 141, 155–60, 205, 208
commands — 201–2, 209, 211
computational linguistics — 111–20
consonantal inventory — 82, 184
consonantary — 56, 60
context-free grammars — 111–13
coordination — 166, 177
Coptic — 54, 59

Cushitic — 1–25, 53, 124, 126, 128, 134, 160
    Central Cushitic — 1–2, 7–25
    East Cushitic — 1–3, 5–25, 160
    North Cushitic — 1–2, 7–25, 156
    South Cushitic — 1–3, 7–25
Cypriote — 55
Cyrillic — 54–55, 59, 62

Dahalo — 1–4, 7–25
derivation — 60, 89–90, 123, 125–33, 135, 144, 150, 170
desyllabification — 207
dialect — 49, 59, 69–73, 81–82, 90–91, 94–95, 97–99, 125, 139, 141–50, 152
dissimilation — 90, 97
Dizoid — 2–3, 6–8, 19, 23
Dravidian — 57
dual markers — 130–31, 133–35

East Sudanic — 2, 10, 13, 16, 19, 25
Egyptian — 1, 3–4, 6, 54–55, 57, 59–60, 82, 95, 123, 126–29, 155–61, 188
    Middle Egyptian — 123, 129
    Old Egyptian — 4, 129
Elamite — 54, 57, 181
ellipsis — 165–68, 170–77
English — 2, 30, 56–57, 115, 166, 168, 171–72, 174–75, 177, 181–82, 208, 210
Ennemor — *see* Inor
epenthesis — 140–42, 147
Ethiopic — 43, 53, 56, 58, 62, 82, 204–9, 211

featural script — 56
French — 55, 181, 187, 210

Gabri — 159
Gatha Avestan — 202
Gandhāra — 61
Geʻez — 45, 49, 123–31, 133–34, 208–10
geminate cluster — 81, 83, 88–94, 96–99, 134, 147–48, 203–4
Georgian — 53–54, 59, 69, 73
Goggot — 159
Gothic — 54, 59
grammaticalization — 203, 206, 210
grapheme — 181, 183–86
graphic system — 183–84
Greek — 53–55, 59–61, 88, 92, 97, 155, 159, 184, 208
Gurage — 155, 208–9, 211
    East Gurage — 45–46
    Gurage cluster — 209

Haphel — 82, 84–86, 92–93, 96
Hatran — 88, 94–95, 97–99
Hausa — 2–3, 6, 21, 123–24, 126, 133–34
Hebrew — 3, 8, 27–28, 30–31, 34, 39–40, 54, 58, 71, 88, 116–17, 119, 124–26, 128, 130–31, 133–35, 157–58, 165, 181–84, 190, 201–11

biblical Hebrew — 82, 88, 92, 111, 120, 161, 165–66, 168, 170–72, 177, 202–3, 211
    Modern Hebrew — 113, 126
    Tiberian Hebrew — 111–13, 119–20
Hebrew Bible — 111, 113, 118–20, 182
    poetry — 165, 168–71, 176–77
    prose — 119, 165, 168–71, 177
Hebrew orthography — 111
Hertevin — 69–72, 139–50
heterogram — 92–93
Hiphil — 28, 38–39, 41, 170, 178
Hithpael — 28, 40–41, 90
Hittite — 159, 181, 187, 198
Hophal — 28, 39, 41, 178
Hurrian — 59, 181, 183

ideogram — 55, 57, 92
imperative — 10, 35–36, 43, 48–49, 78, 144–48, 150, 172, 178, 201–2, 207
imperfect — 35–36, 43, 48, 92–94, 96, 167, 169, 171–72, 178, 202
Indic scripts — 56, 61
Indo-European — 17, 57, 60–61
Indo-Iranian — 202, 208
inflection — 60, 82, 90, 123, 127, 202, 204, 207
injunction — 43–50, 201
injunctive — 43–50, 202
Inor (or, Ennemor) — 205, 209
Iranian — 13, 57–58, 60, 92–93, 98
Iraqw — 1–4, 6–25
isogloss — 2–3, 5, 7, 158, 160

Jibbali — 45, 49, 207–8
Jilu — 70–71
jussive — 43–49, 178, 201–2, 204, 209

Kabalai — 4, 159
Kharoṣṭhī — 56, 61
Kirfi — 156
Kurdish — 71–73, 78, 145–47
Kwang — 159

Latin — 146, 208
lexical analyzer — 112, 114, 116
lexical items — 1, 28, 97, 145, 160–61
linear script — 188–89
Lithuanian — 208
loanword — 5, 59, 81–84, 87–88, 97–98, 130, 142, 146–48, 155–61, 187
    see also borrowing
logogram — 55, 57, 60, 92
logography — 55–56

Malayo-Polynesian — 60
Mandaic — 58, 61, 82, 90, 95, 97–99, 159
Mandean — 98
Manichaean — 58, 60

Mao — 2–3, 5–8, 16, 23
Mayan — 57
Mbara — 159–60
Mehri — 45, 49, 124–25, 207–8
minimality — 139, 143–44, 147–48, 150
Moabite — 205–6
modality — 171–72
Mofu — 159
Mokilko — 158
Mongolian — 55, 58, 62
Mon-Khmer — 60
monophthongization — 206
mora — 144, 146–48
morphology — 43, 69, 72, 79, 97, 139, 143–44, 150, 165, 202
morphophonological — 88, 90–91
Muher — 205
Mupun — 159–60
Musgu — 160

Nabatean — 82, 91–92, 98
nasals — 81, 87, 208
Nilo-Saharan — 2, 5, 10, 13, 21
Niphal — 28, 37–39, 41, 170, 173–74
Northwest Semitic — *see* Semitic
numerals — 59, 142, 145, 149–50

Omotic — 1–25
optative — 43, 45–46, 48
orthography — 2, 58, 60–61, 81–82, 89, 91, 94, 96, 111, 123, 133

Pael — 90, 93–94, 96–98
Pahlavi — 60
palatalization — 205
Pali — 60
Palmyrean — 81–82, 84, 91, 98
Palmyrene — 58, 95
Parthian — 58, 60, 92–93
Peal — 82–86, 88, 91, 93–96
perfect consecutive verb — 171, 178
Persian — 58, 60, 89, 92, 95, 205
Phags pa — 55, 62
Phoenician — 53–55, 58, 61, 183–85, 188, 202, 204–8, 211
phoneme — 56, 140, 181, 183–84, 189
phonemic inventory — 183
phonetic system — 183
phonology — 1, 57, 59–60, 62, 69, 81–82, 88–91, 94–95, 98, 127–30, 134–35, 140, 143, 145–46, 148, 150–51, 168, 172, 204, 206, 208–9
Piel — 28, 39–41, 170
plural markers, external — 123–35
Polish — 142, 205
Prakrits — 56, 60–61
predicative adjective — 128, 131–35
prefix conjugation — 43–46, 49–50, 131–32

prenasalization — 81–99
prepositional phrase — 29, 33, 35, 165–68, 170, 172–73, 175, 177
prohibitive — 202, 208–9, 211
Proto-Sinaitic — 54, 60, 182, 189
Pual — 28, 39, 41

Qabyle — 158
Qal — 28–30, 37–41, 170
Quechua — 57

root — 1, 5–6, 15, 21, 28, 38–41, 43, 46, 81, 83, 88, 90–94, 98–99, 125, 128, 130, 133, 135, 139, 143–44, 159, 187–88
    biliteral — 1
    triliteral — 1, 155, 157
    structure of — 139, 143

Sabaic — 43–50
Sanskrit — 60–61, 208
Sassanian — 58, 92–93
semantics — 1, 4, 27–29, 38, 44–45, 49, 56–57, 60, 93, 98, 113–14, 130, 135, 148, 151, 156, 160, 165, 168–70, 173–74, 177, 206, 211
Semitic — 1–25, 53, 55–57, 60, 62, 81, 90, 92–93, 123–29, 130–35, 139–41, 143–44, 150, 155–60, 181, 183, 187, 201, 204–11
    Common Semitic — 2, 57, 123, 126, 211
    East Semitic — 204, 207, 211
    Northwest Semitic — 56, 59–60, 88, 183, 185, 204, 206, 211
    Proto-Semitic — 1–2, 123, 128, 130–33, 140–41, 149, 204, 207–8, 210–11
    South Semitic — 43–50, 185
    West Semitic — 2, 50, 53, 55–56, 59–60, 62, 88, 157, 161, 183–84, 187, 201–11
Semitisms — 160
Soddo — 205, 209
Sogdian — 58, 60
Somali — 126, 159–160
sonorant — 140–41, 148–49, 209
Soqoṭri — 45, 155
spirantization — 140–41
stem shape — 141, 143
stress — 70–71, 139, 142, 144–47, 151
suffixation — 127–28, 132, 141, 148
Sumerian — 53–55, 57, 60, 155–57, 159–60, 181
Sura — 159–60, 206
syllabary — 55–56, 58
syllable structure — 112–13, 142
syntax — 29, 32–33, 39, 44–47, 49–50, 111–14, 116, 131, 148, 150–51, 165–68, 170, 172–77, 202, 205–6, 209–10
Syriac — 54–55, 58, 71–72, 74, 82, 88, 90, 98, 124–26, 128, 130, 139–42, 144, 149–51

Tai — 60
tense — 70, 72, 150–51, 171, 202–3, 209–10
Tera — 159
Tibetan — 55–56, 61–62
Tigre — 133–34, 204–6, 208
Tigrinya — 155–56, 204–5, 208
Tocharian — 55–56, 58
Tuareg — 123–24, 133
Turkish — 58, 145, 147
Turoyo — 71, 139–42, 149–50

Ugaritic — 54, 59, 82–83, 88, 92, 123–24, 127, 135, 158, 161, 175, 181–89, 202, 205–6
Ugaritic script — 59, 88
    see also alphabetic cuneiform
Urartian — 181
Urmi — 72, 139–40, 142, 147, 149
Uyghur — 58–59, 62

Vedic — 202
vetitive — 201–11
vocative — 49, 167
volitional — 204, 211
vowel lengthening — 141

writing system — 55–59, 61, 181–89

Ya'udic texts — 124

Zakho — 139, 141–42, 145–49, 152
Zay — 205